Topic Sentence

OTHER BOOKS BY STAN PERSKY

Wrestling the Angel
Buddy's: Meditations on Desire
Then We Take Berlin
Autobiography of a Tattoo
The Short Version: An ABC Book

Topic Sentence

A Writer's Education

STAN PERSKY

NEW STAR BOOKS
VANCOUVER
2007

NEW STAR BOOKS LTD.

107 – 3477 Commercial Street | Vancouver, BC V5N 4E8 | CANADA
1574 Gulf Rd., #1517 | Point Roberts, WA 98281 | USA
www.NewStarBooks.com | info@NewStarBooks.com

Publication of this work is made possible by the support of the
Canada Council, the Government of Canada through the Depart-
ment of Canadian Heritage Book Publishing Industry Development
Program, the British Columbia Arts Council, and the Province of
British Columbia through the Book Publishing Tax Credit.

Printed and bound in Canada by Marquis Printers
First printing, August 2007

LIBRARY AND ARCHIVES CANADA
CATALOGUING IN PUBLICATION

Persky, Stan, 1941–
   Topic sentence : a writer's education / Stan Persky.

Includes bibliographical references and index.
ISBN 978-1-55420-028-3

I. Title.
PS8581.E75T66 2007   C814'.54   C2006-906859-3

for

Thomas Marquard

---

hommage à

Jacques Derrida, *The Work of Mourning*

Contents

After

Introduction

A Writer's Education
by Brian Fawcett

First, let me declare my non-objective stake in this book: Stan Persky and I have been friends for forty years now, and for at least the last twenty years he's been my closest intellectual companion.

Neither our friendship nor our intellectual companionship arose out of a commonality of interests or similarities in our respective characters. Persky was born in Chicago, and the roster of his identifications include being Jewish, homosexual, and a committed social democratic citizen. He's also left-handed and plays tennis the way you're supposed to. I'm a blue-eyed Anglo heterosexual liberal anarchist from northern British Columbia who plays tennis like a ping-pong player but wins anyway. We couldn't be more different in outlook, social and domestic habits, and temperament. He is reasonable, calm, and philosophically temperate, while I am, er, not.

What we share is a belief in the political, personal, and even erotic necessity of writing clear sentences that neither minimize nor inflate the weight and reach of what is being said. We also agree, after long and very different experiences within the world, that human curiosity — which is neither an inheritance nor a burden but an elusive and always mobile privilege — hinges on the clarity of written language to secure and articulate it.

A first clue to how this book is going to work lies in the book's title, *Topic Sentence*. In the title story, written in 1970, Persky took on the two questions that dog every artist in the post-modern: What is the subject matter? and, How can it be articulated? Since both questions are unanswerable, Persky twists them: How am I supposed to isolate the subject matter from the myriad of things in which it is lodged? and, How do I elude the distortions of conventional exposition and its self-serving selectivity? How do I make what I write as alive and dynamic as the things I write about?

Take this seemingly innocent and slightly whimsical passage from the story:

> I'll have to get back to my mother and the piano sometime — I can almost hear my cousin Sherwin, son of my mother's brother, Uncle Irving, and his wife, Aunt Rose, playing the piano, the strains of "Malaguena" (I hope I've spelled it right. A Spanish tilde over the "n"?) rising in their living room, much larger than ours — the importance of the size is simply that it is the actual display of the superiority of their social status over us as the poorer segment of the family — his back to us, my mother and his mother, my aunt Rose, sitting on the sofa, where was I enduring it? — I'd like to drag by the scruff of the neck, like a cat, that teacher who taught me composition and make her find the fucking topic sentence in this scrawl. Underline it! Find it and underline it, damn you.

What Persky recognized here, at the beginning of his writing career, is the political and psychological frame of postmodern composition. Everything is allowed in because it's going to get in anyway, and the writer's job is to find forms that ensure that an enforced order of composition doesn't exclude any possibilities. In one sense, he's echoing Charles Olson's dictum that writing has to move at the speed of perception. But he's taking it a step further by tying it simultaneously to the uncontrollable dynamism of human memory and to the architecture that particularity imposes. Mastering that frame has turned out to be a lifelong project. Writing has to be articulated the same way its subject matter is known: there are no set pieces in Persky's opus, no playing out of conventional formulae.

The book's subtitle is "A Writer's Education." What that means is that this book is not a writer's summary selection of his work, designed to convince readers that certain things are true and that others aren't. Nor is it artifactual testimony that the author has produced finely crafted art-widgets that deserve an elevated position in literary history or on the bestseller shelves of the nearest chain bookstore. Rather, this is an exemplary demonstration of a fundamental mode of human understanding, an accumulative instrument of investigation that may well be disappearing from our civilization at a point where it is most needed.

Persky would never make so apocalyptic a statement. That's another of our differences. He'll cheerfully do the investigation, sort the results, and posit his report, citing the fascinating details of the journey without complaining about the rumbling gears offstage. What matters to him is the exercise and education of his faculties, reading and writing it through to understanding.

The book has three slightly cryptically named sections: *Before*, *During*, and *After*. They do not mean beginning, middle, and end. Instead, they mark, without having discrete boundaries, the three stages Persky has traversed to become a writer: self-articulation, ideology, and dissidence; sexuality; and the still-in-progress open field that lies beyond commissioned intentions and self. Persky began as a poet, morphed into a fine political writer, then wrote about homosexuality, and now is a writer prepared to examine every- and anything with a fully deployed sensibility that includes his political and sexual commitments and passions without being governed or limited by either or by anything else. The problem with this sort of explanation is that it makes it appear to be linear, and that's not how Stan Persky's mind — or this book — operates.

Before is a set of pieces that treat the particularities of Persky's origins, which for him are always tangible things with wires that lead elsewhere — sometimes to the self, more often to the myths and abstractions by which social and individual life is supposed to be guided but mostly isn't. (I noted, when I first read the manuscript of this book, that Persky has made a lifelong practice of refusing both abstraction and desire unless its wires are firmly attached to physical bodies of some sort. It reminded me that he once suggested to me that we not write poems in which the line "Please pass the tunafish sandwich" could not comfortably fit, a suggestion that more or less instantly changed the way I wrote.)

Virtually all of the *During* section is an exegesis of homosexuality. "Every writer," Persky told me recently, "because of his historical / social location, has to deal with something or other. In my case, it happened to be homo. A writer has to write 'through' this or else he doesn't make it." The term therefore also means "for the duration," as with military service during wartime.

That pretty much characterizes Persky's political treatment of homosexuality, which has existed as a virtual state of emergency throughout his adult life. Not surprisingly, as liberalized public attitudes move toward normalization, or (to persist with the war metaphor) at least a nominal cessation of hostilities, Persky has successfully integrated it into the range of other concerns and curiosities he pursues.

Which brings us to *After*. It is the book's longest section and demonstrates the range of the mature Persky's field of enquiry and the breadth of his curiosity: after you learn how to be a human being and how to write like a human being, you have to practise what you've learned. I won't comment on this section except to point out that the writing is breathtaking in its skill and generosity, and that Persky could not have gotten to it without that exercise conducted in the story "Topic Sentence." I'll also point out, although it will swiftly become obvious to readers, that this book does not mark any "winding down" of Stan Persky's remarkable intelligence, but, rather, its opening out.

Read on. Enjoy. Learn. This is a remarkable writer cheerfully at work.

Toronto
January 2007

Before

Topic Sentence

We were forced to make "outlines" in school. When? Elementary school? As early as that? I can't pinpoint any specific teacher from either elementary or high school who required the outlines. But I feel the importance of them, of the outlines. I've hit something. The subject here is the painful emergence of a formalized organization of sentences ... they want to teach us — as they, the teachers, had been taught, in places as lousy as the university education faculty no doubt — suddenly I remember my father's sister, my aunt Patty, a schoolteacher, slight humpback, her "no-nonsense" but genial voice ... to teach us, the students, but to teach us what? Composition. (I wish I had a more definite age for us. Between eight and fourteen? No, later than eight. After the time when we could understand an idea like "science." That would be after sixth grade, age twelve.)

I'm preparing an essay for Mrs. Barry, the sixth- or seventh-grade science teacher at Sumner Elementary school in Chicago, *circa* 1953–54. It's on nuclear something or other. Atomic energy. Lester. There's someone named Lester. No, can't get that. Or, rather, I'm getting too much, a cascade of faces, images, relationships, kicked open by the sudden memory of the initial experiences of "composition." Lester was a schoolmate — bright, quirky, unpredictable — but more than that, a prototype of a kind of friendship I have maintained throughout my life. Lester had a similar relation to me then that my oldest still-current friend George Stanley does now. That's why he's here, because even as I'm seeing the origins of an autobiographical idea of composition, the possibility of a parallel, crosscutting history of "friendship" appears.

The essay for Mrs. Barry was fourteen pages long, double-spaced, one side, in ink, large handwriting, maybe even devising

3

a way to leave the bottom *two* lines of the paper blank to intentionally increase its length, which is vaguely connected to showing that you really "worked" on it. On the first page, the cover of the essay, I made a drawing of an "atom," intersecting distorted ovals, without understanding a thing about atomic energy (nor possibly did Mrs. Barry), just that nearly a decade after the United States dropped the atomic bomb on Japan, it was exactly what American seventh graders properly wrote about, which was apparently the main thing I had figured out.

The "topic." Stuck. I'm stuck. The idea of topic strikes me. I had to learn that, too. "Stick to the topic." I had to learn what a topic was in order to stick to it. Eureka! Someone in the world had invented the following item:

In each paragraph there is one "topic sentence." Locate it and underline it. Underline the topic sentence. I can't remember what I looked like. There's a hiatus in my memory between the utterly lovely photo of myself as a four-year-old in a child's version of a sailor's uniform, a framed photo that sat on the piano lid (my mother wanted the damned spinet, scene of hours of fruitless scales practice for me), and the other photo of me, also in a sailor's uniform, this one real, placed on top of the same piano — did I again dream of re-enlisting in the navy a couple of nights ago? — taken sometime around my discharge from the navy or possibly "graduation" from boot camp (1958) —

Somewhere in my childhood I must have been told, You're making a big fuss over nothing. I wildly exaggerate any feeling I have in order to get it up through me (layers of fatty tissue?) and out into the world so that contact will be established with another human being.

I'll have to get back to my mother and the piano sometime — I can almost hear my cousin Sherwin, son of my mother's brother, Uncle Irving, and his wife, Aunt Rose, playing the piano, the strains of "Malaguena" (I hope I've spelled it right. A Spanish tilde over the "n"?) rising in their living room, much larger than ours — the importance of the size is simply that it is the actual display of the superiority of their social status over us as the poorer segment of the family — his back to us, my mother and his mother, my aunt Rose, sitting on the sofa, where was I enduring it? — I'd like to drag by the scruff of the neck, like a cat, that teacher who taught me composition and make her find the fucking topic sentence in this scrawl. Underline it! Find it and underline it, damn you.

Let me push aside this whole thing of the relatives, the room, the status — no, I can't — the details breathe life into it — the stiffness of his hands (Sherwin's — I won't go into the whole relationship with him) as he strikes large chords in certain impassioned moments of "Malagueña" — I'm trying to get a sense of my mother's emotions during these scenes — I mean, I'm imagining myself as her, feeling the pleasure of listening to her nephew Sherwin perform

— mainly I remember being required to visit him after he had developed colitis — later the strapping father of four children and getting rich in the accounting, slum management and assorted real-estate-holdings businesses — then, decades afterwards, when I look him up on the Internet, there's a single reference, to the emeritus board of the Chicago Film Festival, of which he was apparently a businessman member, and a small black cross in memoriam next to his name —

but back then, when we were teenagers, I had to sit at a considerable distance across the room from his agonized bowels to decrease the discomfort of the visitor forced to endure the enormous foul gaseous effusions of his intestines, monster farts, and didn't he get that hysterical stomach (the hockey player Derek Sanderson, he-man and womanizer, formerly of the Boston Bruins, had it too) — didn't he get it precisely from being trotted out x million times to that Steinway Baby Grand (ah, the magnitude of that phrase — "Steinway Baby Grand" — in terms of goals and strivings of various upper-middle-class Chicago Jewish families of the 1950s) — my aunt Lilly, ten or more years later, shrieking at me her defence of the right-wing future vice-president in the Nixon administration, Spiro Agnew, denouncer of the liberal elite as those "nattering nabobs of negativism" — I had just marched in my first protest demonstration against the Vietnam War — as she passed before the sleeping face of the television, used as an altar on the occasion of my mother's death, 1965?

One clue, when you were given an utterly innocuous paragraph and required to find the topic sentence, was that it was likely to be the first one, or the second sentence after the initial sentence, whose function was to engage the imaginary reader's "interest" and "attention." I say "imaginary reader" because although these paragraphs were purportedly lifted from real essays or stories published in real magazines like the *Saturday Evening Post*, the only subsequent probable readers of them, now thinking about this retrospectively — at the same time as this writing is falling to pieces, sentence by sentence — were those of us looking for the topic sentence and wishing that the fucking topic sentence (possibly buried in the middle of the paragraph) could somehow, despite all, as if it were a neon sign or a drowning swimmer in the ocean, frantically signal to us so that we could underline it.

So the theory was — I finally learn the lesson that the teacher, Mrs. Somebody-or-other, was trying to pump into my brain, now, so many years after the fact, half-crazed by compositional delirium — that in each "well-written" paragraph there is one sentence that succinctly contains the "main thought," or rather, the most important thought in that paragraph: "What the writer is trying to get across." And the well-written paragraph also means, of course, the "well-behaved" paragraph, just as we were meant to be well-behaved, because in learning the rules of composition there was an allegedly parallel process going on, of absorbing the rules of being, the rules of self. Equally astonishing: a half century after the inculcation of that lesson, the topic sentence lives, only now it is rhetorically inflated as the "thesis statement."

In the history of contemporary alienation, I have just staked a claim to a gold mine. Therefore, all the surrounding sentences had only a decorative function or, from my point of view (and I haven't even gotten to "reading comprehension" and "outlines" yet), the function of obscuring the topic sentence in a jungle foliage as thick as the scrub we went through the night I climbed Mount Tamalpais in California because I wanted to be with Mike Dodd, even on a drunken, hare-brained, middle-of-the-night mountain hike. And then, out of nowhere, again, years later, I happen upon the photo whoever was with us took of Mike and me that very dawn, on the mountain, at some slight distance from each other, our faces as innocent as deer.

The paragraphs themselves were stapled into paperback-book-sized cardboard folders and kept, upright, in a box on the teacher's desk. There was a routine whereby, when you finished the "worksheet" on a folder, you brought it to the teacher and could select . . . oh no, no, no — there was not only this organized *activity* (and the idea of "activities" by which to structure our day), but also a *system* for performing this task, and it has some emotional tug, a combination of excitement, anxiety, and competitiveness, as I completed the worksheets, delivered them, got them marked by the teacher as correct, selected the next folder, went back to my desk — demonstrating my speed, my rapidity of "comprehension," able to not only underline topic sentences, but also to choose the correct "multiple choice" answer to related questions ("Who was Bobby's uncle?" "How many members in the family?" "What was Uncle Ted going to buy?" — "A car!!"), thus demonstrating my genetic? "brightness" — was my mother called to school to be told by someone, a vice-principal perhaps, the exceptional results of my IQ test? which she, in turn, was not allowed to repeat to me for fear of inflating my ego, turning my head? But turning my head from what? The topic sentence?

The paragraphs in themselves were meaningless to us, despite the professions of their worth (I'm sure educators at conferences still assure each other of the value of this kind of thing) — in short, how can a story be interesting when you know it's been selected, in the first place, to increase your "reading skills" — I mean, didn't they know that we were reading not because we would be interested but because we were required to become "fluent" readers? I mean, if there was something interesting to read — a John R. Tunis sports novel, say, that would generate my own invention of baseball leagues of imaginary teams, or a Walter Farley Black Stallion book — I would get it from the fucking library with the four-fingered librarian, Mrs. Spiegel.

"I'll give you five more minutes." A sentence lifted out of school exam talk. The teacher announces there are five more minutes to write, then papers have to be handed in, some students scrambling to get answers down under the diversionary clatter of papers being passed forward, bodies moving, able at this moment to ask questions of the students around them, violating the rule of "not talking to your neighbours" — the degrading use of that word, "neighbour," to smother the actual competitiveness of the situation.

I wasn't one of the students trying to get last-minute answers. Either I had it — let's see, there was also some behavioural instruction for those who finished the test early. Yes: "If you're finished, then check over your answers" (thus inculcating the lesson of avoiding hubris) — or if I didn't have them, I was fatalistic. I knew that no amount of thinking would produce them, though once, when I didn't have the answers, I wrote across the test, criticizing the inadequacy of the questions, thus bringing, during the next period, Mr. Markowitz — the medieval history teacher, who was also writing historical novels that had some "juicy" parts inappropriate for us to read — thus bringing him, the one person who understood the concept of a "story" and its relation to learning something, right down into the sweaty gymnasium to actually talk it over with me, genuinely upset at the possibility that his questions were indeed unfair or irrelevant. Charlemagne! AD 800!

Now, turn in your papers. No dawdling. Pass them forward, please. And that whole process is another seed of my revolutionary and/or reasonable *being*?

I don't *know* if I knew that. If I knew *all* that. Probably we mainly knew that we had to get it done, whatever it was at any given instant. But look, I learned composition somewhere. And I learned it *there*.

They are trying to teach us "good organization." They admit that real writers don't do this. Or rather that real writers "break the rules." Perhaps the teacher is thinking of Faulkner. The slogan is: You have to be able to follow the rules before you are allowed to break them. Somehow we were to imagine ourselves related to "real writers" by the fact that they too had come through this business of "outlines" and all the other deadening devices of composition, and had even found it helpful? before becoming "mature" enough to abandon all that.

Ironically, the outline that we were to make to "help" ourselves eventually becomes a formal assignment in itself. The teacher, perhaps from reading the badly organized "final product" (yes, an essay was called a "final product"), deductively concluded that we were failing to make an outline. Thus, we were required to "turn in" our outlines along with our essays. The final irony being that *after* I wrote an essay, I would then be faced with the further task of abstracting from it the "outline" that had to be turned in. They thought we were mentally unable to carry in our heads an entire essay we were going to write, and that what we needed was an outline, the empty form of the essay, whose blanks we could thus more easily fill in, when in reality it was exactly the other way around, the specific item (mother, piano, "topic sentence") leading to the next, and the next, until a perception, an idea, a thought emerged into a world in which it had heretofore never existed. That's the something out of nothing, or nothing-but-the-language-base, that is creation!

Lake

It was not *the lake of the heart*
It was the load

taken from the sea
and the seen is not enough.
To know the poetry

You have to go into the poet's country,
which is a darkling wood,
to dream of making love

to the handsome son of a fisherman
This wasn't seeing
not flounder, mussel or cod

Last night again I saw and met the lover
on stairs   a museum of heavy stone
again there was the guided tour   in a ship

the substance of the dream
I believe what's seen there
sharks and sea-monsters

these silent men bring the nets in
all through the morning inch by inch — bring —
it's a hard business
you wanted to jump in there and help
drag that heavy thing from the water

We didn't trade a word
                or look in the eyes
And I've never bought a fish
Not herring, whitefish, eel or crab

The Day

The Mountain

Of course, the day isn't anything you want it to be, anything but that, though sometimes loosely enough arranged in those nothings that it's there to be done with, whatever you want. Or pass it by, and it's morning again. The events of the day, if that's what they were, can be put here and there. We've made it through. Or we're here, in the house, with these plans, mumbled, a dog barking outside, for instance, and that's that.

Where does it start. Each thing having its intensity, you sat there, you lay there then, in the dark, you sing now, you speak, you come around the door to ask whether I want cereal for breakfast, my head turns, my eyes go past the owls,

we're in your centenarian grandfather's basement, in a house outside of Victoria, in the workroom, and then the other room, the room for the display of wooden bowls (your grandfather is upstairs, making oatmeal for us), which pass between our hands, you tell me the names of various kinds of wood, that had been shaped by the lathe in the basement workroom, by your grandfather, and your father in that too, the red cedar that he hadn't used, hadn't gotten around to before his death, there in your grandfather's basement,

my eyes go toward you, past the owls, past the picture of your father on the wall of our bedroom, now that was yesterday too, come to think of it, I was clearing up the desk, and seeing no need for that picture to be lying there on the pile of books on the bookcase, next to the desk, thought about the fact that you brought it here, with some intention surely, had brought it down from your family's home, upcountry, as they say, and so I placed it, holding it in my hands, up against the wall, over the oak case, near the picture of the owls, and it fit immediately, felt right in the first motion,

simply, of your father, the image fuzzy, on a horse, in the mountains, the Chilcotin pass, your father who drowned in a lake, I wanted you to be able to see his photo whenever you wanted, to see it again and again, until it was simply there, in our room,

and your head is around the door, asking, playfully, about breakfast, accompanied by a waft of cinnamon from the kitchen. We can't get used to being moving all the time and in something that's also moving. I can't remember when, or what occasioned that.

Then, another turn in the road. Another place to select into, and then the mind will follow, and we let it. That's the way it works. We were on foot, but left the trail and switched back onto the wide dirt road, wide enough for a truck, a jeep, that went up Windy Joe mountain, dropping off along the edge, into trees,

we passed a man and woman, there was a greeting, that friendliness of being outside, and then not to see a person but each other for hours, or even not to see you, until

you're flying down the mountain, the slag slopes, in bounds, and to call you, from where I've crouched and waited, with not enough sense to put my shirt on, letting the mosquitoes get at me, huddled in a bush, the name of it now gone from mind, though I knew it, with thick mushy leaves, knobby rubbery branches, the *jade bush*, that's it,

at a turn in the road, there's a stream, much later, as we kneeled to it and drank going up, so now also,

but even here, in the house, the body goes on. There are intervals, we shit, coffee and tea are made, now some music plays, or someone whistles, the tune is familiar, you've had your breakfast, or it is really raining again. In the time I go away and come back, there is a space,

I don't want to go over the edge of the mountain, not yet, and the rock-chip tilted path looks as if it does do that, go over the edge, though of course it turns, and I'm merely looking out a long way, the day in mind.

The Shortstop

A field, maybe late summer, or at least something of the fear of when a season turns, in the bones, that's where you say you have a feeling, there, the trees, we're standing near them, as if we're slanted toward them, so that standing right where we are is always an effort not to slide off into the trees, the leaves speckle the ground, we're playing baseball, under a very large blue sky, not much going on, there's nobody watching, we're bunched together, talking to each other, quietly, near the trees,

this dream comes after many of them, at night, as a spilling over of the day's images, lying in the dark room, grinding my teeth together, and little pieces of enamel cracking off, hurting, my mouth, the teeth again and again, or peeing, getting up now in the night to do that, the white rooms, white hall, and light from various sides, from the building across the way, a lighted dulled rectangle of window, is it about 4 AM, someone going to work, has Gladys been up to get the cooking on, a pot of chili, baked bread,

at Gladys and Cliff's wedding, there were several ministers — a local pastor, and George Stanley's brother, Gerald, a priest, and then, the other one, a poet, Robin Blaser, having an epithalamium for the wedding: may you have a shining world, on stairways, he wished them,

then I'm in between the sheets, my friend's asleep, I do, after pondering whether I should, get up, it makes us awake, it's late in the game, we're standing by the trees, grouped together, I'm supposed to be the shortstop, not much has been hit my way, and I have the fear of dropping it, of making a mistake, we are that way, then the batter hits it toward me, the ones nearby casually move away, or I break off from them, I grab it firmly, it's not a ball though, and the batter is running toward first, it's so long to throw it,

the green apple, from the trees, he's going to second, but there are not many of us in the field, or they've gone off, the grass is longer than in a real ballpark, this meadow, and somehow no one is covering third, I see what's going to happen, we haven't given up a run and now this guy is going to get an inside-the-park homer on a dinky infield hit, I run down to home plate, and he does, as I'd anticipated, decide to try for it, to come in from third, it's thrown to me, he slides, I tag him, the hard apple in my hand, I say, he's out, I hold up my thumb and closed fist, giving the sign, who'll believe me, there are no umpires, or there are

there is a slope of ground off the meadow, through salt grass, leading to a beach, a strip of sand, they're in their black suits, standing on it, chatting, by the sea, umpires or priests, from Gladys's wedding.

In So Many Words

Fred Wah is there, in the perennially not-quite-finished Kootenay house that he and Pauline live in, parts of it wrapped in tarpaper, he's in his kitchen, sitting in a chair, I see his Chinese mustache droop at the edges (how he looks this year), his eyes set far back, for a second, I'm trying to hold this face, as we blur by in talking, this is Fred, I think, even as his mouth moves, and behind him, through the window, there are chickens, a woman walking among them, the neighbour, Brassy Ball, and his upland pastures, a few dairy cows, the dog Loki, cats, baby, child, a rooster, all this life moving

(keep it still?)

He's a quiet man, his voice is soft, in the poem (his poem about driving) he follows only the movement, he drives up his twisty road to his house, the poem turns, left, right, in the increasing surge of energy needed to get up this steep incline, we're in the car, I think as I often do that we'll go over the edge rolling over and over through the weeds, the metal of the roof crumpling, on our way to the house, which puts me here, I look out through the squares of glass behind him, around him, to his left, seeing him in it, before me.

We gossip about one person and another, and now it's clear that all of this, including my "portrait" of Fred, unfolding as I speak and listen, is our version of that old Petrarchan genre, "the lives of the poets," then, much later in the day, we're seated around the table, now other people are here, each in his or her chair, as

I listen to one person and then the next (I stray in a memory of what someone looks like, the person we're talking about), and a voice from another place starts up, who's speaking, Pauline, Fred's wife, brings me back.

We drove to Passmore, in the pickup truck, gotten from Fred's brother, for which we had to go down to the mill, in Nelson, the burners blowing up clouds of dirty smoke, it's the fire-ash, landing on everything around in black specks, on the shiny fender of the truck, Fred and I are standing next to it, above the mill, in the street, for a minute, saying something, but the overriding fact is that this is where the men work, along the river, webs of wooden catwalks over the machines.

We leave it behind, to drive into Crescent Valley, and pick up six-foot lengths of birch and a few round slabs of cedar, we're in a thicket of scrub, heaving the wood into the bed of the truck, bark bits sticking on our arms, our breath changing, saying something, we bring it back, the load of wood.

And later, reading and talking all afternoon, I feel a little worried about her, Pauline, I didn't have the slightest idea of what to do with my concern, perhaps misplaced, irrelevant, but make some vague effort, conversational at least, to ask her, how she felt, was it hard, living up here, do you find time to write, things like that, eating beef and beets.

This morning the fog, in the trees and upland fields for grazing, Loki lying there, outside, a St. Bernard, a hulk, thick headed,

                                                              I saw

those late ink drawings, of heads, Jackson Pollack's,

                                                                he's lying on

the ground of yellow leaves next to the grey wooden ladder resting against the apple tree; and yes, talking to Fred, seeing the chickens being fed, or the rivers beyond, but closer, outside the window, their vegetable garden and a few cabbages or bok choy? is that it? that's it.

Osiris

no more day, but night
we've been in this room, for months
    it has heaped up our clothes
       it has our smell
outside, in other rooms
    talk, and people moving
       rivers and islands
the visitor
    here, a shirt over a chair
       out there, dishes we ate on
the work's done, all of it
    and new work is ready for the morning
       all strategies put away
I go across the lake, a boat
    drifting, on that river we saw
       a Sunday afternoon
with watery patches, glaring, expanding,
    slicks, where the sun falls
      the bridge clatters
we're over it
    month upon month

I was with an old man in a boat that plied these waters, which were like canals — he was showing me what to do —

were we inside? at first I was going to say no, then I thought of such things as the passage from *Secret Name*, a book in my hands, as I push my glasses forward to rub my eyes, to rub the sleep away, the lamp on my left, with the yellow shade, the inside of the lens becomes a mirror, reflects my eye, eyebrow, magnified,

was everything there alive last night? we passed through the objects, was it alive, dead, or the opposite of alive-dead, uncreated? in my nervousness, at the beginning my whole body tight with stage fright, in this room with all these others,

I'm

in this boat, Arab air (thick with incense, perfumes), there's a lot
of river traffic here, men in boats, half shell-covered, punts, with
headdresses, robes, sometimes the boat is very cramped, at one
point he asks me what time it is, am I a dead man, where am I
going, what are we crossing, I look up, 1:10 AM,

I look up now,
seeing there's an outside, outside this house, the room where I
am,

we went through room after room, with paintings, old
friends, lamps, cats of stone for the garden, did each thing come
alive, what can be said, what can be explained, all I could imagine
was that we are in a room, with like sympathies, and would read
back and forth, to each other, passages, responding to each other,
and what we knew outside of that would be unspoken,

yet there
must be some other thing, we feel that too, when we are at unease
with one proposition about the cosmos, that this is stasis, this is
the world once and for all, that this is drowning, or drifting, when
we are dissatisfied with that line, the teacher says, it is streaming,
flowing, that this order, year after year, is a streaming, that his
body is streaming itself into the river,

the right word, I think,
worth doing, worth feeling, it is not all image and text then, the
same word to solve the issue of the drowned god, who was not
drowned, who floated on the river, but did not float, as he moved
in it, giving it his life, his body streamed into the river, the whole
order a streaming —

I put my foot out, it hits something, warm,
like an animal coat, I've forgotten there's a footstool before the
chair and think I've kicked the side of a dog, the ridge of his back,
a black labrador, I jerk away,

the boat and the objects, these
foods, one of which has the name of a man, *Paul Latargue*, are
in a room, it's very tiny and cramped, awkwardly boarded up, or
held up, as people crowd in and out, a museum apparently, with
this little unexplained room, or is it a tomb,

in this room, there's
a palm plant,

we pull over to the dockside, cupped in his palm
is a round cake that splits in half, it has the texture of a muffin,

some meat-paste thinly spread on it, I ask what is it, he tells me, the name of a man, what can this be all about,

here, or stumbling through the kitchen, the day will be here, soon, any minute, any hour, what time is it, they did this year after year, what time, three thousand years,

am I crowded in the room, the tomb, with the boat, the dried food, all of this looks so faded, so dry, so crumbling, I think, this is all meaningless for them, it can't mean a thing, they probably wonder why all this stuff has been thrown in here, it's so small, so crowded, there are no labels, what's the point, they wonder, why have they had to wait outside, and then squeeze in here, to see this, only this, as I see them come in I know it'll be disappointing, how can they know, I have ridden in the boat, a little scared, I have seen the food.

Reasonable Beings

What does Immigration want from me?

Between waking up, walking to the bathroom, then downstairs to tend the cats — god, "tend" is such a pretentious word when it comes to cats and feeding them — Puck was acting like such a shit to Tiger (pronounced "Tigger"), whose personality as a cat I don't much like anyway, that I wanted to kill her on the spot, finally picked up that grey furry squalling lump, Puck, that is, opened the door — both of them were on the back porch getting hysterical about getting fed, snapping and hissing at each other, fighting over some anticipated amount of cat crunchies they were going to get done out of (I can feel how dark the city of Vancouver is, pressing in through the windows at the edge of my vision, which is outside the black borders of eyeglass frames that I'm occasionally conscious of — Benjy Foureyes! Benjy Foureyes! he's about to pitch the softball toward home plate that Johnny Murphy in the batter's box is crowding, etc. — okay, excise all memory of childhood in order to attend to the cats, the city, the present — as though I have to account for every instant of consciousness while I'm here ((here on earth?)) but account to who?? and somewhere in the last patch ((of "thought," moments before "this")) I also thought I could revise my lengthy letter to Paul McAfee, which is almost a history of *City Down Below*, the newspaper he edits all by his lonesome, now that the rest of the voluntary writers who formed the bulk of that heroic brigade have broken with him and founded *Opposition Press*, etc.

— the point, the blessed point being that I awaken myself, the dark city pressing in, my mind chewing on that idea) and flung Puck back into the kitchen just to separate the two of them while I pour the cat chow and milk into their various respective bowls. I mean, what the fuck do they

19

think I'm doing if not feeding them when I go out on the back porch? I wish they'd just sit down like reasonable beings — Oh yeah, like *us*, we're reasonable beings, huh? — instead of going off in a cat sulk or charging the milk bowl —

Horace Wilson is in his shag-carpeted living room defending Paul — I'm skipping the whole digest-version biography of Horace, English prof and mentor to a generation of local poets, of whom Paul was once one, and now of course I see Horace distinctly in my mind's eye, at this moment and also decades later, after his death, after his departure not from earth but from us, a less and less reasonable being in direct proportion to the amount of alcohol in his bloodstream, and hear his wife Evelyn's voice saying with forbearance, "Oh, Horace," to excuse, mitigate, forgive in advance some excessive remark or gesture of his — defending Paul on the simple anarchist grounds that he *knows* McAfee, thereby accusing me of the crime of politics just by virtue of not putting personal loyalty ahead of whether I think it's right or wrong for gentle, mild-mannered Paul to have obtained, in the best tradition of small shopkeepers and factory owners, a court injunction against the sit-in protest of his former staff, etc. Well, you (whoever "you" is) can see how complicated *any* thought, fantasy, memory, actual human contact is.

Are you a homosexual?

I walk into his office in a temporary prefab building, while the permanent institutional edifice next door, which will eventually house the Canadian Immigration bureaucracy, is under extended renovation, down by the Vancouver harbourfront, though even the prefab has already acquired, as if automatically, an institutional patina of pea-green walls and grey cubicle dividers. His name is Mr. Eliot and he's in his cubicle. What I started out to say is that in between waking up, feeding the cats, and whatever else, and the late-afternoon contemplation of the events of the day, I applied to become a Canadian citizen. In the interim between my arrival in the country six or seven years earlier and now, I'd become, among other things, a fairly notorious student and civic radical whose pontifications and manifesto-like writings had been regularly reproduced in print and on the air. I hand my application to the man whose desk nameplate says "Mr. Eliot," and who is as unprepossessing as his name and surroundings suggest.

He has a question for me. His hand rests on a file that contains a thick pile of clippings that have been gathered for him by one of the nation's branches of the constabulary. "Are you a homosexual?" Mr. Eliot asks. He's not hostile. In fact, I intuit (and since this grey cubicle is so nondescript there is little to do other than intuit) that he might prefer a simple denial. He doesn't, particularly, want to know.

At the time, the early 1970s, homosexuality in Canada had been recently legalized when the justice minister (and later prime minister), Pierre Trudeau, declared that "the state has no business in the bedrooms of the nation." His omnibus bill, striking down proscriptions against homosexuality, was passed by parliament with less fuss than might have been anticipated. However, the immigration laws still contained an anachronistic prohibition against immigrants who are homosexuals.

What are the implications of answering that question? I ask, managing a pleasant no-nonsense tone (or at least that's how I sound to me). He explains (and again I'm aware that he doesn't particularly want to press this) the section of the immigration law concerning proscribed people, working his way past prostitutes, junkies, and those with contagious diseases right on down to my subsection. I'm afraid I don't know what my legal rights are in all this, I say, and perhaps we'd better set another meeting after I've consulted with counsel blah blah.

I'm out on the pier, walking across the wooden slabs of dock, looking at the tugs in the harbour and the trucks that get unloaded at a nearby ramp, noticing the messy disarray of parked cars jammed in behind various fences. Mr. Eliot has no objection. It's fine by him. After all, he does not expect to budge from behind that shabby oak desk. He'll still be there.

I'm just buying a little time in order to figure out what he is actually asking me. I figured out that he certainly isn't asking me "Are you a homosexual?" Mr. Eliot and Canada couldn't care less about that. Most Canadians I'd met over the years weren't particularly interested in my sexual orientation either, but were more curious about whether I was a draft dodger from the American war in Vietnam. Nope, military veteran, I reported. Of course, every time I open my distinctive yap, Canadians do say, Oh, you're American, eh? No, I'm Canadian, I say, once I'd become a Canadian, but that's not what they mean. They mean

I have an audible American accent, Whitman's "barbaric yawp," despite my efforts to pronounce "about" and "been" in a Canadian accent. Perhaps they also mean, Once an American, always an American. In reality, I'm probably not a citizen of any nation, but instead a "rootless cosmopolitan," a Wandering Jew. Still, rootless cosmopolitans and Wandering Jews tend to be better Canadians than most. I decide that Mr. Eliot is asking, "Are you planning to make a fuss about the homosexual clause in Canada's immigration laws?" I'm not, at least not at that moment. No political martyrdom, thank you. At an even deeper level, the answer is, It's none of your business.

"I'm ready to answer your question," I say, some days later. Mr. Eliot doesn't blink. He looks as though he hasn't left his desk in the intervening days. "Mm-hmm," he says, politely not repeating the offending question. "No," I say. That's good enough for him. He immediately, insofar as he is capable of it, or his position allows, seems to warm a bit as he checks some appropriate box on the appropriate form, and in due course I'll be sworn in.

Do I smell the salt air, once again gazing out from the pier that is becoming my home port? I'm still arguing, past midnight (the night before answering Mr. Eliot's question, before the cats, the revised letter to Paul McAfee; I'm not, as you can see, very adept when it comes to the chronological flow) at the printing plant, with the staff of *The Student* about whether the story of some minor scandal in the English department should be page 3 or page 1, haggling among the lighted layout tables (and in the back, at the corner of my eye, in half darkness, hulks of the old Linotype machines, punching out type from hot liquid lead for the *Racing Form*, a bucket at the typesetter's feet in which to deposit used type for re-melting, all of it being bypassed in the wave of computer technologies) with Merv Albert, Cindy Glass, even Jessica Peabody. In a way, they're delighted (for them, "crisis" is reality. I'm caught up in the heat of it, too).

How'd I get out here anyway? The pier at Aquatic Park, San Francisco, a Saturday afternoon, walking out to the end, passing the backs of people fishing, cruising a little but without much intent, looking at the water lapping the pylons, and at the tip I come to a little locked shed. The pier from which people catch shiners, according to Jack Spicer, the poet *grise* of the park. Kids with crab cages is what I remember. Then, looking back to the city, at Telegraph Hill and its jumble of houses piled up to the tower on its crest. The landscape produced by this mental effort reignites a particular emotion my heart is searching for. I'm young, it's okay to feel whatever I'm feeling, slightly lost, slightly annoyed by the wind. I was trying to light a cigarette by the little shack, door always locked, at the end of the pier, in the lee of the shelter it provided, and only had so many matches left.

The university newspaper staff members read the copy for themselves, slouched around their curved desks. They don't see it. Don't see it like I do. Or is it, don't see it my way? I'm pissed off at Harvey Cochrane, even though I don't see or talk to him. And Pam O'Hara — well, I was pissed off with her as soon as I realized she was actually "going with" Al Bradley. Rant and rave. There I am, past midnight, making everyone I can feel miserable. The "front page" is one of the absolutely few weapons we the students have, I tell an imaginary audience of 50,000 student newspaper workers. It's the place where we can put the most important thing we think people ought to know about, and when we slap the pictures of our enemies on it, they scurry like rats. Ranting and raving like a reasonable being. We're wasting the precious little ammo we got — until, in the conversation, I feel we're at the horrible conciliatory moment when, under the influence of two beers, Cindy Glass, I think it is this time, is sincerely saying, We really need to hold another staff get-together to — No. I'm not going to give up my place.

In the language, I mean. I'm not going to give up my place in the language. Goddammit, you haven't seen me half-angry yet you- you — you goddamned world! I feel like I'm putting you together piece by fucking piece, like I'm piling the houses onto Telegraph Hill one by one, white and yellow, and making that shiny thing shine upon them, that sun shine like a gold paper cut-out, cut out from I don't know what first-grade art class, age six. Stop bothering me. Stop messing with me, someone says in an alley behind my father's store at 45th and Prairie, Chicago, 1954. I saw men on the ground passing nets through their fingers, gnarly brown stubs from where the salt has eaten them for years, Amalfi coast, Italy, 1960. My romanticized image of their feeling is how I felt when I was making the world a minute ago.

Oh, I'm feeling old in you ("you" is world) amid the freshly laid-out nets or in my blue chair. The bay of water spread at our feet is surely Dante Lake.

At the end of everything there's a hooded figure far ahead in the prow of the boat, poling into smoky water as we move soundlessly in the fog.

Sitting in a blue chair, wrenching the eyeglasses off for a second, rubbing my eyes with the flat of my palm, twisting my neck. Wait, that's me, stretching my body up, out of this, the pieces dangling from my clothes like trinkets, not wanting to let me go up into —

Chicago Blues

One Saturday afternoon in Chicago in 1948, when I was seven years old, my mother Ida took me downtown to the Loop. It's known as the Loop because of the elevated urban railway. The tracks of the "El," as it's called, are raised on black metal pylons and form a loop around part of downtown Chicago. We went to the big Marshall Field and Carson's department stores and, after shopping, to the movie theatres on State Street. I recently found a night-time photo of that street while I was thinking about this incident — it's on the cover of Alan Ehrenhalt's *The Lost City*, a book about Chicago in the 1950s. The lighted marquees of the Chicago and State-Lake theatres face each other across the traffic-crowded thoroughfare.

My mother took me to the Chicago Theatre for the matinee. In those days they still had live stage shows before the movie was shown. That afternoon the star act was Carmen Miranda, the Portuguese-born Brazilian samba singer who wore elaborate, glamorous costumes and was famous for headdresses on which a pile of fruit was arranged atop her thick red hair. She performed a couple of numbers and entertained the crowd with some between-songs patter, which included an invitation for children in the audience to come up on stage. The ploy was Miranda's refutation of the claim that she was wearing a wig, that her lush, red hair wasn't her own.

The theatre's ushers quickly herded a half dozen of the children in the audience up on stage. I was one of them. We ordinary, real kids suddenly crossed the boundary of footlights into the magic world of the stage and its larger-than-life figures. There I was, tugging on a proffered lock of Carmen Miranda's red hair and offering mutely nodded testimony in reply to her question, "Ees it real?"

I was both frightened by the amusement of the audience of mostly women shoppers and thrilled to touch Carmen Miranda's hair. Of course, I didn't know that Miranda was "a Brazilian samba singer" or anything else. I probably thought of her as a fairy-tale princess come to life. What's interesting to me now is seeing that this incident has a meaning, has something to do with who I am and how I see Chicago. My mother's reaction after I came down from the stage and was back in my seat next to her is the emotional hole in the memory, since I've no idea what she felt, either then or on many other occasions, and now I've become curious about her feelings. That hole is why my autobiographical portrait of the city begins with my search for my mother. But before that, there's one more thought about theatres and cities.

Carmen Miranda was my first encounter with the space between the magical and the mundane. But it was at another stage venue, when I was fourteen or so, that I glimpsed the idea of the city as a theatre of history. What I saw was a production of Tennessee Williams's play *El Camino Réal* (The Royal Road), in which characters both real and fictional, from all periods of history, appeared on Williams's road of life: Don Quixote, Casanova, Lord Byron, Marguerite Gautier from Alexandre Dumas *fils' Camille*, and even a post-World War II GI that Williams called Kilroy, named for a ubiquitous chalked graffito of the era that declared "Kilroy was here."

An older, "artistic," second cousin of mine, Anne Thompson, gave me the ticket to the theatre because she saw in me a potential literary sensibility. The play was considered to be a failure (too sprawling, too "ambitious"), and Williams was criticized for his pessimism in the mid-1950s era of President Dwight Eisenhower's America. But I was completely entranced by the possibility that time and person were far more fluid than the linear version of our experience. This time I knew I was understanding something beyond the dramatic scenes on stage. I took the idea of time-shifting history on a theatre stage and transferred it to the city itself. Now I saw the city as a theatre in which, as Czesław Miłosz puts it, "Daily occurrences lean every day into history."

I

I was born in Chicago in 1941. A quarter century later, a group of white Chicago musicians, the Paul Butterfield Blues Band, recorded a song, "Born in Chicago," in which that sentence, "I was born in Chicago in 1941," repeated twice, provides the opening lines of their blues anthem.

I was born in Chicago, in 1941, on January 19, a Sunday, at about 3 AM, into the hands of the attending physician at Lutheran Deaconess Hospital, Dr. Nathan Kane, my uncle Docky. Actually, he was my mother Ida's uncle and therefore my great-uncle; his wife, Dora, a sister of my mother's mother, was my great-aunt. Before she became Dora Kane, she and my maternal grandmother had shared the family name of Alpert — I eventually saw photos of the patriarch, Sam Alpert — but my mother's maiden name, acquired from her mother's married name, was Malis, itself probably an immigrant's abbreviation of something like Malinowski. This gradually exfoliating genealogy seemed to me more a tangled vineyard than a family tree.

It was a horrendously long labour for my mother, some forty hours. The story of my prolonged birth, occurring only after my mother had endured three miscarriages, and told to me variously by several relatives, is the founding episode of the legend of my life. "You almost killed your mother," they would say, laughing because the story had a happy outcome.

By the year of my birth, France had already fallen to the Nazis in World War II; by the end of the year, the Japanese attacked Pearl Harbor. One side effect of my arrival — again, this is a vaguely recalled family tale — is that it may have exempted my father, Morrie, who was almost forty, from military service in the war, thanks to a regulation by which men of a certain age who were parents couldn't be drafted. Though I was my father's son, my birth belonged solely to my mother.

Yet she was but an affectionate stranger to me through my childhood. She was an utter paragon of the virtues recorded on the gravestones I saw when we made periodic Sunday visits to the cemetery to pay homage to the family dead: dutiful daughter, loving wife, devoted mother. And the next day, during her regular round of telephone calls to her sisters-in-law — Rose, Lily, and Pearl, the wives of her three brothers — I'd hear her reporting that "we were at the cemetery yesterday."

I was puzzled by her and by most of her family. Not by Uncle Docky and Aunt Dora, though. He was a lean, severe, ramrod-straight man with silver hair, politically a left-winger. Often, before the Friday (or occasionally Saturday) night dinners at their house, sitting in the living room and listening to the sonorous bass voice of radio newscaster H.V. Kaltenborn, intoning, "There's gooood news tonight," or gravely announcing "bad news tonight," some item in the broadcast would provoke an escalating, angry discussion that centred around Uncle Docky and ended with someone, his son Herbie or his daughter Marge's husband, Harry, shouting, "Well, if you think it's so great there, then go back to Russia!"

On some Saturday afternoons, my mother and I went to Aunt Dora's to join her and her daughter as they prepared the meal for that evening. The radio brought us music from the Metropolitan Opera in New York, and during a lull in the cooking, the women would repair to the dining room table for a few hands of canasta. Among the treats that Aunt Dora prepared were *gribinets*, as they were called in Yiddish, the bits of crusted chicken skin left from rendering the chicken fat to make *schmaltz*, and a sweet roll she baked in the oven, *kickels*, an airy, crisp, tan-coloured confection covered with speckles of sugar.

Aunt Dora is the one who is clearest in my mind. I see the pouches under her melancholy eyes as she dries her hands on her apron (do people still wear aprons at home when they're cooking?) while going to answer the doorbell. One night, just before dinner (was it in 1945?) when the bell rang — Marge's husband, Harry, or my father were expected, back "from work" — I announced presciently, "It's Herbie." The genius of four-year-old babes was confirmed when it turned out that Uncle Docky's and Aunt Dora's son Herbie had been discharged from the army a couple of days early and was now at last home from the war, a big stolid man still dressed in his military uniform. I glimpsed Aunt Dora as she rushed from the kitchen toward the apartment foyer, closed off from both the dining room and the living room by doors with small glass panels, drying her hands on her apron, her eyes welling with tears as her medal-decorated son came up the stairs.

After dinner and the clearing away of plates, the family would remain around the table for a friendly but loud game of penny-ante poker. Noticing her reluctance, while they played, to enjoy the pleasure of a cigarette — for obscure reasons of economy connected to memories of the Depression of the 1930s — Marge or Herbie would press upon Aunt Dora one of their own. And when she reluctantly accepted a long Pall Mall from one of them, she would cut it in half with scissors, saving one half and announcing, "I'll smoke it later," pronouncing the word, with a Yiddish accent, as *schmoke*. While they slapped their cards on the table and impatiently urged each other to "Play, play already," I crawled amid the animal-claw legs of the mahogany table and fell asleep at their feet, only to briefly half-awaken in my father's arms later as he and my mother walked to the car for the ride home.

But the rest of my mother's family, her brothers and sisters-in-law and their children, and my mother herself, were a puzzle to me. Her family bored me, and I quickly learned that I didn't have much capacity for that kind of boredom. I didn't understand their interests or passions — mostly connected to businesses like currency exchanges, insurance companies, accounting, and grocery stores — and instead identified with the many brothers, sisters, and offspring of my father's side of the family, who were raucous bohemians, or at least interested in books, conversation, stories, tall tales. My mother's stories, on the other hand, came from the radio soap operas broadcast during the day and the occasional *True Romance* magazine. Who were these people? I wondered about her and her family. At one point I actually voiced that question to my father, who gently explained to me that all of her relatives were part of the package that came with my mother, whom he, after all, loved, and who loved us. The important thing, he indicated, was to navigate these relations with a sort of social courtesy or, as he put it, "Even if you don't like them, at least you can be a *Mensch* and have a drink with them."

It was from my father that I tacitly learned a lesson about love, a rather terrible lesson: that *for love* (to recall the title of Robert Creeley's book), I might have to become intellectually discreet, that I might love someone with whom I couldn't fully share my thoughts, with whom I couldn't talk about certain things because they wouldn't understand them.

My father was an intellectual. He read books, thought about the cosmos, engaged me in serious conversation. On his rare holidays from work, he would spend his free time reading. With the autodidact's eccentric sense of selection, he read anything from Eugène Sue's *Mysteries of Paris* to the six-volume official history of the Mormon Church that he'd bought in Salt Lake City during our trip to the West Coast when I was thirteen. In the mornings, as I was getting ready for school, I'd find him at the dining room table, head on his arms, asleep after a night of reading, surrounded by books, an overflowing ashtray, and the little tin coffee percolator with its glass knob that showed you when the coffee had fully perked.

Something traumatic had happened to him before my birth. I only have a sketchy version of the story. It had happened during the Depression, which was the always recurrent, and for me mysterious, reference point upon which were founded all economic warnings of the present. ("Money doesn't grow on trees, you know," someone would intone and then launch into a tale of the unimaginable deprivations of the Depression.) The Depression, which was the great issue of my parents' generation, is now almost completely forgotten — as are issues that were contentious during most of my lifetime — but in my childhood its resonance was immense.

During the Depression of the 1930s, when my father was in his twenties, he had been on the road, riding the boxcars, living in hobo camps, bumming around. The road had led to youthful trouble, and the trouble — something about safecracking (the story was kept from me until my twenties) — involved a several-year stretch in jail. When he returned home to Chicago, he made a decision, essentially to save his life. The decision was his compromise with society. The package included marriage to the unmarried, late-twenty-something niece of Uncle Docky and Aunt Dora and help into small business from her family, some of whom were the owners of prosperous wartime grocery and meat markets. The prosperity, I recall from family anecdotes to which I inattentively listened, was dependent on access to fresh meat supplies beyond the officially rationed quotas.

That decision provided my father with social stability, however economically shaky, but more importantly with love, which was a mystery to me. Love, I learned, entailed intellectual sacrifices. My father was interested in the abstract questions and aesthetics I was interested in, but he couldn't talk about them with my mother, or with her family. His learning, insofar as it involved them, was reserved for something like parlour-trick displays of bits of knowledge. This disjunction between what was on his mind and real life was connected to the need for love. Or at least this is the way I perceived it. Although I wasn't conscious of how deeply I absorbed this model of affection while an adolescent, as soon as I entered into similar relations of my own, I saw that in some (neo-Freudian) fashion I tended to reproduce the model of my father's idea of love. More often than not, the beloved other was someone "simpler" than myself, someone whose reciprocal love for me included respect for my intellectual complexity, a prowess they could recognize but not fully participate in.

It is that experience of love, I think, that makes me recognize (and resist) the partial truth in the contemporary feminist demand for egalitarian love relationships, a demand I've always felt a trace of guilt about ever since I first heard it. We should love and be loved only by those who are our social, generational, economic, and intellectual equals, the feminists propose. But that is not the world I was given.

My mother had another, final miscarriage when I was four, after which she was told, by Uncle Docky, that any further pregnancy would be life threatening. While she was in the hospital, and even after she came home to recuperate, Alice, a black cleaning woman, was hired to come every day to keep house, cook, and babysit me. After my mother recovered sufficiently to resume her domestic duties, Alice was kept on to help with the housecleaning on a weekly basis.

Her great effect upon my life was based on an innocent lie she told that instilled in me a perpetual anticipation. One afternoon, after finishing her work, perhaps in response to a desire I'd voiced, Alice told me, "Child, next week I'm going to bring you a puppy dog." The next week I awaited her arrival with unbearable expectation. But there was no puppy dog. The puppy was still in transit, the puppy was getting its shots, the puppy would surely

arrive the following week. The amazing thing is that I never figured it out. Every week I awaited Alice's arrival with puppy-like
enthusiasm, expecting her to bring the dog.

After her miscarriage, my mother increasingly retreated from
my view, a semi-invalid wracked by severe diabetes and associated ailments. She died in her mid-fifties, in 1965. I was living in
San Francisco and flew home to be with my father for the funeral
and the Jewish ceremony of sitting *shiva* for the dead, which followed over several days. It was the year that the Paul Butterfield
Blues Band recorded "Born in Chicago," but on the airplane to
Chicago, a current sentimental English ditty that went "Mrs.
Brown, you've got a lov-e-ly daughter" turned in my mind. I
thought of my mother, with her enclosed, blameless, physically
painful life now over, as Mrs. Brown's lovely daughter.

So I didn't really know the woman from whose body I was born.
But if I didn't know her, I retained the songs I learned, so to speak,
at my mother's knee. They were mostly tunes by Sophie Tucker,
a hefty nightclub singer, then in the waning days of her career,
but who was still billed as the "Last of the Red Hot Mamas."
My mother also crooned snippets of Yiddish tunes that had filtered into the American culture of middle-class Jews. Among the
songs my mother sang were "Bei Mir bist Du Schön" ("To Me,
You're Beautiful"), Tucker's version of "St. Louis Woman," and
"The Anniversary Waltz" ("Oh, how we danced / on the night /
we were wed . . . "). But the one that most often comes to mind
— perhaps her muted call for recognition, valorization — was
"Some of These Days," which went "Some of these days / You're
gonna miss me, honey."

That's the word I was looking for in looking for my mother
among my vocabularies: "Honey."

II

Time turns hometowns into memory palaces and ghost cities. I was born and raised in Chicago and left it in summer 1958 when I headed out into the world at age seventeen. It now appears to me retrospectively in two ways. First, I see that theatre of history populated by all the figures who were present but unknown to me during my years there. Second, in a more literal sense, the city returns in the details of the narrow but specific geographic zones of childhood and adolescence. So, for instance, in the romantic sense of Chicago I've invented for myself, I'm a six-year-old in spring 1947 on my way to Mrs. Valentine's first-grade class at Sumner Elementary School on the West Side, confident reader of the Dick and Jane first-grade textbook ("See Dick run. Run, Dick, run. See Spot run. Run, Spot, run. See Jane ... "). I was a confident reader because my father had already taught me to read, so I was spared puzzling over the inanities of Dick and Jane, but I was puzzled by why we had to read about them.

Meanwhile, partway across town, around the intersection of Milwaukee and Division streets, the Polish section of the city (where my uncle Gob has his drygoods store), the novelist Nelson Algren, soon to be the author of the 1950 National Book Critics' award-winning *Man With the Golden Arm*, a novel about the hell of heroin addiction in Chicago's back streets, is in the midst of a passionate transatlantic affair with the French existentialist writer Simone de Beauvoir. She's about to write *The Second Sex*, the founding document of modern feminism. He's showing her around the grubby taverns, backroom gambling dens, and B-girl hotels that are his bailiwick, and the elegant, brainy Parisian is swept off her feet by the rough-edged authenticity of her Chicago boyfriend. Chicago as a city of literature and romance.

Or I'm fourteen years old, in fall 1955, in love for the first time with a schoolmate, and we're erotically horsing around in the boy's gymnasium locker room at Marshall High School, with barely a language in which to recognize our incipient desire. And somewhere out there in a swanky Chicago-area mansion ("swanky" is a word from that era) is the sophisticated Hugh Hefner, puffing a pipe, garbed in a brocade bathrobe, the recent founder of *Playboy* magazine, a glossy, cleverly respectable, and very profitable packaging of soft-core porn with fashionable fiction and interviews. He's lounging at his heated swimming pool, surrounded by a "bevy" of "Playboy bunnies." That night, in my bedroom, I've unfolded the picture of the nubile Playboy centre-fold-of-the-month, and as if I were doing an experiment in chemistry class, I'm checking my reactions to make sure I'm "normal." The experiment is technically a gooey success, but with the cool objectivity of a budding scientist, I recognize that I prefer the locker room to the Playboy mansion, and I say to myself, foreseeing future social difficulties, "Uh-oh, this is going to be a problem." Chicago as a city of desire.

Or I'm within a year of graduation from Austin High School, the 1957–58 school year, and I'm deciding whether to "Join the Navy and See the World" (as the recruiting poster has it) or make use of an invitation from the University of Chicago to drop out of high school and join the university's innovative "accelerated program" as an undergraduate. Meanwhile, on the far South Side of Chicago, even farther south than the black ghetto where my father's grocery and meat market is located at 45th and Prairie Avenue, there are a host of people in the classrooms of the University of Chicago whom I'll eventually come to know through their books.

Although I'd never been to the University of Chicago campus, during those years I was growing up, the future philosophers and social critics Richard Rorty and Allen Bloom, then grad students, were listening to the lectures of Leo Strauss. Was aspiring novelist Philip Roth there, too? What about Saul Bellow? Bellow would become a friend of Bloom and decades later write a very good, late novel about him, *Ravelstein*. In my reconstructed mirror of the past, he has already published the prize-winning *Adventures of Augie March*, whose opening lines declare, "I am an American, Chicago born — Chicago, that sombre city — and go at things as I have taught myself, free-style, and will make the record in my own way." Chicago as a city of the mind.

Even an odd television incident fits into this picture of imagining a larger Chicago than the one I knew. On the city's new educational channel one evening in 1957, the city's great architect, Frank Lloyd Wright, and its most famous poet, Carl Sandburg ("Chicago, city of big shoulders ..."), respectively eighty-eight and seventy-nine years old, are chatting amiably and blandly about the prospects for the city. After the moderator signs off and the old guys think they are off-air, Wright turns to Sandburg and says, "We'd better get out of here, Carl, before somebody starts telling the truth." The point is that there wasn't a lot of public truth-telling in the Chicago of that era. And elsewhere on that soon-to-be-pervasive TV, far from the truth, lurks the jowly bulk of recently elected Chicago mayor Richard J. Daley.

III

The literal city begins for me in an empty lot behind the three-storey apartment building and its navy grey, wooden, back porches at 1110 South Keeler Avenue on Chicago's West Side where I lived with my parents. In the post-war summer of 1946, the lot is filled with tall milkweeds, there's a raggedy path diagonally bisecting it, and we dig foxholes from which to replay imaginary scenes of the just-concluded World War II. Kitty-corner across Fillmore Street is the sandlot baseball field belonging to the adjacent red-brick Calumet Baking Powder factory. The cans of baking powder are dark red and have a drawing of the head of a Calumet Indian on them.

The outfield boundary is a cement railroad viaduct, and when one of the local heroes, a sixteen- or seventeen-year-old kid named Archie, with muscular biceps and wearing a white T-shirt, hits the ball onto the tracks, it's a home run, and one of us younger kids has to go around behind the viaduct, climb the grassy slope, retrieve the ball from the tracks, and toss it back onto the field. The viaduct runs through the neighbourhood, and where Keeler Avenue crosses under it there's a dip in the asphalt so trucks can get through without their roofs scraping the viaduct overhead. During the summer rains, the dip gets flooded and cars are shipwrecked.

From our empty-lot foxholes amid the milkweeds, armed with wooden toy rifles, we can see the railroad viaduct and occasionally, running on the tracks, long dun-coloured passenger trains. In their windows, we can see the uniformed soldiers coming home from World War II, like my older cousin Herb Kane. The boy in the foxhole with me is six-year-old Johnny Tallone, who lives with his parents in a semi-basement flat in our apartment building. Johnny's father, Frank, works in a metal fabricating factory, and from the lead scrap he makes toy soldiers for us. I have a Lionel electric toy train, and Johnny and I stuff the lead soldiers into the windows of the passenger cars so that the train looks like the ones we see on the railroad viaduct.

This is my world, the tiny patch of less than a square block, my Chicago, whose gradual expansion I can trace year by year as I venture out from the empty lot. In one direction, north, I walk under the viaduct along Keeler toward Sumner Elementary School located on the diagonally-running Fifth Avenue. In the other direction, south, I head toward the main neighbourhood intersection of Roosevelt and Pulaski roads. It is a world of origins: first friends, first learnings, first city (even though Chicago was known in America as the "Second City," second to New York). The details of it, which flood in at the instant of recall, explain almost everything about the shaping of self: sex, adventure, relationships, intellect. The images are like a Tinkertoy set from which I can put together my childhood past. Tinkertoys were a package of wooden spokes and wheels out of which one could construct buildings, trains, Ferris wheels, and imaginary animals. In the contemporary world, they've been replaced by video games in which kids practise killing other people.

I have a tricycle, Johnny Tallone has a red wagon. The older boys in the neighbourhood, like teenage slugger Archie and his pal, Jackie, conduct races by pushing me on my tricycle and Johnny on his wagon as fast as they can along the sidewalk on Fillmore Street. The speed is incredible, the ride precarious, the tricycle tipping onto one wheel as we make a perilous corner. Then comes the crash. We've hit the stanchion of a metal fence enclosing a patch of grass. There's blood everywhere. Mine. A gash just below the knee. I still have the faint scar, the first scar.

I'm of two minds about the specificity of those images that spill out of the cornucopia of the past. There's Callico, my first stuffed toy animal with its multicoloured, slightly greasy oilcloth covering. I see the dented two-cup tin coffee pot with a glass knob that violently jiggles when my father's coffee brews. Then the second-hand Tom Mix and Red Ryder and Little Beaver comic books being resold for a nickel from the top of an orange crate by one of the Murphy kids down the block, which I urgently need to buy. I'm looking at the framed photo of me at age four in a sailor uniform, the picture sitting on a spinet piano, my cheeks and eyes colour-tinted by my cousin Bob's mother, Marge, at the photo shop that she and her husband, my father's brother Lew, run at the intersection of Van Buren and Canal streets downtown near the Passport and Immigration office. Finally, in this strange sequential rush of objects, there are the John R. Tunis sports novels, with shortstops named Bucky and outfielders called Jeff and Chad, that I devoured as an adolescent reader and that I've only seen referred to once in my entire subsequent reading career, in Philip Roth's novel *American Pastoral*. On the one hand, these things, and dozens of others, are irreplaceable, are what the real is made of. On the other hand, they're just lost, obsolete, meaningless (or only idiosyncratically meaningful) artifacts, the stuff of elderly nostalgia.

The first enlargement of my backyard world is a few paces south along Keeler. There's another empty lot, grassless, which backs onto the three-storey rear brick wall of our building. You can throw a rubber ball high up against the wall without any fear of breaking a window since there aren't any. I play games of solitary imaginary baseball, or if there's a playmate to act as a combination infielder-outfielder, then, as the batter-first baseman, I also have to be the radio announcer broadcasting the game as we play it — my first idea of narration.

Behind the batter's box of this imaginary field are the wooden back porches, painted with the same navy-surplus grey paint as the ones on our building, of another three-storey apartment house that fronts on the next street, Grenshaw. The paint blisters in the summer heat, and one of our games is to break the bubbles of paint. I only know the back of the building. That's where the Murphys live — three brothers, Steve, Johnny, and Tommy, a sister, the parents — all crammed into a small basement flat that I see as being so poor that I think it has a hardpacked dirt floor rather than the linoleum kitchen floors in our building (the actual floor must have been cement). Through the open door, I spy Johnny Murphy, the brother closest in age to me, walking around in the gloom of their cave-like dwelling, wearing white underpants. He's exotic and, because he's tough, also a little scary. Once, referring to some adventurous feat he was preparing to attempt, jumping off a high diving board I think it was, he said to me, "If I can't do it, I'll kiss your ass." In the erotic confusion of age ten or eleven, I didn't realize he meant the phrase figuratively rather than literally, and I was uncertain if he was threatening that I would have to kiss his ass if he succeeded.

On the corner of Keeler and Grenshaw, on the main floor of the building where the Murphys live, is the grocery store where I take my pennies to buy gummy candies, licorice strips, Popsicles in summer — two columns of flavoured, sugary water frozen on two pine-wood sticks. Discarded Popsicle sticks are everywhere and easy to collect. When you have twenty or so, the flexible pine wood can be plaited (my first craft) into a toy raft that floats in rain puddles — not much different in principle from plaiting these bits of childhood into a life raft floating on a sea of time.

Chicago now includes friends, a gang of neighbourhood kids, but it also embodies a first sociological recognition. It's a neighbourhood more or less evenly divided between Jews and Irish. When we choose baseball teams to play on the sandlot — late into long summer evenings until the ball at last becomes invisible in the darkness — a meritocracy of hitting and fielding skill reigns, indifferent to ethnicity. Everybody wants Eddie Lacy on their team. But there's also an underlying rivalry of religion and class, and the occasional scrap between leaders of the hostile ethnicities. Bobby Greenspan, Jewish, who lives next door to me, and Steve Murphy, Irish, are rolling around in the dirt of the lot between our buildings, one of them with a bloodied nose that stains the other's dirt-smeared white T-shirt.

What strikes me now is how little I knew of the city's geography. The literal city returns to me in the form of non-contiguous island neighbourhoods. There's a horizon: to the northwest, on summer evenings, a glow of fire from the steel mills in nearby Cicero (or is it more distant Gary, Indiana?), and from the south, on those same hot summer nights, an olfactory horizon as the smell of the Chicago stockyards wafts across the city, comes in the open kitchen window.

I have almost no sense of direction in the city — even now, to read the past, I need a streetmap of Chicago at my side. My fuzzy sense of geography and direction, even in places I supposedly know, is one of the motifs of my life. I never know where I am, and I'm always afraid of being abandoned in the middle of nowhere. Yet I plunge deeper and deeper into far-flung urban jungles in a nutty effort to be somewhere. I think that explains some of my persistent fascination with cities and why portraits of cities are part of everything I write.

Though I'm fuzzy on geography, I know some of the transportation corridors that connect one relevant neighbourhood-island to another. For instance, I know how to get from my house to my father's economically precarious corner store on the South Side, where I help out after school and on weekends. Looking at another photograph in Ehrenhalt's *Lost City*, this one of the intersection of 43rd and Prairie, just two blocks from my father's store — a photo taken in 1954, when I was thirteen — I strain to identify the corner restaurant / drugstore where I went up to the counter and ordered lunch (macaroni and ground beef in tomato sauce), almost unaware of being the only white person in a sea of black people. I can see the black woman in her starched uniform putting the plate on the counter before me and saying, "Here you go, sugar."

But all I see in this photo are the sun-bleached sidewalks, the wide traffic-free street with its brick paving and embedded streetcar rails on what could be a spring Sunday morning. The few people out walking are so distant that I can't identify them by skin colour. But the point to reiterate is that my experience is phenomenological rather than political. My nascent politics, shaped by my father's sense of respect for people and by what I've seen on television, are liberal, supportive of the civil rights movement on the march in a distant, feudal, anachronistic American South. But my sense of that, while I'm delivering a bag of groceries up a rickety flight of wooden back-porch steps to a middle-aged black couple and am rewarded with a shiny twenty-five-cent tip, is simply that these are people. So are the young black men in the neighbourhood, who work in the store and teach me to shoot a basketball in the alley. The baskets aren't nets but peach baskets with their bottoms punched out, nailed up to telephone poles.

The other distant neighbourhoods simply float like islands, sudden landfalls that we unexpectedly arrive at in my father's car. Uncle Gob — he's another of my father's siblings, three brothers and four sisters — has his drygoods store in the Polish neighbourhood on Division Street. That's where I learn to say "How are you?" in Polish and where they call me "Staš" or "Stashu."

Cousin Marge, the "high-strung" daughter of my mother's aunt Dora and uncle Docky, and her husband, Harry Fertig, a soft-spoken insurance salesmen at Prudential Life who always asks me how I'm doing in school, live in a high-rise apartment on Lake Shore Drive along Lake Michigan, a status-conscious address that Marge has anxiously insisted on acquiring. Her anxiety will eventually turn into "mental illness." I remember the distinctive, individual sounds of their laughter better than I do the geography. Downtown is the Hamilton Hotel, site of the monthly Cousins' Club meetings that bring together my mother's extended family. Eventually, I learn how to get downtown by myself to go to Kroch and Brentano's bookstore.

IV

There's also a real, larger, historical city that I was only dimly aware of during my years there. It's run by two great entities, the Machine and the Mob. The Machine is the Democratic Party of Chicago and Cook County, and its Boss, as of 1955 and for the next twenty years (until he died in office), is Richard J. Daley. One middle-of-the-road account of Daley's long tenure that I've been reading just to fill in the facts I didn't know as a kid is Adam Cohen and Elizabeth Taylor's *American Pharaoh*. A more pungent, harder hitting biography is Chicago journalist Mike Royko's *Boss*.

Daley rose to a position of almost absolute power from the humble Irish-Catholic, bungalow neighbourhood of Bridgeport, north of the stockyards. The machine he came to control, abetted by church and business elites, consisted of his lieutenants, city aldermen and county commissioners, thousands of "precinct captains" responsible for getting out the vote at election time, and an even vaster population of people holding patronage jobs — city clerks, garbagemen, building inspectors, judges — doled out by the machine. The corruption was deep and the payoffs huge. Though Daley's minions regularly got scooped up in periodic waves of moral fervour and even went to jail, Daley himself was untouchable. That's because the secret of his politics was not stealing money but exercising power — and Daley's power was almost as absolute as that of any feudal ruler who ever lived. His lieutenant in the Jewish ward where I lived was Alderman Jake Arvey, whose name was uttered in tones of reverence. If the local precinct captain couldn't get your parking ticket fixed, your alley paved, your kid into summer camp, he would utter the magic formula, "I'll talk to Jake Arvey, don't worry."

I knew even less about the Mob. An Italian kid at school might boast of some cousin or uncle with mob connections, but it was an invisible power, like the grace offered by the Catholic Church. The Chicago Mafia's dramatic glory days of the 1920s and Al Capone had been succeeded by a quieter, more businesslike generation, headed by Tony Accardo and the younger Sam Giancana. Accardo, like Daley, lived a long life and died peacefully, still in office. Between the Machine and the Mob was the institution that served both masters, the doubly corrupt Chicago Police Department. It was, by all accounts, perpetually on the take, racist, and vicious. A decade after I left Chicago, it would be found guilty of a "police riot" against protestors at the 1968 Democratic National Convention held in Chicago.

The Lost City by Alan Ehrenhalt is a book about the allegedly "forgotten virtues of community in America." The reason I'm reading it is because I'm trying to figure out how to understand the past, including my own past. When people talk about their childhoods, they invariably get onto the subject of whether there was something wonderful about their childhood neighbourhoods and times that has now been irretrievably lost. When I listened to such talk as a kid, I rather typically regarded the adults' memories as mere nostalgia. Ehrenhalt's book is set in various neighbourhoods in Chicago in 1957, the year I was preparing to head out into the world, and Ehrenhalt offers a political defence of what he believes are lost virtues. The lost virtues he laments are authority, religious belief, loyalty, obedience, and the value of community.

Ehrenhalt is no dummy. He's an intelligent conservative. His lament has some appeal and isn't mere nostalgia. Rather, it is the political proposal to somehow restore those lost virtues which makes him dangerous in my eyes. Ehrenhalt is what's known as a "communitarian" thinker, part of a school of contemporary political philosophy that had some prominence in the closing years of the twentieth century. I'm reading him as a negative example of how to see mid-twentieth-century American life. I think that what he has in mind leads to a political dead end, one that is still popular in contemporary American urban life.

Ehrenhalt remembers that the Chicago Cubs' black short-stop of the late 1950s, Ernie Banks, loyally stuck with the team despite being drastically underpaid during a decade or more of annual Most Valuable Player-level performances. Ehrenhalt also remembers Chicago alderman and congressional representative John Fary, a tavern owner by trade, whose claim to fame was his humble boast that he had faithfully supported Mayor Daley for over twenty years and "the mayor was always right." As Ehrenhalt more broadly puts it, "People just stayed married in the 1950s, to their spouses, to their political machines, to their base-ball teams," and he suggests that this was basically a good thing.

"If it is true to say of 1950s America that it was a world of lim-ited choices," he says, "it is also fair to call it a world of lasting relationships." What grieves Ehrenhalt is a contemporary world of bewildering, unlimited, individual choice and the concomitant loss of authority, faith, and community that it entails. He blames this loss on the coming of age of the self-indulgent baby boom generation of the 1960s.

Ehrenhalt's paean to lost values and virtues is clever. Not only is he aware of the danger of mere nostalgia, but he also knows that a great deal of the loss he grieves over was primarily caused by the developments of American capitalism during its mid-twentieth-century boom years. Ehrenhalt recognizes that the responsibil-ity for moving factories to regions with cheaper labour costs was purely a capitalist decision, not something decided by communi-ties. The cozy corner stores he lyrically recalls, like my father's, were doomed not by the neighbours, but by the advertising and pricing power of national supermarket chains. But his partial rec-ognition of capitalist power also serves to cover up that power. Instead of saying that neighbourhoods were irrevocably changed for the worse by capitalism, Ehrenhalt blames the abstraction of "choice," which is tied to the willful, rebellious youth of the succeeding decade. It is true that the next generation challenged complacent authority and that we made stupid mistakes of our own. But the point is that the authority we challenged was unrea-sonable, not some beneficent form of order whose passing should be lamented.

Ehrenhalt is also shrewd enough to note that "there are few among us ... who mourn for the rigidities and constrictions of American life in the 1950s." But there is a mourning, he says, for a sense of community that many remember to have existed in their childhoods and that no longer exists now. "Authority," he admits, "is something else again. It evokes no similar feelings of nostalgia." Ehrenhalt's argument is that one can't have the virtues of community without also endorsing, in some significant measure, the virtues of authority, faith, and loyalty.

Yet when Ehrenhalt looks at "the whole array of social institutions [that] still stood outside the grip of the market and provided ordinary people with a cushion against it," something curious happens. The authority of the day, whether embodied in Mayor Daley, the bishop of the archdiocese, or the cop roughing up a black motorist, is monstrous, undemocratic, and far from reasonable. The faith with which people were imbued, whether embodied in the Catholic catechism or the revivalism of black storefront churches, was bizarre, authoritarian, and if not plain false, a permanent mystification. Finally, his defence of the virtues and pleasures of the oppressed black community is risible at best and never comes close to recognizing that virulent racism in Chicago was part of the nation's national disgrace. Ehrenhalt's political project is to restore authority, but the actual authority he examines as a historian is hideous.

Ehrenhalt tends to gloss over all the imperfections, but he concedes that "there is no point in pretending that the 1950s were a happy time for everyone ... For many, the price of the limited life was impossibly high. To have been an independent-minded alderman in the Daley machine, a professional baseball player treated unfairly by his team, a suburban housewife who yearned for a professional career, a black high school student dreaming of possibilities that were closed to him, a gay man or woman forced to conduct a charade in public — to have been any of these things in the 1950s was to live a life that was difficult at best, and tragic at worst." He, nonetheless, continues to mourn. I don't think we should mourn this particular past. Chicago, though it wasn't all that different from other big American cities in the peaceful, prosperous era of President Dwight Eisenhower, was an authoritarian, racist, corrupt model of life. For us kids, it was just life, filled with the little, specific objects and relationships that make up childhood. That's not a cause for mourning either. We ought to save our mourning for things that matter to us — for the dead, for faded beauty, for *temps perdu*.

∪

What interests me is not elegy but what I think of as "windows" into a world that I might enter. I found those windows more in painted images, books, and conversation than I did on television, in the movies, or from the radio, although I duly absorbed the stories they told. At around age six, I was stirred by a reproduction of John Everett Millais's *The Youth of Raleigh* — the first painting I ever "saw" — that hung in the waiting room of Uncle Docky's medical office. Two boys sit in the sand on the seashore, at the feet of a veteran sailor, who sits on a log and points out to sea as he recounts an old salt's tale, inciting them (and me) to adventure.

The emotional charge I get from painting is explicitly connected to the initiatory childhood experience of being taken to see the sumptuous collection of the Art Institute of Chicago — the Impressionists, Picasso, Georges Seurat's pointillist *La Grande Jatte*. The idea I crudely developed had to do with the way art reflects the world to create another heretofore non-existent world. What begins as a mirror or representation of the world becomes an independent landscape, one whose figures and objects we can enter in imagination so that we, too, are doubled, multiplied, as either personae or as an additional figure in the new landscape. At the same time, the painting and our psychological relationship to it are simply part of the world, but our conception of reality has become more complicated. That idea was barely articulated at, say, age twelve, but I was intuitively certain that I was seeing something from "out there."

Even more fundamental to my developing sense of a geography outside us, and a temporality behind and/or under us, were the books my father gave me to read and those I found on my own in the public library. The library was the one "social institution outside the grip of the market," as Ehrenhalt puts it, that was of use to me. My sense of Chicago expanded beyond its present-day streets to Frank Norris's *The Pit*, about the Chicago wheat pool traders; Upton Sinclair's *The Jungle*, about the Chicago stockyards; and Jack London's *The Iron Heel*, with its imagination of socialist revolution in Chicago. Soon I found the books of Bellow and Nelson Algren set in present-day Chicago.

Equally important as the books about Chicago were the sea stories my father started me reading to give me an idea of the wider world: London's *The Sea Wolf*, Jules Verne's *Twenty Thousand Leagues Under the Sea*, Richard Henry Dana's *Two Years Before the Mast*, and Melville's *Typee* and then *Moby-Dick*. My father's personal repertoire of stories about running away from home and riding boxcars across America in the 1920s also had their effect. When I eventually announced that I wanted to go to sea, he wasn't surprised, or displeased. What's more, I could count on my father's authority — the sole authority I trusted to be reasonable — to fend off dissenting relatives who knew that aspiring children went to college, not to sea. "It's what he wants to do," my father declared, settling the familial matter, as he had earlier settled the matter of my not wanting a bar mitzvah.

My literary interests were crosscut by the lure of the media. I didn't understand the difference between real writing and slick journalism until much later, when I actually worked as a journalist. Both serious books and sensational tabloids seemed like equally glamorous instances of being in print. So, for example, my first book review (I think it was in fifth grade, age eleven), based on a patchy reading of *Moby-Dick*, was titled "Bloated Whale Beached." I got the idea for the snappy title from the headlines of the tabloids. The teacher was impressed, I believe, by this hatchet job, at least in light of my youth, but I now cringe at what I see as a tendency toward glibness. It only meant I would have to read *Moby-Dick* again, later, and this time pay attention.

I was also a reader of the *Chicago Tribune* and its tabloid sibling, the *Chicago Sun-Times*, which I was soon inspired to emulate. I became the publisher, editor, writer, and sole reader of the *Oswego Times*, named for the obscure town of Oswego, New York, which I had goofily selected at random from the *Rand-McNally Atlas of the United States*. Since I was simultaneously reading John R. Tunis sports novels and running an imaginary baseball league, the *Times*, under my editorship, mostly reported sports scores.

The imaginary baseball league was based on a board game called All-Star Baseball. The game consisted of circular cards of famous ballplayers, which were divided up into a map of the players' actual records. If they hit lots of home runs or struck out a lot, the respective spaces for home runs and strikeouts on the card reflected that. The cards were placed on a cardboard mount to which was attached a metal spinner. You flicked the spinner with your fingernail — it hurt a little — and wherever the spinner stopped on the card determined whether it was a hit or an out or a walk. I dutifully kept the stats on the teams I made up and faithfully reported the results of the games the teams played in the *Times*. The interesting feature of the game, and the point of this memory, is that it included players from all historical eras. So it was possible for Babe Ruth, Honus Wagner, or Rogers Hornsby, all historical figures, to play in the same imaginary games as such contemporary players as Johnny Mize, Ted Williams, or Ernie Banks of our own Chicago Cubs. The sole reader of the *Times*, namely me, was immersed in this time-shifting theatre of baseball history.

Finally, I put imaginary print behind me for real print. My first publication was a letter to the editor of the *Chicago Sun-Times*, *circa* 1952–53, in which I urged readers to take a balanced view of the congressional hearings pitting anti-Communist senator Joseph McCarthy against Joseph Welch, counsel for the US Army, an institution that the senator alleged harboured thousands of Communist agents. I had even too-cleverly figured out that appending the words "8th Grade" to my signature would significantly improve my chances of appearing in print.

My first reader was an older, Jewish high school kid in the neighbourhood, Ben Rubin, who coolly asked me, "Did you write that letter?" "Yes," I proudly replied. He didn't say anything more, just went on his way. I was never able to determine whether he was simply verifying my authorship or displaying a young radical's contempt for liberal wishy-washiness. But his tone made me suspect that appearing in print wasn't so great if what you wrote was stupid. I suppose, in my defence, it could be said that at least all these activities kept me out of trouble and spared my parents the fashionable worry of the day, namely, "juvenile delinquency."

Fortunately, beyond my flair for the merely facile, I had some idea of wanting to be a writer. In the last years of high school, age sixteen and seventeen, having settled in with the bohemian crowd that hung out in drama class — I appeared as a prosecutor in Ayn Rand's play *The Night of January 16th* and as a sheriff in William Saroyan's *Hello, Out There* — I began writing a series of prose poems, sketches, vignettes, and verse. After I had written a sufficient amount, twenty-five pages or so, I stapled it all together under the title *How the Night Comes to Me*. My first book.

My cousin Anne Thompson, the one who gave me the ticket to Tennessee Williams's *El Camino Réal*, also gave me a subscription to a magazine, the *Saturday Review of Literature*. One day in 1957, I read a review in that magazine of Jack Kerouac's novel *On the Road*. The reviewer hated it, describing Kerouac's stories of his and his friends' madcap adventures across America as tiresome, amateurish, and jejune. I had to look up "jejune" in the dictionary, but it got my attention. The reviewer also made the mistake of quoting sizeable chunks of Kerouac's breathless prose to make his critical point. In one passage, the book's narrator, Sal Paradise, is recounting the story of the novel's hero, Dean Moriarty, and

his street buddies, his innumerable girls and sex parties and pornographic pictures, his heroes, heroines, adventures. They rushed down the street together, digging everything in the early way they had, which later became so much sadder and perceptive and blank. But then they danced down the street like dingledodies, and I shambled after as I've been doing all my life after people who interest me, because the only people for me are the mad ones, the ones who are mad to live, mad to talk, mad to be saved, desirous of everything at the same time, the ones who never yawn or say a commonplace thing, but burn, burn, burn like fabulous yellow roman candles exploding across the stars and in the middle you see the blue centerlight pop and everybody goes "Awww!"

Those quotes were enough. I had now read books by most of the major contemporary American writers and I had never seen any prose like the quoted paragraphs of Jack Kerouac. I didn't hesitate. I put down the magazine, left my room, got on the Washington Boulevard bus, and went straight downtown to Kroch and Brentano's bookstore. I was as excited as I was the time I rushed down with a nickel in my hand to buy the used copy of the Red Ryder and Little Beaver comic book the Murphys were selling. By the time I was back on the Washington Boulevard bus, reading the first pages about Sal Paradise and Dean Moriarity, I was in Jack Kerouac's America.

Soon after reading *On the Road*, I also found the *Evergreen Review* at Kroch's, a magazine that published Kerouac and a group of his friends — Allen Ginsberg, William Burroughs, Gregory Corso, and others. A widely scattered community of the very people I might be looking for existed. Like someone on a desert island putting a message in a bottle, I put my own pamphlet of writing, *How the Night Comes to Me*, in an envelope, along with a note explaining that I was a sixteen-year-old in Chicago who had read *On the Road* and wanted to be a writer, and I sent it to Kerouac at his publisher's address in New York. A week or so later, I came home from school, opened the family mailbox, to which I had a key, and inside I found a postcard filled with typed writing from top to bottom and along the sides. "Dear Stan," it opened, "You neednt ever worry about not only your reputation as a poet but about my great wild admiration of your poetry and I think the same will be said by Ginsberg, Corso et all, when they see your stuff." It was from Jack Kerouac. The "outside" had sent a message in a bottle to my desert island in "Chicago, that somber city." The rest of the message contained similar enthusiasms, practical advice, and Ginsberg's address and noted that my "great name" had a ring similar to that of "Johnny Pesky," third baseman of the Boston Red Sox, 1942–54.

I was soon on the road myself. My first stop: Great Lakes Naval Training Center, which put me on a bus and shipped me to the US Navy boot camp in San Diego, California. The rest is, well, a history that I've documented elsewhere.

VI

My cousin Bob Perrey is the family chronicler, archivist, and ring-master of our particular familial circus. I'll skip the story of how he got to be a Perrey instead of a Persky, except to note that the name change was predicated on a grain of half-truth connected to his parents' exaggerated fears about how anti-Semitism might affect their offspring's career. Bob is a year or so older than me and is the person in the family closest to me in terms of irony, wariness, and intellectual interests. There are others in our clan who have the same kind of minds Bob and I do, particularly the daughter of Aunt Emma, our younger cousin Karen Loeb, who is also a writer and teacher, and Joe Persky, who teaches economics at the University of Illinois in Chicago. Joe is the son of my father's youngest brother, Harold, a biochemist who was the first person in the family to go to university and become a professor. But Bob is the one I hear from most often.

Bob stayed in Chicago twenty years longer than I did, leaving only in mid-life, in the late 1970s, for California, where he and his wife Heidi raised a sizeable brood of children. He has a sharper sense of Chicago than I do because he lived there and was politically active during the 1960s and '70s. He is one of those talented people who has been a jack of many trades, from college professor to theatrical producer to technical manual writer to proprietor of a tobacco shop. More to the point here, he's also an enviably competent composer-musician, and at one stage in his career he portrayed Chicago as a theatre of history in a cabaret-style political satire. Produced soon after the 1968 riots in Chicago, his theatre piece, *City in a Swamp*, took a dig at the civic motto, "City in a Garden," and played on the aboriginal word "Checagou," which meant something like "stinking swamp." The show was also a local hit, sometimes even outdrawing the road-company production of the Broadway musical of the moment, *Hair*.

So Bob does other things besides remembering family lore and keeping the rest of us up to date on whereabouts, marriages, births, and deaths. But it was in his role as family ringmaster that he gradually cajoled us all to Chicago for a couple of days at the end of summer 1999. I was in Berlin that summer and would return there a few days later. But for a little while, for the first time in decades, there we all were in my cousin Joe's living room in a Chicago neighbourhood on the North Side, close to Lake Michigan. There were now only cousins, spouses, and their children, who were also cousins. All of our parents were dead. They were the ghosts in the circus tent.

We hadn't all been together for at least thirty years, yet everyone was instantly recognizable and we were, in the family tradition, as garrulous as I remember our parents being when they were all gathered at my aunt Emma's house, telling tales, arguing about who was born when, and who lived where, and where the stars were to be seen on a summer night.

By mid-life, most people have acquired a veritable sea-chest — just like the locker at the foot of my bunk in the navy barracks — full of yarns, our own and those we've acquired from other people, and we continue to add to them into old age. We tell those stories again and again, more than twice-told tales, recycling them for new acquaintances. But the art of that storytelling is in the interpretation of their point, the discovery of a detail that changes the story's meaning. It's not a matter of "stop me if you've heard this one before," but of what we see in them at any given moment.

It was at these various houses, Emma's, or Uncle Gob's, where all of the Persky siblings were gathered (minus Aunt Jane, who was crazy and institutionalized, and Aunt Babe, who had moved to California), along with their husbands and wives and us children, that I first heard the uproar and cacophony of this great repertoire of stories rolled out, interrupted with gales of laughter, urgent interventions, disputed meanings. I was my father's son, and the great family divide for me was between my mother's family, who were mostly shopkeepers I wasn't interested in (with the exception of Uncle Docky and Aunt Dora), and my father's family, who were all fabulists. From the beginning, I recognized that I belonged to my father's tribe. Now, here we were, their descendents, as loud, raucous, and laughter-filled as they had once been.

As well, there was Chicago, a big, prosperous American city. I was unaware of its politics, except to note that the mayor was now Richard Daley, son of the former Mayor Daley, and perhaps that was all one needed to know. Bob, Heidi, and their kids went with me on an architectural boat ride up the Chicago River (I'd never been on the Chicago River before), and I took a trip out to the University of Chicago for the first time and was eventually the only white person on the bus as it moved south through battered black neighbourhoods. On the last day, the whole family reunion boarded a chartered bus and drove through the old districts, none of which I recognized. The area where I grew up, on Keeler, had been levelled during the city riots in the wake of Martin Luther King's assassination in 1968, and anyway, the ghosts I wanted to see, principally my father, were only available in the photos Karen Loeb had collected for us. It was probably exactly like all family reunions, except that it was *us*, and it was perhaps slightly more jovial than the average such gathering. In each person, I could see both the trace of the child I had known and the parent from whom he or she had come. So Bill looked like Bill, the present-day successful commodities trader and parent, and also like the chipmunk-cheeked kid I remembered, and in him I could also hear an echo of the laughter of his father Gob, standing in his store on Division Street in 1952 and calling to me, "Hey, Stashu, come over here for a minute."

Sometimes the cities we describe are the fabled, distant metropolises that the thirteenth-century Venetian traveler Marco Polo spoke of, and that Italo Calvino reconstructs in *Invisible Cities*. Sometimes they are just our own little Venice — not the famous canals and the doge's palace, though they are present, too, in the background — but some otherwise forgotten alleyway where we kicked a ball, or a neighbourhood bridge against whose railing we rattled our stick. As Calvino's crafty Marco Polo says to Kublai Khan, intending exactly the opposite meaning of his utterance, "No one, wise Kublai, knows better than you that the city must never be confused with the words that describe it."

The Hedge

The guy from the city said that we had to trim the hedge.

The hedge he was referring to is a succession of large laurel bushes that border the whole length of the eastern side of the Kitsilano property on which the house where I live in Vancouver, 2504 York, is sited. It's on the corner, a two-storey house running about half a block up the hill along Larch to the lane between York and First, part of the long initial slope that peaks around Third or Fourth Avenue, from which it rolls back down to the edge of Burrard Inlet at Kitsilano Beach.

Actually, now that I think about it in this way, the whole south shore of that inlet is a series of hills and slopes that makes its way downward, in a northeasterly direction, from about 33rd Avenue (many years ago, when I first came to the city, I used to go up that way to see the Tallmans, who lived on 37th Avenue), and of course, thinking about it in this way immediately causes me to imagine the whole place before it was the city of Vancouver at all, or even an aboriginal fishing camp, when it was just thickly forested hills and slopes rolling down to the unnamed shore, but I really don't have time right now — as much as I'd like to, since it's probably the only way that we can understand any of this — to give you the whole lay of the land. Instead, I've got to focus on the hedge.

Still, it's only fair to, well, not warn you, but simply note that I'm not really an outdoors person, or a nature lover, or someone much moved by the sight of natural scenery or landscapes at all. I remember my mother saying, a long time ago when I was a child — I believe my father was driving us across America to see the Pacific Ocean, and we were in a motel in some place like the Dakota Badlands — my mother saying, "The scenery is so beautiful," and I recall being struck by that sentence, by the odd-ness of her use of the almost abstractly indefinite term "scenery" rather than saying, for example, "That's a beautiful mountain" or river or sunset or whatever. So, from the beginning, I experienced a confusion of some sort. Actually, I'm more of what you might call a protector of the Great Indoors.

In any case, the house itself was built in 1912 I'm told, and the hedge, as far as I can remember, was already there when we — who were then a group of students — moved in sometime around 1970. In fact, all I can really remember about the hedge is that it wasn't nearly as tall then as it is now. I vaguely recall having seen, sometime in the last year or two, a photo taken back then of the hedge and perhaps one or two of the student-communard inhabitants of the house standing there, and in my increasingly blurred memory it's not much higher than a person's shoulder. Whereas, at present, the hedge is, roughly, a height of about a dozen metres or thirty-five feet, which is pretty high for a laurel hedge, rising to a point nearly halfway up the sharply sloping roof, so that, coming at the house from the east, you literally can't see the house at all, but instead see the lengthy, towering hedge, with its thick foliage of shimmering, glossy layer upon layer of laurel leaf, leaning out from behind a low stone wall, arching over the sidewalk.

At first, letting the hedge grow had a somewhat practical function because the last high-rise apartment building — eleven storeys — to be permitted in that part of Kitsilano is located directly on the other side of Larch Street. Once it went up, apparently a lot of people in the neighbourhood got together — I may have been one of them, my memory on these matters is patchy — and successfully demanded of the city that no building above three and a half storeys be erected anywhere below 4th Avenue. The idea was to avoid reproducing in Kitsilano the development that had occurred in the 1960s in the West End of downtown Vancouver, on the northern shore of the part of Burrard Inlet known as English Bay, where the thicket of towers can be readily seen any morning from Kits Beach. So, at first, leaving the hedge to grow offered us some privacy from the people across the street living in the eleven-storey apartment building, people who were no doubt peering down at us, curious about the goings-on that might be going on among the hippie, artsy, student types (i.e., us) living in the old house.

But as the years went by, I began to appreciate the hedge for itself, even as, from time to time, irregularly, without any pattern, I would trim it back myself, using a rusty pair of ordinary pruning shears with handles that gave you blisters whether you did or didn't wear a pair of grey buckskin work gloves that you got from Gandy's Home Hardware up on 4th Avenue.

The best time to see the hedge, I think, is at night, under the illumination of the street lamps or the moon, because it's then, suddenly coming upon this huge mass of glistening greenery, that you have the best chance of appreciating its hallucinatory power — I mean, you're driving or walking along, say, York Avenue at night, in this ordinary neighbourhood of walk-up condos, fruit trees, gloomy old houses, parked cars, and the one eleven-storey high-rise building, etc., when out of nowhere — pow! — there it is, a massive wall, in the dark, of laurel hedge, rising up and up into the night sky with its smoky shards of cloud and star punctuation, and then stretching along for what seem like blocks and blocks, kilometres even, so long and so high that I've long since come to think of it as the Great Hedge of Kitsilano, somewhat in the way that we think of the Great Wall of China and other wonders of the world, visible even in satellite photos, so that if someone's looking at pictures of the earth and asks, What's that green line here off the Pacific, anyone would reply, Oh, that's the Great Hedge of Kitsilano. Or when tour buses full of Japanese and German visitors roll through the neighbourhood, the driver brakes a bit as he glides the smoky-windowed vehicle down the hill along Larch and says through the crackly hand-held public address system, "And on your left now . . . is the Great Hedge of Kitsilano."

But to come back to the issue at hand, the guy from the city said that we had to trim the hedge. He was a guy in an orange plastic hard hat from the City Engineering Department, I guess, wearing one of those fluorescent red-orange vests that would presumably prevent his being run over by a speeding Jeep driven by a coked-up drug dealer or eaten by a grizzly bear if any grizzly bears happened to be roaming around Kitsilano.

As I said, I'd done some hedge trimming now and again over the years. The principle of my trimming — and I offer these details in case any computer programmer is seeking some of what is now called "expert opinion" for a computer program on hedge trimming that he or she is putting together — was to trim the hedge whenever it occurred to me or caught my eye, or whenever I suspected that its overhang was obstructing the sidewalk that ran alongside it, thus putting us in danger of being cited for violating the city's Unsightly Premises Bylaw. I call this a Principle of Benign Neglect.

I'd go out in the summer afternoon with the pruning shears, whose wooden handles had now broken and been cinched up with duct tape to keep you from getting a handful of splinters on top of the blisters that you'd get whether or not you wore the gloves from Gandy's Home Hardware on 4th, and I'd cut into some of the lower part, trimming it back from the sidewalk, and then reach up to get some of the overhang — I was always meaning to bring along a stepladder, but I never did — just chopping enough so a normal-sized walker-by wouldn't get an eye poked out by a stray low-hanging laurel branch, and while I was at it, just for variation and to keep myself from getting bored, I'd also pull out some of the morning glory that had hopelessly entangled itself in the laurel, and I'd do this until I was sufficiently soaked in sweat and dirty enough for a bath on a summer's afternoon.

Before going back in, I'd sweep up the cuttings with a bamboo rake and stash them in the diminishing space between the hedge and the house, leaving them to peacefully rot over the course of the rainy season, or if not to rot and compost, at least to pile up, no doubt violating some city fire regulation about creating natural tinderboxes, but the business about the house and grounds in relation to a whole passel of civic regulations is another story entirely, which I'll spare you for now.

Rather than concentrating on the trimming part, I increasingly focused on the tending of the hedge. That is, when visitors came by and asked me to offer an exposition on the hedge, I would emphasize my tending rather than my trimming of this laurel hedge over the previous two decades.

I regarded the *tending* — and I'd underline that word in saying it — as the core of my horticultural triumph. And, of course, someone would sooner or later ask me for some tips about tending, or about the philosophy of tending, you might say, and it is then that I would point out the principle that was the secret of my success, at least as I viewed it. The fundamental principle of tending, I would say, is benign neglect, *just leave it alone*, or more or less leave it alone, and apply the principle in inverse proportion to the degree of knowledge possessed, which is to say, and I think I would apply this in general to most of nature, the more you know you don't know, the more you should leave it alone.

But on this particular rainy morning I'm talking about — and it was one of those days in early autumn with a fine, cutting West Coast mist falling and running down the asphalt slope of Larch Street alongside the hedge — on this morning the guy from the city in an orange hard hat and fluorescent vest was saying that, far from leaving it alone, we must *do something*, and from the sobriety of his tone of voice, I took it that he was speaking on behalf of Western Technological Civilization.

I saw no way out. Or rather, what I saw as the alternative to doing as he said — namely, doing something — was a series of bureaucratic encounters, something like one of those demonstrations of perspective in painting, stretching out to an infinite horizon, except that in this case it would take place in an endless set of offices, probably in City Hall — I think I have a memory of going there once for some sort of permit and waiting in lines with guys with long rolls of blueprints under their arms and eventually being shunted from counter to counter — until, at last, the apotheosis of the vision I had while standing there with the guy in the orange hard hat (I myself may have been wearing a baseball or tractor hat) was that I would at last progress to one of the City Hall committee rooms in which the humiliation of being cited for violation of the Unsightly Premises Bylaw would be visited upon me. And this fantasy of being cited would fuel some small amount of paranoia about whoever had turned us in to the city, followed by outrage at being complained about by some unknown sneaky neighbours — so that, suddenly, I, who had opposed the concept of private property under capitalism with near-revolutionary fervour, was puffing myself up as a property owner, full of shop-worn maxims about a man's castle.

As much to intercept this gloomy train of unproductive thought as anything else, I said to the hard-hatted civic employee, "Well, so could you guys trim the hedge?" My quick move, shifting me into the guise of a responsible property owner eager to cooperate with the authorities, seemed to slow him. As we stood in the fine morning mist, he reached into one of his fluorescent vest pockets, pulled out his plastic pocket calculator, and began punching in numbers. While he did his calculations, multiplying trucks with cherry-picker-extending stepladders by the rate of civic labour divided by gas-powered chainsaws, etc., as I was waiting I got an imaginary glimpse of us, shot from overhead, as if from one of those blimps that hover over sporting events and crucifixions: two bulky men standing at the foot of a slope in the West Coast morning rain. "Well, it'd cost you around $1200," he finally said. ($1200!! my mind yelped.) "I'll think about it," I said.

Then, a few days later, I was standing outside the house, beside the hedge, with the thirty-something-year-old brother of somebody we knew, a guy not in a hard hat and fluorescent vest, not driving a large city vehicle, but a guy in jeans with a pickup truck with some gardening gear in the back, and he pulled out a pencil and a crumpled notepad from his back pocket and began scrawling some numbers on it. "Umm, we could do it for about $500," he said. "Oh," I said encouragingly, "I'll think about it."

And then a few days after that — we're getting to the denouement (I've always liked that word, denouement) of this shaggy-hedge story — I was talking to my friend Rob about the hedge. "The city says we've got to chop it back," I explained to Rob, a sturdy, twenty-something, suburb-bred, young man with dirty-blond hair and blue eyes, and with whom I'd had a lengthy relationship involving various intimacies — although I have no intention whatsoever of elaborating on the intricacies of it or of Rob's hard-knocks experiences of the world as an orphaned tyke. Suffice it to say that Rob owned no civic vehicles or pickup trucks or gardening equipment and did no calculations with pocket calculators or pencil and paper. He didn't even have to look at the state of the hedge; he *knew* the hedge, and anyway it was just outside my bedroom window, each year pressing in more closely on the glass, its branches scraping against the house and roof when the wind from rainy season storms rustled through its foliage. "I can do that," Rob announced. "Fifty bucks ought to do it," he said. I didn't even have to think about it.

"But won't you need a chainsaw?" I asked.

"We can rent one from Gandy's on 4th," he said. "All's I need is a stepladder."

"Like the one under the porch?" The one I'd always been meaning to haul out when I tended the hedge.

"Yeah, that oughta do it."

I stayed in, at my desk, reading a book, the day Rob cut back the hedge. All I heard was the roar of the gas-fed chainsaw hacking away, and Rob up on the stepladder, crashing through the brush, like the sound of a two-point buck bolting through the woods, and the occasional merciful pause in all the racket when my sweat-drenched employee took a water break in the kitchen, grinning crazily, burrs and bits of laurel leaf caught in his dirty-blond hair, exulting in honest endeavour. Eventually, late in the afternoon, he called me out for a formal inspection and praise of his labours. Naturally, the poor old hedge looked like a glowering cat who'd been unwillingly subjected to a bath, with hacked-off branches poking up here and there, the sidewalk covered in amputated laurel fronds, a botanical and aesthetic mess, but nonetheless chopped back, reduced, trimmed to satisfy those offended by its exuberant foliage. I helped Rob gather up the cuttings, and we piled the refuse alongside the house, then we stood at the garden gate, taking in his handiwork and gazing down the slope to the inlet as the sun finished its traverse of the sky for the day.

I suppose there's some economic lesson to be drawn here, or some moral to the story, some overarching truth. I can't think what it might be, other than it's often best to allow only those whom you would trust in your bed to work in your garden. As for the hedge, the Great Hedge of Kitsilano, it looked like hell now, but I took the long view, knowing that in a year or two it would heal itself and, with a little luck and benign neglect, outlast us all, or at least outlast me, its faithful keeper from *circa* 1970 to whenever. And the only overarching truth is that the hedge would once more arch over the sidewalk, providing a shady midsummer bower to grateful elderly folks on foot, trudging down to the sea.

During

Autobiography of a Tattoo

Prologue

I bear a blue tattoo of a ship's anchor on my left forearm, acquired shortly after the completion of my "tour of duty" in the US Navy (1961). This is its story.

1

So much depends upon . . .

W.C. WILLIAMS, 'THE RED WHEELBARROW'

This: at fourteen, I fell in love with Martin W. in a high-school gymnasium locker room in Chicago. Between the wooden benches and the metal cabinets where we dressed and undressed, we lingered and "horsed around" in the nude, pushing, shoving, crashing into lockers, mock-wrestling in order to be able to "accidentally" and fleetingly touch the other boy's genitals. I checked the signals emanating from Martin's grey eyes in order to determine the permissible boundaries, surprised by his apparent interest, since I was barely aware of my own. Once we were caught by the gym attendant, not for sexually "fooling around" but simply for lingering, and were punished by being made to clean the soapy residue from the tiles of the showers. As we sponged down the shower room, working in the nude, and exchanged occasional mutual glances, I again recognized our inarticulate desire.

Neither of us, as far as I knew, had ever had sex, either with each other or anyone else, and the kind of sex we were "inventing" (namely, homo sex) — this was *circa* 1955 — was considered beyond imagining. Despite my innocence, I knew (in remembering this, I'm surprised by my knowledge) — maybe just from the way he hung around Martin and me — that another classmate, Don B., was also attracted to Martin, and I immediately pegged him as what I would later learn to call an "evil queen" (but maybe I was an evil queen, too) and intuited that I would have to head him off at the pass.

In the school cafeteria, having lunch with Martin, I devised a language or code in which we could discuss our desire without others knowing what we were talking about, and perhaps also to reduce our own embarrassment at recognizing that desire. Since there were available conventions about the Romance of Boyhood — e.g., passionate friendships, "my best friend," "pals" — it was linguistic explicitness about sexuality that constituted the act of stepping across those boundaries. The little private code consisted of two terms that described sexual acts we hadn't ever engaged in, but that we were prepared to consider: "JOB," which stood for "jack off both," and "Baby Ruth" (the name of a vaguely cock-shaped chocolate candy bar), which stood for "blow job."

My memory of the next step is a little blurry, though the denouement isn't. We must have agreed to get together for sex. It would be at my house, which was available since both my mother and father were away at work.

One more crucial fact in the mix: Martin was moving away, almost immediately, and would be going to another school, another life. It was now or never.

I phoned. I can't remember if he gave me his phone number or if I looked it up in the phone book. (Years later, on several occasions when passing through Chicago, I checked the phone book to see if I could find a "Martin W." — no luck.)

What if his mother answered? I had carefully scripted my gambit: "Oh, hello, Mrs. W. It's Stan P. I'm a friend of Martin's. Is Martin there? I have to ask him something about our Spanish homework." The last would set her up for Martin telling her that he had to come over to my house and help me with the homework. (Had we discussed this plan in the lunchroom? We must have.) Of course, if Martin answered, I could say, "Do you want to come over and have a Baby Ruth?" and he could just tell his mother that he had to go and help a friend with his homework.

The line was busy. I hadn't counted on that. As I listened to the sound of the busy signal, which left me with an instant in which to become too self-conscious, I convinced myself, in that absolutely nutty way teenage boys convince themselves of impossible things, that she would see through it all, would know immediately what I was up to, and the thought of her knowing mortified me. Worse, since the line was busy, I knew it was her who was on the phone — since "women are always talking on the phone" — and therefore, even if the line wasn't busy, she would be the one to answer it.

I hung up. Didn't call back. Too scared. I never saw Martin again. And almost everything in my subsequent erotic experience flows from that adolescent "tragedy," that phone call I didn't make.

2. The Barracks

In the US Navy's San Diego boot camp barracks one night shortly after lights out, one of the four of us (not me) suggested that we jack off to see if the chemical (saltpetre) that was allegedly put into our food to reduce our sexual urges really worked.

We happened to be billeted at the end of the barracks, afforded some privacy by a wall of lockers, in two bunk beds, slim Donnie from New Mexico above me, and in the next bunk over, beefy Bruehl from Arizona on top, and, in the lower bunk, a boy from somewhere in the South, curiously named Richard Richards. Although he tried to get us to pronounce his surname "Reichart," we simply dropped the "s" on his last name and subjected him to the accusation that his hillbilly parents were so dumb that they couldn't think up another first name for him. "Richard, on the double!" the company commander or drill sergeant would call out. "That's Reichart, sir," he would plead, in a doomed effort at correction.

Name-play was crucial in the ongoing daily struggle over the barracks pecking order. My own name was easily elided from Persky to Pesky to Pussky to Pussy, and to be a "pussy" — i.e., a girl — was tantamount to social death. As if to confirm it, I was relatively inept at accomplishing the tasks that constituted our training, and yet the distinctions made were fine-grained enough that I was considered a real, if mediocre, guy and spared the contempt of being consigned to the category of the lowest of the low, occupied by a whiny, uncharmingly awkward kid named Gorney — who was instantly dubbed "Horny Gorney" and who was eventually dumped, headfirst, into the barracks' metal garbage can. Whereas I, for all my failings (unable to swim, not very good with guns, etc.), managed to elicit the sympathetic attention of one of the barracks tough guys, a kid aptly named Harsh, also from Arizona, who invited me one day to do some practice wrestling with him, thus publicly demonstrating that I wasn't to be considered a complete wimp.

The companies were assembled in random fashion on the basis of the coincidental arrival of busloads of recruits from various parts of the country. We were a group of Midwesterners, bused out to the Coast from the Great Lakes Naval Training Station near Chicago; a gangly, giraffe-like, prematurely sober guy from Milwaukee named Brinkhoff was named our recruit company commander, a position he retained once the whole company was put together. (I remember him offering me some fatherly "buck up, kid" consolation once when I was feeling homesick.) We arrived in the middle of the night, were issued blankets and some other gear, and were bundled off to the barracks.

The next morning, on the "grinder," a vast, asphalt-paved, sun-fried marching area in the centre of the San Diego boot camp, we sleepily met our company-mates, a group of boys from the American Southwest, mainly Arizona, and were marched off in raggedy order to the mess hall. I'm not sure how Richards (or Reichart) got to be with us; maybe he was from Tennessee or Kentucky and got lumped in with the Midwesterners.

In the semi-darkness, perhaps illuminated by some stray moonlight pouring in from a nearby window, we reached into our underwear (there was a navy word for them, what was it? — now I remember: "skivvies"! and I also now see how much our learning of "navy words" was part of what was making us into sailors and, by extension, men), or maybe we pulled our skivvies down to mid-thigh, and began to masturbate. Although it didn't occur to me at the time, the proposal (whoever made it) had the function of alleviating our embarrassment about the problem of secretly jacking off. To the sounds of the gentle ship-like creaking of the metal bunks and our own increasingly excited breathing, we entered eternity. I came easily.

Then there occurred the moment that further changed my life forever. While Bruehl and Donnie were privately occupied above, Reichart — though we refused to call him that, as he wanted, I always thought of him as Reichart — whispered to me from his bunk. In memory, our bunks are shoved closer together — only inches apart — than they could have been in actuality. I can't remember his precise words, though from time to time I'm still able to see him in memory, not so much beautiful as sexy, freckles across the bridge of his snub nose, skinny hips. It went something like, "Hey, I can only get it up halfway," and then he asked me to help him, to jack him off a little with my hand. I refused. "Aw, come on," he said, in his sly, cajoling, half-promising, persuasive way.

I reached out from my bunk to his. His hand took mine and placed it around his velvety but hard cock. I remember feeling, just before being overwhelmed by other emotions, an instant of confusion — he had claimed to be only semi-erect, but his cock in fact felt pretty hard to me — innocently unaware that his small fib was in service to his seduction of me.

Guiding my hand with his own, Reichart moved it up and down the sheath of his foreskin, instructing me in the motion he liked, hoping that once I learned the movement I would continue it on my own. I was in ecstasy, terrified ecstasy, ecstatic terror. But instead of continuing to masturbate him, I withdrew my hand. He tried to coax me. I wasn't to be persuaded.

(He would have his revenge the next day, saying to the guys at our table in the mess hall — to Bruehl and Donnie immediately, but others were also within hearing — "Hey, you know what Pussy did to me last night when we were jacking off? He played with my dick," thus, not only confirming my lowly status as a pussy, but raising the prospect that I was also a "fruit." Naturally, I furiously, but carefully — not wanting to excite further suspicion by protesting too much — denied Reichart's charge.)

Meanwhile, above us, in their respective bunks, oblivious to the whispered drama below, Bruehl and Donnie carried on. Shortly after I'd come, Donnie triumphantly declared, "I came!" He was a teenager with fine, delicately shaped facial features, almost feminine in his beauty, and had, by way of self-protection I suppose, developed a slightly nasty, pugnacious edge to his personality. "I don't believe you, you're shitting us," Bruehl said. "Here," Donnie replied to the challenge, stretching out his cupped hand containing his come in the direction of Bruehl's nose. Bruehl took a whiff. "Pee-uuu!" Bruehl reported, confirming Donnie's success. At which point, memory breaks down, dissolves, but that's not at all the end.

First, what if I hadn't refused Reichart? What if I'd continued, on my own, to slide his foreskin up and down the column of his dick? What if I'd brought him off, his come running over my hand as he unclenched his thigh muscles and sighed in contentment? Would he have then told the others at "chow" the next morning? Or would he have kept it a secret, using the secret to get me to do it again (and again), whenever he wanted? Would he have kept me for himself?

I had another scenario, which preserved the original scene. Reichart tells the others, and they begin mildly teasing me. I get him aside and urgently appeal to him, "You've gotta stop telling them I touched your dick. You're going to get me in trouble." As he smiles that lazy smile of his, I make my proposal: "Look, if you tell them you were just kidding, I'll jack you off." He knows he has me, but sizes me up with his shrewd, narrowed, farm-boy eyes. "How do I know you will?" I look around hastily, see that there's no one to see us, and, taking a chance, grab his dick through his denim workpants ("dungarees" they were called) and then rub and fondle it just long enough to convince him. "You better not chicken out," he warns me.

But he promptly brings off his end of the bargain. We're at lunch in the mess hall, and one of the other guys, maybe Bruehl, is ribbing me. "Pussy, did you really play with Richard's dick? Did you?" At which point, just as it's about to get nasty, Reichart intervenes, in a slow half-drawl, "Boy, you-all sure are hicks. You didn't believe all that stuff, did you?" And now the spotlight shifts to Reichart, chuckling and ducking his buzz-cut head as Bruehl tries to whack him with his sailor's boater. "You dumb shithead!" Bruehl grumbles, as Reichart sends me a telling glance.

That night, Reichart's on guard duty, and I make my way out of the back of the barracks to the little shack outside of which he's standing watch, passing through the concrete area where we do our wash and where clotheslines are strung up, on which we hang our sheets and cambray shirts and dungarees. In the night, the whites move slightly in the breeze, like sails, strangely glowing. "It's me," I say, before he ritually asks, "Who goes there?" "Hey," he says, pretending to be a little pleasantly surprised. "I said I would, didn't I?" I say, mock-offended that he might've doubted my word.

Inside the dark shack — we know when the patrols come by to check that the watch isn't asleep, so we're safe for time — I unfasten the buckle of his navy-issue cloth belt, undo his fly, and take his skivvy-covered cock in my hand, then reach into his underpants and hold it directly, intentionally, consciously, impressed by the heat of its flesh, and his body involuntarily leans against, into, mine, and I put an arm around his waist as I jack him off.

There's an elaboration of my fantasy of his seduction of me. His dungarees and skivvies are down around his ankles, and as I lean over, my shoulder against his flat belly, jacking him off with my hand, Reichart suggests, gently touching the back of my neck, "Why don't you put it in your mouth?" "No," I refuse. "Aw come on, just a little. You know you wanna," he drawls. It's the last sentence — "You know you wanna" — his making explicit his knowing my knowing that's the clincher.

Now I make my counteroffer: "I will if you'll jack me off." "Sure," he agrees, increasing the pressure on the back of my neck. "How do I know you will?" I ask, lifting my head up to look into his blue eyes. "What if I do it and you just go and tell the others I sucked you off?" Without hesitation, he reaches into my pants, takes hold of my already-hard cock, and jacks me off enough to prove to me that if he said anything to the others about what we're doing, I'd be able to tell on him, too. "Just put it in your mouth," he urges, continuing to hold my cock and returning his other hand to the back of my neck. I slowly bend my head toward his erection, looking at it with awe as my lips get closer to its tip.

This fantasy operation proceeds in stages. Now he's playing with my butt, wants to fuck me, offers to suck my dick if I let him, etc. And step by step I let him do everything he wants.

Reichart knows everything about sex. We urban kids were astonished to learn that Southern farmboys regularly fucked barnyard animals; they casually assured us that fucking a cow's ass or a lanolin-smooth sheep's orifice was "the next best thing."

When our marching instructors ordered us to close our ranks to "cornhole distance," they knew all about shoving corncobs up asses. Apparently that was a favoured farm product for anal stimulation — in fact, I once saw an ear of corn so used in a porno flick about French rural life. Eventually "cornholing" became a general term referring to anal intercourse. And in assembly and marching terminology, "cornhole distance" jokingly meant close enough to fuck the guy in front of you.

In one version of these imaginary scenes, in which Reichart now has me trained and admitting that I like it, he turns up one night with Donnie in tow, generously prepared to share me with his mates.

In this masturbatory scenario played out so many times, persistent for so long, fantasy has come to seem almost indistinguishable from memory; the importance of distinguishing the two seems increasingly less important. Though I have a memory, I've little sense of it being a memory of myself. If Reichart, Bruehl, and Donnie are still alive (now men in late middle-age — married, divorced, fathers, failures, successes), they've most likely completely forgotten that trivial, boyish incident. I once imagined or dreamed about Reichart in his late twenties, living in a trailer park with his wife and a kid, maybe talking up the waitress at the coffee shop in town where his work crew take their breaks.

Though the boy I was, aflame with desire, seems like someone else, his adolescent passion continues to influence me; it shapes my pleasures, circumscribes my sorrows, beckons me on. Forever afterwards, when I was making love with a real person — someone who invariably resembled those boys I knew in the navy — I was also back in the barracks, reliving the adolescent thrill of homosexual desire. Don't get me wrong. The real person in bed is no less real, with his own life, desires, and otherness, but the ghosts of desire are there too, and they're also real. I think: So that's what I'm left with; or more accurately, that's what I've been given; that's what I've got.

3. Ginsberg

At sixteen, as a teenager in Chicago in 1957, I discovered, more or less on my own, a newly published novel titled *On the Road*, by a writer named Jack Kerouac. Reading a few passages of it in a review was enough to get my attention.

I immediately went to the Kroch and Brentano's bookstore in Chicago's downtown (I lived in a middle-class neighbourhood that bordered the city's burgeoning and expensive suburbs) and bought a copy of *On the Road*. Even now, I can remember my excitement, sitting at the back of the Washington Boulevard bus going home, as I read the first sentences of Kerouac's book.

On the Road is a novel about a group of post–World War II young men in their twenties. They were a quarter-generation too young to have gone to war, as their immediate literary predecessors, Norman Mailer, James Jones, and Gore Vidal, had done. Instead, in 1950s America — a nation of conformists, hysterical Senator Joseph McCarthy-led anti-Communists, and "organization men" in "grey flannel suits" working for corporations — these blue-jean-wearing and T-shirt-clad "beat generation" rebels described by Kerouac spent their time "rushing madly" from coast to coast in search of adventure, "kicks," sex, and life's meaning. Although Kerouac's writing was to age quickly, and rather badly, its romantic "spontaneous prosody" was enthralling to a sixteen-year-old.

Part of its enticement, both literary and social, was that it answered both the question, Where do writers go from here? stylistically as well as in terms of subject matter, and the related question, Where does adventure go from here? "Adventure," I think, was my basic organizing concept then. I'd been raised on literary adventure books: Jack London, Jules Verne, Herman Melville, the writers of World War I and II, and Ernest Hemingway. Kerouac proposed a new way to conceive of adventure, or at least an updated, high-velocity version of Hemingway's 1920s "lost generation" novel, *The Sun Also Rises*. In life, I would shortly solve my own adventure problem by joining the navy, going to sea, and seeing the world. In terms of writing, when I came to the end of reading Hemingway (he'd recently published the parable-like

Old Man and the Sea), with his blunt sentences and studied rep-
etitions, which mirrored the taciturn posture of his male heroes,
Kerouac answered several questions. Hemingway's heroes gave
way to an improvisational, Whitmanesque prose that described
a more amorphous, androgynous male figure.

In fact, Kerouac's stories even included homosexual characters
and treated them as unremarkable in the context he was portraying. One of them was modelled on the poet Allen Ginsberg.
I can't recall if I'd heard of Ginsberg previously, but I soon figured out the *roman à clef* aspects of Kerouac's autobiographical
book and eventually (at Kroch and Brentano's) found a magazine
called *Evergreen Review*, whose contents included "Howl," a
notorious poem by Ginsberg (it had been the object of an obscen-
ity trial) that directly referred to homosexual experience in what
were then called "graphic" terms.

There'd already been modern novels about homosexuality
— Gore Vidal's *The City and the Pillar* and James Baldwin's
Giovanni's Room — although I hadn't read them prior to finding Ginsberg. The one work that touched on homosexuality that
I read at about the same time as Kerouac and Ginsberg was a
novella called "The Childhood of a Leader" in a book of stories
titled *Intimacy* (I still have my very tattered copy of it) by Jean-
Paul Sartre, of whom I'd otherwise never heard. In it, a young
man allows himself (for not altogether straightforward motives)
to be seduced by an older male. When the young man, who'd
attempted to represent himself as quite sophisticated about the
situation, is in fact sickened by his first homosexual experience,
his vain former pretense becomes the object of his seducer's contempt. Whatever Sartre's intentions were — the point of the story
was to account for the social influences leading to the formation
of a fascist personality, I think — the novella included an oblique
representation of homo sex. If Sartre intended the description as
cautionary, it had the opposite effect on me.

The publication of Ginsberg, Kerouac, and others, as well as
the account in Kerouac's novels of a group of adventurers, suggested the existence of a "movement" or "Beat Generation," as
it was being called, that one might join. Perhaps it was an idea of
joining up that led me to put together a series of fragments, stories, and prose poems that I called *How the Night Comes to Me*.
I mailed my pamphlet of writing to Kerouac, in care of his pub-

lishers in New York. In retrospect, it seems like a daring thing to have thought up and to have done. I find myself rather admiring that now-vanished sixteen-year-old boy who, apparently, had been me. A couple of weeks later I received a postcard from Jack Kerouac. Far from being a perfunctory acknowledgment of fan mail, the message, which filled the card from edge to edge with typewriting, was an enthusiastic welcome to the literary world, and news that he'd passed my writing on to Ginsberg and others. Soon Ginsberg also wrote to me, delighted that a Chicago teen-ager had been turned on by their work.

I met Ginsberg in San Francisco a year or two later. After I completed boot camp in 1958, the navy had stationed me, with unintended foresight, at the radar school on Treasure Island in San Francisco Bay. Since I had light duties as a company clerk, there was considerable free time to explore San Francisco, especially its coffee houses and cafés in "beatnik" North Beach, where I maintained a weekend room in the San Gottardo Hotel on Columbus Avenue, a few doors down from poet Lawrence Ferlinghetti's City Lights Bookstore (under whose imprint "Howl" had been published as a book). I soon met Ferlinghetti, who had been alerted to my presence by Ginsberg, as well as some of the other artists and writers from various intersecting circles.

It was in San Francisco that I met Ginsberg, an energetic, black-bearded man in his early thirties, whose lively dark eyes were magnified by the glasses he wore. Although he wasn't "rushing madly" around with as much velocity as Kerouac had intimated in his portrait of him in *On The Road*, Ginsberg displayed a vivacious innocence — a mixture of frankness and playfulness — and, less noticed, an effective and practical side in literary and other politics. He introduced me to his boyfriend, Peter Orlovsky, and others he was close to and let me tag along to various performances, meetings, and on sundry errands his recent fame required of him.

I immediately (and ever since) took Ginsberg to be not only a friend, but one of my teachers. As it turned out, he wouldn't become my poetry teacher — that role was reserved for a moon-faced, pear-shaped poet named Jack Spicer — but one of my teachers in life.

Jack Spicer was the same age as Ginsberg, one of a triumvirate of poets consisting of himself, Robin Blaser (who was in Boston at the time) and Robert Duncan — a poet five or six years older than the other two — who were the acknowledged masters of the "San Francisco scene" that gathered under the image of the White Rabbit (from Lewis Carroll's *Alice's Adventures in Wonderland*). Spicer, Blaser, and Duncan guided a group of men and women about ten years younger than themselves. Interestingly, I had been warned away from the White Rabbit poets by a young poet in Los Angeles whom I'd met through Ginsberg. When I ran into the LA poet in San Francisco (where he later became a professor of literature), he ominously advised me that the leaders of the White Rabbit group were "faggots."

One night I went to the Bread and Wine Mission, at the top of Grant Avenue in North Beach, where Spicer was reading. I'm not sure if I understood Spicer's poems, but I was impressed by the poet's gravity, so I hung around afterwards and met him. He gave me a copy of his recently published first book, *After Lorca*, pulling it out of a wrinkled brown paper bag and making the point, so that I might understand the value of his gift, that it normally sold for one dollar. Later, I was invited by one of the young members of the circle, George Stanley, to attend the weekly Sunday afternoon poetry meetings that were then being held at George's apartment on upper Montgomery Street.

It was here that a new world opened out before me. What astonished me was not merely its novelty, but the recognition that the world, as transmitted through the intelligence of poets, was considerably different from how I had previously pictured it. For one thing, the world was "larger," denser, faster, and more complex than I'd thought. For another, it was connected by a logic and meanings that I hadn't known about. Up until then, I thought that "the world," as I'm calling it, consisted merely of immediate personal events and objects, and that whatever was outside only existed in newspapers and on television. In poetry, I learned that the world included all of time, history, the story of the earth and its beings, and everything that had been thought by human beings. Imaginary and invisible realms were as much part of the world as its more tangible manifestations. What's more, the content of the world of poetry, unlike the ephemeral phenomena of everyday existence, was the stuff of life and death. The poems that we read, criticized, and tried out on each other were crucial to how human beings might understand the world.

Spicer, to whom I soon became passionately devoted, was a difficult teacher. He was lonely, depressive, harsh, manipulative, and, apart from his nightly contact with other poets in a North Beach bar, The Place, and afternoons with them at Aquatic Park, hermit-like in the shabby, filthy succession of rented rooms in which he lived (and died). His redeeming feature, which inspired our loyalty to him, was his love and knowledge of his art, which he regarded as the only redemptive feature of a politically deterministic world that he saw (often to the point of paranoia) as seeking to corrupt poetry.

At the time, he was working on a part of a book, called *The Heads of the Town Up to the Aether*, that consisted of prose-poems ostensibly about Arthur Rimbaud, and it was through this that he gave me a "first work." Any competent writer can give a protegé, if the latter has minimal talent, a work — since the accomplished writer can "see" what the protegé/student might be able to write in a way that the student can't. Spicer casually suggested one Sunday afternoon that I ought to write some "imaginary lives" of poets. Within a week or so I appeared, not much older than Rimbaud had been when he wrote his poems, with *Lives of the French Symbolist Poets*, a pamphlet of made-up brief lives of some modernist twentieth-century French poets (the "symbolist" part of it was simply an ironic "mistake"). They were a little miracle, sheer beginner's luck, and the delight of the elders who surrounded me as I read them aloud was evidence of both the power of art and my acceptance into the ranks of writers. Their success also made me realize that the "politics" of poetry, if not a democracy, was a pitiless meritocracy. Whoever, on a given Sunday afternoon, had written a real poem, was, for that moment, as important as Jack Spicer, my teacher.

There are two asides I want to toss in about all this. One is that in the course of writing about, say, Jean Cocteau (later I was taken by Spicer and Blaser to see Cocteau's films *Orpheus* and *Testament of Orpheus*) or Rimbaud, I also inadvertently learned something about homosexual history, including the still-surprising fact that it had existed in the past. Indeed, I eventually made my own "discoveries" in homo literary history. About two or three years later, when taking an English course at San Francisco State College with a wonderful elderly professor named Wilder Bentley, I began "researching" the work of Walt Whitman and, in a long paper, exuberantly encouraged by Bentley, discovered Whitman's sexuality and its animating role in his poetry long before the official Whitman scholars admitted that Whitman was homosexual.

The irony of all this was that while we poets, even of the merely budding variety, could recognize homo simply by reading a text or looking at a work of art, in the scholarly world such discoveries were still a struggle. When a scholar named Janson published his magnum opus about the Renaissance sculptor Donatello, insisting on the artist's homosexuality as relevant to understanding his work, it was considered an academic "event." At the same time, the contemporary world treated homo as though it had only existed in the past, since it refused any real recognition of homo in the present, except as an aberration.

Second, I had a very short public career as a poet, even though it went on privately for many years. Although you can be given a first work by a master, the discovery of your own "voice" is another matter altogether. Eventually, a couple of years after *French Symbolist Poets*, I had the luck of doing so, in a poem called "Lake." I wrote it in Italy, where, in a fishing village near Naples, I was reading, among others, Dante, from whom I took the phrase that gave the poem its opening line: "It was not *the lake of the heart* / it was the load / taken from the sea / and the seen is not enough / to know the poetry . . . "

When I returned to San Francisco from the navy in 1962, I showed it to Spicer, who gave it his imprimatur. He patted my shoulder shyly with his clumsy, balled fist, his gesture accompanied by one of his exaggerated "best poem I've seen in two years" pronouncements, which also served to chastise and control the other young poets who, it was implied, through laziness or corruption, had not been writing the "best" poem Spicer had seen in two years. Much of what I wrote was in a version of Spicer's dominant, unforgettable voice, but "Lake" was more my own, as much of a distinctive voice as I would acquire in poetry, a voice that I eventually saw was better suited to "writing" than to poetry.

Spicer died of alcoholism — and, one should add, his devotion to language — only a few years later, in 1965, at age forty. I was working in a warehouse then, standing at a packing table, when I was phoned by the doctor at the hospital (I was listed as the

contact person on his next-of-kin form) who told me that Spicer
was dead. Upon hearing the news, I felt a thrill run through my
body. I was astonished at the power of Death, that it could kill
this godchild of Cocteau who, like Orpheus himself (in Cocteau's
version of the story), had transmitted the voices of the dead.

Ginsberg was a much gentler teacher than Spicer. The two of
them met only rarely. Spicer disliked Ginsberg's work, particularly disagreeing with what he regarded as its utopian idea of
love. Their most famous encounter occurred at a party held in a
mansion in nearby Berkeley, where, according to the minor legend of it, Ginsberg proposed sex with a drunken Spicer. God
only knows what in fact happened.

Ginsberg's gentler teaching also included instruction in the
homoerotic history of poetry. Once, he recited for me, in his
infectiously rhapsodic way (I suppose it was a bit of a parlour
trick that he also performed for others, but if so, it was a marvel-
lous trick), long sections of Hart Crane's *The Bridge*, the masterpiece of the American gay poet of the 1920s, which Ginsberg
had memorized.

But of all the lessons in life that Ginsberg offered, the most
important one for me at the time was about homosexuality. First
of all, he simply seemed to assume that I was homo, which gave
me the idea that homosexuality was a possibly normal identity,
and he did so without any apparent ulterior motive (such as, say,
making a pass at me, which he didn't). Second, when I saw him
on the street (traffic-crowded Grant Avenue) or some other place,
he often, after greeting me, asked, "Do you have a boyfriend
yet?" This question, sometimes called out over the roofs of cars
from across the busy street, was extraordinary in its assumption
that it would be alright to have one and to announce the fact of
it in public. "Not yet," I'd reply in kind, thus accepting the possibility that I might one day acquire such a creature.

In fact, I soon fell in love. At the time, I often spent the night
when I was in San Francisco at a large two-storey apartment on
California Street, an artist's commune called East-West House.
One of the poets from the White Rabbit group, Joanne Kyger
(who was working on a set of poems, "The Tapestry," written
in the persona of Penelope from Homer's *Odyssey*), lived there,
as did a black woman named Samantha. They were both six or
seven years older than me, and I thought they were infinitely

wise. Various friends of the East-West House residents casually crashed there. One of them was a boy named Tim who was in the army, a student at the military's nearby Monterey Language School. I was immediately infatuated and trailed after him helplessly, yet I also noticed that my infatuation with Tim, far from arousing disapproval among the others at East-West House, particularly amused and charmed the two women. Joanne and Samantha were moved by my affection, but I couldn't tell if Tim even knew I was there.

One night I was sleeping on the floor in the spacious dining room of the East-West House, halfway under a table. Someone else was sleeping at the other end of the room. Tim arrived late that night, from a party or bar, stoned on pot and half drunk, and lay down on his back not far from me, appearing to fall into a loggy slumber.

I had longed for him for days and weeks. His arm stretched out in my direction and I could no longer resist. Lying on my stomach, I edged toward his hand, crawling in the dark room more or less the way we'd been trained in boot camp to advance under barbed wire. After covering that infinite distance (about two feet or less), I positioned my crotch upon his sleeping hand.

After a few seconds of rubbing against it, his fingers began to respond to my movements. He was awake. My pants were undone, fly opened, and he gently played with me until I flooded his hand with my come.

While he was doing that, I reached for his own genitals, rubbing the erection that was under the rough denim of his pants, then awkwardly unbuttoning the catch at his waist. In the indirect spill of light coming from an open doorway, the ball-shaped head of his cock, which had risen above the waistband of his white underwear, glistened.

He was a large, powerfully built, blond-haired young man of nineteen or so. Although he permitted me to touch him, once I'd come, when I began to do to him what he'd just done for me, he said unreproachfully, "No, don't . . ." He then got up, holding his cupped hand so as not to spill my come, crossed the room, and went down the hallway to a bathroom. Returning, a few minutes later, he lay down next to me and fell asleep again.

In the morning, Tim had to catch a bus back to the army base. Though I gazed at him with soppy adoration, even when I caught his eye, nothing was said, no sign was given of what had happened in the night. He got a ride to the Market Street bus depot from one of the guys in East-West House, and I went along. Even when we had a minute to ourselves in the bus depot, his blue eyes looked through me. It was as if, from his point of view, nothing had happened, or if something had, it was something that couldn't be spoken of. I was crushed, heartbroken by our silence.

Some days afterwards, up in the attic of East-West House, I was having tea with Joanne and Samantha. In response to their amused sympathy for my obvious lovesick condition, I told them obliquely what had happened between Tim and me, and registered their unexpected approval. But it was the general silence about homo that made Ginsberg's open inclusion of it in his articulated vision of the world all the more remarkable. That inclusivity was also present, if less underscored, among the writers in the White Rabbit group, gay or straight. Despite all I'd been told by the world until then, homo was a legitimate possibility of desire.

Once, a year or so after our encounters in San Francisco, Ginsberg and I were living next door to each other in a cheap hotel in Paris. Because of some domestic entanglement, Allen needed a place to sleep for the night and asked to stay with me. Once we were in bed, he asked if I wanted to have sex. I didn't.

Now, it may be that he wasn't particularly hot for me and that the whole thing was inconsequential to him, but I was impressed by how he didn't push the issue, didn't resort to cajoling or complaint, didn't "use," as he easily could have done, our friendship. We slept companionably, without incident. Once again, I was given a lesson, about manners, a lesson in life.

I last saw Ginsberg in the early 1990s, in Vancouver, where he was giving a reading. He had just come back from China and had written a series of poems somewhat in the ancient Chinese manner. In the poems, Ginsberg traversed the classic landscapes of the old poets, offering a subtle homage to their work, but maintaining a fresh and modest accuracy about what he himself saw (sailing down the Yangtze, looking at the trees, whatever).

Afterwards, several of us ended up in a pub on Hastings Street, in Vancouver's Downtown Eastside. Allen produced the folder of his recent poems for me to reread in the bar. As I read, I was moved by his anxious human desire to be reassured of their value. Once more, in poetry's democratic meritocracy, his public reputation was of little import compared to the judgment of a fellow writer.

One summer, a couple of years before his death in 1997, I happened on a column in a newspaper, occasioned by Ginsberg's seventieth birthday. It was a stupid bit of journalism, trading on old clichés about drugs and "beats," parading its irony about the supposed naïveté of the writers of the late 1950s, and at the same time indulging a nostalgia for the past. I stopped reading it.

Instead, I thought of the lines of another of my poetry teachers, Robin Blaser: "there are shining masters / when I tell you what they / look like some of it is / nearly false . . . " I thought of my teacher in life, Ginsberg, shining master.

4. Conduct Unbecoming

When I arrived at US Naval Air Detachment VR-24, based at the Capodichino military airport a few kilometres outside the port of Naples, Italy, I almost immediately met my invisible double.

At the barracks, located a short way from the hangars, someone showed me to the bunk I'd been assigned, a rack of criss-crossed strips of metal and a rolled-up mattress, the place where I'd sleep for the next two years. There were four bunk beds to a cubicle that was partitioned from other identical cubicles by a wall of metal lockers in which to stow our gear. One of my cubicle mates, a shrewd wiry kid from Arkansas named Birdsall, mentioned that the bunk and locker I was about to occupy had belonged to Charlie S., whose replacement I was.

When I reported in at the hangar to Petty Officer First Class Parr — I'd been assigned to work as a clerk in the detachment's administration office, which was located upstairs at the back of the hangar — it turned out that I had been given Charlie S.'s old job as well as his desk. From the office windows one looked down onto the oil-stained hangar floor, where the small T-37s and medium-sized cargo-carrying DC-3s were wheeled in and maintained by the company's electricians and mechanics, who were, among the enlisted ranks, the "real men" of the outfit, compared to us "pencil pushers."

Parr was a gruff, not especially friendly man, a career sailor who had somehow not risen to the rank of chief petty officer, which he ought to have attained, given the number of hashmarks on the forearm of his uniform, signifying years of service. Perhaps that soured him somewhat. It may have been from him that I learned that Charlie, who I was replacing, came from Chicago, as did I.

But it was Birdsall who told me the story. Though unschooled, he was worldly-wise, possessing a kind of commonsense sophistication that I frequently encountered among boys raised in farming communities in the American South. He told me that Charlie — who was now in a navy brig in Norfolk, Virginia — was in the process of being dishonourably discharged for homosexuality. Charlie, Birdsall insisted, wasn't a fruit. He wasn't even necessarily a homo; he was just a friendly, joke-telling, regular guy who simply liked sex a lot. It was clear that Birdsall had been friends with Charlie, as had many others in the company.

What had happened was that one night Charlie, along with a couple of other guys from the outfit, had gone out to an abandoned plane parked in a nearby field behind the barracks, ostensibly to drink a few beer. The little party, enlivened by the entertaining, joke-telling Charlie, became ever pleasanter, looser. Talk turned, as it often did, to how horny everyone was. In any case, one thing led to another and Charlie sucked off the two other guys. Birdsall figured that it was mostly a matter of high spirits rather than exclusive sexual preference, since Charlie often went with the guys into Naples for a night of drinking and sex with the women from the local bar (a sailor's hangout that I would in due course also come to know).

"Shee-it," snorted Birdsall. "If he'd asked me, I'd probably have gone out to the plane with him, too." Since Birdsall was telling this story in the presence of several of our cubicle mates, all listening attentively and none objecting to his account, it was clear that the lack of disapproval was a generally shared opinion.

Word had gotten around. Charlie and the guys he'd blown were called in for questioning by the company officer responsible for such matters. They got scared and blabbed. Now all three of them were being kicked out, since the navy regulation prohibiting homosexuality underscored the fact that no distinction was made between "active" and "passive" participants. The official phrase was "conduct unbecoming" a member of the US Armed Forces. Birdsall saw it as just bad luck that they had been caught. All of this had happened only a month or so before I arrived.

There was a recent letter from Charlie to Birdsall, written from the Norfolk brig. Birdsall handed it to me, and I can still see the lined paper, the blue ink, and Charlie's looping handwriting, which I occasionally ran across in the files at the detachment office, where Charlie had made written entries on documents. The letter was a chatty account of life in the brig, which wasn't at all pleasant for prisoners about to be discharged for homosexual acts. But his account showed that Charlie was taking it in stride, irrespective of the public humiliation to which he had been subjected (humiliation whose magnitude, at this late date, is barely describable or imaginable). It was a friendly letter, unapologetic, and it struck me as the kind of thing one might write from summer camp to one's pals back home.

How extraordinary this all was. I'd been assigned more or less randomly to a place in the world in which I was figuratively stepping into the shoes, and literally occupying the bunk and doing the job, of a boy from the same city and with the same desires as me. The odds against such a coincidence must have been enormous. If Birdsall would have gone off to the abandoned airplane and let himself be blown there by Charlie, I would just as surely have been willing to go there too and perform the very act on Birdsall (who was certainly attractive to me) that Charlie was no longer available to do. How strange and oddly thrilling to come so far only to encounter a mirror image of oneself, a genuine *Doppelgänger*.

In the event, I never went out to the plane or blew Birdsall. But I was passionately, crazily in love the entire time I was there, infatuated with one boy after another, with several at once, with groups of them. I was also sufficiently terrified by the evident consequences of acting on my desire to — as they say in the military — proceed with utmost caution. There are dozens of tales in this sea-locker — of sailors, longing, some sex, friendships, landscapes, art, Naples itself, flights in airplanes, leaves to Paris — the dowry of a future storyteller. But in the autobiography of how I came to bear a blue tattoo of a ship's anchor on my forearm, there are only two I absolutely need.

I fell in love for what seemed like a surprisingly long time, a year or more, with one of the guys in the barracks, a dark-haired, lean-limbed boy I'll call Bob Cassidy. At the same time, I became best friends with David Martin, a sturdy, sensible, old-family Californian with whom I shared intellectual and artistic interests. We often went drinking together, took trips to nearby sights, read the same books.

Cassidy may have been a Californian too. If he was, he was probably a transplanted one, raised in some fringe eastern urban centre and then, probably through parental breakup, shifted to an equally seedy southern California version of same. The other guys didn't much like him; they considered Cassidy fundamentally untrustworthy, a bit rat-like with his sly grin. And indeed, when he crawled out of the sea onto the sand, his black hair slicked back, there was something slightly feral about his dark, glistening eyes. I took a set of photographs of Cassidy in which he was wearing black-and-white vertically striped bathing briefs, exuding precisely the combination of sexy charm and deceit that made others distrust him and me love him. The photos were taken on Ischia, an island in the Bay of Naples, where we spent a weekend together some time after the incident I'm thinking of now.

I'd rented a room in a villa-like building quite close to the base, another place to sleep, where I could spend time by myself, have friends over, make a routine slightly different from the enforced collectivity of the barracks. One night I invited Cassidy over. I don't remember the details, or what phase of the relationship we'd reached, except that I was in pretty deep. In fact, I've clearer memories of confiding my yearnings for Cassidy to my all-purpose artistic and romantic adviser, David, than of being with Cassidy himself. Except for this incident.

We spent the evening talking and drinking. It got late. I suggested to Cassidy that he could sleep over. That was okay by him. I didn't have a plan, maybe not even an intention, simply a mixture of self-deceptively high-minded ideas about love, and lust rubbed raw.

He snoozed. He was wearing white underwear, Jockey-type, that I could see in the dark along with the slight bulge at the crotch. Once again I reached across an infinite gap. I tried to persuade myself that my touching him was tentative enough that I still had an avenue of retreat if he "woke" and objected.

I crawled between his legs as I fondled his growing, hardening cock. He lifted his small butt an inch and in a swift single movement slid off his underpants. Cassidy knew exactly what was going on all along and had no objections. My mouth closed over his erection.

I was surprised by the generous thickness of a sexual organ I had failed to imagine adequately, a size that seemed much larger against the general leanness of his body. Inexperienced as I was, the actual dimensions of reality bumped up against the image of a dream boy whom I'd totally etherealized.

As I strained forward to get more of him into my mouth, lying between Cassidy's spread legs, my belly pressed into the bed, the slight friction of my body against the sheets was enough to release all those months of pent-up passion. After I came, I stopped blowing him. He turned on the bedside lamp. Still half-mesmerized by the sight of his fully erect cock, but already feeling the discomfort of the night air cooling the sticky goo in my crotch, I asked, "Do you want me to go on?" Cassidy utterly kept his aplomb. "It's up to you," he said. Instead, we talked. He slipped his underpants back on, I used a towel to dry off.

In retrospect, it was an idiotic beginner's mistake not to finish him off. It would have given me some much-needed experience, him some pleasure, and would have cost neither of us anything, as well as creating future prospects for the repetition of the experience. What others saw as Cassidy's untrustworthiness was exactly what I trusted to keep his mouth shut and us out of trouble. In the ensuing talk, he asked one slightly grammatically and semantically tangled question that I see as the point of this story.

"Is it me or is this a . . . a problem for you?" Cassidy asked. I immediately understood him. Skip the sociological word "problem." I could tell from his tiny stutter that he just couldn't think of another way to put it at the moment. What Cassidy was asking was, Has this happened because you're in love with me specifically, or are you a homosexual? Intentionally or not, it also offered me an easy way out. I took it. "It's you," I said truthfully enough. But the point is — and this is what it would still take me a while to sort out — both halves of the equation were equally true. I would love specific others, *and* the desire was homo.

There's not much more. I reported in excitedly to my confidant,

David, who seemed suitably impressed by my daring. I described it all in the third person, as if we were characters in the story I'd been trying to write about Cassidy and myself. And just now I'm suddenly remembering — that is, I can "hear" — David's throaty chuckle, a unique sound never heard before or since.

Despite my attempts at art, I remained as stupid as ever in interpersonal affairs. Cassidy and I spent a weekend together on the island of Ischia some weeks after that incident. We slept in the same room, there was all that changing into and out of vertically striped black-and-white bathing suits, showers, generous views of butts and balls; it never occurred to me that Cassidy was offering me a chance at a repeat performance if only I had the minimal grain of sense required to make a move.

Then it was about a year later. I remember the time fairly precisely because on August 13, 1961 (a day that falls within this period), the East German government began building the Berlin Wall, and there was a good chance, if things went wrong, that my tour of duty, which was almost over, would be extended indefinitely — "for the duration," as they say in military-speak. As it turned out, the "crisis" passed and I was discharged as scheduled.

If I were writing fiction, I'd probably turn Cassidy and a boy named Jimmy Joe K. into a single composite. But I'm not (writing fiction), and I won't (turn them into a composite).

I was certainly as much, or as desperately, depending on how you look at it, in love with Jimmy Joe K., a blond-haired apprentice airplane mechanic, as I'd been with Cassidy, who had since shipped out. Our sexual play consisted of some fooling around in the showers, and long dinner conversations in Naples in which I tried a number of arguments (all rather weak) to persuade Jimmy Joe to try it out.

Although he'd been sufficiently excited by our shower-room jostling to be willing to hear my arguments, he was afraid that if he did it with me, he'd turn "queer." The whole prospect was really troubling for him. Instead, he was still hoping to be rescued from temptation by some satisfactory experience with women in one of the cities he went to on flights as an on-board mechanic. In the end, that's precisely what happened.

By that time, my duties had expanded to include some flying time as a cargo handler on the DC-3s that delivered stuff to other

American bases in Europe (which was the primary mission of the detachment). Although I still worked under Petty Officer First Class Parr's supervision, I was now assigned to the detachment's legal officer, Lieutenant Fitzpatrick, whose duties included the investigation of the outfit's internal affairs.

One night I returned to Naples from a flight that had gone to Port Lyautey, Morocco. Instead of turning in, I headed downtown to a basement nightclub where some of the guys drank — the same one where my "double," Charlie S., had partied with his mates. I no doubt hoped to run into Jimmy Joe. In the smoky, low-ceilinged room that featured a circular bar, I shouldered my way through the crowd and got a scotch and soda. Standing across the bar from me, I noticed, was Parr, well into an evening of hard drinking.

I'd worked for Parr for two years and I don't recall that we'd ever exchanged a word, friendly or otherwise, outside of the office. This was the first time I'd run into him "on shore," though occasionally I'd silently noted the morning-after effects of his nights on the town. He saw me and made his way around the bar until he was at my side. We exchanged a perfunctory greeting.

Parr then said in a dead-sober voice, in a tone as casual as if he were ordering me to fetch a file, "Some kid said something to Chief W. [and here he named the airplane mechanics' chief petty officer], and he went to Fitzpatrick. So you'd better be careful." I knew exactly what he was talking about and so, to my astonishment, did Parr. That was it. No questions. No moral judgments. No commiseration. Just a flat-out warning. Parr then crossed the room to join some men of his own rank.

The next morning, I found Jimmy Joe. "Are you out of your mind?" I asked and drew him off to a quiet corner of the hangar. First I found out how far it had gone. Jimmy Joe had gone to his chief for some fatherly advice. It had stayed pretty vague, on the level of, What should you do if you think someone's coming on to you? Jimmy had mentioned my name, but made it clear that nothing had happened. After I'd surveyed the damage, I explained to Jimmy in mostly one-syllable words, except for the phrase "conduct unbecoming," what all of it meant and exactly what kind of trouble both of us could get into. He seemed to understand.

I then scampered up the ladder to the upstairs office at the back of the hangar, breezed in, went up to Fitzpatrick as I normally did at the beginning of the day, looked him in the eye, said, "Good morning, Lieutenant. Ready for some coffee, sir?" and awaited his orders. That was that.

Parr never mentioned the incident again. I was indeed more careful, and Lieutenant Fitzpatrick subsequently found no cause to raise the matter with me.

If Parr hadn't warned me, a number of things could easily have happened: getting caught (if not with Jimmy, someone else), getting kicked out (of the navy), getting stuck with a fate worse than death. Instead of inventing "gay liberation" (along with a few hundred thousand others) in 1969, I would have had years of psychiatrists and, after several twelve-step-program failures and decades of closeted self-hatred, would've had to re-come out as a man of thirty-five or forty.

What I don't know is why Parr warned me. I don't know (won't ever know) if Parr was gay and thus had some idea of protecting his own, or if a more complex set of reasons and loyalties motivated his decision to warn me. I only knew — and perhaps that's all we can know at certain times — that I had been saved.

5. Les Enfants du Paradis

The tattoo's autobiography is not all hesitations, false starts, *coitus interruptus*. If it were, no tattoo would have been inscribed on my left forearm.

I made my way to Paris in 1960. I was still in the navy, stationed outside Naples, still continuously in love, dodging the naval anti-homo authorities. I went by easy stages. The easy stages were made possible because two friends from San Francisco, a couple named Harold and Dora Dull, part of the White Rabbit circle of poets, had moved to Europe for a couple of years. They started in Italy, at a small fishing village on the Amalfi coast outside Naples, a couple of hours by bus from my military base.

Their idea was to stay in a place for a couple of months and then move gradually north. Each week, when I finished work on Friday afternoon, I would take a bus or train to wherever they were and spend the weekend with them. I was six or seven years

younger than them, and they regarded me as a bright, slightly barbaric, younger sibling in need of education. They gave me books
to read, took me to museums, walked me through churches and
ruins, spun out theories about history, art, life.

They were a doomed couple (but that was still a few years down
the road), mainly because Harold, a tall, stooped, very light-
skinned man with washed-out blond hair, pale blue eyes, and
fluttering hand gestures, was a monster of selfishness. He was
also intelligent and, I thought, a very good poet. His selfishness
was charming, since he was genuinely delighted to share his pleasures with others. So if there was a piece of recorded music to be
played, or a kind of food to be chosen, or a decision to be made
on the particular way or route to walk to some destination, he
was passive-aggressively insistent on his preference, but equally
so on ensuring your opportunity to enjoy what pleased him.

Dora eventually made a joke of his insistence, as if it were a
childish thing he couldn't help. I had hardly any preferences at all
at the time, so it didn't matter to me. She was short, dark haired,
of Germanic descent, wonderfully cheerful (with a bell-clear tin-
kle of laughter), and at the same time practical and competent.

Over the months, my weekend train trips grew longer, and
the time for leaving on Sunday evenings became a little earlier
— from the Amalfi coast, then from Rome, Florence, and across
the border into France. Each weekend I became more educated,
more civilized, before plunging back into unfulfilled barracks
boy-lust and listening to the yarns of coffee-drinking "old salts"
at the military base.

Eventually, my trips required making use of my accumulated
leave time. Over the two years, I made three or four month-long
trips to Paris where, at least at the beginning, Harold and Dora
were living. So was my friend and mentor Allen Ginsberg. I got
a room in the hotel where he, Peter Orlovsky, Gregory Corso,
William Burroughs, and Brion Gysin were staying, a tiny, unpre-
tentious, dark-corridored *pension* at 9, rue Gît-le-Coeur, about
a block from the Seine (you could see the river if you stuck your
head out the window), just behind Place St.-Michel in the student quarter. The *pension* eventually became known as the Beat
Hotel.

Harold and Dora shepherded me through the Louvre, took me
to cafés and jazz bars. Ginsberg introduced me to the writings

of Jean Genet, starting with *Our Lady of the Flowers*, told me about or accompanied me to a showing of Marcel Carné's 1945 film, *Les Enfants du Paradis*, and let me tag along as he introduced himself in his forthright, Whitmanic way to various artistic celebrities — the photographer Man Ray; Tristan Tzara, the elderly Dada poet; the American novelist James Baldwin.

Soon I was scrupulously following Arthur Rimbaud's celebrated, if not entirely wise, advice advocating the "systematic derangement of all the senses." I snorted heroin, read Surrealist and "cut-up" writing (the latter by Burroughs and Gysin), ate chocolate mousse, listened to recordings of Ornette Coleman, and eventually made love with boys in Paris — all, excepting the last perhaps, with characteristic moderation. The last, I think, is what's relevant. The tattoo isn't just sex; it's about an education, but given the particular shape of my desire and the historical moment, sex was the part that was most difficult, which is why it commands disproportionate attention.

I found the Café Bonaparte more or less by accident. On the main boulevard of the St.-Germain-des-Prés quarter were the famous cafés Les Deux Magots and Café de Flore, where Jean-Paul Sartre and Simone de Beauvoir spent much of their time when they were in Paris, and where Roland Barthes could also be found, though I had little idea then of who any of these famous intellectuals were. The Café Bonaparte, on the ground floor of a four-storey building, was on the corner of the narrow Rue Bonaparte at the bottom of the square.

The Bonaparte was a hybrid café-bar and attracted a mixed crowd of local artists and intellectuals, some foreign visitors, and a gang of French boys and girls my age who occupied some tables near the pinball machines, which they played. The first people I met in the Bonaparte one afternoon were an English couple living in Paris, two men in their late thirties, who were in the art business. The Bonaparte had sets of glass doors that extended around the café and could be opened, giving the place a pleasant outdoors quality. Soon I was invited to join the two men — who I'll call Lindsay and Clive, since I can't remember their names — at their regular table, which was situated in one of the open arcades of the bar, facing the square.

Lindsay and Clive took me in hand, taught me to drink Pernod, and helped me with my French (which quickly became passable, at least for street use), but, more important, through their conversation they began to educate me about how things worked. One of the ways things worked at the Bonaparte, I learned, was that it was possible to go with the boys there. Some were students, some were about to be drafted (these were the years of the Algerian War), others were what we would now call Parisian street kids, who hung out at the Bonaparte with their girlfriends and sometimes, Lindsay and Clive told me, went to bed with the customers at the bar when they needed a place to stay or pocket money, or just for pleasure. Often a small gift or "loan" was involved, my English mentors added, but the amount was so small as to be more symbolic than noticeable, even to an on-leave sailor who didn't have a lot of money. Now I looked more closely, and with anticipation, at them. The fashion for young men that year, *circa* 1960–61, was a plain black sports jacket and denim jeans, and white or sometimes pink shirts, the tails often left hanging out. Lindsay and Clive explained to me in an avuncular way how to go about approaching the boys I was interested in and satisfied themselves that my pronunciation of the sentence "*Voulez-vous allez a coucher avec moi?*" was acceptable. I became friends with a guy my age named Luc.

Finally, one day, I took a little walk around the square with Luc and, with my heart in my mouth, asked him my magic "*Voulez-vous*" question, which seemed to me about the most daring question one person could ask another, especially another of the same gender. "*À condition,*" Luc amiably replied. The "condition" mainly had to do with whether I had a place we could go. I did — the Beat Hotel — but as we went off to my room in the rue Gît-le-Coeur, I also absorbed the larger point that all of life is presented to us "on condition." Subsequently, there were other boys — Jacky, Peter, Willy — to whom I put, with increasing confidence, my "*Voulez-vous*" question, and, frequently enough, they said, "*Pourquoi pas?*"

The sex with Luc, Jacky, and most of the others was different from anything I'd ever experienced. It wasn't furtive; it was utterly pleasurable without being terrifying or accompanied by the thought of being terrorized. It was — most of all — *normal.* Normal and *fun.* Curiously enough, in between those month-long sojourns in Paris and that leisurely, relaxed, normal lovemaking, I was also, back in the barracks in Naples, pining, yearning, lust-ing after my naval mates and dodging the scrutiny of the company's legal officer. I'm not sure how I dealt with the distinctions between the two settings or if I had to or if it mattered. Just as I had fallen in love with Bob Cassidy and Jimmy Joe K., I fell in love with Luc and Jacky, but now my ardour was slaked in and on their bodies, leaving no troubled emotional residue.

There are two points I want to make about this, and I don't know which is the more important. The first is that I had the approval of my elders. The two English art queens made it clear that I was doing fine, even if my tastes seemed a trifle indiscriminate to them. Ginsberg always took a friendly, encouraging interest in my having boyfriends. At parties, he introduced me to likely companions. He was as explicit and frank in conversations as he was in his poems.

And my older siblings, or adoptive modernist parents, Harold and Dora, thought it was all wonderfully cute. Harold would stretch a long, bird-wing arm around my shoulders and squeeze me to him as we stood at the bar in the Bonaparte, laughing over my evident anticipatory joy as I was about to go off to bed with some Paris pal. Dora, casting an eye in the direction of Luc or Jacky, pursed her lips in approval and uttered a soft *ooh-la-la* to confirm that she thought my choice was hot.

In various homo autobios and novels of people growing up in the 1950s, early '60s — I'm thinking especially of Martin Duberman's *Cures* and Edmund White's *The Beautiful Room Is Empty* — there are lengthy, invariably painful accounts of years and years of failed psychotherapy to reconcile them with their homosexuality. I was spared all those shrinks by the casual, loving approval I got from Harold and Dora, and the others. And by my own lack of any tendency toward guilt, as I want to make clear in a second point.

This I can attach to a specific sexual memory. One night in my room in the rue Gît-le-Coeur, I was about to go to bed with a boy named Willy. He was wearing one of those black sports jackets and a pink shirt with the tail hanging out. He took off his jacket, shoes and socks, jeans, white underwear, and stood there for a moment in his pink shirt, his genitals covered but sturdy bare legs on view. Then he slipped off his shirt and lay down in my comfortable, if lumpy, bed, with its brass bedstead facing the window and a bright green corroded metal mansard roof across the narrow street. I crawled between his legs, one hand on the muscle of his left thigh, and took his cock into my mouth, its soft, rubbery texture quickly growing stiff.

While I sucked him, I had a thought — precise, clear, indubitable as that of the French thinker Descartes, who invented a lot of such thinking. Usually we aren't aware of abstract thoughts in the midst of lovemaking, but this was an exception. The thought was simply this: I like *this* — I like doing it, I like being here, feeling as I do — and I will never deny that the exquisite pleasure of it *is* a pleasure, unless compelled by force. That thought, never since forgotten, didn't take care of love, but it did take care, once and for all, of the issue of homo desire.

6. The Tattoo

My father had a tattoo of a three-dimensional five-pointed blue star on the outside of his right biceps. When I was a child, the tattoo was an object of endless fascination for me, one that was made magical by his ability to make the star wiggle (or "blink") by moving a muscle in his biceps without perceptibly flexing his hand or arm. Again and again, I would ask this vigorous, bald-headed man in a white T-shirt to make the star move. He had infinite patience for me.

The secret of social relations, he pointed out to me when I was about eleven or twelve, was the willingness to have a drink with your in-laws (my mother's brothers and their wives), even (and especially) if you didn't like them. "Show them you're a *mensch*," he advised, using the Yiddish term for a human being. He took down two shot glasses from the sideboard and poured us each a slug of Old Grandad or Old Taylor whiskey. We clinked glasses and downed the burning whiskey in a single gulp, as my mother, a non-drinker, watched, slightly shocked at the sight. I now understood how to be a gentleman.

Of my father's many teachings, the first and most important came when I was about four: he taught me to read. He bought a blackboard on an easel, with the letters of the alphabet inscribed across the top. When I asked him to draw something for me — a cowboy, say — along with the drawing he would write the word, until, in due course, I was able to see the relations between the letters, drawing, and word.

When I came home from the navy toward the end of 1961, my father picked me up at the airport. As we drove into Chicago, a city I hadn't seen in the more than two years that I'd been stationed outside Naples, he asked me about my experiences in the world, and I sensed his paternal pride in my adventures. He parked in front of our building and paused a moment before we got out of the car and went into the house to greet my mother.

"I suppose by now you've experienced pretty much everything in the way of sex," he said. "Yes," I acknowledged. "Both with girls and — ?" "Yes," I said.

He inquired delicately if my desires were by now firmly determined. "Well, pretty much," I said. I didn't have to say anything more explicit than that, since we both knew I was talking about homosexual desire. What was striking to me was the non-judgmental nature of his questions, and his clear concern for my freedom. It was also clear to me for the first time that he, too, had had similar experiences.

"Well, old salt," he said, rather jovially, and heaved my duffel bag onto his shoulder, his tattooed star bulging, leading me home as he had led me into the world.

In Naples, I had admired the tattoo of a ship's anchor in blue on the forearm of a boy named Ferinde, who had a bunk in my cubicle in the barracks. I admired more than that about him, but Ferinde made it clear that advances would be unwelcome. The anchor was an "unfouled" one, which meant that it didn't have a rope (or "line") tangled (or "fouled") in or around its eye, arms, torso, or pronged feet. If I were ever to get a tattoo, I knew that was the one I wanted.

A few months after I'd been discharged from the navy and visited my folks, I returned to San Francisco to live for a while. I got a job in a warehouse and a place to live, both thanks to an older artist named Bill McNeill. I showed Jack Spicer the "best poem" he'd seen in two years and sat at his table with other young writers in the bar he frequented at night. On weekend afternoons we went to Aquatic Park and gazed out across San Francisco Bay. I was about to enter into various relationships for the good, classical reasons of learning wisdom and goodness. Of course, none of this was a tenth as calculated as it sounds in retrospect. But on the other hand, neither was it any longer the case that I was simply and luckily falling into things without thought. There was one more thing to do in relation to what I'd learned so far before doing whatever I would do on the way to wherever I was going.

One night, two young men burst into the bar, like young gun-slingers out of nowhere. In fact, they'd come out of the Great Salt Lake Desert in a jalopy. The tall, lean, blue-eyed one was named Tony; the other was his sidekick. I fell in love with Tony at first sight. Others also claimed to have fallen in love with him, and several poems that season contained images of him, but only I was prepared to endure the arduous trials that are proof of the lover's true devotion.

Tony was primarily het, but he was not insensible or indifferent to the desire he evoked in me. He had no literary ambitions but was instead a "noble savage" in modern capitalist society. He got a job as a car-park at a fashionable restaurant at the foot of Tele-graph Hill, and I often hung out there with him. Before parking a snazzy sports car in the nearby garage as he was supposed to, he'd invite me in and we'd take a spin up the twisting hill to Coit Tower at the top, and then we'd race down the hill as death-defy-ingly fast as possible, my life completely in his hands.

Tony's authenticity was rooted in excess: speeding, drinking, whatever could be pushed to the limit. I trailed after him, rode with him, took LSD with him, moved him into a room in my apartment where, for some insane reason I can't remember, he kept a shotgun — but I was allowed to retain possession of the shells. I wasn't any smarter in love than I'd previously been. It was just a sweet, long, painful, physically unrequited hell. He did eventually permit me a single night of sex with him, though he made sure it was boozy enough that it was deniable (by him), and he made clear to me afterwards that it had meant little to him, although he could hardly deny that it was both a recognition of my "need" and a gift to me.

In the middle of this romance, one night Tony and I were in downtown San Francisco. Around Seventh and Market we saw a tattoo shop, and I said I wanted a tattoo. Tony accompanied me. The tattoo artist was a locally famous man named Lyle Tuttle. The shop wasn't busy at that hour, and Tuttle had time for me.

Tuttle's fame was that he was an "illustrated man" (to recall the title of a Ray Bradbury science-fiction story of the period).

There'd been articles about Tuttle in the weekend magazines of the local papers. His entire body, except for his hands, neck, and face, was completely covered by a tapestry of tattoos. The absence of tattoos in the other places meant that he could dress up like a businessman and pass. In between heating up the inks and laying out the tools, he showed us some of his body. He even unzipped his fly and pulled out his cock, revealing a tattoo of a meat stamp used in butcher shops certifying "Grade A Beef."

Tuttle was a little disappointed that I wanted such a timid example of his craft, but business was business. While he was preparing, I had the curious fantasy of wishing I was a black man so that I could get the tattoo of the anchor in white ink, but of course that wasn't possible, and I settled for the traditional blue.

I sat across from him, but close, our knees touching, and he held my forearm firmly to the table as he drew, freehand, an unfouled ship's anchor in blue ink into my skin. It wasn't painful, and to a passerby it looked like no more than the usual thoughtless dumb-kid whim of the moment, to be regretted the next morning.

I've never regretted it. My father, who saw it some time later, was predictably pleased that I had turned out to be "a chip off the old block" and immediately understood its import. My mother was a little unsure, since a tattoo was a rejection of social class — in her view, only "common" people would get a tattoo — as well as religion, given that it was a clear violation of the Jewish injunction against "graven images."

Getting the tattoo wasn't a mystical epiphany or anything, merely a little weird as a physical sensation. But I was aware of its significance. The tattoo came not at the beginning, when most sailors get them, as a promise or a vow of things to come, a hope-ful boast of manhood, but at the end — of my "tour of duty," of an initiatory education in desire, art, the world — as a document, testimony, as a vow of *memory*.

Eros and Cupid

On Condition

In Paris, long ago, a French boy my own age, about nineteen, whom I had asked to sleep with me, replied, "*À condition*." I have ever since retained the sense in which all of life is presented to us "on condition." We slept together many times.

Eros

It's probably not a good idea to see either of them at their best. Blinding Eros, charming Cupid. Better to catch them off guard, as they do us.

For an instant they stand revealed in the merciless fluorescence of a public building, or their voices grasp at optic fibres. For instance, B., scruffy, unshaven, stoned to the eyeballs, making me drive him to the airport through rush-hour traffic and then getting the flight info all wrong, forgetting his I.D., so I have to use my credit cards for his fool's errand across the mountains. Or M., phoning collect in the middle of the night from some other time zone, with an incomprehensible tale of loss. So, one starts, and moans, as did Jack Spicer:

What have I gone to bed with all these years?
What have I taken crying to my bed
For love of me?

But there is no denying how they marked us, broke our hearts, wrinkled our souls. One even left a blue anchor tattooed on my forearm.

94

The first time I saw B. was in the Ambassador Pub in Vancouver. It was during the rainy season.

I cajoled my drinking crony, Mr. Stevens, who had a special talent for such chores, to intercede on my behalf with a blond, curly-haired sprite sitting several tables away. *Mister* Stevens was the camp name of this thin, fortyish man with pale, thinning hair and wire-rimmed glasses that corrected only about a third of his myopic sight. Because I was the member of our troupe most identified as "political," he liked to subject me to his conservative diatribes, the intensity of which were directly correlated to the level of alcohol in his blood.

I rather preferred Mr. Stevens's drunken and savage self-caricatures to his attacks on human equality. "Well, what am I?" he would wail, and then pathetically answer himself, "A third-rate hag in a fifth-rate faggot bar in a ninth-rate town." I appreciated in this the grain of half-truth that applied to all of us. In fact, we made a comic duo. Squinting behind inadequate spectacles at a hazy youthful shape in the middle distance, he'd ask, "How about that one?" It was like cruising with Mr. Magoo, the short-sighted cartoon character likely to mistake a tank for a toadstool. I felt like a seeing-eye dog reporting in, "No, not him."

He was not without his redeeming features. Simone de Beauvoir once wrote, "Sometimes man seeks to find again upon the body of young boys the sandy down, the velvet night, the scent of honeysuckle." Some nights in the bar, only Mr. Stevens could adequately verify this text by his rapturous description of teenage flesh — someone he had slept with the night before — as he ran his feathery fingers over my own forearm to illustrate his story.

Mr. Stevens returned alone from his mission, dropping into a vacant armchair alongside me at the terrycloth-covered circular table several of us were clustered around. "He'll be over in a minute," Mr. Stevens said.

This is perhaps the most tremulous moment in desire, equal even to the first sight of the desired one nude. The mildly entertaining or boring evening is about to go on without me. Our friend Lolo, with his heavy-lidded eyes and magisterial manner, is grumbling his displeasure over Mr. Stevens' and my lascivious gossip, his hopes for a literary turn in the conversation dashed. Mr. Stevens, by now, is listening to a plaintive anecdote by Ed T., an accountant. As Norman, the waiter, glides down the aisle with a trayful of beer, B. pulls up a chair at a tangent to our crude circle. On my lips the unimaginable yet utterly banal language that will cloak the arrangements for a startling intimacy. Equal even to the first touch, a hand placed around the curve of his side, just above the waist.

■

"Look, I'll be blunt," B. began, without preliminaries, but half-apologizing in advance for the commercial proposition he was about to make. I unhesitatingly agreed to the terms of the contract.

Once we were in the streets — we had quickly collected our things, made our farewells to our respective friends; "I'll call you," I yelled to Mr. Stevens, as if we were erotic scientists and I was promising to report my findings from the laboratory / bedroom — and had walked about a block and a half in a driving rain toward my parked car, B. surprised me by confessing he was too drunk, stoned, or otherwise out of sorts for sex.

I was taken by his candour. Instead of our agreed-upon destination, B. requested a ride to the other side of town where he proposed to spend the night at a friend's house. Although this was something of a violation of the code governing such affairs — i.e., it suggested a relation based on respect rather than rapacity — I said okay, having long ago been persuaded by my father's example that courtesy is a true virtue. In any case, I could enjoy the anticipation of our next meeting.

■

Even in such arranged circumstances, there is an element of seduction. At first, B. was a casual pleasure. That is, I almost immediately forgot what had initially possessed me, namely, Eros. But I sought to entice him, laying myself bare, openly admiring his evident charms, initiating a discourse of admissions. Soon he delighted me by the frankness of his expressions of pleasure.

B. was from a rural town upcountry. There was a monstrous

but typical family: younger brothers in Prince George, alcoholic and physically dangerous father, a sister in Edmonton. B.'s sexual tastes were distinctly bifurcated between female age-mates and older men. Presently, he was at the tail end of a deteriorating relationship with a man in the suburbs, a salesman with whom, by B.'s own account, he had fallen in love — this casual acknowledgment itself opened a horizon.

Like many others his age, B. was living more or less by his wits and the welfare system. Capitalism, or, more specifically, its disemployment of youth, rendered B. economically powerless. I was, naturally, for him, at the other end of the spectrum of financial and other powers. For, as ridiculous as it often seemed to me, the world — or at least that part of it known as the media — was for the moment demanding of me an almost daily exercise of minor intellectual authority. I was called on, often at dawn, by the local radio station, for ceaseless commentary on a range of current issues, including the economy and the high rate of unemployment, especially among youth.

I'd have to be particularly obtuse — more so than in my dimmer moments — not to recognize the inequalities in class power between B. and myself. Worse, there's also, as it's known in Marxist argot, a cash nexus, which poses its own set of inescapable culpabilities, but I think I'll save that one for a rainier day. As I began seeing B., I was struck by how the structure of the homoerotic tends to even out the standard imbalances in relationships — class, age, education, whatever. Partly, it is the forbidden character of this desire (especially in this particular form of age disparity and commercial transactions, itself a distinctly minority taste in the homo milieu) that accounts for its egalitarian current, that causes its relations to be fundamentally a collusion, a conspiracy, a project. But more: in the sex of homosexuality, how often those who are, by definition, the dominated become the dominant.

I'm not saying that homosexuality eradicates differences, just that it reshuffles the cards one is holding. It may seem as if I'm claiming some superiority for gay relations and, perhaps — if somewhat sneakily — I am, but I also know better. I've seen enough heterosexualities that are sufficiently dense, tangled, and constructed of sub-basements of charged feeling that I'm little tempted to engage in a bidding war. Among the pleasures of that celebrated homoerotic sexual preference, then, are its *equalities*, *reciprocities*, *reversals*.

I once saw a movie called *Trading Places* — an update of the old prince and pauper fairy tale — with a boy named Michael. When it ended, as we were about to go home for sex, I suggested that we could "trade places" also. He was immediately enthused by this verbal play and the ease with which it could be enacted.

Similarly, the assumptions one makes about many stereo-typical sex roles are often surprised by a reversal. One night in Numbers, a Davie Street gay bar, Mr. Stevens and I were taking pleasure in viewing the affectations of a faggoty but exception-ally pretty youth as he played up to various men in the room — "outrageous" gestures, poses, swoons. Yet, how often these effeminate youngsters startle us later in the evening with the cer-tainty of their desire.

In sum, I succeeded in arousing a hitherto unexplored region — a utopia — of B.'s ardour. I can't say I *gave* B. power. The very presumption is arrogantly self-defeating. The most that can be claimed of my volition is that I *enticed* us to an edge, or perhaps, since it all occurs within the boundaries of a code, I conducted us to, not a play-within-a-play, but rather a reality-within-a-play, occurring within the sexual drama itself. Herein, a reversal that offers the possibility of countering the endemic will to possess. This also happens to be the key to sadomasochism: the appar-ent exaggeration of possession harbours the abandonment of the will to possess. In all this, for de Sade as for Socrates, the consid-eration is ultimately moral or else it is without interest.

B., from our first encounters, sought to diffuse the boundaries of the code, to make them ragged as a fjord, invoking ambiguous borders between coded and open relationships, in sex as well as in economic matters. In bed, one or the other of us being pen-etrated, it was soon mutually obvious that we were engaged in something more than a protocol. And how often he transformed monetary transactions, for his own sake as much as mine, with the utterance, "You're helping me out," as though it was but a munificent loan whose return was not pressing.

The recurrent spatial metaphor for me is "beneath" — beneath the arena of the code, under the stairway of childhood, in the basement, where a friend and I, as adolescents, fantasized "initiating" another boy whom we desired.

Just as I began to acquire the illusion, like Proust's Charlus, that my life would become considerably easier were B. to enter it on a more permanent basis, he announced a brief visit to his sister in Edmonton that, instead, turned out to be a temporary disappearance.

●

When B. phoned one crisp morning in early December — he had the uncanny ability to announce himself or appear out of nowhere — I was in the backyard, seated on a kitchen chair in front of the Japanese plum tree, working (. . . well, pontificating) before a television camera, constituting myself as an imaginary being.

I hadn't seen him in three months. In the meantime I had discovered Buddy's, a gay bar where I often brooded in contentment after a day's work on the book I was writing about local politics, and had even met a campy young man there with whom I was having an affair. The young man was one of those wonderful people from another planet, solely interested in clothes, haircuts, interior decoration — a devout reader of *Gentlemen's Quarterly* — but who thought sex rather messy, sticky, smelly. In contrast, B. loved to get in and unpretentiously rut. Indeed, he appeared within the hour, stripped, announced his "horniness," which was visible, and promptly, to paraphrase the Homeric poets, entangled me in his limbs. In the hazy enchantment of afternoon, the room grew languorous with smoke and flesh.

B. had changed, or wanted to be seen by me, among others, as having changed. Though it was his relatively unchanging hyperkinetic "essence" that was of interest to me, he was at that nascence of adulthood when it seemed urgent that his identity become more comprehensible. He wanted to "get it together," as if he saw his life as a scattering of fragments that he now sought to gather in one place or link into a network. B. had returned to school and had decided, apparently, that there was a role for me in this scenario as unofficial tutor. To all this I found myself sympathetic — because it was B., of course, but perhaps also as a characteristic of getting older. Increasingly, as I observed human striving from the minuscule distance of imagined immortality, it seemed to me that what people wanted was often reasonable, even modest. At the same time, the charnel house of a society in which they sought to realize their ambitions appeared ever more appalling.

●

In those days, not yet in love, I would arrive at the upstairs bar in Buddy's around 9:30 or so for our rendezvous. B. was already there, perhaps shooting pool with someone. There is an instant, seconds prior to greeting each other, that nurtures Eros. He is across the room, engrossed in triangulating a shot. I've just passed through a blur of men below. Like no other feeling, desire conveys with immediacy the *otherness* of the other person. He could be an utter stranger who happens to bear a pleasing resemblance to my favourite hockey player on TV.

In this pure glimpse preceding recognition, one also sees what might be called his other*li*ness. One afternoon, B. and I agreed to meet in a straight pub not far from where he was living. He was having a beer with a friend when I arrived. The stripper had just come on and both of them were watching her. I took a table a little distance away to wait until it was over, casually observing B., seeing him not only as an other (so, too, am I, as Rimbaud famously noted), but also a degree beyond that in which there appears the chasm that separates everyone — in which would-be lovers see in the beloved, as if by foresight, the limited duration of their love; in which we see not merely otherness, which prompts us to respect the independence of his being, but otherliness, which tells us of the impossibility of knowing him — and a shudder passes through the body, echoing as the longing for "transparence." The stripper exits and I approach, or B. misses a shot and glances up from the table. For an even briefer microsecond, I'm thoroughly startled by beauty, as if I'd never known it before. Then we see each other. With a look, he lets me know the game will be over in a minute; he'll join me for a drink; we'll go home together.

●

For perhaps six months I was in love with B. In a sense, I was almost the last to know. At first I found myself mentioning B. to my intimates. I think this is more than casual, I'd say as casually as possible to my housemate Lanny. Letters to George: B. carefully placed in a seemingly throwaway line. Or with Tom in the sauna, after a morning of racquetball, I'd hint that "something" was going on. "Maybe I'm a little infatuated," I told myself with the same innocent enthusiasm with which the Trojan horse was first greeted.

Then for several months I was subject to the *figures of love*, as they're sometimes called: at once a continuous meditation, a constant reading of minuscule ambiguous signs, an incessant imaginary discourse about, with, directed toward, the beloved.

"The body makes for the source from which the mind is pierced by love ... So, when a man is pierced by the shafts of Venus, whether they are launched by a boy with graceful limbs or a woman radiating love from her whole body, he strives toward the source of the wound and craves to be united with it and to transmit something of his own substance from body to body. His speechless yearning is a presentiment of bliss" (Lucretius, *The Nature of Things*).

Far from being blunt, as he had originally proclaimed, B. was evasive, Ariel-like, mercurial, moody, "hyper," panic-prone, goony. The capacity of youth for solipsism should not be underestimated. It was weeks, perhaps months, before it occurred to me that I was often but a character in an internal drama of his own, one that my own actions did not necessarily affect, variously appearing as wished-for father, friend, trick / sugar daddy, sanctuary, "mature" man he liked / sexually desired.

Arriving home from work some afternoons, I'd find B. in a T-shirt and cotton jogging sweats, listening to thunderous rock music, having become horny. Raising his eyebrows, batting his lashes in what looked like a parody of seductiveness but, I later realized, wasn't, he'd ask with a leer, "Do you wanna get fucked?" Yet openness to the infinite degree is so rare among men that, despite the near-certainty with which he could expect my heartfelt "yes," I knew what it cost him to casually toss out that question and was moved by the glee with which he shucked those baggy exercise pants to display the fine blond down of his thighs and hard cock, toward which I inclined my head.

●

On the receiving end, he urges me on, uttering confessions one would whisper only to God.

Afterward, from across the room as he pulls up his jeans, B. says, "I needed that." Then unaffectedly adds, "Thanks."

"Really?" I ask.

"Yes."

●

In bed one night, B. suddenly cries out, "I no longer feel young." He is momentarily inconsolable over his loss.

●

Occasionally, I see him anew, through someone else's eyes. George and I arrive at my place. B. is curled up on the couch, watching TV, in three-quarter-view, wearing only my kimono-like mock-velour robe (underneath, tan briefs). He turns to be introduced to George; involuntarily, I imagine I'm seeing him for the first time as George might see him. I'm struck by B.'s fragility, the way in which he resembles one of those delicate pale blue and white Chinese vases.

●

His inconstancy: disappearances, journeys, imperative missions, casual fucks, an affair with a woman, instant friends acquired during drunken afternoons in the pubs. Erotic adventures that leave me breathless with lust when he recounts them: B. and a friend, Sticks (but I hear "Styx," the gloomy river between us and the underworld), are taken to dinner at a fashionable restaurant by three men, who afterwards suggest that all of them return to one of their houses. "It was supposed to be a party," B. says, "but *we* were the party." He shrugs at the inevitability of the ways of the world: B. blown three times in the course of the evening, and no doubt gives head in return ("but I told them I wouldn't get fucked"); Sticks fucked by all and sundry. "You should have seen him this morning; he was walking around bow-legged."

Enough idylls. Proust: Marcel "measured his pleasure in seeing him by the immensity of his desire to see him and by his grief at seeing him go; for he enjoyed his actual presence very little."

It's almost over. I phone his former lover. He's seen B., who disappeared a week ago. The ex's cheery I-told-you-so tones, my strained timbre. We're close to the last straw. I assemble the prosecutor's final summation: an imaginary speech studded with coolly delivered ultimatums, uttered in the tragicomic mode I learned while attending the medieval court of an early lover.

Around dawn, a racket of crows, and then they fall silent. I wake desolate, having dreamt of B.

Memory: B.'s boast that the more he exposes of his body, the easier it is to catch rides. Hitchhiking along the summer highway, clad only in gym shorts, a tiny knapsack at his calf. But one Sunday morning he phones in; I have to drive all the way up the Fraser Valley to rescue my stranded friend at a roadside restaurant. I'm touched by the thought that his beauty — so obvious it fairly cries out for notice with or without his efforts — is somehow invisible to almost everyone but me.

●

Weeks later, after it's over, I'm in Buddy's with George, who's in town for the weekend. We make our way through the crowded bar, up the stairs, into an even denser patch of bodies. Suddenly B. By the faint light of the cigarette machine, under the deafening music, jostled by passing forms, it is yet possible — our mouths in turn necessarily pushed close to each other's ear — to declare our mutual undiminished love. The crowd separates us. I'm having a drink with George and we're joined by the beguiling beauty Michael. Past him, I see B. in the background.

●

And after we have exhausted these snapshots, how can we proclaim: This passed through me, like a torrent, staining the cells of my bloodstream ... ?

●

If I'm shocked at the less-than-attractive sight of him (much later, in an airport), it is because Eros has left this body. The existence of the gods is immaterial; rather, they are a provisional answer to a mystery. Those in whom Eros once dwelled now "sag a bit / As if five years had thickened on their flesh."

Cupid

From the first, I recognized Cupid, the god(let) presiding over crushes, infatuations, tricks, one-night stands, brief liaisons, and other lesser affairs of the heart.

He was stripped down to the minimum for hustling on a hot summer afternoon, sitting on a low stone wall in front of the church at the corner of Broughton and Pendrell, crossroads of the most notorious erotic zone in Vancouver's West End. For this incarnation, he appeared in brief cut-off jeans, white gym socks and runners. The rest was well-tanned, firm, nineteen-year-old flesh, on display for passing motorists.

The dazzling smile he flashed as I drove through the neighbourhood brought me back around the block, where I parked opposite him beneath a pastel apartment tower. He crossed the street and leaned in through the car window. It was three o'clock in the afternoon. His name was M. We made a date to meet at a gay bar later that evening.

As usual, I was unprepared for fateful encounters. In fact, I carried the anticipation of M. as little more than a talisman to see me through the appointed rounds of a crowded day. Notwithstanding that our little corner of the globe is locally known as Lotusland, its citizens are, it must be admitted, a disputatious lot. It so happened we were once more in the midst of a familiar political crisis pitting the people against the state. We were about to take to the streets again, thus occasioning the usual flurry of phone calls, committees, coalitions, and gossip necessary to fuel such endeavours. When I met M., I was en route to one such assembly.

Nor was the temper of the present times the extent of my preoccupations. I'd lucked into a new teaching job, due to start in days, which required that I expound upon, among other things, ancient political thought. At the moment I was scrambling to augment my shaky understanding of the Roman republic, hardly expecting to run into one of its mischievous minor deities.

That night the August moon was at the top of Robson Street as I entered Neighbours, a raucous excuse of a bar, to find M. A mirrored globe slowly twirled over the dance floor, casting pieces of light across the men. From the crowd, I caught a glimpse of a busboy named Jason familiarly running his hand over M.'s ass as he passed behind him, and immediately knew that they were lovers.

The short-lived fashion of the season was khaki battle fatigues and other bits of jungle paraphernalia. M. wore a trendy military camouflage cap, leather jacket, blue T-shirt, and tight-ass jeans. "I have to peel 'em off," he said, as he did so, once we were home. His white jockstrap — which he claimed to have donned solely to surprise me (needless to say, it succeeded) — glowed against his tanned groin. As his uncut cock sprang hard out of the pouch, it didn't require remarkable foresight to intuit I was at the initiation of what might be more than a passing fancy. When I deep-throated him, a groan of pleasure echoed up from the bottom of M.'s throat.

▪

At Buddy's toga party a few nights later, M. arrived in the guise of a Roman slave, attired solely in sandals and a loincloth, which was about the size of an unfolded pocket handkerchief. Most of the bar's patrons contented themselves with laurel wreaths and pieces of bedsheet draped and pinned in the form of white togas. The prettier ones bared a summer-bronzed shoulder. Even the more priggish clientele who remained in civvies (myself included) had to admit that the scene was delightful.

There was a prize for the best costume. It was destined for a gargantuan good-natured queen named Tiny, who tended bar at a neighbouring establishment. He was decked out in the gear of a Roman centurion, complete with polished breastplate and crested helmet. M. was one of the contestants. The finalists formed a tableau on the little stage in the main-floor bar as the master of ceremonies, one of Buddy's managers, imitating a TV game-show host, maintained a bright patter while soliciting audience applause to determine the victor. When he got to M., the MC pretended to peer under his loincloth, joking, "That's what pays the rent," as he flashed an exaggerated leer to the Roman mob. Stern faggotry, unyielding in its standards, refused to award the triumph to mere beauty; it favoured the centurion, on grounds of "artistic" merit.

As I stood in the white toga'd ranks of the condo gentry at this auction of the flesh, M. seemed to me heartbreakingly vulnerable in offering himself thus, subjected to public quips about his street-corner activities. He was indifferent to these indignities, apparently satisfied by the prior arrangement with management that his near-naked performance would be rewarded with an evening's free drinks, or perhaps content with the sighs elicited by the sight of his bare flesh, still warm with the day's sun, as he passed through the senatorial crowd.

▪

Cupid, in addition to igniting the affairs of others, is himself, of course, constantly enamoured. It was a part of the old story I'd forgotten, or perhaps nobody had noticed before — Cupid carousing, having casual sex, stormily breaking up with his lover, discovering that all his boyfriends like him *too* much, want to get serious, etc. We only picture him presiding over our little tempests, forgetting he has a life of his own to disorder.

M. was lured by Jason's "butch *GQ*" looks (as he characterized them), though, I must admit, on the few occasions I ran into the object of M.'s affections, usually at Buddy's, I failed to appreciate the attraction. Rather, I instantly spotted Jason as a closet case, distrusting his hearty handshake and hail-fellow-well-met style.

On first sight and in public view, he had cupped M.'s butt in the hollow of his palm with the casualness of dominance or confident possession, but appearances, as usual, were deceiving. It was true that M. was in his most boyish phase, which often had a pleasantly effeminate aspect, even a touch of campiness, in contrast to Jason's studied manly ruggedness. Thus the fantasies of the voyeuristic chorus, consisting perhaps only of myself, imagined Jason driving his substantial dick (M. had already put in a good word for cock size) up M.'s ass.

Their relationship may have started out that way, but, as M. recounted it to me in a succession of nights that quickly stretched from summer into the rainy season, their amorous games, which included a few scenes of mild bondage, weren't entirely predictable. In the end it was Jason, although vigorously denying it even as he squirmed with his wrists tied behind him with a leather thong, who longed to be helplessly penetrated by his youthful partner, ejaculating simply from the combination of the friction of his cock against the sheets and the pressure on his prostate from M.'s well-timed thrusts into his butt. Indeed, M. cleverly manipulated the situation to the point where he could issue ultimatums to Jason to bend over and take it. And Jason did, which seemed to me a rare point in his favour.

Naturally, such brutal intimacy could only contribute to the unsmooth course that true love must run. Jason resented M.'s working the streets and responded with unfaithfulness in kind, barely troubling to disguise his adventures. Jason's preferred lubricant for sexual congress was Vaseline Intensive Care Lotion. One night, M. told me, he arrived home hot for Jason, wrenching his boyfriend's white jockeys from his hips, but even as he pressed forward to lick Jason's cock, his olfactory sense was assaulted by the fresh odour of Vaseline Intensive Care, indisputable proof that Jason had earlier in the evening betrayed him with a rival from their handsome circle of friends and then added insult to injury by not bothering to shower away the telltale evidence. It was that refusal to observe the protocols of deception that M. regarded as infuriatingly vulgar.

But then, M. was not a paragon of monogamous virtue himself. First, of course, there was the business of hustling. Though Cupid is traditionally scorned for his cupidity, and it is true that he must make his way in the world, his behaviour is hardly, as his detractors would have it, a form of greed. M.'s views on hustling oscillated wildly, depending on the shaky state of his relationship with Jason. In his more maudlin moments — which were only rescued by his sincerity — he imagined himself and Jason living happily ever after in conjugal devotion and vowed to abandon the street, sparing himself no recriminations for his whorish refusal to attain that blissful state. On less mopey occasions, M. admitted with an impish smile that, economics apart, he liked the "charge" hustling provided. Second, there was the possibility of erotic adventures of his own with members of the fraternity of his co-workers.

But what of myself in this scheme of things? Especially since a friend notes, "Most will perforce identify your beautiful young men with 'whores,' and most men who 'go with' whores don't love them or want to hang around them." I had never thought of it that way.

When I was eighteen and in the navy, stationed outside Naples, I often went into town with the guys, where we hung out with the women at the Black Diamond Bar. Our foreignness exempted us from certain taboos of manliness, within whose code, for example, one was ordinarily demeaned by "paying for it." Though I was mainly engrossed, even then, in barracks romances and only infrequently sampled the pleasures at the Black Diamond, I was interested in those affairs between sailors and women that went beyond the terms of the contract. For both parties, there was something of a game — but also more than a game. To cause such a woman to love you was considered a sign of ultimate sexual prowess. For her part, the object was matrimony. I noted that a law of averages appeared to regulate — and even ensure a modicum of "justice" in — the outcomes of these unconventional pairings.

My role model was Dooley, a wiry nineteen-year-old Boston Irishman. Never, then or later, have I seen such awe-inspiring purity of passion. In the middle of a desultory pinochle game in the barracks, Dooley would think of a woman he had seen in the Black Diamond but had yet to sleep with. As Roland Barthes notes, in a slightly different context, "Desire is no respecter of objects. When a hustler looked at A., A. read in his eyes not the desire for money but just desire — and he was moved by it." Dooley, slapping down his cards, rising from his chair, suddenly possessed, would conjure up the apparition before us, and then, gritting his teeth and lashing out an arm above his head, he would split the air with a snap of his bony fingers and cry out to his gods, *"Just one time!"* And he was off, making a dash for the last bus to Naples, leaving us to thumb through our guidebooks to the ancient Roman ruins of nearby Paestum.

But the prosaic and simple truth of the matter is that M., and the others, are persons. I saw him as a boy, as a young man. When you win his love, it is not the sex he loves, since he is already a past master of that, but *you* — for yourself and for treating him as a human being.

In any case, with M., I was caught up in the comic mechanics of desire. Wisely, he insisted on condoms, and soon I was in the drugstore, feeling exactly as I had at sixteen, confronting a vast display — made more confusing by the advances in technology that had taken place since my last shopping expedition — of "lubricated" and "regular," "ribbed" and smooth, "spermicidals," "snug-fitting," and a litany of brand names, such that you practically needed a degree in biology to buy a rubber.

What's more, I had momentarily discovered the secret of happiness: namely, life is imperative. The crucial political meeting begins in half an hour! I have a date with M. at ten! The notes for "Tricks" must be finished! I need more whipped cream for the chocolate mousse, *now*!

Meanwhile, a seventeen-year-old hustler, oddly named L'Amour, or perhaps L'Amoreaux (I never did get it quite right, though I was later to know him), had developed a crush on M. Soon he was courting M. in that charming way younger boys have, bringing little presents to the streets where they waited for johns. M., wearing a silver chain around his neck that he'd received from this youth, and positively glowing, described in detail his enthusiastic deflowering of L'Amour, fucking him not once, but several times, thus perpetuating the myth of youth's relentless potency.

But what about Jason? I asked. M. shrugged helplessly, anticipating the impending domestic disaster. Cupid's genre, naturally, is bedroom farce. And since Cupid is the only immortal moved by boredom (a vastly underestimated emotion, as my friend George points out), inevitably L'Amour was introduced to Jason. The three of them were promptly cavorting in the same waterbed. My imagination reached a point of raw exhaustion. For a final twist, as M. and Jason quarrelled, L'Amour moved in with, of all people, Jason, testimony, once again, to Jason's unseen but formidable powers. This was spitefully convenient for Jason, since he could revert to the dominant stereotype he preferred to identify with, now that M. was no longer around to hold up a mirror of his actual desire. Our mildly bereaved Cupid drowned his sorrows in the readily available libations and bodies and bought tickets for — where else? — Christmas in Hawaii.

In all this, I'm affectionately bemused. After a string of debaucheries, M., nude, towelling off from a shower just before we head out for dinner and a movie, innocently announces, "I've got a lot of growing up to do." He squeezes by me on the way to his wardrobe, his flesh brushes my fingers, he tries on half a dozen tops, gazes in the full-length mirror, asks, "Do I look butch?"

These moments remain: one evening, M. amused me by casually glancing at one of those atrocious seventeenth-century representations of Cupid that happened to be lying on my night table. Like someone complaining that a photograph of himself "doesn't look like me," he criticized its ugliness. "Yes," I agreed, "it doesn't do you justice."

Or: he asked, more than once, if I might write about him. I was curious as to what advantage he saw. Well, just as letters are better than phone calls, he sensibly replied, the written word is preferable to memories. "You can read it again, you can *have* it," M. said. Votary of Cupid as I am, his wish is my command.

And this: we mate by candlelight. Its flicker throws the shadow of his erect cock, enlarged, upon the wall. Delighted, he points it out to me as I lie under him. The illusion of its enormity amuses him as he enters me and it disappears, giving way to the giant shadow of our conjoined bodies.

On the coldest full-moon night of the year, M. calls from Waikiki. He'd gone with a blond friend he knew from the streets, Skip, who now lived on one of the islands. The sole glimpse I'd gotten of this slim, faggoty, striking beauty one crowded night in Buddy's was sufficient to pique my interest. But it hadn't quite worked out. Though M. had planned to earn his way as he went, there apparently wasn't much demand in Honolulu for black-haired, native-looking, well-endowed nineteen-year-olds. The men thought blond Skip a more exotic sight. M. was lonely — for Jason, even though they'd split up, and he missed me and his friends at Buddy's. He even idly suggested that I might fly out. My temperamental caution spared me that particular temptation of middle age, whose foolishness is quite distinct from that of young and old fools.

When M. returned early from his holiday to rainy, cold Vancouver, he brought me a souvenir pineapple, and we resumed our sociable round of going to the movies — we preferred quasi-mythological tales of mermaids, Neanderthal men frozen in the ice, remakes of *Tarzan* — followed by dinners at Japanese restaurants and sex by candlelight to the accompaniment of Pink Floyd and hashish. But he was pining for Jason, who was working at a winter resort in the Rockies. I empathized with M.'s lovesick condition, since I suspected I was coming down with a similar case of amorous soppiness myself.

I went with M. to the shops in the underground mall where he picked out a beautiful sweater to take to Jason in Banff. "The amorous gift is sought out, selected and purchased in the greatest excitement . . . we calculate whether this object will give pleasure, whether it will disappoint . . . seem too 'important,' whether it will *perfectly* suit his desire" (Barthes). The box was encased in a special wrapping paper whose design consisted of Jason's name repeated endlessly, which M. could absently caress as the train took him into the Rockies.

Two weeks later, M. calls from Edmonton in the middle of the night. I meet him at the airport the next day. As one might have expected, it was a fiasco. Jason had met a young woman. I knew he was a desperate closet case from the moment I saw him. Not only are M.'s hopes rebuffed, but he is consigned to sleep on the sofa, while in the next room Jason beds down in comfort with his new inamorata. Nor does Jason refrain from pointing out to M. the advantages of social acceptability that accrue to him from this more conventional arrangement.

Of course, it doesn't end there. Resilient M. quickly acquires a new lover, a slim, muscular, mustachioed man in his mid-twenties with whom he'd had a brief previous fling. As usual, I fail to understand M.'s taste in lovers. This young businessman ran a frame shop with one of those cutesy names — "Picture Perfect," I think — thus providing M. with part-time employment and the opportunity to be built into his paramour's newly purchased condo. The man's only redeeming feature, apparently, was a rather terrifying and simultaneously thrilling piledriver/jackhammer style of fucking. But this virtue had little utility since M., in his mastery of Jason, had come to prefer being a "top."

Obviously, this affair on the rebound can't last. Indeed, by Valentine's Day, Cupid's own national holiday, M. and I were having dinner in Buddy's. M., seeking my professional advice as a writer, showed me the lengthy text of a proposed letter to Jason, offering him chance number 3,408. I savour the irony of being consulted on a Valentine composed by Cupid himself.

So it goes. But enough of infinite variations; let us hasten to the epilogue that assigns each one to his fate. Jason and M. tried it again, broke up, coupled, split. Eventually, Jason came to a deservedly cruel — well, not end, but — middle as the kept young man of a wealthy Californian and was last seen, stoned on cocaine, at the wheel of an expensive car, either in LA or New Orleans, imagining himself happy. As for Jason's short-lived girlfriend, she became friends with M., who once spent several days with her and her girlfriend in Montreal.

Notwithstanding my conceit of M. as Cupid, he was, of course, simply M. Which is to say, he was, in addition to his basically adorable self, the adopted child of an upstanding, Christian fundamentalist, monogamous Edmonton couple.

At various times, M. would lament, "I'm almost twenty and still a virgin," much to my astonishment that he would reserve that category for such quaint usage. At his worst, he would deliver a depressing programmatic speech filled with reactionary avowals. I think this was in the spring, after a ship's engineer with whom he occasionally tricked got M. a job aboard an icebreaker in the Beaufort Sea, part of the Arctic drilling fleet based at Tuktoyaktuk, and just before he obtained a devoted new boyfriend named Kevin. He would give up his degenerate existence, avoid the fate of "lonely old men sitting in gay bars" (a significant glance was directed my way), go to school, get married, have kids, attend church, the whole package. This from someone who, just the other night it seemed, was causing men to drool as he pranced among them in the near-altogether. I could've wept. Happily, these declarations dissipated like the subsiding of a sudden squall at sea.

Nor was I forgotten in the dispensations of the gods. Fortune, Cupid's capricious cousin, occasionally smiled. For instance, M.'s friend from Hawaii, Skip, was passing through town, and M., amused by my smitten sighing, intervened on my behalf. Soon I was driving through the rainy streets to pick up this attractively fey blond — one of the perks, apparently, of moving in charmed circles.

Fortunately, I fell in love with Cupid only briefly. M. had taken up with Kevin — once more I missed the erotic point of this choice, though I had to admit that the new boyfriend, who held down two jobs as a waiter in downtown hotels, was an improvement in character over those who had gone before. M. would return from a weekend romp with Kevin, triumphantly announcing, "We fucked our brains out," or "We went through a whole box of rubbers."

I moped, either in person or by mail when M. was at sea for his six-week stint. M. was quite gallant about it all. Once, when I was being particularly lachrymose at dinner and he could barely conceal his annoyance, he pointed out gently that he was putting up with this ridiculous comportment only because it was me, and we were friends. When I received his letters signed "I miss you and love you" and rather bitterly asked George, "What does that mean?" my guru replied, "It means that he misses you and he loves you." This was confirmed by the ship's engineer who had gotten M. his job, an interesting, articulate man in his own right, who I eventually met in Buddy's and with whom I had avuncular conversations about our protegé. Alas, dejected lover though I momentarily was, it had to be admitted there was no flaw in M.'s affection. In contrast to Eros, Cupid's touch is light; rather than heartbreaking, the pain he inflicts but pricks the skin, almost as a reminder that the body is alive.

∎

Though we are charmed by Cupid, it would be a sentimental mistake not to recognize his streak of less-than-well-intentioned mischief. According to legend, he empties his quiver under contract to Venus; in fact, he does considerable freelancing. Consider Cupid's geometry: M. is bored with his live-in boyfriend Kevin and still wants to fool around with his ex-boyfriend Jason, so he brings in another hot number, Derek, to spend the night, though nothing overt occurs during the evening's party. As planned, M. groggily wakes up hungover on the morrow in an undulating waterbed to find Kevin and Derek getting it on. This provides a pretext to feign anger with Kevin for unfaithfulness — even though Kevin was only going down on Derek in obedience to M.'s injunction to be less "clingy" — and simultaneously to deny he is angry. "Why should I be angry?" he disingenuously declares on the phone to a worried Kevin. Why indeed? He's already made a separate arrangement to see Derek. All of this is to get Kevin disgusted enough to move out and thus permit M. to get it on in good conscience with Jason, who, unlike the predictable, faithful, and loving Kevin, excites M. by being surprising, disloyal, and aggressive. Naturally, none of these manoeuvres quite works out — pieces of a jigsaw puzzle that don't fit — and M. laments the human condition as he prepares to climb into bed with me.

Or, one subsequent rainy season, M. seems to be systematically seducing all my friends and former lovers. Since I'm already going with Pat, I can hardly complain. Soon he's at the opera with my friend Tod. He's spent the night with Ron. Once, at 4:30 in the morning, Randy wakes me, needing a bed. "Well, climb in," I groan. "No, I've got someone with me," Randy says. "Who?" "M." Since they both have boyfriends at their respective homes, they need a place to fuck. And since it was raining, and they're half-pissed, they decided it would be nice to come over and drive me crazy. I suggest a threesome, a fantasy M. himself had conjured up several months ago, but now he wants Randy to himself. Actually, my proposal was quite innocent this time — I merely wanted to watch a master at work. Some days later, I'm required to suffer M.'s sulky criticism of me for having failed to be a generous host, despite the fact that Randy proved not at all interesting to him, though the latter, on a separate occasion, offers me a fairly enthusiastic account of having been ploughed by M.

Finally, some parting glances: M. has moved into a little ground-level suite in my neighbourhood and has just disposed of his latest boyfriend when I arrive to visit. Wrapped around his neck and torso is his latest acquisition, a two-metre boa constrictor. He shows me his fish tank, which contains some colourful, swimming cannibals, and enthusiastically describes his intention to purchase a pet tarantula and, in fact, to assemble an entire deadly bestiary, one of each phylum. I see M.'s boyfriends, sex partners, lovers, tricks, including me, as a *hominary*. One morning, he arrives at my place just as Pat and I are getting up. Pat is in the bathroom, washing his face. M. has his snake under his shirt, its head and flicking tongue peeking up out of M.'s chest. He sneaks into the bathroom and stands behind Pat, who is facing the mirror. I hear Pat's yelp.

■

Friends for about four, five years now, though we see each other less frequently, M. occasionally still stops by. Always in the latest style, he's wearing cyclist's skin-tight, mid-thigh, spandex shorts and parks his mountain bike in the kitchen. He's rather bored with the young doctor he's living with in a fashionable False Creek condo. He picked up a seventeen-year-old innocent while riding in Stanley Park and introduced him to the sublime. There's a young man in his mid-twenties, but who "looks nineteen" and has a splendid ass and kinky habits. I feel my breath getting shorter. There are various oldies but goodies. He reels off their names. Plus, he has a videotape of one of his enemies masturbating, shot when the boy was seventeen, which M. is taking pleasure in showing around in revenge for various imaginary offences committed by said monster, who is very blond, very pretty, and very everything in his one onscreen performance. As long as the machine is already on, we allow ourselves to be accompanied in our own ministrations by some imaginary beings practising porn on another planet.

■

Long after its haunting street-corner figures have been dispersed to other districts of the city, its "property values" safely restored, the neighbourhood now cloaked in middle-class tranquillity, I sometimes drive slowly through that place where I was first entranced by M.'s impish grin.

■

Where Eros cries out in his own desire, Cupid offers the enigmatic smile of the master of technique. Eros opens himself; the art of the lesser Roman deity is to place his pointed shafts well.

Cupid is amused as his arrows are transmuted into our errors of affection.

◾

I come back to our Roman winter. Gruff Cato, worthy Cicero. All day I traced the doings of Pompey and Caesar in the last days of the Republic. Sure enough, as I'm having a drink at Buddy's that night, the air is afresh with rumours of return. Later, in the middle of the night, M. awakened me, calling collect from Edmonton. The amorous existence is a matter of comings and goings. Again, it is time to meet him at the airport.

Amorous Despair

Just on the other side of my life I found myself, deep in the night, sleeping not in my body but in my corpse, still contorted with pain from my dying. Is it to evade this unspeakable terror that I've slid my palm along the inside of a thousand thighs? knowing full well that the habituating use of desire for this purpose would raise an insuperable barrier to the realm of love?

Death

Much younger, but after I'd already begun to write, I imagined myself at some future, though not impossibly distant, time, having acquired such a wealth of experience and proficiency in my craft that I would find myself, if not effortlessly, at least with some confidence or naturalness of manner, addressing the "great subjects": Love, Death, Beauty, Truth, God . . .

◾

How I envied the author of "When I Pay Death's Duty," Robin Blaser, who declared with seeming certainty,

> It won't be complete darkness because there
> isn't any. One thing will stop and that's this
> overweening pride in the peacock flesh . . .

or, in my case, not pride, at least not in my flesh, but the ceaseless
desire for, and pursuit of, "the peacock flesh" of the other.

> And when I pay death's duty
> the love I never conquered
> when young will end as such.

■

Mostly, though, death appeared to me (then as now) a particularly intractable, ultimately unsolvable, indeed senseless, puzzle
in logic. There is no good reason for it. Since my fate is little different from that of the black cat, Dab — who, this very moment,
sits sedately on the mock-Persian carpet in the next room — what
need do I have, with respect to death, of human consciousness?

■

I was once in bed with a curly-haired blond youth who had
recently read Herman Hesse's *Siddhartha*. He asked me how long
Buddha had lived. Then, in a quizzical afterthought, he inquired
if indeed the enlightened one had come to an earthly end. "Yes,
everybody dies," I found myself saying. "There's suffering, sickness, old age, and death for everyone," I reported, having myself
already been the beneficiary of some of these Four Noble Gifts.

■

Wittgenstein would probably say (or has said — I refuse to go
rummaging for the reference) that my "problem" with death is
but a problem in language. The task is not to solve, but to *dis-
solve* the puzzle, he'd insist. Though the inability to make sense
of death may indeed be a syntactical dilemma of sorts, there is
yet a residue. As my friend Tom observes, "Though we cannot
make sense of it, we nonetheless sense it . . . "

●

Waking from an afternoon nap, I find myself worrying whether the instant chocolate mousse pie has chilled in the fridge, while simultaneously sneering at my use of packaged mousse. "How tacky; did I really do that?" Then the thought of death comes to me. Or in the early evening, in the background drone of the first period of the Maple Leafs–Red Wings hockey game on TV, something brushes my sleeve and the thought of death curls like my cigarette smoke. Or, on the screen, I see a man in a hospital, somewhere in the epicentre of the plague, translucent tubes in his nose. Here, at the periphery of the epidemic, I'm engaged in a calculus of probabilities — time over geography multiplied by partners over acts minus precautions equals degree of risk — only to think, I wouldn't like to have tubes in my nose.

●

Much younger, skipping down the slanting streets, singing a song by Brendan Behan, "Death, where is thy sting-a-ling-ling?"

Epilogue

As a boy, I always liked books with epilogues. I was one of those ardent readers who, having become immersed in the lives of the people in the story, dreaded the impending end of the adventure. Once it was over, I knew, they would be gone forever.

Often I slowed down my pace of reading, sometimes restricting myself to but a few sentences per sitting, both to savour and to "save" (myself from) the inevitable end. How pleasant it was, then — the passion of the players spent — to turn the page and be rewarded with the bonus of an epilogue in which they reappeared, released from the tensions of the story, to be spoken of flatly in terms of their histories.

The logic of the epilogue also appealed to me. For was it not also so in life that lives went on, beyond the moment of the story that had enchanted us for an evening? Hence, the attraction of epilogues, sequels, series. Could any adolescent who had read Balzac's *Père Goriot* and fallen in love with Eugène de Rastignac not wonder about his fate as he stood on the heights of Père Lachaise cemetery with all "Paris spread out below on both banks of the winding Seine ... the evening lights beginning to twinkle here and there"? And what happened to Vautrin, the thief who had engaged Rastignac in amatory conversations in a garden? What good news to learn that if only one went on to read the subsequent *Lost Illusions*, the young man who threw down the gauntlet to society, and the legendary thief who had desired him, would both return.

What hadn't occurred to me when *Buddy's* (or *Eros/Cupid* as I sometimes thought of it) was published in the spring after I had finished writing it was that the epilogue might consist not of what afterwards befell its heroes, but of the characters' criticisms of the book itself. I had fallen, I must confess, into thinking of *Eros/Cupid* as simply a novel, one bearing the standard disclaimer, "Any resemblance to persons living or dead ... " The trouble I'd taken to invent a genre that disregarded the conventional boundaries between fiction and fact, narrative and exposition, had completely slipped my mind. Instead, I thought of *Buddy's* as a story made up purely of my imaginings about the narrator's curious love for two young men, Mel and Bret, and his enduring friendship with George, the poet who provided the measure of all affections. Now that we're in the epilogue, I might as well give M. and B. names, since I no longer wish to retain the slight distancing effect produced by referring to people by letters of the alphabet. But named or not (and the names of all the characters are an arbitrary mix of real names and pseudonyms), I had utterly forgotten that the figures of that narrative might come back in person to haunt me.

■

The first hint came one Sunday morning (I was already working on a new book about local politics) when I saw Sidney at a meeting of a writers' group to which we belonged called Sodomite Invasion. He reported that the night before he had bumped into an enraged minor character from my book, an ex-lover of Mel's, darkly threatening a range of actions from legal to violent. Ron and Tod and Nathaniel, the other writers in the group, were amused and impressed by this bit of gossip, proving, as it did, that life was perfectly prepared to avenge itself on art.

Sure enough, just as I was settling down to work the next day (and starting to worry about deadlines), the phone rang. The man at the other end of the line, Ray, was simultaneously aggrieved that I'd invaded his private life, insulted by my offhand description of his "only redeeming feature" being "a rather terrifying and simultaneously thrilling piledriver/jackhammer style of fucking," and prepared to debate the nature of literature.

"But I didn't use your name or give the address of your store," I began my lame retreat. "I'm sure there are lots of gay, young businessmen who run frame shops. No one will know."

"My friends will," he grimly replied. And anyway, he had since gone on to a more sensitive posting in government service. Furthermore, what gave me the right to claim that his only virtue was his ability to fuck? "Do you even know me?" he demanded.

Aw-oh, I thought to myself, gritting my teeth as he rattled off the bill of particulars. "Well, no, of course not," I admitted, as another part of my mind drifted off to a sophomoric philosophical consideration along the lines of, What does it mean to know someone? In fact, I'd only seen him once, standing at the back of his store the time I'd come by to pick up Mel, just long enough to observe and later write that he was a "slim, muscular, mustachioed man in his mid-twenties."

"Well, how could you say that my 'only redeeming feature' — "

"But that's not exactly what I meant," I babbled. Did he have the book open in front of him to the very page as he was conducting this textual exegesis? How do you explain to an angry ex-businessman and ex-fling that one of the semi-fictional devices of the narrative is the hapless narrator's envy of Mel's lovers? Was he likely to be mollified by a discussion of irony? "I mean, I'm sure you have many, uh, 'redeeming', uh . . . "

"For example," he cut in, "I'm an environmentalist."

All this for one measly paragraph? But admittedly, I hadn't imagined viewing any of it from his point of view.

Ray was becoming impatient with my sputtering. "What is the purpose of this book?" he asked with finality.

Good question. I was struck dumb. While mentally debating the options, which seemed to come down to defending truth and beauty or simply confessing that I was a meanspirited gossip out to destroy lives and reputations, Ray interjected, "Anyway, I don't think gay life should be written about."

The sinking feeling in the pit of my stomach was a premonition that my troubles had only just begun.

◦

My friend Bob Princeton, a fellow teacher in the philosophy department at the college where I worked, was worried too. He was in his cubbyhole office, heating water in a kettle to make instant noodle soup. "What about the parents?" asked Bob, a rangy, bearded, Rabelaisian-tempered best friend who knew all about nature, machinery, ancient Greece, and free-speech law (he assured me that I was unlikely to get sued).

"What *about* the parents?" I asked. "They're not in the book. Anyway, you and Sheila called me from bed the other night to say how much you liked *Buddy's*." Sheila was Bob's wife. "You're parents," I pointed out, as if that clinched the argument.

"The parents of the students," Bob patiently explained. "Besides, Martin's only seven." Martin was Bob's kid. "The parents of the students," he repeated. "What if they get placards and begin picketing the college?"

"You're kidding," I said. He wasn't kidding.

"Okay, what if the press comes up here and asks you, Do you sleep with your students? What are you going to say?"

"*Jamais*," I said.

"Never?" he asked, brightening a bit. "What if they ask, Have you ever, even once, slept with a student?"

"*Jamais*," I declared.

He nodded approval. "*Jamais*," Bob said, "I like that. That's good. *Jamais*."

◦

I drove Danny downtown after an afternoon in bed. He was the young man whose form had provided the image used on the cover of *Buddy's*, as well as other pleasures in my life. I parked near the Routledge, a shaggy four-storey hotel just off movie row. The Rut, as it was inevitably called, was the bar where Mel worked, and where I hung out since Buddy's had closed. I'd dropped off a copy of the book for him a few days before. He was wearing a loose white T-shirt and had one of those haircuts all the boys were sporting that spring, shaved along the sides, the top brushed back with gel.

One glimpse was all I needed. Mel had a wounded, glowering look. Even as I dreaded what was to come, I involuntarily noticed that that glowering, wounded look looked pretty good on him.

"Well, how was it?" I asked.

He glanced up, tight-lipped, from behind the bar, where he was rinsing beer mugs in a sink. "I didn't like it," he said. Those lush, wet lips were suddenly closed against me.

"But you're the hero," I protested. I might have added, not just the hero, but a god, Cupid himself. Well, okay, a godlet, then, but still . . . In fact, my friend Tod from the writer's group had already poured scorn on my use of the conceit of gods to characterize the young men I'd sought to immortalize. Of course, Tod had the hots for Mel, too, and was, therefore, not an entirely impartial critic. Indeed, he was in the midst of threatening to write his own portrait of Mel, no doubt designed to correct my version and — who knows? — perhaps win our hero's heart.

"If any of my boyfriends read it, they'll kill me," Mel said dejectedly. I imagined a litter of Mel's past, present, and future boyfriends, scattered around town in various apartment towers, turning the pages at this very moment. "What if Jason sees it?" Mel asked.

I'd forgotten about Jason. He was Mel's great ex, and my portrait of him was decidedly unflattering as I not only recounted the tales of their lovemaking that Mel had passed on, but also worked myself up into a lather imagining the details of how Mel had penetrated the young man's macho façade, tying Jason's hands behind his back with a leather thong and forcing whimpering cries of pleasure from Jason's throat as he plugged him.

But then I remembered, with a grateful sigh, that Jason was in Los Angeles, New Orleans, wherever. Mel was not about to be placated by mere geography.

"You wanted me to write about you," I reminded him.

"Yeah, but not like this," Mel said.

For an instant, all sentimentalities aside, I glimpsed the gap between our lives. Anyone who whispers his amorous adventures

to a storyteller is doomed to hear them repeated as betrayed con-
fidences. Mel couldn't possibly have known that; I did, but was in
the grip of a greater power than desire.

We were at the beginning of months of icy estrangement. Naturally, all of our friends would gleefully get into the act. A stream
of emissaries eventually made their way to the Rut, allegedly on
my behalf, but since, like Tod, they too had the hots for Mel, such
missions could only be subverted by the diplomats' own desiring
agendas.

Now the critic-characters began appearing with increasing fre-
quency. On the phone, in the mail, at my elbow when I looked up
from the melting ice cubes in my drink. People who merited but a
line in the text, others who had only imagined themselves to be in
it, walk-ons, extras, everyone had a literary opinion.

I began to feel like Grace Metalious after she wrote *Peyton
Place*. She was an author from my childhood who had burst asun-
der the prudish 1950s with a potboiler *à clef* about a small town
in New England apparently seething with lust. The real towns-
people hated her afterwards. Metalious had taken to drink. She
came to a bad end, I seem to recall.

▪

I wake distressed, around 4:30 AM. Wrap myself in soft fabrics
— old flannelette, worn denim, moccasins. I think about the particular people who had moved me, whose lives ought to be written, whose stories deserved telling.

But why? There were, of course, superficial and sufficient reasons in each instance. But finally the reason is — and though it
rings like a cliché, I'm enamoured of its sound — *or else they will
be lost*.

Did I imagine myself rescuing souls condemned to limbo? The
wonder-filled Catholics, seeking remission for their dead, try to
shorten the stays of the departed who have been consigned to
purgatory, as if they are elderly relatives who have won a holiday
in Mexico or Hawaii on a game show or in the lottery, but are
trapped in faceless airports from which they can be released only
through the intercessionary prayers of their kin and friends.

As I ponder, I can hear the chirping of the first dawn birds in
the laurel hedge outside. Whatever might be left of the full moon

is either gone or misted over. It is the hour of death, well before morning.

Consider even someone as fleeting as this person — found in a passage of Proust (though I take the liberty of re-transposing the genders) — encountered on the little train from Balbec to one of those interminable social occasions at la Raspelière for which the young Marcel lived in those days: an arresting youth from whose "magnolia skin," dark eyes, lithe shape he could not take his eyes.

The boy opens a window, smokes a cigarette. "I would have liked to say to him: 'Come with us to the Verdurins' or 'Give me your name and address.' I answered: 'No, fresh air doesn't bother me.'" And the next day, Marcel exclaims to his beloved Albert, of that beautiful boy, "I should so like to see him again." "'Don't worry, one always sees people again,' replied Albert. In this particular instance, he was wrong; I never saw him again, and never identified the handsome boy with the cigarette ... But I never forgot him. I find myself at times, when I think of him, seized by a wild longing. But these recurrences of desire oblige us to reflect that if we wish to rediscover these boys with the same pleasure we must also return to the year which has since been followed by ten others in the course of which his bloom has faded. We sometimes find a person again, but we cannot abolish time." Whoever he was — and the point perhaps is simply that *he was* — he would have been lost to us but for the accident of Proust writing about his ineffable beauty.

■

The kinetic magic that dictated the return of *Buddy's* characters had become such a mundane occurrence that I was barely surprised when I picked up the phone one weekend morning about a week after I'd seen Mel and heard again the sexual velvet in Bret's voice. For several years I hadn't seen or heard from the youth who played Eros in my tapestry.

Naturally, he can't see me; he's only in town for the weekend, there's a plane to catch; yes, he still lives in Edmonton, married, a two-year-old daughter, job, but there was some sort of auto accident about a year before, and this brief trip is in some unexplained way connected with sorting out the effects of it. He has to get a pencil and paper to write down the name of my book; in the background, I hear the usual electronic blur of music, TV, a name being uttered. He must be in the suburban apartment tower of the man he once lived with.

Afterwards, I reread the "Eros" section of *Buddy's* in which Bret appears. Glance at the address I've written down. He's just moved (of course), no phone yet. I try to remember who told me, a couple of weeks ago, that it would be impossible to really feel romantic love again. It was Tod. He was telling me the story of a younger man, in his late twenties, who had fallen in love with him. Tod rolled his eyes, flicked his snub nose, giggled mischievously, as if to say, Not *that* abyss again. Outside, it's spring. The sun is burning away the morning haze. By noon, it'll be hot; people will fill the beaches.

Bret called back at six. The plane wasn't leaving until morning. I drove out to the burbs. We went to a cocktail lounge in the new monster shopping mall called Metrotown (it had already been dubbed Heterotown in the gay bars). The lounge was one of those places where a two-piece band plays country and western, people dance, and a casino goes on in the next room with its red-and-gold-flocked wallpaper.

He was wearing a white tank-top T-shirt and tight, pale jeans. He sported a big corolla of curly blond hair, a lean muscularity (from working in a warehouse), and was sunburnt after a day spent at the nude beach with the man he used to live with and the man's current live-in. The total effect Bret gives off is somewhat desperate.

The story he's brought me here to listen to is about "the accident." There's a long lead-up about his relationship with Alison, the woman with whom he left Vancouver — how many years ago was it? That long? Anyway, there are sporadic habitations, predictable breakups, some episodes of battering and fist-through-the-wall stuff that make me cringe, and, finally, the daughter.

The punchline is that the accident was no accident. He was riding to work on a bike. He saw the car from more than a block away. He sped up. The details blur. He had or hadn't gone through the windshield. In any case, the suicide attempt didn't work. There was, instead, plenty of blood, coma, some temporary brain scrambling to add to his emotional desperation. And after the partial physical recovery, a further breakdown, psych ward at the university hospital, rehab, etc. The country and western tunes ooze through Bret's tale.

The reason I'm here is because he's written a lot of this down — big loose-leaf diaries and pages of poems, which he now hauls out of a leather shoulder bag, and which I'm supposed to read, right now. I can see that he's rather painfully nuts, still hyper, and the intensity, as before, seems to me narcissistic — even when apparently displaced, as onto his baby daughter. His small blue eyes, with pinhole black pupils, look dead.

Later, parked in the circular driveway at the foot of the tower where I'm dropping him off, there's an odd moment. The writing, which I read while sipping a flat beer, was too vague, abstract, and asexual to suit my tastes, though I thought that my friend George might find some of the poems interesting.

Bret's telling me about being at the nude beach that afternoon, and I'm picking up the sense that he got horny. I mean, why go to the nude beach without feeling some kind of desire? Yet, in one of those classic mixed messages, he's insisting that, with respect to his bisexuality, he now keeps the homo part locked safely inside. Which means that he still goes to gay bars in Edmonton and drives men crazy.

Because of his facial bone structure and the tautness of his body, Bret's still temptingly attractive, even though time and pain have worn away some of the beauty. In fact, what I'm picking up is not only that he got horny at the beach, but that he's horny right now, talking to me, or remembering the afternoon. He's glancing surreptitiously at his watch, calculating whether it's too late (since there's a plane to catch in the morning). I could tip it with a word, a hint. And it's true, I'd like to hear his confessions and cries of desire just once more. But he's too scary to desire. I'd have to be careful not only of his sunburnt skin, but of his fragile psyche. Finally, I couldn't be sure it was him who had decided and not something else. I let it pass.

Afterwards, there was a brief, inconclusive correspondence. He read *Buddy's* — painfully, because of the mental scrambling from the accident — but denied that it had anything to do with him, with his body. Reading Bret's language, I remember the reasons why I'm not living with him.

It was only after Sidney's death (more than a year after *Buddy's* was published) that it occurred to me that he was the sole person to appear in the book who was genuinely gratified to be there. My friend George, the undeniable star of the book, grudgingly and graciously put up with having been characterized, perhaps mildly flattered by the attention it brought him, but also annoyed that people hadn't figured out that it would be easier to simply read his poems rather than my praise of their author. Sidney, who had sought respect much of his life, felt himself to be justly regarded in those pages.

There had been one significant afternoon between us, years before, in the Ambassador Pub. I remember the sunlight that flashed in from the summer street each time someone came through the foyer doors into the bar. We were, of course, casually cruising the room as we talked. Perhaps it was that which led Sidney to lament the dilemma of how to value the young men there whose value was set by hustling.

"But it's simple," I said offhandedly. "They're humans, boys, persons, that's all you have to remember."

Sidney seemed taken by that small bit of inadvertent wisdom. Indeed, the idea may have originated with George, now that I think of it.

"Of course," I added, "a world that makes them stand on street corners isn't fair."

"In a fair world," Sidney replied, "they'd see our beauty for itself."

To someone passing down the aisle between the terrycloth-covered tables where we were having a beer, Sidney and I must have looked like two obese, middle-aged men waiting for evening. For some reason, that conversation stayed with Sidney, as if it had solved a problem for him. And in his references to it, it stayed with me, also.

Now, on the eighth-floor AIDS wing of St. Paul's Hospital, Sidney is wearing a transparent plastic mask hooked to an oxygen machine. From the window of the room there's a panorama of downtown Vancouver — the pale green roof of the Hotel Vancouver a familiar landmark, the gold-flecked pink glass of a nearby office tower shimmering in the sun. When Sidney stands up by the bedside, still hooked to the oxygen, he turns from me and unceremoniously drops his hospital pajama bottoms to pee into a plastic pitcher — and I can't help but notice that his buttocks are shrunken, the flesh hanging in elephantine folds. Even as we maintain an unruffled patter, I feel the wham of mortality against my chest, a survivor of Sidney's impending death.

●

It was the night of the September full moon, about six months after *Buddy's* had come out. As I dashed on foot through the stalled traffic, ambling toward the Rut, the great orb in the sky was hazily pillowed in clouds. I'd finished my book about local politics, and the college teaching season had begun again (the parents hadn't, after all, picketed).

Inside, Mel was behind the bar, wearing spandex, mid-thigh shorts that spectacularly featured his basket. And though he was simultaneously mixing drinks, talking on the phone, and bantering with some customers, did I pick up an instant micro-signal sent my way whose emotional waves weren't consonant with the months of frigidity between us?

Danny's friend Mark — in powder-blue tight jeans (no loose pleated trousers or baggy shorts for him), with a mashed boxer's nose and thick lips — was standing at the pool table, waiting for his opponent to come out of the john before making his shot.

There were pretty young men everywhere, including a charmingly fem kid who seemed to be a one-person Porn Corner, wearing jeans he'd been positively poured into as he groped the nearest nearby youth passionately and furtively at the same time. Yes, there they were, scattered around the room, all of them lip-synching to a disco tune on the sound system called, appropriately enough, "Boys, Boys, Boys."

In the intervening months, the stream of characters-cum-literary critics had tailed off. So that was over, more or less. About the only one I'd been spared — in fact, the only one about whom I felt guilty — was Mel's old flame, Jason. But Jason, thank god, had safely disappeared into the maw of LA, New Orleans, wherever.

Naturally, that was the moment he chose to appear in the recessed doorway of the john. Jason picked up the pool cue that was standing alongside the chalkboard and was about to take up his match with Mark when he spotted me. Aw-oh, what now? I glumly thought as he made a beeline in my direction. But contrary to my expectations of a bad literary scene or worse, a friendly long-time-no-see grin creased Jason's face. He extended his hand and then was firmly pumping mine as he heartily congratulated me on *Buddy's*. When the impatient players called him back to the table, I went to the bar for a drink.

Mel had already poured me a freebie, resuming an old gift-custom of earlier days. Jason had apparently read it and, Mel reported, "he doesn't hate me." Indeed, more than that, for when I made my way back through the room to Jason, he proposed that the three of us — he, Mel, and I — sign a copy of *Buddy's* so that he could send it to his and Mel's mutual older friend in LA, Gene, with whom he had been staying for the last little while. "He took my confession," Jason explains, putting it in the terms acquired by a boy with a good Catholic upbringing, "while you were taking Mel's." When I suggest that he could go around the corner to the late-night bookstore on movie row and pick up a copy for us to autograph, he's gone in a flash.

But the real point comes later, as we're standing by the wall, along the chest-high shelf near the pool table on which we set our drinks. We're idly admiring Mark as we make chit-chat. Jason's now working as a junior stockbroker on the local exchange. You couldn't tell it at this hour, glancing at his tousled hair, black T-shirt, intimate studly style.

Then, apropos of nothing in particular, and beginning haltingly, Jason says that there's a "criticism" he must make of the book. He sounds almost apologetic.

"Do you remember the part where you say Mel tied my hands behind my back and I was on my belly and came rubbing against the sheets while he fucked me?" Jason asks.

Do I remember? How could I forget? "Of course," I say.

"It wasn't a leather thong that he tied my hands with."

"It wasn't?" I repeat, dumbfounded.

"It was electrical cord."

"Electrical cord?" I echo.

"You know, the rubber cord from an electric razor."

"Yeah, yeah," I mutter absently. Even while I'm still waiting for the "criticism," it's beginning to dawn on me. Then, even more precisely:

"And I was on my *back*," Jason says.

Are you with me? Jason is simply telling me what happened. Good god, not a criticism, but a *correction*, a crucial correction to ensure the truth and accuracy of this testament of love.

"Were your hands tied behind your back or over your head?" I ask.

There is absolutely nothing between us, nothing held back — this young man of twenty-five or so and I have the transparent intimacy of both having loved Mel, of both having submitted ourselves, many times.

"Over my head," Jason reports. The cord was tied to the metal bedstead in a room in the Guildford Hotel on Robson Street (I had been there once myself) and held Jason's hands in place over his head while he lay on his back, his legs in the air, over Mel's shoulders, as he squirmingly imagined his embarrassment should a mutual friend come through the door to discover that his butch cover story concealed a boy begging to be fucked. Jason blew his wad without his dick being so much as touched. His come gushed onto his rippled belly solely from the force of Mel's cock in his ass. I marvel at this rarest of gifts, the literal truth.

▪

At the end of the epilogue, the author at last understands that conventional phrase, which concludes so many prefaces, whereby all others are absolved and it is declared that "whatever faults remain are my own."

A History of Homosexual
Desire in Montreal,
1642–1992

His name, unaccountably enough, is Jimmy. I'm still a time traveler, having been stripped of all being by airports, taxis, metal detectors, freeways, buses, hotel rooms with punch-card "keys," and, worst of all, in-flight movies at 10,000 metres above the earth. On this Vancouver–Montreal direct flight, which is taking me to a gay literary conference to which I will contribute, although I've yet to know it or to have written it, this very account, we're subjected to a terrible in-flight melodrama — as I scrunch down in my seat and try to read a paperback edition of the philosopher Blaise Pascal — called *Far and Away*, starring Tom Cruise as an improbable nineteenth-century Irish immigrant fleeing the potato famine. The film is so horrible (even with the sound off) that it can't be saved by the sole sexy scene in which he lies in bed unconscious and completely naked, except for his genitals, which have been covered by an inverted, ordinary, kitchen mixing bowl placed there by the hardy pioneer women who have somehow rescued him from whatever and dragged his konked-out, fast-fading cuteness onto a bed. His co-star, Nicole Kidman, I think it is, sneaks in and covertly lifts the bowl a couple of centimetres or so, but out of camera range, to get a peek at the organ that presumably all the rest of us are dying to see, but I'm sufficiently bored that instead of following the plot or trying to read a dense paragraph of Pascal, I find myself wondering if nearly bankrupt Canadian Airlines and its film censorship board, in editing this version for outer space, have cut (or uncut, puns intended) any crucial frames here of that which will inflame Nicole's imagination through the next hour and a half of implausible adventures across two continents.

And yet, as soon as I materialize in a recomposed body, like they do in *Star Trek*, on the corner of St.-Laurent and St.-Catherine, gazing east down the length of the narrow thoroughfare, a dim blaze of red and orange neon that blurs like streaked techni-colour mascara into the wet, rain-slicked surface of the street itself, I approach the 350 years of desire in Montreal.

In the Club David, I find a free barstool just inside the entrance at the corner of the bar, two people talking to each other on my immediate right, and the bartender, to my surprise, is able to hear and understand my request for vodka and orange juice despite the level of a throbbing sound system that accompanies a boy dancing through progressive states of undress on a small stage, across an aisle just beyond the bar. There will be a more or less continuous succession of such eighteen- or nineteen-year-old boys, dancing, stripping, sinuously melting into mirrors, running their hands across their smooth torsos, each one a kind of story that never fails to engage my attention. How do they get such per-fectly flat bellies? I ask my friend Don on a subsequent evening in the same bar. How do they get so skinny? I moan, while getting a glimpse in the mirror on my left of my own frog-like paunch growing up into my jowls, exactly like Günter Grass's drawing of same on the cover of his new novel, *The Call of the Toad*, which I'd packed for the trip. "They don't *get* skinny," Don points out through a cloud of his cigar smoke, "they *are*." "I know," I sigh, "God made them like that."

In the first moments of that fragment of a history, I'm in such a panic of information absorption — from the display, in the foyer of the bar, of photographs of the nude dancers, whose images I'm trying to match up with the actual dancer on the platform, smooth long thighs, in my field of vision, to the pure nausea of all the senses of a fevered body (I've arrived with a winter cold) tast-ing the acrid underlay of alcohol beneath juice, checking the pool table located diagonally behind the island bar, picking up the nar-rative of a jagged pelvic thrust of the dancing boy whose limber cock slithers from the jockstrap that he's down to — that the cou-ple on my right are barely registered and receive only secondary initial attention. He's a young man — his Walkman earphones worn as a necklace around his long neck — talking to a nonde-script man in his thirties, who almost immediately departs.

He turns to me, beginning with a casual remark that's a lit-tle beyond my French linguistic capacities despite our national commitment to bilingualism, and though I reply haltingly in his mother tongue, he graciously switches to mine. I can forego, can I not, an account of the two or three centuries that lead to analysis of the Quebec National Assembly's Bill 101 and whether it is a reasonable defence against linguistic imperialism? Okay, consider it skipped, which allows me instead to notice that he's not a young man in his middle to late twenties, as I'd at first thought, but a schoolboy, twenty at most, with chopped dirty-blond hair, exquisite lips, etc. He's attractively skinny and, I will discover when he stands up, surprisingly tall.

There is no way, really, to describe what constitutes a "beautiful boy." Despite whatever details of clothing or gestures can be provided, their utterly diverse and always particular beauty must be rendered as a kind of absolute uniformity, as a degree zero of the beautiful, so that one might as well read off the items on an application form for a job or a medical checkup: nineteen or twenty, aforementioned dirty-blond hair, eye colour already forgotten, six feet tall, uncut cock, and so on. And in fact, I'm still shielded from the extent of his beauty, muffled in padded jacket, pantaloons from ninth-century Damascus, Just Do It sneakers, by the sweat-and-light-slickened torso of the dancer in the middle distance, but I've already registered, rather to my surprise — and this is perhaps the point — a decision about him, a judgment as final as mortality and eternal life as portrayed in Claude Jutra's film *Mon Oncle Antoine*.

He's drinking a beer, from whose bottle he's already peeled the label, and is explaining through his lush lips (the kind that young women models acquire through the injection of collagen) the obviously complex story of how a boy born in Quebec City, heart of the land of winter, could be named Jimmy. In due course he produces a student identification card with photo, name, and birthdate, which occasions the introduction of a cast of grandfathers, adoptive parents, distant and lost kin of every sort. I don't quite get whether his grandfather, because he had been named Jimmy by a stubborn mother, would or wouldn't speak to him on the grounds of an offence to Québecois culture.

To further complicate matters, Jimmy, who is remarkably loquacious in both national languages, is simultaneously launching a multiple discourse that, as near as I can recall, includes the following files: action-movie actor Steven Seagal's new film, *Under Seige*; a lengthy story about Jimmy's trip to Calgary; his bets in a sports lotto game of which he has several receipts, some of which are dependent on the outcome of the Montreal–New Jersey Devils game, at the moment in the second period, the score 3–1 for the Habs as we will eventually learn; the fragmented running autobiography with appropriate trials and tribulations; and, finally, a learned disquisition about the rock group Genesis and its former lead singer, Peter Gabriel, which is now providing the soundtrack companionship for a new dancer, a nearly naked slim boy with close-cropped wiry blond hair (I think his name is Pierre), whose beauty and dancing skills are so remarkable that I interrupt Jimmy for a moment to point him out and am pleased and reassured when the boy confirms my opinion — "Oh yes, he's very beautiful," Jimmy says, with unfeigned enthusiasm. For some reason, the open recognition of one boy's beauty by another also beautiful boy thrills me in exactly the way that a successful bit of science assures us of the notion of objectivity. Though running a dangerous fever, lost in his narrative litany, dazzled in the best sense of that word — in short, at last alive — when Jimmy says, "Would you like to go have some fun?" with what relief from calculation, second thoughts, the sort of dither one has in a restaurant trying to decide whether to have the *boudin à la Lyonnaise* or the *côte d'agneau*, I am utterly unhesitant for a change. "Yes, *bien sur*," I reply.

We can say it is a matter of intuition that permits this choice, though, speaking as a working philosopher myself, I think that intuition, despite the recent resurgence of popularity it's enjoyed in feminist discourse, is less reliable than we think. Indeed, much later, an hour or so from now, Jimmy will chide me for my naïveté, my lack of precaution, warning me of the considerable dangers — from robbery to homicide — implicit in taking a boy like him to a hotel, but, in fact, it was exactly the sorting of mere scraps of information that produced the intuition not merely that Jimmy was a safe pickup but, beyond that, of his inexhaustible repertoire. Although I could as easily be wrong. In which case I would appear in a small newspaper item, near the bottom of an inside page, as, to invoke one of the more belaboured words of our times, a "victim," perhaps "not yet identified," as journalese puts such mysteries.

But rather than intuition, what I'm trying to distinguish, since I happen to be reading Pascal (a not altogether easy task on a bumpy flight with a bad inflight Tom Cruise movie playing), is the difference between accident and miracle. In discussing those miracles that "are supernatural ... in substance, *quod substantium*, as when two bodies interpenetrate or when a single body is in two places at the same time," Pascal worries about the distinction between "false ones and true ones. There must be some sign," he says, "by which they can be recognized, otherwise they would be useless." A page later, he observes, sounding more like Wittgenstein than a seventeenth-century metaphysician, "If there were no false miracles there would be certainty." But as a good pragmatist, I'm willing to settle for the view that Jimmy's presence is a lucky accident rather than a true or false miracle.

In the small, futuristic hotel room — a punched card functions as the room key to get us in — the possibly false miracle named Jimmy, having turned on the Montreal game and checked his sports lotto tickets, asks if it's okay to take a shower. In the half-open doorway and in the bathroom mirror, as he at last discards those baggy pantaloons, his white underpants are half pulled off, snagged on a boyish hip, revealing a large, already partially hard, uncut cock, which, for a microsecond, he is modestly shy about exposing or whose image he wishes to keep from the reflection in the mirror, but he immediately abandons this chaste (but sincerely demure) moment when he invites me to join him inside the tiny shower stall. The scalding water runs down my chest, and Jimmy, who has slid in a film of soap behind me (after we've kissed, his tongue darting forcefully but birdlike into my mouth), presses his swelling groin against my butt — I willingly return the incipient pressure of the first of what will be many thrusts — one arm tightly across my clavicle (I make a last consideration of the possibility of his strangling me), and offers an elegant finger to suck, between my lips into the cavity of my mouth ... that's the instant in which I recognize that although this is strictly a one-off event, I'm prepared, on the basis of this accidental meeting, to considerably reorder the complete itinerary of my life. For a few hours, anyway.

On Certainty

Between the anticipations of the evening and the loss of the day's memory (and more, no doubt), we occupy the present tremulous moment. While Manuel sprawls in sleep above the gathering traffic of Hamburg's Reeperbahn in that interlude dividing the end of the afternoon from the early evening, I, having woken from our nap before him, sit reading at a small dressing table at the foot of the bed, pausing occasionally to glance up at his tousled blond hair.

I first happened upon Ludwig Wittgenstein's *On Certainty* while reading Ray Monk's biography of the Austrian-born philosopher. The work is, like almost everything Wittgenstein wrote, unsystematic, fragmentary, and unfinished. It was also the last thing he wrote; he worked on this topic right up until two days before his death in April 1951. My admiration was roused by the fact that Wittgenstein simply kept on, scribbling thoughts into his notebook, to the very end: "I do philosophy now like an old woman who is always mislaying something and having to look for it again: now her glasses, now her keys." There's really nothing else to do. Impending death ought not be treated as something out of the ordinary, he seemed to imply.

On Certainty was, as well, about exactly the subject that was most on my mind. I was immured in the mixture of my body's certainty of desire for Manuel and my puzzlement over almost everything else, from the identity of the other person to the identity of the new societies emerging from the wreckage of the Communist states in the 1990s. Wittgenstein seemed to offer at least another way of asking about what we knew.

In addition to Manuel, there was another person in my life, Alexander Goertz. He was the one with whom I had begun reading *On Certainty*. Goertz (everybody called him by his surname) was a rosy-cheeked, blond-haired music student in his early twenties, of Hungarian-German parentage. I had met him in Berlin through Michael Morris, a painter friend of mine, and Thomas Marquard, a high-school teacher and musician who was destined to become a long-time friend as I began to live part-time in Berlin. I was introduced to Goertz perhaps a week or two after I'd met Manuel. There wasn't anything sexual to our relationship; Goertz was, insofar as those terms apply, heterosexual and often lamented his misadventures in the minefields between the sexes. It had been intimated to me that Goertz might in some fashion become my intellectual companion in Berlin. I immediately saw the need for such a person in my life, and his arrival was welcome.

Goertz's interests in music ranged from the medieval composer-nun Hildegard of Bingen to the obscure American musical experimenter of the 1940s, Harry Partch. Goertz was in his period of walking down stairs backwards; he was a vegetarian, so we regularly went for lunch at a cheap Indian restaurant on Grohlmanstrasse; he was one of the few people who could recount a dream in such a way that I wasn't bored by it; he invented devices to "purify" the sound of electric guitars, and so on. Though some regarded him as merely quirky, I had no difficulty in recognizing his genius. When I mentioned Wittgenstein's name (I had just read the biography), Goertz at once declared his interest. Thus we began reading *On Certainty* in Berlin — in the room in Michael Morris's apartment where I was staying for the summer — puzzling out the book's fragments rather randomly, since the form of its composition seemed to lend itself to such a reading.

The problem Wittgenstein set himself was roughly as follows. In 1939, the English philosopher G. E. Moore published an article, "Proof of the External World," in which he claimed to *know* a number of commonsense propositions, such as "Here is one hand and here is another." In an earlier paper, "A Defence of Common Sense," he made similar claims: "The earth existed for a long time before my birth" and "I have never been far from the earth's surface." Moore was attempting to defeat philosophical scepticism about objective reality by a number of "obvious" assertions.

Wittgenstein replied (in his notebook), "If you do know that *here is one hand*, we'll grant you all the rest." The sweep of that opening gesture delighted me. The question he posed was, "Now, can one enumerate what one knows (like Moore)? Straight off like that, I believe not — for otherwise the expression 'I know' gets misused," adding, "We just do not see how very specialized the use of 'I know' is."

Instead, Wittgenstein turned the problem of knowing around: "What we can ask is whether it can make sense to doubt it." He meant that quite literally. "Do I, in the course of my life, make sure that I know that here is a hand — my own hand, that is?" Then he tried to explain why such an announcement would be most odd and to think of conversational examples where such a claim might make sense.

Now, pondering *On Certainty* in the Florida Hotel in Hamburg, Germany, I wondered if its author, himself homosexual, might be amused to know that he was being read in a gay brothel, for it was slowly dawning on me that that's what the Florida was, though Manuel had simply proposed it as a place he knew in Hamburg where we could stay for a weekend. Or perhaps it was simply I who was pleased that philosophy could be at home here, as much as it could be in the classroom back in Vancouver where I taught.

That evening, behind the Exquisit bar in the hotel, Manuel's best friend, a bartender named Detlef, was the host of his own birthday party, which was one of the reasons for our trip to Hamburg. Detlef poured drinks for the men and boys who filled the barstools and tables, while deftly accepting little gifts from new arrivals — they were buzzed in to the second-floor establishment through a locked steel door — as well as taking phone calls offering best wishes on his thirtieth birthday.

Detlef was a solidly built, dark-haired man in a denim shirt and jeans, the edge of his butt perched on a tall stool, legs confidently spread. I was introduced to him, and he poured Manuel and me glasses of champagne with which we toasted him. I could see that when he was twenty, Manuel's present age, he must have been strikingly handsome. Had some of the middle-aged men who now crowded the bar once slept with him? Undoubtedly. He was taciturn, cool. His style was more *noblesse* than *oblige*. Manuel's enthusiastic greeting was returned rather indifferently, I thought. When Manuel asked if he should take up my invitation to visit me in Canada, Detlef dismissively replied, "Sure. Why not?"

as though he had left the invitations of men far behind him, as though he knew exactly what they were worth. He soon turned his attention elsewhere. Manuel had told me that he and Detlef had never slept together, that they were just friends. I wondered if their friendship was as close as Manuel supposed.

After a while, Manuel suggested that we visit some other gay bars of Hamburg. Outside, in the cold drizzle, we hailed a taxi that took us to the St. George district on the far side of the train station at which we had arrived the day before. We aimlessly traipsed from one bar to another — the Universum, the Club König — each slightly differing in décor and demeanour, but all of them strangely empty. Back at the Exquisit, Detlef's party went on. We had a nightcap before going upstairs at midnight.

When we went downstairs for breakfast in the morning, we discovered that the entire bar had been ripped apart and was in the process of being renovated. Wiring dangled from the ceiling. The furniture had been piled up against the walls. To Manuel's annoyance, the breakfast room was temporarily housed in a suite off the corridor; the coffee was cold, the bread stale. We escaped the wreckage, taking a cab across town, where we found a basement bar that was just opening. There was hot coffee, fresh croissants, and a pinball machine to amuse my guide in this labyrinth.

When Manuel asked, "What do you want to do?" I said, "Let's see Hamburg," and soon we were on a tour bus, whose oversized windshield wipers swept away the rain pelting its smoky grey windows. It was one of those standard city sightseeing tours for visiting strangers, probably boring for Manuel, who knew Hamburg, but I liked it. I liked being inside out of the rain, being with Manuel, not having to do anything, while the city, with its narrow, villa-lined streets, a fountain in a lake, all suggesting its wealth, floated by us in a wet haze.

At the harbour, where there was a shopping stop as the tour more or less ended, we got off the bus, hunched under a small umbrella. I was too cold to imagine that I was looking for the homoerotic photographers Herbert List or Herbert Tobias, whose ghosts and images were among the other reasons that had brought me to Hamburg. Although I wanted to see the places where they had made their daily rounds in the 1920s and 1950s respectively, I could barely make out the harbour cranes and anchored ships through the mist and slanting rain. Certain jumbled streets that angled toward the slate-coloured water tempted me (was I looking for some long-gone bar of the 1920s — the Parrot's Perch? — where List had gone?), but I saw that Manuel had had enough.

On the Reeperbahn we searched for an open restaurant or café — not easy to locate on a boulevard of pleasure that only awoke with dark — until, just as we were about to give up, we stumbled upon a place that served traditional German cooking. A television mounted high behind me was showing a Chinese comedy film. Manuel watched it with pleasure, while I enjoyed looking at him and his grey-blue eyes following the slapstick. We had no idea in the world where we could go from here.

Though the surfaces of the city were cold and wet, inhospitable even, I was deep inside it, looking out, rather than the other way around. Manuel was attentive to my desire; his manners charmed me. I could never have found my own way into and through that garish maze. If I had entered the Exquisit myself (using one of those gay guides that offered the symbol "R" for "rent boy"), I would have been faced with the opaque backs of the men at the bar, or by Detlef's cool demeanour. Instead I had been led by the hand. But to where? In one sense, to no more than a slightly shabby waterfront sex hotel. But in another, was it not into the heart of the body's, or the city's, secrets? Back in our room, we lay in the tangle of white sheets.

Manuel liked me to impale myself astride his condom-covered erection. He said he got hot seeing me jack off on his belly as he came inside me. It amused him to watch me cry out in pleasure as I reached back to place my hand on his bare thigh, feeling the convulsion of its muscle as his groin bucked up into me. Afterwards, he napped.

I sat naked in a chair by the little table, once more looking out over the Reeperbahn as I returned from the animal world to the uniquely human one that Wittgenstein wrote about. My body involuntarily quivered, still shaken by its recent fucking, so that it took an effort of will to keep my hand steady enough to turn the page.

At first, when I was reading *On Certainty* with Goertz, we

dipped into passages playfully, in no fixed order. "Suppose some adult had told a child that he had been on the moon," Wittgenstein speculated, thinking of Moore's claim that he had never been far from the earth's surface. "The child tells me the story, and I say it was only a joke, the man hadn't been on the moon; no one has ever been on the moon; the moon is a long way off and it is impossible to climb up there or fly there. — If now the child insists, saying perhaps there is a way of getting there which I don't know, etc., what reply could I make to him?"

Goertz and I liked the unintended irony of that passage. A decade or two after Wittgenstein's death, the impossibility of being on the moon had itself been dissolved. That season, they were playing a song in the bars that included, amid the blur of techno-sound and the interstellar static, the voice of astronaut Neil Armstrong proclaiming, in slightly botched grammar, "One small step for [a] man, one giant leap for mankind."

I had been reading *On Certainty* as though I were seeking the answer to a Zen riddle, but in that hotel room — my body, the ground of first knowledge, still alive to the place where it had been recently penetrated, and the boy who had done so now innocently asleep — I came as close to understanding Wittgenstein as I would.

Since Wittgenstein saw the human realm as residing in language — the rest of the world being an unspeakable mystery — doubting and certainty were simply possibilities in the practice of language. "A doubt about existence only works in a language-game," he proposed. "We should first have to ask: what would such a doubt be like?" Certainty, Wittgenstein says, is, "*as it were*, a tone of voice in which one declares how things are ..." Later he adds, "Do I want to say, then, that certainty resides in the nature of the language-game?"

That is, "it's not a matter of *Moore's* knowing that there's a hand there, but rather we should not understand him if he were to say, 'Of course I may be wrong about this.' We should ask, 'What is it like to make such a mistake as that?'" Because "the *questions* that we raise and our *doubts* depend on the fact that some propositions are exempt from doubt ... certain things are *indeed* not doubted." In the end, "if you tried to doubt everything, you would not get as far as doubting anything. The game of doubting itself presupposes certainty."

It was not that I knew something with certainty, but that my doubts depended on my not doubting certain things. I had thought I was looking for a Cartesian kind of certainty. What Wittgenstein wanted to show me was that there was no separating certainty from doubt; what was of interest were the doubts, and the set of undoubted propositions — the language-games or, simply, the "background" — necessary to sustain them.

If I had translated my desire for Manuel into the equation "Desire is the body's first epistemology," Wittgenstein solved at least half the riddle of how we know anything. I had still to discover the other half of the maxim that I sensed might complete my declaration about what the body knew, or where its knowledge led.

That night the bars were again a failure. At midnight on a Saturday, they yawned in emptiness. I was uncertain if the explanation — for which various bartenders offered their versions — was to be found in a seasonal economic downturn, was due to the lateness or earliness of the hour, or was simply an unaccountable mystery.

Manuel and I sat up in bed till three or four in the morning, gossiping through the baffle of language. Those leisurely conversations — in the middle of the night, or dawdling long after breakfast — were what took the relationship from urgent desire to a more diffused enamourment. Manuel claimed to make a good living from hustling and held up Detlef as a role model, a possibility of how one could make the successful transition to a later stage in life. Detlef was how he imagined himself ten years down the road. But since I didn't seem to fit the picture of one of those lavish-spending gentlemen from whom he drew sustenance, what was he doing with me?

"Because I said I would go to Hamburg with you," he replied. I asked him if he had any regrets. "Not at all," he said. "You like doing sex?" I asked. "Yes," he answered, "like you love writing books." (Did he really say that, or had I misunderstood, mistranslated?) When he asked, just before we fell asleep, "What do you like best about Hamburg?" I answered, "Making love in Hamburg with you," and I wasn't just being polite.

▪

When I woke in my familiar bed on a cool, cloudy Berlin morning, feeling the little aches and pains of middle age, it was a reminder that Manuel was twenty. The thought of him bore with it reflections on the transience of our intimacies. About twenty-four hours earlier, I'd been fucked, and yet now it was utterly forgotten by my body, while *I*, on the other hand, remembered that he had taken my pen, written my name on the bottom of his big toe, then his own on the bottom of the other one, and brought his feet together, pressing our written-on-flesh names against each other, making me laugh. But what was this "body" I separated myself from? Who was this "I" that I thought about apart from the body's sensations?

Meanwhile, life went on: I obeyed the orders of the day. At dinner with Michael, I pondered the differences between pornography and the erotic, and Michael showed me his latest snapshots. Goertz turned up for lunch, and again we attempted to untangle a passage of Wittgenstein. I moved to an acquaintance's apartment in Moabit district to house-sit for a month while he was away.

One night, as I walked partway home from the bar, I turned into the Ku'damm and found the great boulevard jammed with honking cars. There were crowds several people deep on the sidewalk, gazing up at a huge electronic news screen on the corner as it announced the narrow vote by which Parliament had chosen Berlin to be recently unified Germany's capital once again. Where the Berlin Wall had turned the thriving Potsdamer Platz of the pre-war years into a Cold War wasteland, Sony and Mercedes were now planning to build new corporate towers. The post-Communist future was unfolding.

∎

Manuel and I appear in each other's lives casually. In the middle of the afternoon, as I stand on a busy street corner across from the Zoo station, dithering over something trivial, he materializes out of the blue — actually, out of one of his favourite hangouts, the Presse Café, which is right next door to the international press shop where I've just bought a newspaper. "Are you free?" I ask him. He laughs. "You're simply impossible," he says, a phrase

I particularly like because it's the same one he uses to admonish his erect cock, shaking a finger at it, as though his body too were distinct from himself. And in minutes we're on the S-Bahn, riding to my place.

After we play for a while, he asks for a rubber. Then he's inside me. I reach behind, cupping his ass in my hand, to press him deeper into my body. Later, while I lie on my back, his teeth nip at my groin as I come. Even later, after he's gone — to meet his "jolly" aunt from Florida? to hustle in the Zoo station? — my body doesn't remember. As is my habit, I seek an aphorism to encapsulate that peculiar dualism I experience: *the body fucks and forgets; I remember and write.* I'm left with inconsequential details of our couplings — the disposal of a used condom, the sight of cloud formations when I open the curtains again.

But what does it mean to say that the body forgets? It experiences the pleasure provided by Manuel, but shortly afterwards, as the sensation dissolves, it's almost as if it never happened. I, having an identity, remember what happened to me — even if memory is unreliable and cuts out at odd moments, like a power disruption — but the body is indifferent to identity. It's concerned solely with sensation, is sense-full and thus "senseless." It doesn't contemplate life or death; I do.

My dualism, I notice, seems to divide in a rather different way from the standard philosophical terms of "body/mind" (or "mind/brain," as it has become in contemporary debates). For me, the set is "body/me," where "me" is a language-rooted (Wittgensteinian?) concept. "I" or "me" is not mind, not brain, but that which is associated with the words identifying myself. In a way, my dualism skirts the question of whether mind can be reduced to the material(ism) of the brain; instead, "me" is more like a fictional character.

And indeed that's how *fictional dualism* seems to work. I can use the body's memories for only a very short time, and then I have to "make up" what it feels like to be in the bubble bath with Manuel in Hamburg. Memory without fiction is incoherent.

For the moment, I see dualism everywhere. I've begun to learn reflexive verbs in German, which makes considerably more use of that grammatical device than other languages I know. "I remember" in German is *ich erinnere mich* — literally, "I remind me," thus implying, at least in terms of syntactic logic, that there is a "me" for "I" to remind.

But if I have a use, as a writer, for what I remember, then what do other people do with the bits and pieces left over from the experiences that the body, perforce, forgets? While we (artists) make art out of it, for others it goes into gossip, anecdotes, ways of presenting themselves, summing themselves up, reminiscing — in short, pretty much what the rest of us (artists) do with it. Is the difference between us — other than artists make art, non-artists don't — merely tautological?

One can't go on believing in "fictional dualism" forever. But I could go on, for as long as it might last, seeing Manuel, reading philosophy, watching the sky over Berlin, meeting Goertz for lunch.

⬤

One afternoon, some weeks later, Goertz came by with his guitar. The windows and balcony doors were open onto the courtyard and the thick foliage of the chestnut tree at its centre. By then, I was again staying at Michael's. It was warm and muggy, though the sky was thick with rain clouds. Goertz played some pieces by Leo Brouwer, a Cuban composer whose name I had mentioned to him. I thought about the obvious fact that I liked Goertz so much more than Manuel, notwithstanding the fate imposed by desire. Listening to the music, watching Goertz's fingers on the strings, I was astonished that someone could do that, that it could be done at all — the skills involved seemed so difficult compared to what I did in making sentences or constructing and deconstructing philosophical puzzles.

"I'd better play some Bach," Goertz joked after playing one of Brouwer's works, "just to make sure I'm not frightening the neighbours." As he played, it began to rain. In the middle of the afternoon, the storm gathered in a fury I'd never seen or heard before. The noise of the deluge, pelting the chestnut tree, echoing in the courtyard, drowned out the music. We sat and listened to its consuming roar.

⬤

Manuel phoned one night, late, from the bar, during the time I was apartment-sitting in Moabit. I was sitting at the black-topped desk, looking into the night sky, which was filled with the whop-whopping sound of unseen helicopters. There'd been choppers over Berlin all day, occasioned by the arrival of a flock of foreign dignitaries from NATO. Perhaps he was bored at the bar (I could hear its disco rhythm in the background); he said he'd come over in half an hour and spend the night (I didn't ask why he couldn't sleep at his own place). When he hadn't shown up an hour later, I fell asleep in familiar puzzlement. I'd never understand his appearances, his no-shows. He'd been agitated of late. Things were going badly, I assumed. Landlords, creditors, bureaucrats were all demanding payment.

At a quarter to three he woke me. I didn't understand all the details of his tale about getting stopped for riding the S-Bahn without a ticket. He crawled into bed with me and quickly dropped off into exhausted slumber. A great deal of the pleasure I took with Manuel, it occurred to me, consisted in simply look-ing at him while he slept; it was a pleasure I connected with that of looking at the moving clouds. He threw the comforter off, and I was filled with wonder to see his naked body. Like the clouds, nature had produced his particular shape, a form that aroused the exact sense of desire that my mind, my brain, had fashioned through a set of encounters and accidents over the years that constituted my erotic experience. The sight of him, the fact that he was *here*, seemed both a lucky coincidence and, since we had both agreed to be together, an instance of freedom, just as the clouds appeared to be both accidentally formed and freely float-ing across the sky.

Manuel slept until noon the next day. Then I gave him some money to go to the bakery for pastries while I laid out the plates, put on the coffee. From the kitchen window I watched him come back up the street, recognizing even from a distance the bakery's familiar wrapping paper, a package balanced in his hand.

After breakfast, he asked, "Do you want to go swimming?"

"I don't swim," I said, puzzled.

"In the bath," he laughed.

In the warm soap-bubble froth of bathwater, we slid across each other's bodies again. We towelled off and went back to bed.

I'd said earlier, over breakfast, that I wanted to go to the Zoo station to pick up a newspaper and smokes. He proposed that he sleep a bit more, that I wake him when I came back and we'd have coffee and the rest of the pastries before he went off to "work." Maybe I could get him a copy of the local tabloid, *BZ*, he suggested. There was a parting sentence as he lay in the comforter, but I missed the verb. He may have been asking if I trusted him enough to leave him alone in the apartment. The thought had crossed my mind.

The errands took a half hour. When I came into the apartment, I noticed from the corner of my eye, passing through the workroom into the room where we slept, something amiss on my desk. Something white on its black surface, something red out of place. The bed, with its tangled comforter, was otherwise empty. The place where I kept cash, tickets, passport, and traveller's cheques had been disturbed. There was an instant of bodily thrill, a rush of adrenalin, at taking in so instantaneously what had happened.

Yet I felt strangely cool about the theft, unlike the first time he had stolen money from my pocket. Then, when it was far too early for a real narrative to have formed, I'd simply experienced the emotions of someone who had been robbed. Now I also saw it as a final "plot twist" in the story. I began to assess the damage methodically, going first to the maroon-coloured bag where I stored my money and documents, but remembering the disarrangement on the desk of white, of red.

The cash (a relatively small sum) was, of course, gone. But what about the traveller's cheques? Some were there, scattered as he'd hastily rifled the bag. If he'd taken any of them, that would mean a dreary sorting out at American Express. I took the handful of cheques with me into my workroom to match the numbers against those I'd written in the back pages of my red notebook. Only the cash was missing.

The white object left on the desk was a note. As I was about to glance at it, I realized that the red notebook itself had been left on the desk, out of its usual place amid the stack of books that was my current reading. Though I was relieved that the notebook was still there, its placement meant that Manuel, for some reason, had been into it.

I went through its pages until I found what was missing: a strip of photo-booth pictures of him that I had pasted into the back cover. Was he trying to make it harder for the police to find him, in the unlikely event I should call them?

I turned to his note, written in German, in capital letters:

Dear Stan,
  I'm sorry I have to do this. I'm really stupid. I'm not doing it because I want to. But because I've got no other choice. We'll never see each other again.
  Tschüss,
    Manuel

At last, certainty filled me. Something had happened, and while there were perhaps doubts about Manuel's conflicting motives (at least, I hoped there were conflicting motives), there was no doubt about the event. At that moment, sometime in the early afternoon, a new batch of clouds rolled in, and the sky darkened again.

The certainty (and doubts) before me seemed curiously distant from the things Moore claimed to know and that Wittgenstein doubted. The material damage was minimal. I still had my documents, my traveller's cheques, and my irreplaceable notebook. His arithmetic was odd, though, since he would've made more money by sticking around.

Did I doubt that this was my hand and that was my other one? It was possible that he had enjoyed the sex and yet decided to steal from me. It was even possible that he liked me, though that was in the realm of uncertainty. He had given me a surfeit of bodily pleasure. What sort of thief left you sexually content and apologized for stealing from you?

Had I been to the moon? I was charmed that our encounter had ended with writing. All that summer I had been deluged with visual images — the photographs of List and Tobias; Michael's drawings; snapshots, porn, ads — even as I insisted on words. I'd feared I would forget what Manuel looked like, and now that he had taken my only pictures of him (although, oddly, while I had them, they never helped me remember what he looked like), all I had by way of remembrance were words.

Had the earth existed for a long time before I was born? I might run into him again, but this felt like a natural end to the story. So what was the nature of the narrative that I'd sought to fulfill by choice and interpretation of accident? Certainly there was no preordained story that wanted me to do *x* — go to Hamburg, become infatuated with a blond-haired boy — no other, greater source that overrode the secondariness of my personal life compared to the primacy of the world. Nor was there a narrative independent of us, discerning some shape to seemingly haphazard events. But our seeing a story made life something it wasn't heretofore.

If desire is the body's first epistemology, the knowledge to which I aspire at last is the story.

I was amused and touched by the wildly romantic, but false, despair of that last line: "We'll never see each other again."

▪

Well, of course we would. A few days later, Manuel called from Cologne (or that's where he said he was; I was only certain that it was him). The rest was lost in the blur of language. "Why did you steal from me?" I managed. "I don't know," he said. He was going off with someone to Mexico. He'd call me again. (In fact, we stayed in touch and saw each other for the next few years. And yes, I left him alone in my various subsequent apartments without incident.)

That night I was drinking sweet vermouth and soda in Tabasco's, the bar where I'd met Manuel. While Henk the bartender listened to one of the customers at the bar tell his tale of woe, a dark-haired boy with a faint downy mustache wandered in and ordered a beer in heavily accented English. I had been vaguely expecting to see a blond boy I'd noticed in Tabasco's once or twice before.

When whoever it is (invariably unexpected) begins the conversation — he's Portuguese, his name is José, he's travelling in Europe, wants to know if I'm looking for a good time — all that matters is to recognize: this is what I requested from the world. Many miss it altogether, deny they've asked for anything, or decide that this is not exactly what they asked for.

He sits naked astride my thighs, his medium-sized hard dick nestled under my balls, the light from the night-time street outside glowing on his smooth torso. My cock slides up and down in the grip of his fist, he tips his head forward and aims a stream of saliva he's built up in his mouth so that it lands where his hand provides a spit-slickened groove for me.

When I walk José to the main drag so that he can get a cab back to the bar, there's a low-key full moon over Moabit.

Rereading Paul Monette's Borrowed Time

I only have to reopen the pages of Paul Monette's *Borrowed Time: An AIDS Memoir* (1988), as I did recently, and a lot of it comes back. From the chilling first sentence — "I don't know if I will live to finish this" — the aura of dread that for years permeated every minute of the time of that plague era returns in force, sending a shudder through my body. The memory leaves me off-centre, with a survivor's mixed feelings of guilt and gratitude, and also a sense of being curiously obsolete for possessing personal recollections of what to others can only be an increasingly distant matter of history. Some twenty or more years after the beginning of the AIDS epidemic in the early 1980s, and after or in the midst of subsequent, if lesser, epidemics (Ebola, West Nile, bird flu), how can I explain what it was like then? Strange to have lived through — strictly by chance — a plague in my own lifetime. Strange that its location in people's minds, including my own, is now displaced, both temporally and geographically. Strange that in one sense AIDS is over but hasn't at all ended, neither here, in North America and Europe, where it continues to afflict particular ethnic and subcultural groups, such as intravenous drug users, nor there. "There" is now Africa, where AIDS rages in catastrophic proportions, with literally millions of people on the verge of death, simply, as far as I can tell, because "we," the rich world, won't give "them," the poor world, the drugs they need and can't afford.

How to give an idea of what it was like then? Through our records of the plague, our dispatches from the front. There is, not surprisingly, a lot of very good writing about AIDS, from novelist Edmund White's fictionalized memoir *The Farewell Symphony* to activist-scholar Douglas Crimp's militant essays *Melancholia and Moralism*. The amount of good writing is not surprising in the sense that a sizeable number of talented, literate men, their minds "wonderfully concentrated," as Samuel Johnson put it, by the prospect of death, applied their intelligence to providing a description of the plague. Even works that are justifiably criticized — journalist Randy Shilts' bestselling *And the Band Played On* and Larry Kramer's shrilly pitched *Reports from the Holocaust* come to mind — offer moments of legitimate illumination. But of all the books written in the midst of the plague, Paul Monette's *Borrowed Time* is the one that had the greatest impact on me.

I

The circumstances of Monette's grief-stricken tale are simple enough. Set in the mid-1980s, Monette and his friend, Roger Horwitz, lovers for a decade, are practically poster boys for the joys of middle-aged gay domesticity. There's "a stucco 1930s cottage high in a box canyon above Sunset Strip" in which they live, and "a view of the city lights through the coral tree out front and between the olive and eucalyptus across the way," while out back "is a garden court shaded by Chinese elms and a blue-bottom pool that catches the sun from eleven to three," as well as a terrace for dinners with friends down from San Francisco. There's a used, balky, black Jaguar (upscale successor to a Mercedes) and holidays to Greece or the California foreshore at Big Sur. There are understanding parents with a house in swanky Palm Springs, fashionable restaurants, and an assortment of therapists and agents. They attend benefit dinners put on by the gay community, and Roger, a lawyer, and Paul can afford to sponsor a table. The occasional movie star, prominent producer, or famous writer passes through the scene of their domestic life.

But there's a darker side to this middle-class homosexual idyll. Monette, a once-promising poet and novelist, the author of *Taking Care of Mrs. Carroll* (1978) and *The Gold Diggers* (1979), finds himself, five or six years later, at age forty, in something of a literary slide, stalled on a novel and reduced to writing sitcom scripts. There's a hint of recent past trouble in an otherwise monogamous relationship. And there is the rumour of the plague.

Monette recalls the "shadowy nonfacts," "the most fragmented of rumours" of the early 1980s. He remembers noting in his diary in December 1981 "ambiguous reports of a 'gay cancer,'" then adds, "but I know I didn't have the slightest picture of the thing. Cancer of the *what*? I would have asked, if anyone had known anything." A couple of months later, in early 1982, driving to Palm Springs to visit Roger's parents, Paul reads aloud from the gay magazine *The Advocate* an article titled "Is Sex Making Us Sick?" As Monette notes, "There was the slightest edge of irony in the query, an urban cool that seems almost bucolic now in its innocence. But the article didn't mince words," providing the first in-depth reporting he'd seen — it wasn't yet mentioned in the *Los Angeles Times* — of a mysterious — was it fatal? — disease that targeted gay men.

"I remember exactly what was going through my mind while I was reading," Monette writes a half-dozen years later. "I was simply relieved . . . because the article appeared to be saying that there was a grim progression toward this undefined catastrophe, a set of preconditions — chronic hepatitis, repeated bouts of syphilis, exotic parasites. No wonder my first baseline response was to feel safe. It was *them* — by which I meant the fast-lane Fire Island crowd, the Sutro Baths, the world of High Eros. Not us."

It wasn't "us," not yet. Nor was it yet known that the disease didn't present a neat set of preconditions. Not until a year and a half later, in autumn 1983, did Monette get a call from his best friend, Cesar, a teacher in San Francisco, who reported a swollen gland in his groin that he was going to get biopsied before the school semester began. "AIDS didn't even cross my mind, though cancer did," Monette recalls. "Half joking, Cesar wondered aloud if he dared disturb our happy friendship with bad news. 'If it's bad,' I said, 'we'll handle it, okay?'" Paul and Roger were busy getting ready for their annual trip to Big Sur. Paul put the thought away. After all, "even though he went to the baths a couple of times a week, Cesar wasn't into anything *weird* — or that's how I might have put it at that stage of my own denial. No hepatitis, no history of VD, built tall and fierce — of course he was safe."

But days after their return from Big Sur, Paul arrived home one evening and "Roger met me gravely at the door. 'There's a message from Cesar,' he said. 'It's not good.' Numbly I played back the answering machine, where so much appalling misery would be left on tape over the years to come, as if a record were crying out to be kept. 'I have a little bit of bad news.' Cesar's voice sounded strained, almost embarrassed." Monette spends the evening working his way through a tangle of telephone calls, bracing himself for cancer news, before he reaches a mutual acquaintance named Tom. "The lymph nodes, of course — a hypochondriac knows all there is to know about the sites of malignancy. Already I was figuring what the treatments might be . . . I had Cesar practically cured by the time I reached Tom . . . But as usual with me in crisis, I was jabbering and wouldn't let Tom get a word in. Finally he broke through: 'He's got it.' 'Got what?'" Monette asks, but he knows at that instant that "it" is something other than a curable cancer.

The best thing about Monette's narrative is simply its accurate accumulation of mundane details. It is like a careful description of weather — a gathering storm — or a slowly advancing, but relentless, artillery barrage, closing in on your little foxhole. Though life will soon be as alien as "living on the moon," Monette's text respects the reality of his experience sufficiently that there is no vain striving to rise above it, to claim that he's anything more than a precise instance of something larger. Roger and Paul are ordinary, middle-class gay men, accustomed to the privileges available to them, not even the sort of gay men I especially like. They're politically liberal but not more than that, fussily self-absorbed (aren't we all?), "out" in homosexual terms, but not *too* out. All of that is part of the unheroic attraction of *Borrowed Time*.

Since Monette's book is a chronicle of a doom foretold, the inevitable happens: Cesar's condition deteriorates, Roger falls ill, is diagnosed with the deadly syndrome, and, in turn, Paul tests positive for the virus. Among their circle of friends and acquaintances, more and more of them are struck down by what is clearly a plague. We know all this from the very beginning of Monette's book, where, as in a Greek tragedy, the chorus opens the drama with a recitation of the plot. Monette, looking back on the wreckage of life, ponders the difficulty of knowing where to start. "The world around me is defined now by its endings and its closures — the date on the grave that follows the hyphen.

Roger Horwitz, my beloved friend, died of complications of AIDS on October 22, 1986 ... That is the only real date anymore, casting its icy shadow over all the secular holidays lovers mark their calendars by," he says in the first pages.

Further, "the fact is, no one knows where to start with AIDS. Now, in the seventh year of the calamity" — the time at which *Borrowed Time* is being written — "my friends in LA can hardly recall what it felt like any longer, the time before the sickness. Yet we all watched the toll mount in New York, then in San Francisco, for years before it ever touched us here. It comes like a slowly dawning horror. At first you are equipped with a hundred different amulets to keep it far away. Then someone you know goes into the hospital, and suddenly you are at high noon in full battle gear."

Once Roger is hospitalized at the University of California at Los Angeles, their life together, with sporadic respites over the next year and a half, increasingly revolves around various rooms and wards at UCLA hospital. Henceforth, they live on time borrowed from the future they will not have. But there's more than one sense of time here. For gay men of their generation, there's the "lost time" of having been in the closet, the years before the declaration of public homosexuality in 1969. Making up for that lost time perhaps explains part of the gay sexual frenzy of the 1970s, a reaction to the recognition that what was once absolutely forbidden can be transformed into a state in which everything is permitted. Nor is time here only borrowed from the future. Recounting an earlier journey to Greece, Monette observes that "people who travel have dreamlike moments where they borrow time from the past, but it's not out-of-body at all. The echo of the ancient image, warrior or monk, is in you."

Finally, time borrowed from the past is the substance of writing. "I can see us so vividly side by side in bed — reading, dozing, roaming — always coming around again to that evening anchorage ... At the time I thought there were no more layers of innocence to peel ... I cannot say what pagan god it was, but I'd gotten in the habit, last thing at night, of praying: *Thank you for this*. I'd be tucked up against my little friend, perfectly still, and thanking the darkness for the time we'd had — the ten years, the house, the dog, the work. I did, I counted my blessings ... I knew what I had and what I stood to lose. I held it cradled in my arms, eyes open even as I slept. The night watch from the cliffs at Thera, clear along the moon all the way to Africa." Thera was the Greek island city they had visited, destroyed by a volcano in 1500 BC, perhaps the source of Plato's myth of Atlantis. A couple of fresco paintings from its civilization survived, and, like Monette, I've seen them in the museum in Athens. I have a postcard.

The rest of *Borrowed Time*, recounted in tones both measured and frenetic, is a mixture of inconsolable sorrow, political rage at governments and media slow to do what they could have done to reduce the ravages of the plague, moments of hyperventilating panic and claustrophobia, and eventually exhaustion and "the desolate waking to life alone — this calamity that is all mine, that will not end till I do."

II

Living in Vancouver, I was on the periphery of AIDS, literally on the epidemiological margins of a fatal viral epidemic. It was transmitted mainly through sexual intercourse between gay men, and its epicentres were in New York, San Francisco, Los Angeles, and other North American cities that contained smaller but sizeable homosexual populations. But even being on the edge of the plague was close enough to feel the horror, to become hysterical in the middle of an afternoon, wake up in a sweat from nightmares (and wonder if it was those symptomatic "night sweats"), visit dying friends on the eighth floor of St. Paul's Hospital in Vancouver or in a bleak Berlin apartment, attend countless meetings that Monette describes as "boredom in a good cause," remember the dead at memorial services. Close enough to read *Borrowed Time* the first time, in 1988, with terror. Monette's account was not so different from the plagues referred to by Boccaccio in *The Decameron* or described in Defoe's *Journal of the Plague Year* and Albert Camus's *The Plague*.

I remember calculating my degree of risk by means of a primitive equation I'd made up: acts plus number of sexual partners minus precautions taken, over geographical location multiplied by time, equalled risk of exposure. That is, if you were the recipient in acts of anal intercourse and had had sex with many people without using condoms, and if you lived in one of the plague's epicentres at the time of the critical mass dissemination of the virus (the early 1970s), the odds were against you. I had lived in San Francisco for five years or so before moving to Vancouver in the mid-1960s, just before the main period of the virus's silent spread, so my comparative safety was simply a bio-geographical accident. The same was true of my bedroom behaviour. It was only at the insistence of a sensible friend in the early 1980s that I began to obey the protocols of a safer sex, so again, it was more a matter of chance than prescience that provided whatever protection I enjoyed.

The human immunodeficiency virus (HIV) was attended by two particular cruelties. Its incubation period could be as long as a decade, so the "safer sex" procedures soon undertaken by gay communities (which successfully reduced new infections) didn't protect you if you had acquired the virus years before. Second, there were no available medications for AIDS other than those to alleviate the accompanying "opportunistic" infections that a deficient immune system invited. From the mid-eighties — the time of Roger Horwitz's death — there were experimental drug protocols, and Monette, with his histrionic energy, *chutzpah*, and middle-class gay privilege, was quick to enroll his friend in available programs, but to no avail. Nothing worked. Retroviral inhibitor drugs, which don't cure AIDS but prolong life significantly, wouldn't be available for years.

In 1989, the year after Monette's *Borrowed Time* appeared and as a half-million mostly American gay men continued to die, I wrote, in a book called *Buddy's*, a fantasy about "How the Plague Ended": "It hadn't ended with a magic bullet, a cure, or even imperfect treatments." It ended, in gay communities, because self-education had dramatically reduced the rate of lethal transmission. "It ended, so it was said, because we had changed. And the change had changed us, in ways that were not yet apparent." And at the end, "we didn't even feel relief. Perhaps we permitted ourselves to take note of our exhaustion." But "what next?" We couldn't yet turn our attention back to everyday catastrophes. There were still committees to sit on, hotlines to staff, the dead to bury, memorials, demonstrations, and the rest. "Yet, we would continue to desire. We had not ceased grieving ... we would continue to cry our eyes out. We would find ourselves numbly staring at the ocean on a muggy afternoon, then come to, recalling a dinner engagement. Gradually, it would become a memory, like the curling, yellow-edged pages of an old newspaper exposed to the air. But when it ended, we barely noticed." As it turned out, that effort to imagine an end of the plague, at least for the limited "us" that comprised gay men in North America — an attempt to provide a bit of sombre political hope — was not that far off the mark. There were "imperfect treatments," but today, more than a decade after my fantasy of it ending, gay friends remark to each other on the eerie disappearance of the mention of AIDS in the media, or even among ourselves.

Both the failure of governments and media to respond to AIDS and the inadequate efforts of scientists to develop effective medications sparked the politics of AIDS. There were two half-truths promulgated by gay activists that were crucial to engendering support for a stricken community, but which can now be viewed in a more balanced, retrospective light. The first was the claim that AIDS is not a gay disease, but one that can strike anybody. That is of course true in a literal sense, but in reality the virus was introduced into a primarily gay male population and, as epidemiologists learned, was quickly and "efficiently" disseminated and contained within that aggregate, aided in part by that population's sexual practices at the time. What "leakage" there was of the virus (through blood transfusion, shared use of needles, and heterosexual transmission via bisexual men) was limited, and the grave anticipation that AIDS would decimate the "heterosexual community" in North America was never realized. Like others, I knew the truth at the time, but in the face of charges by evil Christian fundamentalists that "AIDS was God's punishment" of homosexuals, the claim that anyone could come down with AIDS was a useful political fiction.

The other half-truth concerned sites of transmission and "promiscuity," and it became a point of contention within gay communities, as well as outside, because it touched on one of the central premises of gay liberation. What public homosexuality proposed at the beginning of the 1970s was that the whole question of sexuality was up for grabs. Conventional — i.e., conservative heterosexual — notions about who one slept with, how many sexual partners one had, the motives for sexual activity, and much more, were all subject to challenge. At the time, homo-sexuality was news from the front lines of human relationships. The subtext of its challenge to conventional sexuality — espe-cially to the shibboleth that sex was primarily reproductive or creational, rather than recreational — was a broader attack on institutional arrangements in bourgeois society. At least that was the case among radical adherents in Gay Liberation Front groups (I was one of the founders of the GLF Vancouver branch). As with other revolutionary proposals, there were excesses — in this case, of sexual activity, as became evident in mounting statistics of venereal diseases, hepatitis, and amoebic infections. When AIDS struck, a decade after public homosexuality, the response was often a barely disguised homophobia. "Promiscuity," it was claimed, violated a law of nature; homosexuals had brought the plague upon themselves.

In practical terms, gay bathhouses, which facilitated sexual encounters, were targeted as dangerous sites of AIDS transmis-sion. Even some gay men themselves called for the temporary clo-sure of such establishments. But for many gay activists, who had adopted the slogan "Silence=Death," such proposals amounted to a betrayal of the principles of the gay movement. Hence their insistence that the vital issue wasn't the number of partners or the circumstances of sexual encounters, but the practice of safer methods of sex. Again, while it is literally true that transmission of the virus could occur in a single act of "unprotected" sex, it was simply an epidemiological fact that the number of partners and the circumstances of the encounters were factors in the rate of transmission. Though insistence on prudence against accusa-tions of promiscuity wasn't the whole truth, its political function was understandable.

If "Silence=Death" was a call to act up against delinquent authorities (Act Up was the name of a prominent AIDS activ-ist movement), then one form of acting out — namely, shout-ing at governments, media, and even at each other — equalled a kind of resistance. With respect to the latter, failure to toe the party line could get you labelled a traitor. I remember one local incident, now almost comic in retrospect, in which I found myself on the wrong side of the line. Through my old friend John Dixon (he was also my colleague in the philosophy department at the college where we worked), I was a member of the board of the British Columbia Civil Liberties Association (BCCLA), over which Dixon presided, and which was actively engaged in issues involving people with AIDS. One of Dixon's contributions was a book, *Catastrophic Rights* (1990), in which he argued for the civil right of access to experimental drugs for those struck by catastrophic illness. I was also a member of the board of the local AIDS organization, one of those voluntary jobs that seemed to have more to do with bureaucracy, budgets, and "boredom in a good cause" than the visible saving of lives. One simply signed up, and, indeed, doing so did some good.

At one particularly untimely moment in the midst of the plague, the local conservative government of the day proposed a quarantine law. The proposal was in response to tuberculosis cases and had been innocently requested by the Vancouver public health officer, someone Dixon and I knew to be an intelligent and sensible medical official. The initial draft of the law was so loosely written that it was reasonable for an already beleaguered gay community to see the spectre of concentration camps. The BCCLA, like other groups, opposed the initial draft, but rather than using the occasion to mount a political outcry against an insensitive regime, we successfully lobbied the government to redraft the bill to remove the threat to people with AIDS, which it did.

Of course, no good deed goes unpunished, as one of my friends wryly says. For supporting the redrafted measure, Dixon and I were called onto the carpet of a gay community meeting one evening and afforded the opportunity to be the target of a couple of hours of angry remonstrance. An intransigent slogan of "No quarantine" was obviously a simpler battle cry than the complexities of moderate legalese. As it turned out — BCCLA, as usual, formed a watchdog committee to monitor the effects of the legislation — no one with AIDS was ever threatened with quarantine. That minor fact didn't prevent the appearance of vitriolic, scurrilous articles, questioning the state of my soul, in the gay press (even in gay newspapers that I wrote for) as long as five years after the fact. Few self-delusions are more convincing than righteous anger.

Meanwhile, the wounded continued to die. In outposts at the margins of the plague, unlike the blitzed epicentres, the deaths may have been epidemiologically proportional to location, but still, those dying were not strangers to us. Fred Gilbertson was a large man in his thirties, a friend of mine from writing groups and the gay newspaper for which we both wrote. His interests included politics, theology, and a demimonde of sexuality with which I was also familiar. He had been a "character" in my book *Buddy's*, and unlike some of the other friends I'd written about, he enjoyed his appearance as a semi-fictional figure, taking it, as intended, as a mark of respect for him. For Fred, AIDS took a swift course. A year after his jovial appearance in my book, when I visited him at St. Paul's Hospital near the end, he was physically shrunken, breathing through an oxygen mask, and without illusions as to his fate. A few months later (I was writing an epilogue for the paperback edition of my book), he was dead.

Other people were acquaintances. Dixon and I spent some time with Kevin Brown, the president of the Vancouver Persons With AIDS organization, working on medical and welfare issues for the disabled. Brown was one of the many people whose lives became more focused, as he told me when I interviewed him for a newspaper article, as a result of AIDS. Suddenly, because of the disease, he had become a spokesperson and discovered in himself a reasoned, gentle articulateness. Another person whom I slightly knew was Jon Gates, a social democratic activist. Even as he was dying, he had foreseen that the epicentre of AIDS would shift to Third World countries, and he campaigned to make drugs available to the destitute parts of the world years before the crisis in Africa was dimly perceived by the rest of us. A fellow member of the AIDS Vancouver board was a psychologist named David. On the last day of his life he held a farewell garden party for his friends and acquaintances. I was one of several people he had asked to provide drugs for his suicide, which he committed later that day among a circle of intimates. There were others, of course. I attended memorial ceremonies for Warren Knechtel, a faun-like photographer; for literature professor Rob Dunham; for political activist Maurice Flood. All people I knew. All gone. Now, as the poet Miłosz says, "all they can do is make use of me ... of my hand holding the pen, to return among the living for a brief moment."

Paul Monette did live to finish *Borrowed Time* and, as it turned out, quite a bit more. His memoir was accompanied by a suite of poems, *Love Alone*, in which he could rage against the dying of the light in another key. Two novels, *Afterlife* and *Half-way Home*, and an autobiography, *Becoming A Man*, followed. Finally, there was a volume of essays, *Last Watch of the Night*, published in 1995, the year of his death at age fifty.

Rereading *Borrowed Time*, the terror of the first reading gives way to measured grief. Grief, as Monette says, "that will not end till I do."

Feasting with Oscar: From <u>De Profundis</u> to Post-Queer

I

In cell C.3.3 on the third tier of Reading Gaol, a prison about sixty kilometres west of London, in the early winter months of 1897, forty-two-year-old Oscar Wilde, serving a two-year sentence for the curiously named crime of "gross indecency," began to write what would become one of the remarkable documents in the history of prison literature as well one of the most memorable testaments in the annals of homosexual life. The work is known to us under the title *De Profundis*, or "From the Depths," and is addressed to Wilde's then twenty-six–year-old, blond-haired, blue-eyed boyfriend, Lord Alfred Douglas, better known as "Bosie." ("Bosie" is a version of the affectionate Scottish term "boysie," for "boy.") The centenary of the letter's first, partial, heavily expurgated, posthumous publication in 1905, by Wilde's Canadian-born literary executor Robbie Ross, provides the occasion for revisiting the text of *De Profundis* and for reconsidering the fate of "the Love that dare not speak its name" in the more than a century since Wilde's death in 1900.

De Profundis is many things at once: it is, as Richard Ellman, one of the best of Wilde's many biographers, asserts in *Oscar Wilde* (1987), above all, a great love letter. It's also a love letter from Hell, in both senses of that phrase: a letter written from a literal human hell, prison, and also a letter from hell in that it savagely flays its recipient and dissects its author. It's the letter everyone (or at least me) has wanted to write to his rotten, no-good, extravagant, reckless, terminally shallow boyfriend, who, for reasons beyond human ken, one still loves. But it's more than that: it's also Wilde's defence of Art against Life; it's an account of his own ruined career (an *apologia pro sua vita*); it's a meditation on, of all people, Christ, not as a god but as the quintessential figure of the Artist; and finally, it's an effort by Wilde to understand his own experience of punishment and come to terms with it through a concept of *humility*, one of the ideas furthest from our image of a man whose notorious pride went before his fall.

In rereading *De Profundis*, as well as in reading the numerous biographies and watching the various films about Wilde — the most recent is director Brian Gilbert's 1997 *Wilde*, starring Stephen Fry and the blond-haired, blue-eyed Jude Law — the part I find most challenging is to imagine Oscar Wilde. The difficulty is less intellectual than characterological. Intellectually, we have available all of Wilde's texts, his testimony at his trials, and a good selection of his letters, including this most famous one. What's more, we know a significant number of facts about Wilde's life, down to the intimate details of who put tab A into slot B, and even the condition of the hotel sheets after various sexually athletic romps that featured not only Bosie but also the young men whom they bedded. So the problem is not the facts, even though new ones have emerged as recently as the latest biography, Neil McKenna's *The Secret Life of Oscar Wilde* (2003). Rather, the intellectual problem is the framework or context in which to understand Wilde.

The intellectual context poses both personal and political puzzles. Why, for example, did Wilde launch a doomed legal suit for libel against Bosie's father, the Marquess of Queensberry, a lawsuit that began the process that ended in his incarceration? And why, after the failure of that suit and before Wilde was charged himself, or even when Wilde was briefly released on bail between his trials, did he not flee to France, as most other sensible, legally endangered homosexuals did? It is said that, on the day of Wilde's sentencing, the ferry boats to Calais, Dieppe, and other French ports were jammed to the gunnels with gay men. Why wasn't Wilde on board long before the denouement? Equally, or more, important are the social and political riddles. What was "the Love that dare not speak its name," a phrase that appeared in a line of one of Bosie's poems, about which Wilde testified at his trial? How did men who had sex with young men conceive of themselves? Was Wilde, in addition to being a prominent writer and a genuine celebrity, also a proto-gay activist? Was there a nascent gay political movement in the closing years of the Victorian era in England?

The intellectual issues can, I think, be resolved. What is difficult is to imagine the personality of a man who more than once quipped, "I put merely my talent into my work; I put all of my genius into my life," and who described imagination as the human faculty that is "the basis of all spiritual and material life," the necessary beginning of both love and art. There are several thespian representations of Wilde by actors such as Robert Morley and Peter Finch, but I'm tempted by the portrayal offered by Stephen Fry, who imagines Wilde as avuncular and gentle in all his relations, who retains a soft-spoken melancholy even amid the pleasures "in the mire," as Wilde described his debaucheries. But I can't know for sure. Perhaps Fry's performance is another well-intentioned but sanitized portrait. Anyway, the truth of personality is, as we know, pluralistic, as are many other truths.

So the desire to have Wilde in the room, sitting in a chair, legs crossed, smoking a tipped cigarette, about to speak, must be the undertow in any meditation. If I can't fully imagine Wilde, there are available glimpses. I've seen photographs of cell c.3.3, with its high, recessed window, its thick door. Upon entering Reading Gaol, partway into his two-year sentence, Wilde was a ruined man. In his last letter to Bosie as a free man, on the eve of his conviction, he wrote, "It is perhaps in prison that I am going to test the power of love. I am going to see if I cannot make the bitter waters sweet by the intensity of the love I bear you." But in reality he was very nearly engulfed by those bitter waters. Prison and its "hard labour" almost killed him, both mentally and physically.

In fact, his sanity was only saved by a recently appointed and kindly governor of Reading Gaol, Major James Nelson (the appointment may have been the result of political pressure by Wilde's loyal friends). Nelson allowed Wilde to have a broad range of books (we have the list of Oscar's book requests) and, for the first time in eighteen months, writing materials beyond those permitted him for simple letter-writing. Now, in his cell during the winter evenings of early 1897, beneath the light of flaring gas jets, on a makeshift table constructed from a plank bed and two trestles, Wilde began to write his letter. We can partially see, in imagination, his broad back, his convict's garb, his prison-cropped hair.

Of course, *De Profundis* is a marred document. Some of it is based on misinformation (especially about Bosie's efforts to rescue Wilde), some of it is self-aggrandizing (Wilde's declarations of his own "genius"), much of it is lost in the fog of self-deception, and yet, everywhere, Wilde's love seeps through the litany of recrimination. At the end, he comes close to turning the bitter waters sweet.

From its opening lines, we hear the inimitable tone and see the direction of Wilde's missive. "Dear Bosie," Wilde says,

> Our ill-fated and most lamentable friendship has ended in ruin and public infamy for me, yet the memory of our ancient affection is often with me, and the thought that loathing, bitterness and contempt should forever take the place in my heart once held by love is very sad to me. . . .
>
> I have no doubt that in this letter which I have to write of your life and of mine . . . there will be much that will wound your vanity to the quick. If it prove so, read the letter over and over again till it kills your vanity. If you find in it something of which you are unjustly accused, remember that one should be thankful that there is any fault of which one can be unjustly accused. If there be in it one single passage that brings tears to your eyes, weep as we weep in prison where the day no less than the night is set apart for tears. It is the only thing that can save you. . . .
>
> Do you still say . . . that I "attribute unworthy motives" to you? Ah! You had no motives in life. You had appetites merely. A motive is an intellectual aim. That you were "very young" when our friendship began? Your defect was not that you knew so little about life, but that you knew so much. . . . With very swift and running feet you had passed from Romance to Realism. The gutter and the things that live in it had begun to fascinate you. That was the origin of the trouble in which you sought my aid.

Wilde is referring to the beginning of their friendship in 1892. They had actually met the previous year, when a young poet with whom Wilde had slept, Lionel Johnson, brought Bosie, his distant cousin and then a twenty-year-old student at Oxford, to Oscar's house, where Bosie was presented as another adoring reader of Wilde's novel *The Picture of Dorian Gray*. But the real relationship began when Wilde received a desperate message from Bosie at Oxford asking for Wilde's help. Bosie was being blackmailed by a young man; he was frantic and could think of no one other than Wilde as a person who might rescue him from the mess. It was Bosie's helplessness that perhaps first ignited the erotic spark for Wilde, as it was later Bosie's repeated and tearful pleas for forgiveness that overcame every attempt Wilde made to break off their affair. In any event, at the very outset, Bosie's blackmailing young bedmate was paid off by Oscar and Bosie was saved. Although Bosie's sexual interests were mostly confined to agemates and adolescents, his considerable experience in bed by the time he was twenty, and his pleasure in being adored by important people, meant that there were few obstacles to a relationship with Wilde that included Bosie's beautiful body. But now, writing his letter, Wilde is thinking of a different operation on Bosie's flesh.

In these early passages of *De Profundis*, Wilde urges Bosie to "read this letter straight through, though each word may become to you as the fire or knife of the surgeon that makes the delicate flesh burn or bleed . . . " Wilde reminds Bosie "that the fool to the eyes of the gods and the fool to the eyes of man are very different . . . The real fool, such as the gods mock or mar, is he who does not know himself. I was such a one too long. You have been such a one too long. Be so no more. Do not be afraid. The supreme vice is shallowness. Everything that is realised is right. Remember also that whatever is misery to you to read is still greater misery to me to set down."

Those two sentences, "The supreme vice is shallowness. Everything that is realised is right," is the mantra of the letter, repeated several times in its course. The first half, describing shallowness as the supreme vice, is principally applied to Bosie, and Wilde warns that the vice is often accompanied by a fatal defect of character, namely, lack of imagination, which is the insuperable barrier to love and the wellspring of hatred. The second, more mysterious half of the mantra, "everything that is realised is right," is Wilde's way of advocating, as he later puts it, the "frank acceptance of all experience," denying conventional measures of morality and insisting that the point of self-examination is not excoriation of sin but full recognition of, and responsibility for, one's acts.

Wilde says to Bosie, "I blame myself terribly. As I sit here in this dark cell in convict clothes, a disgraced and ruined man, I blame myself." This self-laceration is slightly disingenuous, since it launches the detailed litany of recriminations directed at Bosie and the recital of the history of bad scenes mainly caused by Bosie. But Wilde's relentless chewing over of the quarrels, bad scenes, and senseless arguments of their love affair is forgivable. In a sense, it's all he has. As Wilde himself writes later in the letter, the "wearisome iteration" of the story of their love "makes all sleep abandon me till dawn, and at dawn it begins again: it follows me into the prison yard and makes me talk to myself as I tramp around: each detail that accompanied each dreadful moment I am forced to recall: there is nothing that happened in those ill-starred years that I cannot recreate in that chamber of the brain which is set apart for grief or for despair: every strained note in your voice, every twitch and gesture of your nervous hands, every bitter mood, every poisonous phrase comes back to me." However, his rants against Bosie aside, Wilde's self-accusations are not entirely a rhetorical trope, and later in the letter they become pertinent.

II

The road to the depths of Reading Gaol was a descent from considerable familial, social, and artistic heights. Born in Dublin, Ireland, in 1854, Wilde was the son of a distinguished surgeon and, more importantly for his aesthetic sense, of a woman who was a revolutionary Irish nationalist poet, who wrote under the *nom de plume* Speranza.

Wilde attended Portora prep school, Trinity College, and Oxford, where for all his flouncing about, and for all his devotion to Aestheticism, as the emerging philosophy of the era was known, he nonetheless took a rare double first, in "moderns" and "greats" (or modern lit and classics), and won the Newdigate Prize for best undergraduate long poem. When Wilde says to Bosie, "There was too wide a gap between us. You had been idle at your school, worse than idle at your university," he's pointing to an actual intellectual divide between himself, the most brilliant of his generation of students at Oxford in the 1870s, and Bosie, two decades later, who was "sent down," as they say, without a degree at all.

Bosie hadn't been entirely idle at school, but his activities were, from mid-adolescence on, mostly focused on having in bed almost every schoolmate he wanted. Wilde would not have counted that a fault in Bosie, or anyone else, if it had not kept him from his books.

In the Wilde scandal, there was an explicit issue of class. Almost as shocking to the Victorian sensibility as the acts of which Wilde was accused was the revelation that he (and Bosie) consorted with working class and lumpenproletariat youths. Wilde regarded this disapprobation as pure British hypocrisy and even on his way to trial managed to quip, "The working classes are with me — to a boy." Among the objects of Wilde's affections were blackmailing rent boys, clerks and shop assistants who had risen from families of manual labourers, and aspiring artists of humble origins, none of whom, Wilde thought, ought to be disparaged for their intellects or habits. Instead Wilde made a distinction within his own social class between those Oxford youths with something on their minds and those who dissipated their promise with the pursuit of nothing more serious than games, the hunt, and other undergraduate frivolities. Bosie was, alas, for all his talents and his ability to turn a sonnet, among the latter group at the time of their love and, as it proved, long afterwards. That was the "too wide a gap" between them.

It might be, and has been, asked, what did Oscar see in Bosie? The extant photos of Bosie do not flatter him. He was, I should note, a particular type that many men have found sublimely attractive. His beauty was ethereal, delicate, and golden, almost but not effeminate, but in bed, from his mid-teens on, he was the active sodomist. The photos show Bosie slumped in fashionable ennui, wearing the uniform of his generation — blazer, white ducks, straw boater — faintly attractive, but hardly riveting. What we want to see (well, what I want to see) is the sort of picture made ubiquitous by twenty-first–century technology: Bosie in the altogether, the seemingly frail torso conjoined to a powerful lower body acquired in those field games at which he was surprisingly good. It's this mixture, this reversal of expectations, a dynamic of domination and submission, that is a source of ultimate desire for some men who love young men. In bed, Bosie was not unlike some of the rent boys in the streets that both Bosie and Oscar took to their bed, separately and together. When Wilde describes his adventures with these boys, he uses the phrase "feasting with panthers." One of Bosie's attractions was that, once out of his lamb-like haberdashery, he was really one of the panthers and, like some other panthers, one who enjoyed feasting with Oscar, especially since Oscar was paying for the feast.

It is sometimes asked, mistakenly I think, whether Bosie was really in love with Oscar. There's no doubt, based on all the evidence, that Oscar was in love with Bosie. But it's silly to ask if the range of emotions a twenty-one-year-old feels for a glamorous thirty-six-year-old man, which include intellectual and social dazzlement, the pride of being seen as "Oscar's boy," the certainty of forgiveness, the ability to rely on a father figure (as he wasn't able to rely on his unstable, mad, real father), and much else, constitute "love." It's enough to say that Bosie made himself available to Oscar, in bed and in companionship, that he was kept by Oscar, that he sometimes bored Oscar with his obsessive conversation about boys, but that in the long run he was loyal in his fashion, whether the loyalty was inspired by love or by a desire to maintain his self-image.

More interesting are Wilde's own sexual preferences and their possible relation to his proto-gay political interests, which is partly the focus of Neil McKenna's biography and one of the reasons that it is "new." According to the legend, Wilde's homosexual desires were first aroused some years earlier, in the mid-1880s, when he was over thirty, shortly after he had been married and fathered two sons. The source of the erotic flame was a seventeen-year-old Canadian, Robbie Ross, then living in England, the son of a deceased former solicitor-general of one of the Canadas. It was Ross, an apparently untroubled young homosexual, who unhesitatingly seduced Wilde, had a brief affair with him, became his friend, and who reappears much later in the story as Wilde's literary executor. He was followed by a series of equally presentable young men in Oscar's life right up to the appearance of the fatal Bosie.

Well, that's the legend. But as Wilde eventually told his friend Frank Harris, a journalist, editor, and well-known libertine himself, Wilde's "sex awakening," as he called it, had occurred in adolescence at prep school. He had "sentimental friendships" there, as was common among boys, and on the day of his leaving school, at the railway station, a boy a year younger than him, with whom he'd had endless walks and interminable conversations, came to the station to say his goodbyes. As the train for Dublin was about to depart, the boy suddenly turned and cried out, "Oh Oscar!" "Before I knew what he was doing he had caught my face in his hot hands and kissed me on the lips. The next moment he had slipped out the door and was gone." On the train, Oscar became aware of "cold, sticky drops" trickling down his face. They were the other boy's tears. "This is love," Wilde said to himself. "For a long while I sat, unable to think, all shaken with wonder and remorse."

Wilde was one of countless middle-class Victorian men, raised in the company of boys, who emerged into adult life sexually undefined and sought what was known as the "marriage cure." The matter was perhaps more urgent for Wilde in that his early fame came from a stylistic dandyism and aestheticism that included a foppishness in dress and manner, a kind of homosexual camp before its time. There were unwelcome insinuations of effeminacy that accompanied his devotion to a fantasy of the Greek mode of life and to art, a notion not so much of art for art's sake, as it's sometimes described, but a devotion to art because it was spiritually superior to life. In any case, Wilde married Constance Lloyd, dutifully fathered his sons, put rumours of sexual irregularities temporarily to rest, and began his career as a critic and essayist, but even as he walked through London's Piccadilly, where available rent boys loitered, he was not unaware of the icy splinter that rent his heart, as he put it.

With respect to Wilde's affections, it's only fair to mention that there is some biographical controversy over Wilde's relations with Constance. While biographer McKenna claims, with some evidence, that Wilde quickly recognized that he'd made a "terrible mistake" in getting married, partisans of Constance like to believe that Oscar truly loved her and deeply valued familial life. It's certainly true that even as Wilde was writing *De Profundis* in prison, he was still negotiating with Constance (now exiled on the Continent) and her lawyers about a possible reconciliation upon his release. Why not give Constance the benefit of the doubt, or at least credit her with living up to her name in matters personal and financial? She travelled all the way to prison to personally deliver to Wilde the news of his mother's death. Certainly there's no contradiction in the possibility that Wilde loved his wife and preferred to sleep with young men.

Up to the moment of his imprisonment, Wilde was the undoubted literary celebrity of his era. His name was spoken in the same breath as those of such late-Victorian contemporaries as Arthur Conan Doyle, Joseph Conrad, George Bernard Shaw, and Henry James. Wilde regarded the work of the latter as lugubrious; the distaste was mutual, since James thought Wilde's productions empty froth. But the point is that Wilde was taken seriously, and justly so. Wilde was, first of all, a brilliant literary critic whose essays, collected in an 1891 volume called *Intentions*, had offered an aesthetic theory which declared that art, far from merely *imitating* life, in fact *creates* life.

In 1891 he also published a controversial novel, *The Picture of Dorian Gray*, a book that worshipped the transient yet eternal beauty of youth, and that many, both devotees and the scandalized, took to be the introduction of homosexuality as subject matter into English-language literary works. As if the accomplishments of critic and novelist weren't enough, Wilde was, as well, the enchanting teller of tales and published two volumes of short stories that year, to go with two volumes of children's stories already in print, stories he had invented for his own sons.

Finally, 1891 was the year in which he wrote his debut play, *Lady Windermere's Fan*, the first in a series of successful drawing-room farces that were at the same time merciless satiric revelations of what really lay at the heart of respectable British social life. (Henry James was in the audience one night, hating every line of it, while his own debut play was bombing a couple of theatres over.) Wilde's *annus mirabilis* was one of the most remarkable literary debuts of the Victorian era. At the time of his arrest, four years later, in 1895, two of Wilde's hit comedies, *The Importance of Being Earnest* and *An Ideal Husband*, were both playing to packed audiences in London theatres. Wilde's claim in *De Profundis* that "the gods had given me almost everything. I had genius, a distinguished name, high social position . . . I made art a philosophy and philosophy an art," was no empty boast.

There was more. Perhaps Wilde's remark that he put his talent into his work, while he put his genius into his life, was intended to get people to notice the genius in his work as well, but the life was, indisputably, spectacular. Its props included gold-tipped opium-flavoured cigarettes; silver cigarette cases, which were casually distributed as gifts to the young panthers; much champagne, too much; late-night banquets; and the rumpled beds of expensive hotel suites, where the green carnations worn in one's lapel faded toward the dawn.

At the center of that life was Bosie, the son of Lord Queensberry. Bosie's sanest brother, Percy, was a Member of Parliament; his slightly older brother, Francis, Viscount Drumlanrig, was a protegé and most likely the boyfriend of Lord Rosebery, the foreign minister and later prime minister of England. The only personage we have to take note of here is Queensberry, who was decidedly not sane. A reactionary aristocrat, given to hunting, drinking, horses, boxing, and fits of violent, frothing rage, he was vulgar in manner and speech, had two broken marriages behind him, and, fatally for Wilde, became fixated upon the friendships of his sons, Drumlanrig and Bosie, with, respectively, Lord Rosebery and Oscar Wilde.

After demands and threats of physical violence that both relationships be permanently ended, Drumlanrig died in his mid-twenties by gunshot wound, most likely a suicide. Queensberry then pursued Wilde, hounding him from restaurant to theatre to club. It was at Wilde's club that Queensberry left his card, "To Oscar Wilde, posing as a sodomite," or possibly, "To Oscar Wilde, ponce and sodomite," but in either case, with "sodomite" misspelled. That was the action that precipitated the denouement of the affair and led Wilde, urged on by a ferocious Bosie, anxious for revenge on his father, and against the advice of every sensible friend, to launch an ill-considered criminal libel suit against Queensberry. Wilde lost the suit and was promptly charged with "gross indecency," and while the first trial ended in a hung jury, at his second trial he was easily convicted. There is some evidence, cited by McKenna, that the vigour of the prosecution against Wilde was inspired by Queensberry's threats to expose others in the government of the day, a damaging political prospect.

III

One of the mysteries of Wilde's life, investigated by friends and biographers ever since, is why he let himself be inveigled into the disastrous suit. There were, of course, some misperceptions and some hubris on Wilde's part. It was not until *De Profundis* that Wilde realized that "all trials are trials of one's life, just as all sentences are sentences of death." He at first thought the trial would be a literary affair, that it would be an urbane debate about the morality or otherwise of his writings — *Dorian Gray*, a few poems in praise of "Greek love," a purloined, purplish love letter or two — and he thought he could easily disarm his opponents and tormenters. He may have thought he was untouchable, a delusion no one should entertain, not even the author of *The Importance of Being Earnest*.

But Queensberry was playing by his own, more pragmatic, set of rules, later enshrined to regulate the barbarities of the sport of boxing. In preparing his defence of justification, Queensberry hired private detectives at considerable cost, and they, without much difficulty, turned up a posse of rent boys who had dallied with Oscar; a brothel and its proprietor, who was charged along with Wilde; and even the linen maids from various hotels, who testified as to the condition of the sheets, upon which, they claimed, were found semen, lubricant, and "soil." The reliability of much of the evidence is shaky — the boys were clearly coerced, threatened with prosecution, and paid off, and no doubt many of the acts attributed to Wilde belonged to Bosie, whose name was carefully left out of the court proceedings at the wishes of both Wilde and Bosie's mad father — but that's immaterial.

It's not until you reread *De Profundis* that this crazy act of self-destruction becomes comprehensible. At every turn, the answer is Wilde's love for Bosie, which may be a thing beyond comprehension. Wilde himself says, "For my own sake, there was nothing to do but to love you." After the initial passages of *De Profundis*, Wilde settles in to a lengthy literal accounting of his affair with Bosie — literal in the sense that it comes down to shillings and pence and includes a description of a bizarre week-long gambling holiday in Monte Carlo just before Wilde's trial that Bosie had insisted on when Oscar should have been consulting his lawyers.

The account of their sweet-bitter relationship takes up half or more of Wilde's letter. Wilde writes, "I gave up to you always. As a natural result . . . your claims . . . your exactions grew more and more unreasonable. Your meanest motive, your lowest appetite, your most common passions, became to you laws . . ." Wilde is the hunted stag when he cries out, "At the one supremely and tragically critical moment of all my life, just before my lamentable step of beginning my absurd action, on the one side there was your father attacking me with hideous cards left at my club, on the other side there was you attacking me with no less loathsome letters . . . Between you both I had lost my head. My judgment forsook me. Terror took its place. I saw no possible escape, I may say frankly, from either of you." If not a hunted stag, then, as Wilde says, "Blindly I staggered as an ox to the shambles." And when you read these passages, you may find yourself saying, as I do, Yes, I can see how it might have happened, how Wilde ended up risking all.

As for the second mystery, why Wilde did not flee to the Continent, either just before his arrest or when, between his two trials, he was on bail, the answer is explicitly given in the letter Oscar wrote to Bosie on May 20, 1895, in the midst of the trial that would almost certainly convict him. Wilde writes, "I decided that it was nobler and more beautiful to stay. We could not have been together. I did not want to be called a coward or a deserter." This is the effusive love letter in which Wilde also says, "It is perhaps in prison that I am going to test the power of love. I am going to see if I cannot make the bitter waters sweet by the intensity of the love that I bear you." Since "noble" was a term regularly used in defence of "Greek love," Wilde's more recent biographers argue, I think rather persuasively, that Wilde's decision to stay, was a political act on behalf of "the Cause," which was another of the many names of the Love that dare not speak its name. Wilde also says that to stay is "more beautiful," which is reasonably read as part of a self-conception that embraces martyrdom on behalf of his love of Bosie. Of course, the mood of *De Profundis*, written almost two years after the love letter penned on the eve of prison, was considerably more experienced.

In the passage of *De Profundis* where Wilde offers one of several summations of his life, the passage beginning "The gods had given me everything," he goes on to say, "I treated art as the supreme reality and life as a mere mode of fiction ... I summed up all systems in a phrase and all existence in an epigram ... Tired of being on the heights, I deliberately went to the depths in the search for new sensations. What the paradox was to me in the sphere of thought, perversity became to me in the sphere of passion ... I grew careless of the lives of others. I took pleasure where it pleased me, and passed on. I forgot that every little action of the common day makes or unmakes character ... I ended in horrible disgrace. There is only one thing for me now, absolute humility ... Now I find hidden somewhere in my nature something that tells me that nothing in the whole world is meaningless, and suffering least of all. That something hidden away in my nature, like a treasure in a field, is humility ... It is the last thing left in me, and the best: the ultimate discovery at which I have arrived."

Wilde's concept of humility provides the transition to his meditation on Christ as Artist, of which I only want to cite a few lines. "Humility in the artist," says Wilde, "is his frank acceptance of all experience just as love in the artist is simply his sense of beauty that reveals to the world its body and its soul." Wilde continues, "I see a far more intimate and immediate connection between the true life of Christ and the true life of the artist ... the very basis of his nature was the same as that of the nature of the artist — an intense and flame-like imagination. He realised in the entire sphere of human relations *that* imaginative sympathy which in the sphere of Art is the sole secret of creation." Wilde adds, "In reading the Gospels" — which he calls "four prose poems about Christ" and which he was reading in his cell in Greek — "I see the continual assertion of the imagination as the basis of all spiritual and material life. I see also that to Christ imagination was simply a form of love, and that to him

love was lord in the fullest meaning of the phrase." I'm not necessarily recommending Wilde's aesthetics here, but simply citing
his notion of imagination as the beginning of love as a clue to
understanding why Wilde's contemporaries took him seriously
as a man with something more on his mind than his ceaseless
stream of cutting epigrams and alluring paradoxes.

Wilde writes at the conclusion of *De Profundis*, "Of course to
one so modern as I am, *enfant de mon siecle*, merely to look at
the world will be always lovely. I tremble with pleasure when I
think that on the very day of my leaving prison both the labur-
num and the lilac will be blooming in the garden." To Bosie, he
says, "I will, if I feel able, arrange through Robbie [Ross] to meet
you in some quiet foreign town like Bruges, where grey houses
and green canals and cool still ways had a charm for me years
ago." And, in the last lines, he reflects, "How far I am away from
the true temper of the soul, this letter in its changing uncertain
moods, its scorn and bitterness, its aspirations and its failure to
reach those aspirations, shows you quite clearly. But do not forget in what a terrible school I am sitting at my task. And incom-
plete, imperfect, as I am, yet from me you may have still much to
gain. You came to me to learn the pleasure of life and the pleasure of art. Perhaps I am chosen to teach you something much
more wonderful — the meaning of sorrow and its beauty. Your
affectionate friend, Oscar Wilde."

There is much more in *De Profundis*. I think all of it is worth
reading — the story of the love affair; Wilde's reflections on art
and artists, including Christ; the idea of humility he propounds
toward the end; even his deluded hopes of a reunion with Bosie.

IV

On the evening in May 1897 that Wilde left Reading Gaol, to be
transported to London for release the next morning, Major Nelson was at the gate and handed Wilde a bulky package. Although
Wilde was not permitted to send it before his release, Nelson had
saved Wilde's pages and, upon his departure, returned to him
the manuscript of *De Profundis*.

It was this large envelope that Wilde handed to Robbie Ross

a few days later when he arrived by the night ferry at Dieppe, where he would spend his first days of freedom. He had already instructed Ross, in a letter that we possess, to make two typed copies of *De Profundis* — typed copies were still a newfangled technical advance in 1897, and he assured Ross that listening to the typist was no more painful than hearing one's sister practise the piano in the next room. Once the copies were prepared, one for Wilde and one for Ross as Oscar's literary executor, the original was to be sent to Bosie, who was somewhere nearby on the Continent. The typing wasn't finished until August, and Ross sent one of the typed copies to Bosie, wisely retaining the handwritten original. Bosie, though urged in the letter to read it again and again if need be, stayed true to character and didn't read it at all. Or perhaps he read a few pages and threw it in the river Marne as he once claimed.

In any case, by early autumn, despite the admonitions of friends, solicitors, and all others, Oscar and Bosie were living together in a small villa outside Naples, at Posillipo. It lasted about three or four months, but the myth of their love quickly wore off for both of them, and they may have been happy when economic necessity forced them apart. Both Wilde's wife and Bosie's mother cut off their respective allowances once the women learned they were together again, attended by the sunnier Italian version of English panthers. But well before that, Wilde had evidence that time eroded beauty more completely than prison destroyed the body or mind.

At Posillipo, Wilde polished a final version of *The Ballad of Reading Gaol*, which he'd mainly conceived in prison. It was published to some acclaim under the signature of his cell number, "c.3.3," but everyone knew it was by Wilde. It is considered one of Wilde's great works, and its famous refrain is still occasionally recited: "And all men kill the thing they love, / By all let this be heard, / Some do it with a bitter look, / Some with a flattering word, / The coward does it with a kiss, / The brave man with a sword!" I tend to prefer, among Wilde's poems, the more economical "Harlot's House." It was a favourite of my poetry teacher, Jack Spicer, who often made me read it to him (so he could hear the words aloud), and it served as my introduction to Wilde:

We caught the tread of dancing feet,
We loitered down the moonlit street,
And stopped beneath the harlot's house.

Inside, above the din and fray,
We heard the loud musicians play
The "Treues Liebes Herz" of Strauss.

Like strange mechanical grotesques,
Making fantastic arabesques,
The shadows raced across the blind.

We watched the ghostly dancers spin
To sound of horn and violin,
Like black leaves wheeling in the wind.

Like wire-pulled automatons,
Slim silhouetted skeletons
Went sidling through the slow quadrille.

They took each other by the hand,
And danced a stately saraband;
Their laughter echoed thin and shrill.

Sometimes a clockwork puppet pressed
A phantom lover to her breast,
Sometimes they seemed to try to sing.

Sometimes a horrible marionette
Came out, and smoked its cigarette
Upon the steps like a live thing.

Then, turning to my love, I said,
"The dead are dancing with the dead,
The dust is whirling with the dust."

But she — she heard the violin,
And left my side, and entered in:
Love passed into the house of lust.

Then suddenly the tune went false,
The dancers wearied of the waltz,
The shadows ceased to wheel and whirl.

And down the long and silent street,
The dawn, with silver-sandalled feet,
Crept like a frightened girl.

Though my teacher Spicer taught me to favour this nightmare of love to the more celebrated funereal ballad, in any case, *The Ballad of Reading Gaol* proved to be Wilde's last literary work. Though there were increasingly faint attempts in his last three years, apart from correspondence, often to beg money, Wilde never wrote again.

When Wilde and Bosie parted, Wilde went off to visit the homoerotic photographer Baron Wilhelm von Gloeden, who was based in Taormina, Sicily, and Bosie continued to traipse around Europe before ending his exile and returning to England. The two of them saw each other from time to time, but were more enamoured of the legend of their past love than their present casual friendship.

Wilde's wife Constance died in 1898, so Wilde's allowance was restored, but it was never enough for him to live in more than an increasingly alcoholic penury. Queensberry died in early 1900, and Wilde himself died at the end of November 1900 in Paris. And, of course, Queen Victoria's death in 1901 made way for Edwardian and Georgian moments in a new century. Robbie Ross was at Wilde's deathbed; Bosie was the chief mourner at the funeral.

It was Ross who took charge of Wilde's estate and literary remains with both skill and care. In 1905 he took Wilde's long letter from Reading Gaol and gave it the title *De Profundis* (Wilde originally titled it *Epistola: In Carcere et Vinculus*, "Letter: In Jail and Chains"). More important for his purposes, Ross removed absolutely all reference to Bosie, edited it down to about a third of its original length, and saw to its publication, the publication whose centenary was marked in 2005. And there the matter might have remained. Ross went on to edit several volumes of *Collected Works* that were published three years later, in 1908; Wilde's literary reputation was posthumously restored, thanks to the diligent Robbie; and Wilde's sparkling plays again amused audiences on London stages. In 1909, Ross deposited the original of *De Profundis* in the British Museum with instructions that it be sealed for fifty years. However, there's one more turn to this little bibliographic tale.

A few years later, in 1912, a writer named Arthur Ransome produced a biography of Wilde. Indeed, bios of Oscar had started appearing as early as two years after his death. But Ransome, who knew Ross, had seen Robbie's copy of Wilde's letter and very obliquely referred to it and to Bosie, in a single line, without naming him, as someone who might be thought of as the source of Wilde's painful prison woes. Bosie was still around — he would live a very long and undistinguished life, not expiring until 1945, at age seventy-five. Between Wilde's death in 1900 and the appearance of Ransome's biography in 1912, Bosie had undergone a transformation. He renounced the Love that dare not speak its name, converted to Catholicism, and married, though it only lasted for a few years, but long enough to have a child (who came to an unhappy end in a mental institution). In general, Bosie, who was really no longer Bosie but Lord Alfred, dabbled at various not-quite-occupations.

As is well-known, hell hath no fury like an apostate of an older creed who has been born again in the Church. By age forty-two, Bosie had acquired much of the temperament and litigious habits of his late father, and not a little of Queensberry's madness. Upon hearing of the passing reference to himself in Ransome's biography, Bosie promptly sued for libel, Ransome offered justification as a defence, and that's how it came about that Wilde's letter was retrieved from the dust of the British Museum, brought to court, and read aloud. A servant of the Crown, i.e. a judge, rather than a servant of the Muse, the shade of Oscar, compelled Bosie to listen to a text that offered a coruscating portrait of his soul, as thoroughly revealing as *The Picture of Dorian Gray*. The jury promptly found Ransome not guilty of libel, and Bosie went on his erratic way, the tedious details of which can be left aside. *De Profundis* was not released to the public in a reliable, unexpurgated edition until the early 1960s, but that this remarkable work has reached us at all we can mainly credit to Robbie Ross.

V

At Wilde's first trial in April 1895, the prosecutor cited two clearly homosexual poems by Alfred Douglas, including "Two Loves," in which the narrator finds two youths in a garden, and asks one of them:

What is thy name? He said, 'My name is Love.' / Then straight the first [the other youth] did turn himself to me / And cried, 'He lieth, for his name is Shame / But I am Love, and I was wont to be / Alone in this fair garden, till he came / Unasked by night; I am true Love, I fill / The hearts of boy and girl with mutual flame.' / Then sighing, said the other, 'Have thy will, / I am the Love that dare not speak its name.'

The prosecutor turned to Wilde in the witness box. "What is the 'Love that dare not speak its name'?" he asked. And Wilde, who in the face of the testimony of rent boys, linen maids, and the rest had been forced into lies, denial, and shifts, suddenly found his voice. He replied,

The "Love that dare not speak its name" in this century is such a great affection of an elder for a younger man as there was between David and Jonathan, such as Plato made the very basis of his philosophy, and such as you find in the sonnets of Michelangelo and Shakespeare. It is that deep, spiritual affection that is as pure as it is perfect ... It is in this century misunderstood, so much misunderstood that it may be described as the "Love that dare not speak its name," and on account of it I am placed where I am now. It is beautiful, it is fine, it is the noblest form of affection. There is nothing unnatural about it. It is intellectual, and it repeatedly exists between an elder and a younger man, when the elder man has intellect, and the younger man has all the joy, hope and glamour of life before him. That it should be so the world does not understand. The world mocks at it and sometimes puts one in the pillory for it.

For once, Wilde spoke not wittily but well, Wilde's biographer Richard Ellman notes. As one of Wilde's friends, Max Beerbohm, who attended the trial, described the scene, "Oscar has been quite superb. His speech about the Love that dares not tell his name was simply wonderful and carried the whole court quite away, quite a tremendous burst of applause. Here was this man, who had been for a month in prison and loaded with insults and crushed and buffeted, perfectly self-possessed, dominating the Old Bailey with his fine presence and musical voice. He has never had so great a triumph, I am sure, as when the gallery burst into applause."

Wilde's defense is straight out of his reading of Plato's *Symposium*, but there's a misunderstanding, I believe, about "Platonic love." As the prosecutor intimated when the applause was shushed, surely this *apologia* could not also apply to relations with rent boys. The misunderstanding is that Platonic love is chaste. Though its emphasis is on the spiritual aspect of such a love, and though it could be thoroughly debased, the Love that dare not speaks its name is also sexual and, yes, might even be applied to rent boys, though Wilde generally preferred to provide material gifts of silver cigarette cases to his panthers.

If we had no other evidence, that speech would be enough to establish Wilde's claim as the first modern homosexual. In addition to Wilde's philosophical advocacy of the imagination, and his articulated style of life (rather than mere lifestyle, as we have it today), there is his writing, which brought homosexuality for the first time into literary discourse in English, and his variegated erotic adventures, his feasting with panthers. What makes the claim modern, I think, is that it is sealed by a public political speech in defence of the naturalness of a form of homosexual love.

This is not to confuse the modernity of Wilde's homosexuality with "Modernism." Although Wilde is casually included in the standard text, Malcolm Bradbury and James McFarlane's *Modernism* (1976), perhaps on the strength of his French-language play *Salomé* and his relations with poets like Mallarmé, he is probably more accurately thought of in literary terms as a Late Victorian Romantic, and he himself used the term Romance in opposition to mid-nineteenth-century Realism. When modernism emerged in the early twentieth century in the work of Proust,

Joyce, Pound, and Eliot, Wilde's epigone didn't understand it and generally hated it.

But with respect to sex and politics, we have considerable evidence, as laid out in the most recent biographic work about Wilde, of something that we can call a proto-gay political movement in England, of which Wilde was a conscious member, and whose political aim was the repeal of the "gross indecency" law of 1885, under which Wilde was convicted. Wilde knew the work of John Addington Symonds, who had written about "Greek love" in the 1890s; he had exchanged frank conversation and a kiss with Walt Whitman, whom he had visited on his American tour in the 1880s; he was a friend of George Ives, who founded a secret gay order in the 1890s and went on for three decades to campaign discreetly but openly against the "gross indecency" law.

Wilde was also aware of the work of the German theorist Karl Ulrichs, who in the last third of the nineteenth century offered a complete defence, up to and including marriage, of what he called Uranian love, the name taken from the Platonic notion of Uranos or heavenly love. Uranian was one of the many names — along with Greek love, the Cause, and others — by which the Love that dare not speak its name went. The word "homosexual" had already been invented in the late 1860s and was coming into use. In Berlin in 1896–97, as Wilde languished in jail, the first formal gay rights organization, the Scientific-Humanitarian Committee, was founded by a gay sex researcher, Dr. Magnus Hirschfeld, who was associated with the psychiatric circles of Sigmund Freud. So I think it's fair to say, as biographer Neil McKenna does, that "Oscar's place in the history of the small but courageous band of men who strove to bring about the legal and social emancipation of men who loved men has rarely been acknowledged."

Nonetheless, there's an irony to be observed a century or more later. "The Love that dare not speak its name," which Wilde eloquently defended at his trial in 1895, the love of men for young men and adolescents (male youths from mid-teens to early twenties), the love whose name is also pederasty, is in our era, in which homosexuality has become a public fact, still the Love that dare not speak its name, even among homosexuals. In an age when homosexuality has succeeded in becoming "the loving union of two people," the other Love, the one that dare not speak its name, remains an embarrassment, an unease, and a source of "bad publicity" among gays; it's a near-crime within the law (especially in the most recent Canadian law of "sexual exploitation" as it applies to relations between adults and youths); and it is often classified as a form of "child abuse" by legions of psychologists and the ever-present evil media. The practices of that Love, more than a century after Wilde's death, are almost as furtive now as then. It is intellectually spoken of, and gossiped about, only among the initiates, but is permitted, now as then, an underground commercial existence since we live in an even more relentlessly commercial culture than that of England at the end of the Victorian era. Though Wilde's defense of the Love that dare not speak its name is taken today as a general statement about homosexuality, its actual definition is more specific.

The story of the gay movement and social life, from Wilde's day to now, is increasingly available to us. It is uninterruptedly chronicled in works such as George Chauncey's *Gay New York: Gender, Urban Culture, and the Making of the Gay Male World, 1890–1940* (1994) and Matt Houlbrook's *Queer London: Perils and Pleasures in the Sexual Metropolis, 1918-1957* (2005). There is an historical anthropology, which includes such representative books as Gary Leupp's *Male Colors: The Construction of Homosexuality in Tokugawa Japan* (1995) and Khaled El-Rouayheb's *Before Homosexuality in the Arab-Islamic World, 1500-1800* (2005). As well, the bibliography of gay literature since Stonewall, the 1969 marker of contemporary "gay liberation," is voluminous. We have passed from the homophile movements in the 1950s and '60s, which finally saw the repeal of legislation like the "gross indecency" law and its equivalents in countries around the world, to the gay liberation movement and beyond.

What I'm interested in is how to conceptualize the present situation — not so much to propose a political agenda as to understand where we are. In contrast to Marx's famous dictum that rather than merely understanding the world, we need to change it, I remind myself that first we do have to understand it if we want to change it. My current conceptualization is based on another Marxist notion, one usually applied to economic affairs, known as the Law of Uneven Development. I think the Law of

Uneven Development can also be applied to cultural circumstances, such as the status of homosexuality. The idea is simple: what we find in the economic world at one and the same time are completely different ways or modes of producing things, so that feudalism, raw capitalism, social democracy, and other forms of production all exist simultaneously and can only be explained by examining the specific historical circumstances, cultures, and power structures of particular nations. I think something similar holds for how we might think about homosexuality.

What I see, and I'm intentionally oversimplifying, is a tripartite global situation. In various countries, which I'll call pre-gay, homosexuality is still illegal, is often punishable by death, and cannot be spoken of, much less named. Yet in all of these pre-gay places there is a considerable amount of homosexual activity. It generally takes three forms: traditional pederasty operating within well-understood but unspoken conventions; sexual relations, often involving specifically designated categories of effeminate men; and, in countries that are visited by global travellers, sex tourism. Though some of the participants in those acts, usually the "top" or active partner, certainly doesn't think of himself as a homosexual or gay or whatever, and doesn't even think of the act he's participating in as homosexual or gay or whatever — rather they think of themselves simply as "men," and they think of active anal intercourse merely as "sex" — nonetheless, we would register all of this as homosexual sex between males. What isn't permitted in contemporary pre-gay societies is discourse about homosexuality, and in that sense it literally remains a relation that dare not speak its name.

In other countries — the United States is a prime example — they're still in the midst of gay struggles. Religious denunciations of homosexuality, referenda banning gay marriage, rollbacks of anti-discrimination laws addressing sexual preference all jostle with gay characters on TV, commercial gay pornography, increasing and/or declining public sympathy for various gay causes. But the US, in the midst of a strange period of religious revivalism, to say nothing of bellicosity, is clearly still in the gay struggle mode. Other countries, such as Thailand, present a more hybrid situation that combines traditional pre-gay modes with sex tourism and a vigorous debate about the conceptualization of modern gay identities.

Then there are countries like Canada, as well as various countries in Europe, that I would describe as post-gay or post-queer. In these countries, being gay is no longer a contested identity, legislation has been passed that protects gay human rights up to and including gay marriage, and public sentiment has clearly moved to the side of people who identify themselves as gay — if they feel the need to identify themselves in sexual terms at all. Indeed, in post-gay societies, work on self-identity tends to move in directions that make the notion of "gay" somewhat obsolete, as reflected in the discussions of the last decade over the use of the term "queer."

All these modes of homosexuality exist simultaneously and, using a loose notion of the law of uneven development, can be traced to specific cultural histories, but post-gay is the term that makes people, particularly those who have been involved in the history of gay struggles, uneasy. People working in gay organizations and gay-oriented businesses may fear that their activism and jobs will be terminated as a result of the political and social success suggested by the term "post-gay." But I don't think that's the case, even if we recognize a notion of post-gay.

First, it really is important to know when to declare victory; otherwise one tediously lives in a past that no longer exists or, worse, persists in a tribalism that is already all too prevalent in the world. Second, the law of uneven development doesn't apply only to entire cultures, but operates differentially within countries. So while post-gay clearly obtains in places like Vancouver, Toronto, or Montreal, in various provinces, and in various specific communities, the issue of being gay or queer remains problematic, and "coming out" is still a major personal event.

Third, and finally, the condition of post-gay doesn't mean that there's nothing to do. As we know too well, crimes like gay bashing continue to occur; anti-gay organizations like the Canadian branch of the US-based Focus on the Family continue to press for repeal of rights; and the plight of various individuals, such as teenagers in regressive school-board districts, is an abiding concern. Furthermore, even when we've achieved a post-gay condition, it doesn't mean it can't be reversed. And one more sociological point: given that homosexuality looks like a more or less permanent minority preference, in which there are ongoing concerns about finding like-minded or like-desiring people, or finding support in the development of one's own identity, whether as a teenager or as an adult in particular communities, it ensures there is no "end of gay" in post-gay. Although the Love that dare not speak its name, as Wilde meant it, is perhaps doomed to marginalization, the Love that just won't shut up, as we jokingly dare to describe it today, will continue to be heard.

■

As Oscar Wilde remarked at the author's curtain call on the opening night of *Lady Windermere's Fan* in 1892, when he appeared onstage smoking a cigarette (the only act of his public or private life that would be more shocking to us today than it was to his Victorian audience), "Ladies and Gentlemen, I have enjoyed this evening *immensely*. The actors have given us a *charming* rendering of a *delightful* play, and your appreciation has been most intelligent. I congratulate you on the *great* success of your performance, which persuades me that you think *almost* as highly of the play as I do myself."

After

Sonnet About Orpheus
(Scar)

It wasn't so much
the body of Orpheus
that the furious women
tore to pieces   rather

the mind of Orpheus
scattered like a broken mirror
among the talking trees
The body is precise

as a scar
just below the knee
(tricycle crash, age six)
the mind a blank

this close to hell
the story splits
one part, the song, borne in the blood
the other, his severed head, carried by the stream.

The Translators

The Toronto *Globe and Mail* reported that the two men, translators in Tirana, Albania, had shared "a tiny, Spartan office" in the state publishing house for most of the previous twenty-two years. That detail particularly fascinated me. "Behind battered typewriters," the article by Paul Koring said, perhaps a bit melodramatically, "they have battled to keep fragments of literature alive in the darkness of Stalinist orthodoxy."

The story had been published a few months earlier, in April 1991. Reading the brief account of the two now middle-aged men, one wondered the simplest things. How had they spent their time? What did they talk about? Keep necessarily silent about? What loyalties had caused them to persevere? How had they maintained their sanity? — for it seemed an ultimate test of sanity. It was something like those stories one occasionally ran into decades ago, in which a pair of Japanese soldiers emerged from a jungle in Burma or Java twenty years after the end of World War II, never having heard that it had ended.

In the case of Mr. Simoni and Mr. Qesku — those were their names — the endurance had been similar, but the cause was rather more recognizable to us. The convulsions that swept away regimes across Europe, from Warsaw to Bucharest, in the late 1980s had at last, in 1991, reached the hills of what was once ancient Illyria. And blinking into the uncertain sunlight — for it was hardly clear that our vaunted free markets would provide a panacea for their woes — there appeared the translators of Tirana, having, you could say, kept the faith. It was a faith that transcended the generations-long remoteness that shrouded their land. Albania was not a Burmese jungle nor an island in the Indies, but a southern European nation wedged between Greece and what was then Yugoslavia. It was a mere eighty kilometres across the Adriatic from Bari or Brindisi in Italy. Yet for all that, it might have been as distant as the moon, so successfully and for so long had its Glorious Leader, Enver Hoxha, sealed it off as the last and purest bastion of Communism.

•

That spring and summer I was in Berlin, thinking about the fall of Communism (it was more than a year since the opening of the Berlin Wall), reading a little philosophy (the subject I teach at a college in Vancouver), and pursuing the amorous adventures that leisurely evenings in bars and cafés sometimes yielded — in about that order.

I was often to be found at a table in the Café Einstein in the late afternoons, engrossed, like many of the other patrons, in a book or newspaper. Though it was something of a reading-list staple when I went to school, somehow I had never gotten around to Joseph Conrad's *Heart of Darkness*. Or perhaps I had and had merely read it carelessly as a student — since, upon taking it up now, it seemed both fresh and yet strangely familiar to me.

As I began (or began again) Conrad's tale of a journey to what had once seemed like the ends of the earth, it called up the ideas I had about Albania. My interest in Albania had been inspired by the brief newspaper story about the translators I'd read earlier that spring. In fact, I'd clipped the article and tucked it into the back of my notebook.

I never really admitted to my friends in Berlin that I intended to go to Albania. At most, I'd say something casual and indirect like "I wonder if it's possible to fly to Tirana from here?" But I made the necessary phone calls, inquired at a travel agency, checked the airline office. One day I got my friend Manuel to accompany me to the Albanian consulate in east Berlin, only to find the dilapidated building locked and to be informed by a caretaker that I needed to contact the office in Bonn.

My method — to use a word that appears prominently in Conrad's tale — was circuitous at best. Indeed, it was a sort of game that I called "following the story," in which one set certain events in motion, or created the possibility of setting them in motion, by some ordinary but deliberate act — reading a book, walking a certain route, going to a particular place. And if something happened as a consequence, the challenge then — the whole point of the game, really — was to attend to the ensuing possibilities in such a way that the pattern of meanings we call a story resulted.

Reading the opening pages of Conrad's story, I found it easy to identify with its narrator, Marlow, the veteran sailor who was making his way about Brussels to secure a posting on a Congo riverboat of the Belgian trading company that, for all practical purposes, ruled that distant African land. I too had been to sea. As I read — while at the same time arranging my own curious journey — Albania seemed as distant as Marlow's destination, and Comrade Enver Hoxha, who had ruled it, was a figure as forbidding as Kurtz, the god-man who gradually becomes Marlow's obsession.

Of course I was aware of the cliché of reading Conrad in this way. The "heart of darkness" was everybody's metaphor, and virtually anyone who travelled to what might be regarded as an obscure corner of the earth invoked it. But there was nothing I could do about it. If you're a reader, sooner or later you read Conrad, and by happenstance, I was reading *Heart of Darkness* at exactly that moment.

In the end, I found myself filling out a visa application for Albania while seated at a table in the Café Einstein. I was in the high-ceilinged room of the villa that overlooked the café garden, which was almost empty that afternoon. Even the garden's tame sparrows, who hopped up on tables to filch a stray crumb of *Apfelkuchen*, had flown off. Wettest, coldest June in memory, the German tabloids moaned, along with the requisite references to climate change and other weather disturbances. And still chilly, even into July. The black-jacketed waiters moved among the bundled-up patrons at a glacial pace, carrying hot drinks on sterling trays.

When I asked my friends, in the studiedly casual voice I'd adopted, "I wonder if it's possible to fly to Tirana from here?" they invariably replied, with barely restrained politeness, "But why would you want to go there?" Or else they would fail to hear me correctly, thinking perhaps, since I was a Canadian, that I had said, "Toronto," and they would make me repeat the name of the Albanian capital. Then they, who had been almost everywhere, would quizzically repeat it themselves — "Tirana?" — in the slightly bemused tones reserved for impossibly distant places or vanished cities of the past.

Sometimes they would attempt to dissuade me by pointing out the difficulties of acquiring a visa. "I phoned," I'd report. "To Bonn, of course," one of them assumed. "To Tirana," I said. "You can phone Tirana?" they asked, warily. "Easier than east Berlin," I replied, drawing a wan smile from my friends for all the times we'd tried to make an appointment across the once-divided city.

The Albanian attaché in Bonn suggested that I needed an invitation from someone in Tirana in order to complete my visa application. When I asked him if he happened to have the number of the state publishing house there, he supplied it, and soon after I attempted to phone Simoni, one of the men mentioned in the newspaper story. After bursts of static on the line and a babble of languages (Albanian, English, German, Italian), then a long pause (he had been walking down a flight of stairs), I was speaking to the man himself. Simoni promised to send a note of invitation. And thus I "followed the story," even as I was following other stories. If the invitation from Tirana arrives, if mail service from Tirana even exists, I told myself, then I guess I'll get some snapshots from the machine at the train station to stick on the application form. And indeed, one by one, each of the items appeared, until at last I signed my name in the Café Einstein and sent the papers off.

A few nights later, while I was in the bath, the phone rang. Annoyed, and dripping down the hallway, I picked up the phone to be told by the Albanian attaché in Bonn — unusual that he should be working on a Saturday evening, I marvelled — that my visa had been approved.

In the post, along with the appropriately stamped papers, he sent me a picture postcard. I didn't know what to make of such an unbureaucratic gesture. It was a picture of an ancient boy's head, marble, from Apollonia, one of the places down the Adriatic coast that the Greeks had set up in the fifth century or so BCE. "Best wishes," the postcard said.

I was on the SwissAir Berlin-Zurich-Tirana flight, with a date to meet the two translators at 7 PM at the base of the Skanderbeg statue in the town square. I hastily acquired the necessary background from *Eastern Europe on a Shoestring*. Skanderbeg, the potted history tersely informed me, fifteenth-century warlord; castle in the hills at a place called Kruje, a bit north of Tirana; fought the Turks twenty times, never beaten. National hero. Once Skanderbeg was out of the way, it was the Ottoman Turks for the next five hundred years. Succeeded by King Zog, then the Fascists, and finally by the Glorious Leader, Comrade Hoxha.

I don't know what I was after. Oh, to find Simoni and Qesku, certainly. And to find out how a country in the middle of Europe could more or less disappear from the face of the earth for half a century. But I also wanted to know what was there. We in the "West" had ignored Albania, even though it, too, was located within Western civilization. I wanted to make up for an inexplicable oversight on our part. Sure, Albania had been sealed off for god knows how long, but was that sufficient excuse for our failure to consider it? Marlow's celebrated utterance (I'd tossed my copy of *Heart of Darkness* into my bag) echoed in my mind: "And this, also, has been one of the dark places of the earth."

So I had a rendezvous. But first there were the "pilgrims," to use Conrad's term. I mean, if I could think of it, then surely the business pilgrims would already be figuring out how to turn a dollar in post-Communist Albania. He was a Swiss engineer, named Weber. Boarded at Zurich. Some Texans were seated in front of us. As soon as we were up, Weber had a powerful thirst. By the descent, he had persuaded the flight attendant to sell him some cans of beer in a paper bag. But he knew the country, I had to give him that.

When Weber wasn't courting the woman in the window seat, I asked him the usual traveller's questions. I'd heard of the Hotel Tirana. No, the Dajti, he firmly recommended. Reservations? No problem, he'd fix it up if it came to that. And was there a bus into town from the airport? *Kein Problem*, I could ride in with him. Hail fellow, well met. Well lubricated too, by the time we were on the ground in Albania.

The airport was a patch of cement in the countryside. It was thirty degrees Celsius at 4 PM. By the time I was walking down the double row of palm trees into the terminal, I was poached in my own juices. Lads in green with machine guns. The usual madhouse — babies, relatives, heaps of baggage. "Fixers" everywhere.

Weber had several thousand dollars in trading goods, by my estimate. Cigarette lighters, Swiss Army knives, textiles, camcorders, the whole store; vast amounts of personal belongings, bottles of Johnnie Walker, cigars, suitcases for an expedition. We showed our papers, then lugged the whole caboodle past the boys with guns, and we were in the courtyard of the terminal. I'd barely a moment to get my bearings. Sheer confusion it was. Crush of relatives, officials, much weeping and kissing on the cheek, the yard crammed with cabs, children begging for coins, the swelter. A whole family to greet the engineer, with hugs, kisses on both cheeks, bouquets of flowers already wilted in the heat; of course I must be introduced, our party divided into two cabs, Weber's trading goods stuffed in the trunk. He was already passing out cigarette lighters to everyone within reach. And then we were off.

It was the moment of pure exultation in a strange place, whether there's anything to be had there or not. Soon enough there would be the practicalities, interviews, putting together bits and pieces of history. But for now we were barrelling down a country road, honking at peasants on horse carts, bicycles, sheep on the road, men without shirts in a field, squinting through the sun at us.

The countryside was dotted with concrete mushroom caps, overgrown now, that were apparently defence outposts, gun emplacements and the like, pointed in all directions. The Glorious Leader was ready to fight the Turks, the imperialists, Titoists, Russian revisionists, the Chinese renegades after Mao, everyone he'd broken with in the name of Marxism-Leninism, in the name of Comrade Stalin, of the truth. I had the unnerving sense, for the briefest moment, of peering into Hoxha's besieged mind.

At the fork halfway between Durrës on the Adriatic and the capital inland, we took the turn for Tirana. And all the time Weber, sitting in back between a pale girl in a white blouse and her father, lectured the lot of us. I missed most of it, I confess. Words lost in the wind, while the driver was running peasants on bicycles off the road with his terrible honking. Of course the pilgrim had a plan to set the country right, something about playing Beethoven on the radio, and the phrase, "They're really children, you know."

Finally we came into the city. All the main roads of Tirana converged on Skanderbeg Square. It was a large open space. I marked the equestrian statue as we passed; that was where my rendezvous was. Around the edges of the big traffic circle in the square there were various official buildings, "people's palaces," according to the old terminology, with windows bashed in and boarded up after the recent rioting. I was informed right off that the towering statue of the Glorious Leader, set in the middle of the traffic circle, had been pulled down some three months ago by the people, the same "people" whose name the regime attached to the palaces and the "people's republic."

We dropped off the girl and her father and some of the engineer's booty. He ordered them about genially, drank his beer, handed out gifts. He was a lean, nervous pilgrim, but no fool. Then back to the square, this time south, past yellow and red stucco buildings — government ministries, Weber said — and down Martyrs' Boulevard a block or so to the Dajti. A four-storey job done by the Italians before World War II, big Mediterranean pines all around, shading it, and facing a spacious public park.

Crowds of fixers, drivers, cadging children, and arriving pilgrims jostled in the hotel driveway. Predictably, no available rooms. But the engineer was jovial, extra bed in his suite, no problem for the night, fix you up in the morning. He'd enjoy a bit of company — more like an audience for his unpacking. I barely had time to splash a few drops of water on the dusty wraith I'd become, and the engineer was off, for business in Durrës, I think it was.

An hour later, just before the onset of dusk, I made my way over to the square. I sat beneath the fearsome Skanderbeg, perched on his mount. Presently two men arrived, as ordained. The younger one, Pavli Qesku, struck me as rather elegant — mid-forties, lean, prematurely grey hair, tinted glasses. The other man was older and had one good ear, so he had to position himself on your left to catch the conversation. That was Zef Simoni.

I'd brought books for them — I suppose it could be said that I was a pilgrim in my way, too — but rather than examine them at once, they suggested we take a stroll down Martyrs' Boulevard. They pointed out where the statues of Lenin and Stalin had flanked the thoroughfare; now only pediments remained. Everything had come down in the last six months, more than a year after the wave that swept the rest of Central Europe, more than five years after Hoxha's death. The Communist Party had attempted to make the transition, had assumed that everything would continue forever — simply parade the image of the old Glorious Leader, gradually insert that of the successor, a man named Ramiz Alia. They figured they would carry on into eternity. But now everything was breaking up. Statues toppled, street names altered.

I'd noticed on a map that the continuation of the boulevard north of Skanderbeg Square had been named for Stalin. I wondered if it still was.

"Oh, we never called it that anyway," Zef said, dismissing the issue in an understated, slightly ironic way I would quickly get used to.

"But this is still the Boulevard of National Martyrs?" I inquired, just to check.

"Well, after all, this is true," Pavli said. "We are still a nation and, indeed, there have been martyrs."

"So there is no need to change it," Zef added. They had been in each other's company for so many years that they had acquired the habit of completing each other's sentences, as old couples do.

I was impatient to get to the heart of it, to the only question I really had for them, namely, how had they survived? As we passed the Hotel Dajti on the left, and twilight came down on the big park facing it, they represented themselves as timid men, unheroic, cautious creatures, never members of the party, though they had worked in the state publishing house translating the Glorious Leader's works and speeches all those years, Zef into German, Pavli into English. Another translator, Jusef Vrioni, had put Hoxha into French. I'd seen Vrioni's name, about a month before, in an article in an American magazine, where he'd been cited as the French translator of the great Albanian novelist Ismail Kadare, who was now living in Paris. I'd even glanced at *The General of the Dead Army*, one of Kadare's novels.

But the immediate answer to my question was relatively simple. They had translated literature — Dickens, Conrad, Lawrence,

Orwell even — I knew that already from the newspaper piece. But there was a new bit, a bit that hadn't been in the newspaper, and that was the key. They made dictionaries. It was an obvious thing for translators to do, now that they mentioned it, but it hadn't occurred to me. "So," I said, "in a sense, words saved you."

We crossed a little trickle of water just beyond the hotel, the Lana River. It flowed in a ditch below us, beneath the boulevard overpass — grass slopes, a paving-stone embankment. To the right, from the west, the last of the light hit it.

"Working with words saved us from the situation in which we lived, sort of," Pavli replied. Then he added, almost more to himself than me, "Yes, to a certain extent, it is true."

"A justification," Zef explained. "In our work as translators, we used words to express other people's thoughts — and we were not in agreement with those thoughts. So we wanted to use the same words to express, not our thoughts, but something neutral at least." It was put with perfect modesty. My curiosity was at once satisfied. Strange how quickly it went. Now we were simply evening strollers, casually conversing.

The boulevard, a broad four-lane thoroughfare, came to an abrupt dead end at the university, which was set at the base of a hill. The students had demonstrated here the previous December, and then again in February. That, apparently, was what had started the overthrow of the regime. Beyond the boulevard, we took a footpath that wound around and up a wooded rise. St. Procopius Hill, Zef informed me.

Somehow we got onto the subject of China. Perhaps it was something about Zef's bad ear. He had been to China during Hoxha's alliance with Mao, and the Chinese had restored some of his hearing. Even now he had only one good ear, supplemented by a bit of lip-reading. Anyway, it got me thinking about my time in China, in 1977, just after Mao's death, around the time of the breakup of Albania's "firm and eternal friendship," as the formula went, with Beijing. I found myself recounting an odd little conversation I'd had with my Chinese minder. We were speaking of sexual practices, and I'd asked, a bit mischievously, if there was homosexuality in China. My guide affected to be shocked. No, none at all, he firmly assured me. None whatsoever. So I asked him if the Chinese masturbated. Oh no, he said, and then, curiosity getting the better of him, he asked me, And you, in the West, do you masturbate? Why, yes, I replied, all the time.

Zef and Pavli burst into laughter, got it right away. "So there was even a correct line on sex," Pavli chuckled. I was about to rattle on when Zef interrupted to point out some buildings to our right. "The barracks of the National Guard," he said, making it clear by his tone that the institution wasn't exactly loved. The path switched back up St. Procopius Hill, but an unpaved road forked off toward the barracks. It was dark now, and all you could see were some lighted windows and young men in uniforms inside.

At the top of the hill we came out of the pines onto an outdoor café, which was our destination. It was well attended, mostly by couples and some guardsmen in pairs. A table was found for us, and the waiter brought us drinks.

"Raki," Pavli ordered. "Perhaps you won't like it," he remarked to me.

It was acrid stuff, perfectly drinkable, of course. And there was bread, soup, and some roasted chicken. My hosts half-apologized for the poor quality of everything, but in fact it was fine. A perfectly good café on a summer evening, and a bit cooler up here on the hill. After the food, more raki, and we smoked cigarettes.

One of the young guardsmen broke away from his mate and came over to our table to ask for a light. I held the flame to his hand-rolled smoke.

"You've just lit the cigarette of a National Guard," Zef said.

"Of a young man," I insisted.

"Who might masturbate in the barracks," Zef quickly added, accepting my distinction. We all laughed at that.

Oddly enough, we didn't talk about politics at all that evening. Zef mentioned that he had learned to read Greek and had read Plato's *Phaedo* in the original. It was a work I was familiar with; I often taught it. Indeed, I had opinions about the death of Socrates.

I confess I did most of the talking. As I said, I had views. The part about Socrates' last day in jail, his weeping friends, the hemlock he drank, all that was true in my opinion. But the part about the immortality of the soul, I insisted to Zev and Pavli, that was added by Plato himself. I don't think Socrates believed any of that. Socrates simply thought you died and consciousness ceased or — well, it doesn't matter about my views. But it was all so wonderfully odd. I'd come all this way, to the moon, to the last outpost, to inquire about the fall of Communism, and instead we were talking about Plato, just as civilized people anywhere might have done. Of course, I had to acknowledge that the places where civilized people could talk of such things were much diminished in our time, even in my own part of the world.

It had grown late, the café had emptied, the guardsmen were back in their barracks. Zef and Pavli walked me down the hill, back into the heat of the town, now in darkness. Behind the hotel there was a sleek building that bore the only electric sign I'd seen. It alternately flashed the temperature and the time, lighting up the night. The Institute of Strategic Studies, Pavli informed me. They came into the Dajti with me for a minute so I could give them the box of books I'd brought, and arrangements were made to collect me in the morning.

The engineer soon returned from Durrës. He produced a bottle of Johnnie Walker and we sat on the balcony outside the room, overlooking Martyrs' Boulevard — little traffic at that hour, only the gear-grinding of the occasional truck, a late-night bus.

■

In the morning, the engineer and I took breakfast together. The other pilgrims were there, impatient with the service, anxious to get on with business, to make the world go. Weber was soon off, the brooding Swiss of last night — he too read some philosophy — giving way to the nervous energy of deal making.

Across the corridor from the breakfast room was the bar. The engineer left me there with one of the fixers he knew, in case I needed anything. I escaped onto the cement front veranda of the Dajti. Even though the flashing digital sign, forever reminding us of time and heat, reported nearly thirty degrees before nine o'clock, a nice breeze came in from the park across the boulevard. Below me, in the driveway, taxi operators were taking the pilgrims off. There were all sorts of kids hanging around. Small ones, and teenage boys, too.

One in particular attracted my attention. He was in his mid to late teens, blue-eyed, with pale sandy hair and a quick smile. He was with a couple of his friends, and at first all I noticed was the kids' friendliness among themselves, the way they leaned against each other, casually draping an arm over the other's shoulders. Then the one with blue eyes and I exchanged glances and there was a brief, wordless encounter, the sort of meeting I might have forgotten if nothing else had happened. Our eyes met again, he offered a smile. It was nothing, really. But as he passed behind me on the veranda, he touched me. He ran a feathery hand across my shoulders, just as he did with his friends. And as quickly as he'd appeared, he was gone.

I would later learn that his name was Ilir. But for now I was on a "mission," a mission to find out about Albania, and agents on missions are not permitted to be distracted. So, the rule was, I was allowed to see him only insofar as that furthered the aim of finding out about Albania. The guiding text, after all, was *Heart of Darkness*, not Thomas Mann's *Death in Venice*, I reminded myself.

Just then, Zev and Pavli turned up to show me around. I tried to make apologies for chattering on about the *Phaedo*.

"No doubt you like the part about the soul," I said to Zef. He had told me he was a Catholic. But apparently there was no harm done.

"It was very good conversation," Zef assured me.

"Yes, nice to talk," Pavli seconded.

We crossed the square and were soon in a maze of side streets and then back lanes. There were some market stalls set up on the walks. Little potatoes, green onions, dark fresh figs, all in small quantities. Housewives spent hours gathering the day's provisions.

"Looking for things that don't exist," Pavli said.

We came to a five-storey building, made of bricks, oddly spaced, a hand-done job it seemed. "Zef's flat is on the top. He built it himself," Pavli told me. Looking up, you could see from the fresh colour of the brick that the top floor had been added recently. One could imagine the difficulties of a man in his fifties hauling the bricks up those stairs, mixing the cement, mortaring them in himself.

By the time we climbed to the top, my shirt was soaked through. Zef's wife met us, and while we settled in she brought us bottled water, raki, some Turkish delight sweets, and then coffee. I reminded myself that I was in one of those southern European cultures where the protocols of hospitality mean that they give you everything they have, even if they have very little.

There were shelves of books along the back wall. With a very slight ceremonial gesture, Zef presented me with a copy of the German-Albanian dictionary he had compiled, which had been published the year before. He quoted Milton on justifying God's ways to man. "I had to justify myself to myself," he said. "To do something useful."

About noon, we went down and made the short walk over to the publishing house where they worked. First there had to be a formal meeting with the director in his suite of offices. Pavli translated. I had been through this sort of thing before. Formalities to be observed, cups of bitter coffee served. I intimated that I had access to paper supplies, something the director — who, of course, was a party member — could note in his report if necessary. Even though it was all breaking up, and the party was in the midst of a chameleon-like effort to appear in more acceptable colours, much of the organizational infrastructure was still in place. And all the old habits. Although the director was the only party member I would actually meet, I was little inclined to question him about his view of the recent political changes. I knew I'd only get the current official line, and in any case the shade of "the last Communist," Hoxha himself, still lurked everywhere. On the stairway, going up to their office, Zef said, "Very good," appraising my performance, and the three of us laughed about it.

Then we were in the "tiny, Spartan office" that I'd read about in the newspaper piece. Well, a small professional quibble here, a detail. It was Spartan in the sense of equipment, the absence of books. But not tiny. Larger than the cubbyholes most journalists and instructors had in the newsrooms and college offices I was familiar with back home. Spacious enough for facing desks, walls a glossy, pale green, and there was a big window, with a breeze coming in, and a view from the second floor looking west to the hills, in the direction of Durrës on the coast.

We talked about making dictionaries; there was a large old one on a revolving stand on Pavli's desk. I'd never thought about them in precisely this way before.

"Where do you start?" I wanted to know.

"You begin from anything you like," Pavli said. "Just collecting words, finding phrases, putting them on cards, keeping files. But that is only preparatory work. The real work begins when you touch a typewriter and put a white sheet in and write 'A.' What shall we write about 'A'?" he asked.

I'd wanted to know how they had survived all those years, and here was a clue under my nose. You know how you're so familiar with an object that you barely notice it? You're looking for a big answer — something about the spirit or history — but the answer is right in front of you in a simple, material thing. In the German-Albanian dictionary Zef had given me, in the old dictionaries in their Spartan but not tiny office. It's a matter of seeing it, of resisting your own familiarity.

Zef said, "We wanted to use the same words to express, not our thoughts, but something neutral at least." Harmless things. Words. And in the pages of his dictionary were thousands of words — tree, sky, beach, sea — each one an expression of thought uncontaminated by the regime.

"Something neutral," Pavli repeated, adding, "despite the fact that sometimes other people, outside us, put in words that expressed the reality that existed at that time. As they did with Zef's dictionary. They put in expressions like 'the dictatorship of the proletariat' and 'scientific socialism' and so on."

"Not very scientific," Zef commented wryly.

"But also the definitions," Pavli said. "Here, look." He turned to the word "liberal." "'One who makes concessions towards shortcomings and mistakes,'" Pavli read, "'who is not exacting toward others; who allows irregularities which harm the work of society.' This dictionary is full of such stupidities."

Over the years, they had slowly compiled words at night, while at work they duly translated documents, position papers, the works of Comrade Hoxha. On the far wall, facing the open window that looked out toward Durrës, there was a bookcase containing the books of the Glorious Leader. Zef went to it and pulled out a couple of paperback volumes to give me. He made a show of banging them against the side of the case to shake the dust from these translated but seldom-read memoirs. On the cover of one, called *With Stalin*, was a photograph of the two men, shot from below, standing on a rampart. Later, in the hotel, I skimmed its hagiographic, childishly humble accounts of Hoxha's reception in Moscow by "Comrade Stalin."

●

Pavli walked me back through the mid-afternoon heat to the Dajti, and we arranged to meet again in the evening. The desk clerk had a room for me. Weber was still out when I moved my things to the new room. It was small but sufficient — a bed, a writing table, lace curtains, a shower, a little balcony, and a roll-down metal shade to keep out the heat. The room faced east, looking directly onto the blinking electric sign with the time and temperature. By the time I came up from the bar, bringing back a litre of mineral water, I was soaked from my small exertions. I showered, made my notes, replenished myself with liquids, read a page or two of Conrad, and then napped.

Pavli came to get me in the early evening and took me to his apartment, where Zef was already waiting for us. Pavli's wife brought us raki and then went into the kitchen while we watched television. There was an interview with a visiting Albanian politi-cal leader from Kosovo, the southernmost, so-called autonomous province of Yugoslavia, but actually under the thumb of the Ser-bians. Two million Albanians lived there, and now, with the war in Yugoslavia, the old dream of Greater Albania was in the air again. I happened to learn a little about it only subsequently, when I read a translation of a novella by Kadare set in Priština, the Kosovan capital, about a failed uprising there a decade or more ago. Zef and Pavli watched the interview intently; such dis-cussion was still something of a novelty on Albanian television.

Then Pavli's wife brought in food and they switched channels to an Italian game show. It was announced as a "light supper," but in fact it was a full plate, carefully laid out. Mussels, olives, tomatoes, onions, hard-boiled eggs, and a fruit compote for des-sert. All the time we were watching the politician from Kosovo, Pavli's wife had been working in the kitchen. I thought of a femi-nist friend back home and knew exactly what she would make of it.

After Mrs. Qesku cleared the table, I turned on the tape recorder for our formal interview. Now I was at work, as I had been a hundred times before, in many places. And later, no doubt far away from where this encounter had occurred, I might hear those voices again, or they would be transcribed into a sheaf of notes that would find a place in a manila folder or in the depths of the maroon-coloured gym bag I lugged around with me, a homely object I sometimes described as "my office."

Zef Simoni was born in 1933 in the northern town of Shkoder, to a well-to-do Catholic family. As in neighbouring Yugoslavia and Greece, the ending of World War II inaugurated civil war in Albania. While Greece was allotted to the Allies, in both Yugoslavia and Albania the partisan triumph was not impeded.

"Immediately when the partisans came into Shkoder," he recalled, "they started shooting people in batches. Behind the town graveyard. And after having a batch of people shot, they put up a proclamation with the names and the crimes they were supposed to have committed." Zef was eleven.

"So they came in 1944?" I calculated.

"Yes. And they were my first exercises in literacy."

I was momentarily puzzled.

"To read the names," Pavli supplied.

"It was just reading matter for me," Zef said. I had a glimpse, no more, of a child peering up at a freshly pasted sheet on a brick wall, absorbing the litany of the newly dead with a chilling innocence. Outside, in the night, we could hear the shouts of children at play.

Pavli's wife offered us brandy. "It is a very fine brandy, made at home," Pavli recommended. "Wild cherry." We each accepted a glass.

"They were people of a conservative mind," Zef said, recalling his family. "Right wing, I would say now. My father was first an import-export merchant, then he had a printing shop, then a magazine, and he made some translations. He was the first Esperantist in Albania."

"He translated *Pinocchio*," Pavli added.

"Into Esperanto?" I wondered, slightly amused. But no, he had put the tale into Albanian.

"He translated the biography of Skanderbeg into Esperanto," Zef said.

"So you're a second-generation translator," I observed.

"Second-generation," Zef nodded, laughing.

Once again it was a matter of words. Words for civilization, words in self-defence. But wasn't the ruling party's concern also the use of language?

"Propaganda is made of words, of course," Pavli agreed.

"But everything is distorted," Zef replied. "You are told you have freedom, which others, you are told, have not. And you have not freedom. You are told you have free speech — it is written in the constitution — and you land in jail for saying the wrong things. You are told you are free to move about, and you must have documents to move from one city to another. Everything is told it exists, and it doesn't exist, or exists its counterpart." Zef spoke rapidly, forgoing the niceties of English grammar in his excitement.

"My own family," Pavli said, "was a little more exposed to such propaganda. My father was a partisan, then a Communist, and fought in the brigades of the national liberation army. After the war, he began to realize that there was something amiss. But he couldn't grasp what it was. He was a tailor. In a small town in central Albania. Slowly but surely he began to realize that the cause of the situation was the party itself, and he began to dislike it, until in 1949, after five years in the party, he refused to be a member." Pavli had been five then. "But in my family there are still some people who believe that the party is good, just that something went wrong somewhere. There are some people who are still utopians, who have the hope that socialism is something good for humankind."

I was curious to know how they had become friends.

"We worked together," Pavli said.

"They just put us in the same room," Zef added, "and they said, work together." The two of them laughed at the simple absurdity of it.

"And this has gone on for over twenty years," I said, laughing also.

"Yes, twenty-two years," Pavli confirmed, "except for a period of three years when I was in Peshpatia, a small town in the mountains."

They had escaped the terror of executions and prison, but not entirely. They had spent the years together carefully. "Very careful," Pavli reiterated. "What we said in the streets, what we said in the café."

"We expressed our more delicate thoughts in English, just in case," said Zef. "We were very careful about where we talked, how we talked."

"Or we had code names for things."

The way their voices alternated reminded me of the strophe and antistrophe of a Greek chorus. "Code names?" I repeated.

"For the government, the party, the leaders, our party secretary." Like a children's game, I suggested. "It was very childish," Zef said, "and very horrible."

"But it was not Newspeak," Pavli added, referring to George Orwell's dystopian novel *Nineteen Eighty-Four*.

Yet their caution did not protect them completely. Pavli was shipped off for three years in 1975 to a sort of internal exile.

"The reason they gave Pavli for sending him to Peshpatia," Zef began, "well, the true reason was that he didn't accept to become a member of the party, but the specious reason they gave him was that you keep too much Zef's company. They kept me in Tirana."

"But Zef was frightened then."

"Because in their sick mind, I was infected, hopelessly. There was some hope for saving Pavli."

So Pavli was shipped off to work as a schoolteacher in a mountain village. "Did you think you would ever return?" I asked.

"It was a closed chapter," Pavli replied. "I just took my bag, my typewriter, and my books."

"Were you married?" I asked.

"Yes, but happily we had no children then. My wife could go on working here. The government needed her work because she was chief engineer of the porcelain factory. She kept working in Tirana, and I went to Peshpatia."

"Chinese style," Zef said.

Pavli's wife was sitting in an armchair, away from the table the three of us were gathered around. For all her fulfillment of the traditional duties, she was an educated woman, skilled, and able to follow our conversation in English, occasionally supplying a correction to their account. I saw her then as if for the first time. I had only a moment to imagine their three years of separation, caused by an ideological whim, which they treated, in retrospect, as a minor inconvenience. Compared to so many others, I suppose it was.

Pavli had gone on speaking of Peshpatia. "The headmaster of the school was a very nice chap, very understanding. He gave me a whole room to myself, a bare room of course, but it was a room. There was a round stove which the schoolboys were careful to supply with firewood. It is fifteen or twenty degrees below zero in winter there. I was all by myself. The dictionaries were there, and whenever those people, security, came from time to time, unannounced, to search my room, they saw they were harmless books. I never gave them cause to suspect."

"And in the place of Pavli," Zef said, picking up the other end of the story, "into the office stepped a chap who had been Pavli's schoolmate. He had some connections with the Minister of Internal Affairs, and I am sure he informed on me, but he informed only on the good side." Zef laughed at this small irony, then added, "I was very careful, of course."

"My former schoolmate didn't do anything while he was there," Pavli noted. "He was supposed to be a translator, but he couldn't do the job. When Zef was away, he just sat there doing nothing."

Sitting there, comforted by cherry brandy, I had to remind myself that I was listening to an account of political terror. Not executions, torture, jailings — though there was that, of course — but quiet terror, everyday terror.

"When we translated that book which I gave you, *With Stalin*," Zef began again, "we worked night and day."

"Three months of hard work in the midst of summer," Pavli said.

"Then they gave us four or five days to recover," Zef continued. "On one of these days, the chief of the enterprise came to me and said, 'You are invited to the Tirana branch of the Ministry of Internal Affairs. I don't know what they want from you, but you must go.' I went there. Certainly, I was very afraid. But I tried to keep control of myself. I told myself maybe they had some translations for me to do. I was ushered into a room and there were two armchairs, and they smelled of sweat, a heavy stink of sweat. Because the people who went there sweated profusely under interrogation."

They asked Zef about various people he knew, and he offered bland replies. The fencing went on for some time. Then the interrogators asked about a certain person. "I said, yes, I know him. I couldn't say I didn't. And what are his opinions? they asked. I said, the generally current opinions. And what are his literary tastes? I mentioned the most conventional tastes I knew of. Then they told me, he has been slandering the party, and you must know. I know nothing, I have not seen him for six months. After that, they gave me a cigarette. They did not make direct threats to me. They told me, look, we are going to arrest this man. If you warn him, first, it will be useless, and second, you will be arrested too. So I went home. On my way home, I wanted to have a double portion of cognac just to steady my spirits." He laughed in recollection of his fear. "Then I thought that I might be followed. If they saw me drinking, they might think I had something to fear. So instead I went straight home and lay in my bed for about half an hour. Only then did I come out and go to the café, where I had my double portion of cognac. In about six months' time, Pavli, who knew nothing about these things — "

"Zef didn't whisper a word," Pavli interjected.

"Had I told Pavli, he would think, first, that I was a hero, and second, that I must have blurted out something. So I said nothing. And six months later, it was Pavli who mentioned to me that so-and-so had been arrested. And still I said nothing."

"You didn't tell Pavli about the interrogation?" I asked Zef.

"I learned of it only last year," Pavli said.

"When did this incident happen?" I asked.

"In 1980," Zef said.

"You only told him ten years later?" I said in astonishment.

"Ten years," Zef said, and we all broke out laughing, but no doubt for different reasons. They laughed at the mixture of absurdity and horror, and because it was now possible to laugh at it, and because it was a small thing compared to what others had endured. And I laughed nervously, almost embarrassed to be made a party to this terrible intimacy.

"After six months, Pavli told me, you know, this chap so-and-so has been arrested," Zef repeated. I turned off the recorder, stuffed the tapes into my gym bag.

It was a story no different from those we had heard countless times in recent years. But that was the point of it: there was nothing "Albanian" about the anecdote. The insidious method was ubiquitous. Anyone, even the most intimate of your friends, might inform. A remark you'd made in the sanctity of your home, thoughtlessly parroted by your child at school, might bring the authorities to your door. No letters unread by the censors, no movement without approved documents, and, of course, no passports. Your fate decided in rooms, committees, none of which you had access to, but in whose anterooms you waited. And though the digital clock recorded the passing minutes, the Glorious Leader had made time stand still.

Yet from the outside, to a visitor, the place must appear but a small, dusty, inconsequential town of barely a quarter-million inhabitants, baking in the sun, poor, but with people going about their business. There was little visible sign of the oppression, or the methods that made it possible. It was as if I had travelled the length of a river — like the river in Conrad's story — to reach, as Marlow did, the kingdom of a madman.

The parallels were eerie. Like Kurtz, Hoxha had not always been mad. He had begun with the intention of improving the lot of humankind, the great dream of our time. And those of us on the left had even grudgingly admired him as the ruler of a tiny, mostly agricultural country who had rather heroically broken with first the Soviets, for deviating from Stalinism, and then even the Chinese, for abandoning Maoism. But in his obsessive effort to perfect human beings, to create, like a god, "the new man, the new woman," he had gradually turned the inhabitants into slaves.

"You translated Conrad," I said to Zef.

"And perhaps you think you are a bit like Marlow?" Zef joked, intuiting my pretension.

But there was no Kurtz at the heart of this darkness, no self-critical last cry of horror to ponder. There was only the rubble of Hoxha's rule. And its survivors. We in the "West" had thought of them almost as savages, just as Conrad had recorded that men of the Imperium thought of distant peoples of a different colour a century ago. Yet I had discovered, as had Conrad, that they were the same as us.

I didn't think all that at the moment; only later, when the voices recorded in my little machine had become words on pages. But there was something more, something that did occur to me as we spoke, though I didn't mention it to Zef and Pavli. I had yet to free myself from the human dream that had given way to the dictator's inhuman methods.

It had gotten well on into the evening. There was more to ask, but they had arranged for me to do interviews with some other people beginning early the next morning, a Saturday, and the following day we would hire a driver and car and go to Durrës, so there would be time to talk then. I couldn't resist asking about the present, now that the nightmare was over, or almost over.

"The change can be seen if you follow a couple of people walking in the streets," Pavli said. "They have stopped turning their heads back to see if we're following them. We no longer turn our heads back."

▪

Zef walked me back to the Dajti through the silent streets of Tirana. From the balcony of my room I faced the electric sign flashing in the night. It was almost midnight. Just under thirty degrees. The sign blinked on and off, flooding my room with pale light and then plunging it into darkness. In bed, I turned away from the wall where light flared every few seconds.

Six hours later, I woke up. Beyond the Institute for Strategic Studies, beyond where the town ended, there were pale brown mountains, with Mount Dajti to the east. A haze lay between it and the edges of town. I stood on the balcony drinking coffee. Directly below me, three floors down, was the raggedy, semi-abandoned garden of the hotel. Palm trees, an empty fountain, untended bushes. A skinny yellow cat prowled through the bush.

The opposition Democratic Party was headquartered in a sort of villa, set back from a busy street, with a wide gate at the front to admit vehicles. Inside, even at 8 AM, clusters of men were gathered in the driveway-courtyard, petitioners, perhaps, or local functionaries. An outside staircase led up to a warren of offices. We were ushered into a large room with a long rectangular table. At the head of it, talking on the telephone, was a stocky young man in his late twenties with unkempt curly black hair. There was a window behind him, covered with shutters through which slivers of sunshine filtered, playing upon the gauze curtains that hung in front of it.

When he put the phone down, we were introduced. His name was Azem Haidari. He was a graduate student at the university and had come from a small mountain village, Treppoja, in the north. He was married and had two children.

"If you want," Haidari said, via Zef's translation, "I will tell you about the democratic movement in Albania, the Democratic Party, the political life, and the Parliament." As a result of the elections in the spring, he now sat as a member of that body. We had about an hour's interview, variously interrupted by the urgency of the telephone and by people poking their heads through the double doors with brief messages for the young politician. It was a standard interview; he spoke as a man with responsibilities. But I saw that both Zef and Pavli rather admired him. They liked his vigour and, apparently, the colourful mountain villager's way of speaking — he didn't mince words. When he was on the phone, I could get a hint of a more animated, indigenous style that no doubt had popular appeal. But with me he was diplomatic, without irony.

Here was the person who, as much as anyone, had loosened the grip of Hoxha's successors. "The dictatorship was so savage there was no possibility of even thinking of establishing another form of government, because the mere thought of it put your life in jeopardy," Haidari said. But the explosions in eastern Europe had had their echoes even in Albania. Hoxha's successor, Alia, had seen, like everyone else, the events in Romania in December 1989 that had resulted in the swift execution of Nicolae Ceauşescu, the long-time Communist leader there.

"Mr. Alia, recalling the fate of Ceauşescu, saw that he had to do something for democratization. But his speeches, his manoeuvres, were only for export," Haidari said dismissively. "They were intended to give the impression that something was being done, whereas nothing was being done." It was that impasse that led Haidari to take political action, organizing the students. The way he put it was very innocent — it was the language of the nineteenth century's "springtime of nations" — and yet it had the self-deprecating awareness of a man standing before a mirror, giving an account that would later be read as history.

"When I was a student, I always recalled President Kennedy's words, Ask not what your country can do for you, ask what you can do for your country. So I decided to give my all to Albania, even my life. At first, the possibility of emerging alive from the first demonstrations after forty years of Communist rule was very slim indeed. Nevertheless, against all these odds, we succeeded in carrying out our peaceful demonstrations. The moment came to do something for Albania, and I am very happy this offer of sacrifice was accepted." That was all it took, if not to topple the regime, at least to shake its foundations.

Later, toward the end of the hour, the mountain man declared, "I love life, but I have the opinion that life should be loved for as long as it lasts, and we should not think to prolong it more than its course. You can't escape your fate." It was not the first time I'd heard young men fearlessly proclaim such things, and I've seldom doubted them. Yet it was always eerie to hear someone say it.

Just at that moment, the phone rang. Haidari picked up the receiver and soon was speaking more animatedly. I saw alarm in Zef's and Pavli's eyes.

"There's been a shootout," Pavli said, following the progress of the conversation. "One of his cousins, a young cousin of his, has been shot."

"Where?" I asked.

"In Treppoja."

"How did it happen?"

"The situation is stable," Pavli said, missing my question.

"But who was shooting?" I wondered. Haidari's voice subsided.

"He made a speech in Parliament about Kosovo," Pavli explained. I put it together in bits and pieces — the arrival of the visiting politician from Kosovo we'd seen on television had heated the political atmosphere — then there was Haidari's speech on the suppression of the Kosovan Albanians by the Serbs — no mincing of words, apparently — and somehow the news of the speech — was it heard as a call to arms? — had triggered the flare-up in his home village, not far from the border.

On the outside staircase going down, Zef said, "In six months he could be dead." Meaning young Haidari, courting fate as he was. Then we were back in the streets, in the unforgiving heat. In the mid-thirties before noon. As we walked, Pavli recalled that the former student leader had accurately predicted that the newly elected government would be forced to form a coalition with the opposition "by the time the cherries were ripe."

"And when do they ripen?" I asked.

"In May and June," Pavli said. "And it happened. Now he says the present government will fall by the time the watermelons are ripe at the end of the summer. By the time the watermelons ripen." Pavli seemed taken with Haidari's agricultural turn of phrase.

(Many years later, in 1998, my brief encounter with the young Albanian politician suddenly returned to mind. In September of that year, Haidari, then thirty-six, was assassinated in front of the party headquarters from where we had taken our leave that day. Most often, reportage is simply the news of the day; occasionally it is a mirror held up to the future.)

Our next interview was with a writer named Trebeshina. It was held at the apartment of a young colleague of his, also a writer. Trebeshina was in his mid-sixties, but you could see he had been badly used. He spoke in a hoarse whisper through yellowed and broken teeth. His was a tale of jailing and neglect. He had been imprisoned twice by the Fascists, against whom he had fought in World War II, and three times by the Communists. The first time, in the fifties, was a literary jailing. "I was always against the socialist realism," he said. "I was of the opinion that if there is realism, there is no need for socialist- or Fascist- or so on." He wrote an open letter to Hoxha and got three years for it.

I didn't quite catch the reason for the next incarceration, but the third one, in 1980, came about when he publicly declared his refusal to vote. For that he got a long stretch. He'd only been released three years ago, in 1988. And though he'd written much after the open letter, none of it had been published. He had been ignored, neglected, always at odds with the Writers' League. He didn't share the conventional estimate of the great Kadare. "A collaborator," Trebeshina rasped. When I asked him about hearing of Hoxha's death while he was in prison, he replied, "He's not dead." At the end of his fragmented recital, Trebeshina said, "I always wanted to ring the bell for the others, but I did not. During all my life, I was a Don Quixote."

Pavli walked me back to the hotel. We went along the Lana River, where a peasant sat on the grassy embankment, tethered to a couple of grazing sheep. The electric sign now registered thirty-six degrees. Pavli left me in the driveway of the Dajti. He and Zef had arranged a meeting with Kadare's translator, Vrioni, for the evening.

I had worn my lightest short-sleeved shirt, but I was soaked through and slightly dazed, grateful to get to the shade of my little room, clutching the bottles of water I'd acquired in the bar on the way up. Before I showered and napped, I made my notes, the paper practically melting under my hand. It was as if all substance had dissolved into a primordial ooze — the water I drank greedily, the perspiration pouring out of me, smearing the ink, dampening the pages. The interviews with Haidari and Trebeshina had been ordinary enough, the sort of tales of courage and suffering in a heretofore almost unknown place, which are then inadequately condensed into the columns of the dailies. I had conducted such interviews before, in many places, though I only practised journalism sporadically. But this time I had been affected. I could feel the ends of my nerves. Perhaps I too, like Trebeshina, was a Don Quixote, or maybe a Sancho Panza. It seemed to me, at that moment, that your entire life as a writer leads to the one street you are walking down, to the miserable little pile of dark figs you are unthinkingly looking at, to the rasping, bitter voice you are listening to. Everything had led to this moment, and its possible description is infinite. And yet you do not know the story, except as it unfolds before you. You do not know the story, I repeated to myself as I fell asleep.

●

I went down to the veranda of the hotel early. The young man was there, the one I had seen before. We greeted each other like old friends. We shook hands, and he touched me on the shoulder. We introduced ourselves. That's when I learned that his name was Ilir. Ilir as in ancient Illyria. It was impossible not to think of the head of the boy on the postcard that the consul in Bonn had sent me.

Ilir was with a friend his own age, to whom he introduced me. They both had a little English, though I had some difficulty following the anecdote they were trying to tell me. His friend was a music student, as was Ilir, or perhaps a dancer. I couldn't quite get it.

They knew all about current music. "Michael Jackson," Ilir said, "he is a great man. And MC Hammer, very beautiful." I was rather amazed by their knowledge, though also appalled that, of all things, this was what had penetrated the ideological defences of their shrouded land. "But how do you know all this?" I asked Ilir. They had seen it on television from Belgrade, which apparently transmitted the European version of the American music channel MTV. So, score one for the Global Village. I was too charmed by Ilir to be contemptuous of the pap the world wanted to feed him. Indeed, it seemed remarkable enough that in this remoteness he was a thorough contemporary of others his age anywhere in the world. If I had to choose between Hoxha and MTV, well, why not?

There was a complicated story about a man named Hussein — "not Saddam Hussein of Iraq," Ilir laughed. This Hussein had promised them some papers, but I couldn't make it out. For what purpose? "Rap," Ilir said, "for the rap." There was something about videotapes, but I got it mixed up.

Then Zef and Pavli turned up for the evening at Vrioni's. I shook hands with Ilir's friend, but the farewell with Ilir was more elaborate, kisses on both cheeks, hand holding, assurances that we must get together soon.

Walking to Vrioni's, I must have babbled, telling Zef and Pavli about Ilir. They seemed amused I was so taken with him, the way you are when a visitor comes to your hometown and enthuses about something there that you've never thought of, but that leaves you pleased for both your guest and yourself.

On the way, they reminded me that Vrioni had for a time worked in the publishing house as a translator. In fact, at the time of Pavli's exile, Vrioni's name had also appeared on the list of those to be sent off to get "closer to the people."

"He was sent too?" I asked.

"He was meant to be sent," Pavli said, "but on special instructions from His Highness — "

" — who knew some French," Zef interjected.

" — who read his own books in French," Pavli continued, "and liked the way they had been rendered in French — "

" — because Vrioni had translated his own works," Zef put in.

"There was no one who could translate his works as well as Vrioni did," Pavli added.

"So he was not going to saw off the branch he was sitting on," Zef concluded.

Vrioni lived in a detached two-storey house with a small front garden. His wife greeted us at the door and led us into the living room, where Vrioni was waiting for us. He was a tall, elegant man. I was told later that he was seventy-eight years old, but I never would have guessed it from his looks or his manner. He was the son of a wealthy landowner and had been raised and educated in France before the war. When he returned to Albania after the partisan triumph, Hoxha had him jailed for thirteen years. Then he became a translator, of Hoxha's books as well as those of Kadare.

His wife brought in a bottle of Johnnie Walker whisky, with glasses on a tray, and, after placing them on the low, glass-topped table before us, retired upstairs, explaining that she was feeling poorly. Our conversation was in French. Vrioni could speak English, but he made it clear that to discuss certain concepts, only French was adequate. Zev and Pavli filled in for my deficiencies.

We hit it off right away. I mentioned that I liked jazz and uttered the name of the legendary French jazz guitarist Django Reinhardt. Immediately Vrioni lit up. He rummaged about beneath the sound equipment at the side of the room until he produced a cassette. The room filled with the instantly recognizable arpeggios of the three-fingered jazz guitarist, joined by a violinist. It was Reinhardt's version of the "Marseillaise," accompanied by Stéphane Grappelli, recorded just after the Allied victory in 1945, Vrioni told us. For a few minutes we simply listened with pleasure and sipped our whisky.

Vrioni was most dubious about Albanian prospects. He began to tick off on his aristocratic fingers the reasons for his doubts in the precise manner of French intellectuals. First, the level of Albanian culture was abysmally backward. I interjected that I had met a sixteen- or seventeen-year-old boy in Tirana who was extraordinarily well versed in contemporary music, having watched television from Yugoslavia. My host was unimpressed. He continued his dissection of the country's gloomy future.

I mentioned to Vrioni that I had seen his name in an American magazine article about Kadare. It was clear that he had more than a proprietary interest in the Albanian writer. His translations into French had made Kadare's reputation outside Albania. Without the translations, which had so pleased the French public, the great novelist might be unknown today. There was even a hint that something more than translation was involved. It was almost as if he regarded himself as Kadare's co-author. And he had also translated the Glorious Leader. Vrioni went to the bookshelves on the far wall and returned with a couple of volumes, opening one to the title page. On it was Hoxha's inscription, in his own hand, to his "Comrade" for his "tireless work" in rendering the leader's writing into "perfect" French. Vrioni translated Hoxha's praise of himself with considerable drollery, assuming our appreciation of the implicit ironies.

I noticed that, on the low table before us, there was also a copy of the French translation of Milan Kundera's latest novel, which I had recently read myself. That led to Vrioni's inquiring about a Mexican novelist he had only heard of on his last trip to Paris. Did I know of Carlos Fuentes? I remarked to him that this conversation we were having might take place in any capital of Europe. Yes, people were always surprised to encounter a cultivated Albanian, Vrioni said. "Of course, you know Montesquieu's *Persian Letters*?" he asked.

In that eighteenth-century work, the imaginary Persian through whom Montesquieu provides his portrait of the ills of France appears in a Paris salon and is asked, with near disbelief, How is it possible for a Persian to be in Paris?

"I, too," Vrioni said, "have been at a salon in Paris, and upon identifying myself as an Albanian, I was asked, by a man who knew his Montesquieu, But how is it possible for an Albanian to be in Paris?"

For all his civility, even the charm of his vanity, there was something unsettling about Vrioni. I remembered the rasping voice of the broken Trebeshina, the Don Quixote; at the mention of Kadare's name, he had spat the words "A collaborator." To be able to write, and to use his fame as a platform from which to criticize the regime, even indirectly, had he not also lent that renown to a justification of the regime? Had Kadare not faced the moral dilemma of the person who sustains the culture, which he imagines as belonging to posterity, but only at the cost of semi-collaboration with the totalitarian power, which he must persuade himself is merely temporary? Was that not also true, albeit to a lesser degree, in the case of Vrioni? Here we were in this comfortable home, with whisky on the table, the latest novels, a modern sound system, and amid all these elements necessary to the maintenance of a civilization was the very hand of the Glorious Leader, the madman, thanking his "tireless Comrade."

Vrioni's ailing wife appeared at our departure. It was already night as Zef and Pavli walked me back toward the hotel. Martyrs' Boulevard was jammed with people on that Saturday night, walking in family groups, sitting on the low wall along the park, milling about in conversation in the hot darkness. I was overwhelmed by the sheer physicality of bodies. When the ideological shroud is pulled away, what you're left with is warm, human sweat.

We wanted to arrange for a car for the following day. Ilir was still hanging around with some friends in the congested driveway beneath the veranda of the Dajti. He dashed off into the shadows to secure a driver, soon reappearing with a man who seemed trustworthy enough. We agreed to meet in the morning, and Zef and Pavli melted into the throng of strollers on the boulevard.

I told Ilir that we were going to Durrës the next day. "I also," he said. "For the swimming." But perhaps we could meet later in the afternoon for a soft drink. "Yes, yes," he said enthusiastically. We would meet at five.

In the morning, as the sun came in through the chinks of the half-pulled metal shade, I could hear the birds below in the otherwise empty garden. The driver proved to be quite reliable, and we were promptly on the road for our little holiday. We passed buses jammed with like-minded weekenders heading for the sea.

At Durrës we inspected the ancient Roman amphitheatre. First century, I was told. It had been but semi-excavated, located as it was right in the middle of a residential neighbourhood. The heat was stunning. It was a relief to duck into the shaded galleries and interior stairways. A Byzantine church had been installed in its midst in the Middle Ages; the whole place was a rockpile jumble of two millennia. At last we emerged into a portal overlooking the whole of the site. They had dug only partway down to the great half-circle stage of the theatre, but it was easy enough to imagine, easy enough to move in time. When we finally clambered off the heap, I was grateful to our thoughtful driver who had found a water tap, which he ran for his parched inspectors of antiquities.

Then there was the local museum to see. It was across the street from a narrow beach at the sea's edge. I only had half an eye for the ancient statuary, for now I was longing for the Adriatic, which I could smell from there. "Where I come from," I said to Zef and Pavli, "it's considered good luck to dip your hand in the sea, if you're a visitor." My hosts apparently felt we had fulfilled our duties as tourists and obligingly led me across the road. It was a scruffy beach, pebbles and shells mostly, but the Adriatic stretched out before us in a long, low succession of thin layers of wave. I reached into it and wet my hand, scooping up some water to my face, while the sea ran over my foot.

Having displayed sufficient enthusiasm for this natural wonder, Zef and Pavli decided to show me the beaches at the south end of town. It was a five-minute drive. Down the wide stretch of sand was an area of resorts and hotels, where the workers and their families went for holidays and where the country's few tourists had been permitted during the old regime, to provide a source of foreign exchange. We stopped at one of the hotels to get a cool drink. We sat in a cavernous hall that gave out onto the crowded beach below and the Adriatic rolling in, and sipped an orange-flavoured concoction. Afterwards the three of us strolled through the mob of bathers, families, groups of boys playing football in the sand, bodies everywhere. What struck me was that when the ideological fog lifted, what you had were the people — not the abstracted version, as in "the People," but the physical fact of them — and these people, the Albanians, were not so different from the rest of humanity, not dissimilar to the Italians or Greeks, who were on their own beaches that Sunday afternoon.

In the car again — now we were travelling inland and north, to Kruje — the image of that human flesh shimmering in the sun remained with me for some while. I turned to Zef and Pavli, sitting in back.

"Communism never talked about the body," I declared.

"It never talked about the spirit either," Zef countered.

"But it had an equivalent to the spirit," I replied. "It had the notion of revolutionary consciousness. At least that was a mental thing. But they claimed to be materialists, and yet they didn't speak, except mechanically, about the body." To be fair, in the world I came from the body was relentlessly displayed, but for all its commodification, it was rendered almost equally meaningless, I added.

Of course, the return of the body is not the same thing as the birth of a citizenry, I admitted. The madman had broken many bodies here, but when the kingdom fell apart — for a variety of reasons, including the simple fact that it didn't work — the body of, say, old Trebeshina was, in a sense, replaced by that of the new generation to which Ilir belonged.

Yet bodies, left to themselves, form only the relationships of a society — at best the wisdom of the elders, at worst the gangs of the cities. Whereas the dictionaries Zef and Pavli made belonged to a culture, even a universal culture, out of which citizens might emerge where there were none before. I had no more idea of how it might turn out here than anyone else. But wasn't that true of so much of that new entity that we referred to by the old name of Europe? For the moment, it was simply bodies that impressed themselves upon me. Bodies that, as Pavli had said, no longer had to turn their heads to see if someone was following. Perhaps I had a touch of sun, I don't know.

At Kruje, in the mountains, there was a reconstruction of Skanderbeg's castle and a sweeping view of the valley below. We dutifully toured the site of the warlord's redoubt. Nearby there was a little outdoor restaurant, and we sat in the walled garden by a fountain and feasted. Below us, at a table placed near the edge of a precipice, commanding a view of the valley, was a party of Italians. They were very jolly, yodelling out into the mountains, hoping to produce an echo. The waiter told us that, far from being the frivolous tourists we might imagine, they had taken in some young Albanian men who had fled to Brindisi — I remembered the footage of overcrowded boats I'd seen on TV the previous spring — and now they had come to visit the parents, to bring them news of their sons.

Sheep wandered about the garden, eating bread from our hands, nudging up against our knees, while we dug our fingers into their white, oily curls. But even as we feasted, dipping our bread into the dish of oil in which the olives soaked — Zef said matter-of-factly, "I haven't tasted olive oil in two years" — and as the Italians hallooed and yodelled, our talk strayed from the bucolic surroundings.

"What did you think the day Hoxha died?" I asked rather suddenly.

"It isn't very Christian," Zef answered, "but it was perhaps the finest day of my life."

"How did you hear about it?"

"We were not together at the time," Pavli said.

"First, there was only classical music on the radio," Zef remembered. "And we thought something had happened. And of course the only thing that could have happened was that he died. So we waited for the official announcement, which was at the twelve o'clock news."

"I was travelling that day, to my hometown," Pavli recalled. "I took my little daughter with me. I went to see my father, who was sick. On the way to the train station, I met an old journalist. He approached me with a sort of — I can't explain what his face was like when he saw me — but he desperately wanted to tell me something. He approached me with half a smile and said, 'He is dead and gone.' I got it immediately. When I reached home, I told my father, I gave him the news. He just rejoiced. 'I saw him go before me. I don't mind if I die now.' Those were his words."

Pavli fell silent. We listened to the water falling in the fountain.

Zef said, "We hoped that his death would be the end, but the regime lingered on for another six years."

"The true end of the dictator," Pavli continued, "was on that famous day when his ten-metre-high statue was brought down. My wife was walking with her bicycle in the square and she saw people gathering, rushing about, and the police throwing tear-gas bombs. Nobody cared about their lives, they just rushed toward the statue and managed to bring it down. Afterwards, a tractor pulled it to the campus, where the students were on a hunger strike. They cut off the head, which was sent to the students. And then the body . . . "

" — it was dragged along," Zef interjected, "like a dead crocodile."

"Without its head," Pavli added.

In the mid-afternoon we came down from Kruje, back toward Tirana. I would be leaving the next day, so, though there would be a farewell, this was in a sense the last of our conversations. And at the end, as we had begun, we spoke of dictionaries. It was as if they hadn't made themselves clear enough, hadn't got it right, and it was somehow important to them that I understand.

"If we had been hot-headed and just burst in a fit of passion and told them everything we had in our minds, we would have been content for a while, but our work would not have been done," Pavli said. "Dictionaries are not our work. It is something which belongs to the whole people, and people who make dictionaries are only a few idiotic, I would say, hard-working asses who take upon themselves the work of a lifetime."

"Eccentrics," Zef said, chuckling. "But it was some sort of justification."

"Or a revenge on our own selves," Pavli offered, alternatively. "After having humiliated ourselves, serving him so devotedly, we wanted to do something to atone for what we had done."

Zef disagreed. "I, for my part, didn't think of it as atonement. I considered it only as a reply to people who, after liberation — I was always hoping for liberation — to people who would ask me, And during these years, what have you done? It was meant as a reply."

"So that you could say . . . ?"

"I did something useful," Zef concluded. The car pulled into the driveway of the Dajti.

∙

I went down to the hotel veranda at five. Ilir was there, in a white T-shirt and jeans. When we went into the bar to get mineral water and soft drinks, he wouldn't let me pay; instead, he made some arrangement so that I was his guest. Upstairs, in my room, we sat on the little balcony facing the electric sign.

He was a dancer, it turned out. His father wanted him to study law, I think it was, but he wanted to dance. There was some difficulty with language. We used Zef's dictionary to get through the rough spots. I would think of a word we needed in English and translate it into German in my mind, and then look it up in the dictionary and show Ilir the corresponding word in Albanian. Then I would say the English word for it. Cumbersome, but a bit like a game.

Ilir was in one of those folk-dance ensembles approved by the regime. But his passion was for ballet. Classical and modern dance, although he called the latter "abstract." "Ballet abstract," he said. He told me, in bits and pieces, the story of a ballet he was in at school, *The Silver Birds*, written by his teacher, his "choreograph." And then I finally got it about "the rap." What he was interested in was rap dancing. He'd seen this fellow, MC Hammer, an American, who was a performer of rap dancing, on Yugoslavian television. And the famous Michael Jackson, of course. I hadn't paid much attention to any of that, but one absorbs it, since it's in the air, so I knew what he was talking about. I'd thought the sound of rap was like the staccato of a firing squad. But Ilir's idea was this: He too wanted to be a choreographer. And the ballet he wanted to create would be a combination of classical ballet and rap dancing. Well, why not?

We sat on the balcony and chatted away for a couple of hours. There were other stories. Something about his sister, or sister-in-law, wanting to flee Albania for the Italian refugee camps, how he'd pleaded with her not to go. And once he'd been to Turkey for two or three weeks — I didn't quite get why — and had stayed with a family who had been very nice to him, but he'd gotten homesick.

Ilir was outgoing, unselfconscious, a little breathless. Perhaps all the pidgin English, pidgin Albanian, made our encounter seem much simpler than it was. I didn't think he represented the "spirit of Albania" or some such nonsense. I could feel the temptation to make that of him, but that's a dangerous sentimentality too. He was simply himself. But he was also of the place; he would have to live here when Vrioni and Don Quixote and the translators had gone on. He might even make a ballet, if the place wasn't overtaken by chaos; if it didn't revert to hill banditry and blood feuds; if, against the odds, Ilir's musical talent and the "deliberate belief" (as Conrad calls it) of the dictionary makers could forge a citizenry. Ilir wanted to see me again the next day, before I left. He would bring me a *regalo*, a gift. He'd come at nine the next morning.

That evening I had dinner in the hotel, in a large hall at the end of the long corridor, beyond the bar and breakfast room that flanked its length. Through the dining room windows you could see the boulevard, filled with people passing up and down in the middle of the wide avenue. The pilgrims, myself included, were at their cutlets. The Texans were at a table on one side of me. I gathered they were off to Cairo the next day. Apparently they'd done a deal for oil rights down at Flore, to the south, below Apollonia, the old Greek town. And at the table on my other side there was another businessman, with a woman, earnestly lecturing a local fellow, who seemed quite deferential before the pilgrim's sermon on efficiency.

I took the air for a bit, among the strolling crowds, and then retired to my room. Before I nodded off to sleep that night, I saw the end of it, of the story I was following here. I envisaged my meeting with Ilir in the morning, the flight back to Berlin, but more than that, I saw how all the conversations, the places I'd seen, and the dictionaries came together. When you're vouch-safed, in advance, a glimpse of the tale in its entirety, you simply shudder with gratefulness to the god for whom the Greeks named that town of Apollonia.

Ilir arrived promptly at nine. The haze was just lifting from Mount Dajti. He had a plastic sack filled with *regalos*: a bottle of Albanian raki, another of wine, some candy, and a collection of video and cassette tapes — Beethoven and a local singer and MC Hammer, which he'd taken off the radio, and some TV footage of the visit of the American secretary of state to Tirana. There was also a snapshot of himself. He emptied his treasury upon me. Would I send him a video of Hammer or Michael Jackson? "Yes, of course," I promised and later did. "But there's one more *regalo* I'd like," I said. He was puzzled. What more could there be?

"I'd like to see you dance," I said.

"But where?" he asked.

"Here," I said. At first he made the faintest show of resistance, but he was an artist and accustomed to performing. Beethoven is not really for dancing, he pointed out, even as he snapped the tape into my little interview recorder with the familiar dexterity of teenagers everywhere.

He placed himself in front of the gauze curtain before the window. It was embroidered with birds, and the faintest breeze moved the cloth. I pressed the button and symphonic strains emerged. At first I didn't think it would come off. There was barely enough room to move between the bed and the doorway to the bathroom, three or four paces at most. I don't know what I expected — that it would be quite provincial or crudely amateur-ish, perhaps.

I needn't have worried. He struck a pose and quickly found space to soar and plunge and turn. When the Beethoven ran out, he immediately found the woman pop singer on the tape and danced a mixture of Turkish and folkloric movements. For the finale there was a performance of rap dancing to Hammer chant-ing the refrain "Can't touch this," repeated again and again. It was one of those boasting songs from the American ghetto, full of aggressive sexual double entendres and self-acclaim for the performer's artistry. Although I'd only paid annoyed attention to it when I'd seen it in passing on television, it now struck me as quite beautiful; I saw the art of it. Ilir simply viewed it as another form of modern dancing. For him, the elements of the culture had no gaping spaces. For his needs, Beethoven and MC Hammer were contemporaries. And the tiny room was as adequate as the stage in the amphitheatre at Durrës.

At the end, he collapsed into the chair at my desk, heaving for breath. I offered him a can of cola. It was soon time for him to go; he had a test at school that day. We hugged farewell. "Can't touch this," I said, echoing Hammer. "Can't touch this," he repeated with a grin.

■

The rubber tires of the plane squeaked down onto the tarmac at Tegel Airport in Berlin as I turned the last pages of Conrad's story. I was left at the end with Marlow, Conrad's yarn-spinner: "Marlow ceased, and sat apart, indistinct and silent, in the pose of a meditating Buddha."

I got up, reaching into the overhead baggage rack for my maroon-coloured gym bag. Coincidentally — and this was one of those thousand things you couldn't possibly make up — my seat companion was a riverboat captain, just returning from someplace in Africa where he worked for a German resource company. We wished each other well at the end of our respective journeys.

That evening, a cool, damp, Berlin night, I had a drink at the Café Einstein. When I said to a friend I'd run into there that I was just back from Tirana, he made me repeat the name and then tried it out himself, as if uttering the name of some place on the moon. I extracted Zef's dictionary from my bag as evidence that I wasn't making it up. "But why did you want to go there?" he asked, tolerantly amused.

The Horses of Instruction

The Secret of Happiness

One semester, on the first day of an introductory metaphysics class I was teaching, as I was rambling on about the technical requirements of the course (how many papers, which books we would read) and making a few remarks about the subject matter, I said something (I can't remember what) and a blond-haired young woman put up her hand and asked, "You mean, like in *The Celestine Prophecy*?"

Since a good deal of teaching consists of following "leads," I dropped everything, signalled to her that I would respond to her question, but first asked the class, as I always do when a heretofore unmentioned "cultural" reference comes up, "How many people know about *The Celestine Prophecy*?"

The Celestine Prophecy is a New Age "wisdom" novel that had been on the bestseller lists for over a year at that time and would remain there even after its author, James Redfield, published the inevitable bestselling sequel (called *The Tenth Insight*).

Usually when I survey students about any cultural reference that doesn't relate to current pop music groups or movies now playing, only about three or four hands uncertainly go up, and this lets me go into a little routine. "What, you've never heard of [Descartes, Proust, V.S. Naipaul, whoever]?!" I say in tones of mock and real astonishment. This time, at least a third of the class of thirty-five students raised their hands, and several of them, when I probed further, appeared to have actually read it.

"Well, uh — " I said, groping for a name. "Jennifer," she supplied. "Well, Jennifer, maybe you'd better say something about what it's about for those who haven't read it."

"It's about this guy," she obligingly began, "who goes to the

231

mountains, in Peru I think it is, and he found these old manuscripts. And they have these, like, 'insights.'" I could see that she
was enthusiastic and about to describe the insights to us.

"Just a second," I interjected. "Do these old manuscripts really
exist or did Redfield make them up?"

She was temporarily nonplussed, as if she hadn't thought about
this question before. After a pause, she said, "Gee, I think they
exist. I think I read in a newspaper that he found this old chest."

Well, if my heart sank a little at the confirmation of the fact
that students were no longer taught the difference between novels and non-fiction, I could take comfort in the further fact that
we were at least in the right place — namely, a metaphysics class
— to investigate the difference. Interestingly, none of the other
readers of *The Celestine Prophecy* offered any correction to
Jennifer's claim. I made my little disquisition on categories of
writing and their relation to reality. Then I offered a bit of further encouragement. "Of course, it probably doesn't really matter whether they exist or not. What we're interested in here is
whether the 'insights' are 'true' or not. Now, what was that first
insight again?"

The insight she recalled was something like "Everything that
happens, happens for a reason." Further, it was clear that she
was taken with this idea and believed it. By now, I was in a good
mood. Instead of having to go through all the boring stuff at the
outset of the semester, by a lucky break we were plunged right
into the course subject matter. Naturally, I began by ascertain-
ing that when he said things happened "for a reason," Redfield
wasn't referring to mere causality, in which case we'd be dealing
with something that was only trivially true. By "a reason," in this
instance, Redfield must mean that everything that happens, happens because some power intends it to happen. Then I wanted to
know if this was a reason we could know, since it mattered to me
whether this was a secret reason we could never know or do anything about, or if the god or power who had a reason for making
something happen that appeared to us as a mere accident was
approachable in some way. We were off and on our way.

If I've given the impression of being slightly sardonic about
the students' knowledge or state of mind, I don't mean to be.
Apart from the mock astonishment (that verbally accompanies
my real astonishment) that they don't know about Descartes,

Proust, V.S. Naipaul, or whoever, there is no mockery involved at all. In fact, all these claims and questions about what happens and the reasons for it happening seem to me perfectly interesting and legitimate, and I take them seriously. I'm interested in the answers, too.

I should report — since I'm not going to go on with the whole story of where that particular discussion went — that I failed with the young woman I'm calling Jennifer. When she turned in her paper, it consisted of an assertion of her New Age spiritual beliefs, unleavened by critical thought or any doubts. My efforts to get her to focus on the possible status of those beliefs, and the problems of how we could know whether something was true or not, earned me a zero. (I tend to mark myself as well as them.) When I gave her a c on her essay (a strictly charitable grade meant to encourage further effort), a lengthy commentary, and heaps of marginalia full of helpful hints ("When you say ... do you mean that ... ?" and "Have you considered the possibility of ... ?"), she came to my faculty office, the doors of which are now left open during student visits to reassure all that nothing untoward is happening.

"But you said ... " she began, angrily launching a litany of blame. When I saw that she was really angry and near to tears, I did my best to explain the grade-appeal system available to her and immediately arranged an appointment for her with my colleague Mark Battersby (he was the elected department head that semester), who's very soothingly good at dealing with this sort of thing.

That semester, I discovered that I had two "lessons" to teach. The lessons tend to change each year because I try to forget everything I learned about teaching the semester before and start all over. The simpler lesson was about "boring" and "interesting." Though the use of the word "boring" as an expletive was no longer the buzzword it had been a couple of years earlier, there was still something to say about whether the students found Descartes, Proust, et al. "boring" or "interesting," since they often reported finding things boring that I thought were interesting. Although I was willing to grant some objective ground to those notions, I also wanted to argue that they weren't simply "natural" categories, and that finding something boring or interesting depended a lot on who you were and how you looked at the thing. That is,

234 • TOPIC SENTENCE

boring or interesting was, in large part, a measure of yourself. If
I didn't push this discussion to the point where it became boring
itself, they usually found it reasonably interesting.

The second lesson is something I call "negative precepts."
There's a part of the metaphysics course that I've informally
dubbed "Gods, ghosts, aliens, angels, and Elvis," although as
time passes and fewer students have heard of Elvis Presley, he's
beginning to fade from the list of entities that may or may not be
alive and well. This part of metaphysics is about beliefs people
have about things outside common sense and what we know of
the laws of physics.

I tend to be ontologically conservative. If somebody says they
believe something (alien abductions, say), I ask for "good reasons" for so believing and request, as well, a canvassing of alternative possible explanations for the phenomena at issue. If it
turns out that the basis of the belief amounts to "Well, isn't it
possible . . . [that aliens exist and that they have a penchant for
abducting earthlings]?" then I turn to a discussion of the notion
of "probability."

If it turns out that there aren't any good reasons, I invoke the
"negative precept," which in its most didactic form goes something like, "If you don't have a good reason for believing in
something, don't believe in it." I also offer its obverse: "If you
don't have a good reason for disbelieving something that you
otherwise have good reason to believe in, don't disbelieve it."

For example, if we ask, "How do we know other people have
minds like ours?" the standard reply is the argument from similar behaviour and similar anatomy. We believe other people have
minds like ours because they do and say things similar to the
things we do and say, they have the same kind of brains that
we have, and — and here comes the negative precept part — we
have no good reason to believe that they are robots or replicants
or zombies. It's *possible* that they're robots or replicants, but we
can do a little checking and quickly discover that robotics hasn't
yet reached the stage of producing believable androids.

I think that most of what I've described is pretty standard
teaching practice, although, as a pluralist, I believe there are lots
of ways to teach well, and I certainly wouldn't require anyone
to adopt the methods I use or tell the jokes I tell. It's odd that so
little is written about what actually goes on in teaching, though

we teachers devote vast amounts of our conversation and gossip to discussing precisely what happened in particular classes on particular good and bad days, and exactly what student so-and-so said when I asked . . . , etc.

Sometimes I teach myself something. One day we were talking about happiness. We were far enough along in the semester that they had noticed I was invariably cheerful. By the way, this is one of those things that I don't think you can fake. Although contemporary students may have been rendered ignorant about their culture, they strike me as psychologically acute about attitudes, self-presentation, and the like. It's true — and they can tell — that I like being with them, having the conversations we have, figuring out the answers to the questions, even though most of the questions in metaphysics don't have answers.

"How come you're always so happy?" one of them asked. Often when I'm asked that (which is, in fact, a tough question to answer satisfactorily), I try to fob them off with an account of my father, from whom I acquired my happy temperament. I have a large repertoire of anecdotes about what a wonderful guy my father was. But when that doesn't work, I have to admit, "Because I've discovered the secret of happiness."

"What is it?" they ask, at last "interested."

"You don't think I'm just going to come right out and tell you, do you?" I tease. "I mean, tuition fees haven't gone up so high that we have to reveal the secret of happiness, have they?" I like to fool around a lot, especially when tough questions are on the table.

Eventually I get around to admitting that although it seems I have discovered the secret of happiness, and they have some available evidence — namely, my persistent if sometimes insufferable cheerfulness — that would give them good reason to believe this is the case, it's a "secret" that's hard to put into words. Still, I try. I point out that part of the secret of happiness is to recognize that happiness isn't as important as they thought it was, but they don't believe that. What it usually comes to, I finally concede, is a recognition that unless life is *imperative*, it's not very interesting. I don't try to explain that all at once, but I'm usually willing to provide an example or two.

The example I gave them was about what I do in the morning. For some reason, students seem infinitely fascinated by the autobiographical details of the lives of their teachers, even though they tend to judge those lives to be fairly dopey and definitely boring. Anyway, after I wake up, go to the bathroom, and make some coffee, I settle in at my desk and read a few pages of philosophy. I like to read philosophy first because it's the most difficult thing and my mind is clearest at the beginning of the day, before the travails of the world have demanded and received my attention. The students usually make a sound of mild disgust upon hearing this — a kind of "ugh, why would anyone want to do that?" sound — but they're sort of interested. There's a slight bias in favour of "weirdness," and this counts as definitely "different," as they currently say.

I also explain that I don't like any electronics sounds in the morning while I'm reading my philosophy — radios, TVs, music players, and the like. I tell them about that bit of personal bias as part of my general campaign against consuming all that junk. I don't even like newspapers first thing in the morning. Their stories feel like little hands clutching at me, each one demanding that I sympathize with their idea of the world.

I say, This is something I like doing, reading a few pages of philosophy in the morning. It's part of what makes me happy, and I've been doing it just about every morning for years and years.

As I was telling them this, I was a little surprised to realize that it was true and that I had never really thought about it in terms of happiness before. To a degree (a limited degree, naturally), and under certain conditions, we can do pretty much what we want, especially if we're middle-class academics in wealthy societies. To a degree, and this is the more important factor, nobody *cares* what I do at 6:11 AM. To a degree, nobody gives a shit about anything we do, and nobody'll give a shit after we're dead whether or not we read a couple of pages of philosophy first thing in the morning for years and years.

"Of course, people not caring about each other is usually bad," I caution. "But there's also a good side to nobody giving a shit. The only one who has to care, at least about certain things I do, is me." The sense of exhilarating freedom and terrifying loneliness contained in the recognition that nobody gives a shit is part of the secret of happiness.

Academic Freedom and Its Distractions

A senior administrator at the college where I teach — a very nice person, committed to liberal education, sensible, decent, and so on — turned up one day to talk to the faculty members of the Humanities division and tell us what our college was up to. The big idea, he quickly revealed, was entrepreneurial education — revenue-generating projects that would increase the institution's fiscal independence, affording us relief from the budgetary whims of passing provincial governments. The first of these projects under exploration, he announced, was China. I must admit that I missed the economic details of this proposal, other than that it was financially favourable to us. Apparently, someone in China was starting up one or more private postsecondary institutions and was seeking some sort of business and intellectual partnership with a North American institution that would provide curriculum and faculty.

My attention was so adrift during the initial part of his presentation that I didn't really wake up until our administrator said, "And so, you would have the choice of teaching on either the Lynnmour campus here or the China campus." I'm pretty sure he didn't name some city in China, like Beijing or Shanghai. He just said, "China." Now, I should mention that my college is a minuscule provincial institution tucked into a patch of woods on the first ridge of hills on the north shore of suburban Vancouver. What got my attention was what seemed like a comical category mistake; namely, the equation of "Lynnmour campus," located here in the bucolic Lynn Valley of British Columbia, and the entire nation of China. He made it sound so easy: Lynnmour–China. Take your pick. Whichever you like.

While I was still figuring out what possible discourse would permit these two items to be fit into a single category of some virtual geography exercise, our intrepid administrator had already moved on to the next project: "We've had an inquiry to mount business management programs in Lebanon." Again, I was nonplussed. Most of us had come to this meeting thinking about things on the order of "Gee, I wonder if we can get a couple of extra 10:30 teaching time slots in next semester's schedule now that the new building has opened." Instead: Lebanon wants our business management programs.

Our visionary was unfazed. The first lady of Panama, he reported, wants to establish a "city of knowledge" — a vast educational complex with students from around the world who would be housed in former, now-abandoned, US military bases in that Central American country. And again I found myself about three steps behind, as I had been all through this recital. While he was on to the military bases logistics question, I was still thinking to myself, "The first lady of Panama? There's a first lady of Panama? And she wants a 'city of knowledge'? What next?"

I didn't have long to wonder. "What next" was the West Coast Express. Only a few loose ends remained to be tied up on the West Coast Express deal, we were assured. Once the deal was in place, teachers from our college would apparently be offering courses to early-morning commuters travelling the West Coast Express train from the suburb of Maple Ridge to their downtown Vancouver office jobs. We already know, our administrator said — I can barely convey the tone of chipper good will and enthusiasm in which all of this was told to us — what courses the commuters want on the way in to work — accounting and spreadsheets or something — but the one detail to be nailed down was that we weren't sure, from the surveys and focus groups that we'd done, just exactly what courses the commuters wanted on the ride home to Maple Ridge.

While you're contemplating the possibilities of music appreciation courses and/or bedtime stories as the commuter train goes clickety-clacking toward the horizon of Maple Ridge and beyond, let me pause in this true tale — although I realize it sounds like something from a wicked satirical novel about academia — to note that it was at that moment I began to understand, for the first time, the dimensions of the bureaucratic phrase "inclusive university." If the administrators at my little backwater — but excellent — arts and sciences college are contemplating such ventures and calling it education, what sorts of deals do you suppose the CEOs of major educational enterprises are negotiating? The moral of the story is: It might be possible and profitable to manufacture widgets at postsecondary institutions, but why call it education? Why not call it a widget factory?

Although what's on my mind is the matter of academic freedom, I feel obligated to first canvass some misleading educational developments, like the one above. These "distractions" from education, as I think of them, come equally from diametrically opposite political directions, right and left. All of them, I believe, will seriously undermine what education writer Peter Emberley, in his book *Zero Tolerance*, calls "the scholarly culture" and "its two predominant animating principles — reading in the tradition of books, and renewal by conversation." The right's long-standing threat to academic freedom emanates from the marketplace demand that the universities see themselves as "engines of economic growth" and "job-training centres." That demand is, I think, more threatening than the dangers from the left. Those left-wing dangers — namely, of behaviour and speech codes, or harassment policies — although trumpeted by the right as the evils of "political correctness," are minor irritants in comparison to the prospect of the entrepreneurial college. As for the spectre and/or promise of new teaching machines, it finds its enthusiasts on both sides of the political divide.

■

Computers can be discussed in the fewest possible sentences because everyone in the field of education already knows all about them and their growing place in whatever institution they're working at. About the only thing the teachers don't know about the computers is how to operate them, which occasions the need for all those nice people from the Information Technology department and their handy Helplines. So I can spare us the disquisition on what the full-scale entry of computers in education and the burgeoning legion of technical attendants they require for their maintenance is doing to university budgets by pointing out that they're bleeding them white.

I'll refrain from indulging in the debate about the vital or not-so-vital role of computers in pedagogy. In fact, I want to offer little more than a definition and a commonsense observation. The observation is that computers are a tool, and if a tool is useful to the task at hand, use it. Of course we know, from Benjamin Barber's *Jihad vs. McWorld*, it's not quite as simple as that, because the matching of tools and needs is not simply a natural process. Rather, needs are often created as addictively felt wants, and technologies become imperative rather than optional.

In the larger view, the computer is the latest solution to a classic dream. Sometimes the dream is called the perpetual motion machine, or the philosopher's stone, or the alchemist's formula to transmute lead into gold. At times, all the versions of the dream seem like blasphemies on the original vision of the transubstantiation of wine and bread into blood and flesh. In this case, the dream is that of the great teaching machine. Those of us who have practised the teaching arts for a while have already been through this once before in our careers when that great oxymoron, educational television, was offered up as a surefire panacea.

A quarter century later, the main function of educational television, as we know, is its use in the *second* amphitheatre where herds of students have been sequestered because the first amphitheatre, where the prof is lecturing live, is already full. I'm sure there are surveys showing that the students in the second amphitheatre are happier watching the lecture next door on a giant TV screen than the students in the first amphitheatre. In many institutions, a similar screen has now been installed in the first amphitheatre, and the students there are able to ignore the live lecturer entirely in favour of the warm and fuzzy feelings that television apparently produces. And naturally, no one wants to discuss whether it's a good educational idea for two amphitheatres full of undergraduates to be "taking" — I use the word advisedly — such courses.

Even in the few minutes I've been thinking about computers, their educational presence has become more ubiquitous. The effect on teachers is that they're now doing more and more of the clerical work formerly done by secretaries and learning assistants, as we call them at my school. The teachers now maintain class lists, enter grades, often receive late papers, fire off memos, etc., via computers. In many cases, these are chores that used to be done by registrars and other helpers. Although the office is increasingly paperless as promised, the flow of memos tends to increase, and just as with the ever-present cellphone, anytime anyone has a passing thought, they copy it to everyone within electronic range and the inbox clutter grows apace. And despite IT's array of "firewalls," encryption, and other protections from mischief, one receives a steady flow of messages from mysterious sources offering to sell sex potions and/or enlarge your penis.

For students, the effect is more serious, if not dire. Certainly, Peter Emberley's idea of education as "renewal by conversation" is under threat, likely to be replaced by such cheapened simulacra as course websites, "chat rooms," "text messaging," and so-called mixed-mode courses, in which more and more of the course is delivered by computer. The students, who have been thoroughly acclimated to the culture of cellphones, digital thises and thats, and a variety of music-playing machines (to which they listen ceaselessly), are at home with computers. The "search engine" has replaced or is replacing the library and books as a source of thought. The search engines also make it easier to buy prepackaged papers, which, in its turn, has generated a whole side-business of automatic computer programs that detect purloined papers. At more progressive schools, there's a push to get the teacher out of the classroom and into the studio so that the lecture can be digitally packaged and ingested, and students can absorb it wherever and whenever, usually while doing five other things at the same time (a practice of distraction known as "multitasking"). One account I read reported that even students who live in dormitories on campus prefer not to attend class but to watch the stored, digitalized version of the lecture at their time and place of convenience.

I've no idea if computers will achieve total dominance. Maybe they will. But the main thing to remember is that the new teaching machine, philosopher's stone, lead-into-gold formula, appeals to two temptations. First, there's the teacher's temptation to get out of teaching, and second, there's the administration's temptation to get rid of teaching and transform students into consumers. The situation is, as one of my mentors often said, another bad idea whose time has come. In any case, the art of teaching can be added to the growing list of endangered species, likely to go the way of the dodo.

■

In terms of distractions, it's necessary to address various subtopics that can be put under the rubric of "therapy."

Some time ago, in the mid-1990s, I innocently attended the

faculty union meeting at my college, where the subject of sexual harassment was introduced as an issue for consideration. I say "innocently attended" because although I had followed and participated in the debates launched by the women's movement over the previous quarter century and had read many of the major texts in the field, I see retrospectively that I was, for a variety of reasons, some social and some personal, something of an innocent about what was at issue. That innocence may be a sort of occupational hazard to which people who teach philosophy are especially prone.

In any case, I was prepared to enter the discussion with the requisite inquiring temperament and a willingness to seek actual remedies. When the issue of sexual harassment was called to my attention, my initial (and continuing) response was that, of course, we ought to do something to prevent it. I had little idea of the possible extent of sexually harassing behaviour at the institution where I taught, but I was assured by various colleagues that it was significant enough to merit specific attention.

There were, I was told, frequent acts of repeated "unwanted" sexual touching or fondling, threatening demands for sexual favours, and proposals of rewards in exchange for sex — what was once known in academia as "an A for a lay." I was (and remain) prepared to hold up my hand at the appropriate time to vote for the resolution to stop that sort of thing.

Well, the appropriate time and the resolution soon appeared. Except that there was something curious about the resolution — which was, I should note, a resolution that was to be inserted into the legal contract between the college and its teachers. Before I get to the curiosity, a couple of preliminary remarks are necessary.

First, there already existed an extensive process of monitoring and evaluating the performance and behaviour of teachers, which included the acts now called "sexual harassment," and also included sanctions such as reprimands, suspensions, and even firing. There was a nice old-fashioned phrase for that sort of behaviour. It was called, back in the 1950s and '60s, "moral turpitude," and we all rather savoured the word "turpitude," bemused by what exactly it might mean. In any case, moral turpitude was eventually succeeded by the clearly more antiseptic phrase "termination for just cause." Furthermore, there already existed a squad of counsellors, division coordinators, deans, vice-presidents, and sundry other administrators with whom one might lodge complaints.

Second, and in addition to this considerable machinery, there was the question of intellectual climate. Our college was one of the leading sites where a critique of sexism, racism, homophobia, and various other discriminations had been developed. There was not only a critique but also widespread advocacy, among the teachers, of values designed to undercut such sexism, racism, homophobia, and so on. Now, a lot of people who aren't particularly fond of academic institutions like to pretend not only that such institutions didn't lead the way in exploring these issues but also that they are among the prime offenders. No one has demonstrated that either claim has any empirical weight, but they're still frequently heard, often from academics themselves.

Despite this context of available mechanisms of remedy and intellectual advocacy against discriminatory behaviours, I was willing to support specific action against sexual harassment, on the grounds of collegiality and with the thought in mind that there were some acts, lying between Criminal Code offences and institutional regulatory codes, that might be captured by such a policy in a way that would be an improvement on existing methods.

Then came the proposed policy. I'll quote the crucial curious section, although members of similar institutions will be familiar with the wording. It says: "Sexual harassment is comment or conduct of a sexual nature, including sexual advances, requests for sexual favours, suggestive comments or gestures, or physical contact when any one of the following occurs: a) the conduct is engaged in, or the comment is made, by a person who knows, or ought reasonably to know, that the conduct or comment is unwanted or unwelcome; b) the conduct or comment has the effect of creating an intimidating, hostile or offensive environment, and may include the expression of sexist attitudes, language and behaviour." This wording was followed by several other clauses that referred to illicit rewards, reprisals, threats, and so on.

The fact that the policy was written in execrably convoluted prose that was grammatically suspect wasn't curious. I understand what committees are capable of doing to language. Anyway, when I asked why it was so badly written and reasoned,

I was assured by a committee member that "we merely copied the wording from the University of British Columbia's policy." I winced at this confession of plagiarism but decided to let it pass. I was more concerned about reasoning. If one parsed the policy, it said, among many other things, "Sexual harassment is comment of a sexual nature when the comment has the effect of creating an offensive [classroom or campus] environment, and it may include the expression of sexist attitudes."

Clearly, we were a long way from the acts that I thought we were trying to prevent. Indeed, it seemed to me acts and mere words had been conflated by the proposed policy. By "mere words" I mean words that aren't acts, such as, say, threats. Worse, the conflation of acts and words depended on ambiguous, undefined phrases that would be left for interpretation to the administrators of the complicated quasi-judicial procedures that the policy's drafters envisaged. Among those phrases are "of a sexual nature," "offensive environment," and "sexist attitudes."

I wanted to know if an utterance, delivered in the classroom, to the effect that pornography is mere free expression protected by the Constitution and that a once-current slogan, "Porn is the theory, rape is the practice," is intellectually imbecilic, qualified under the proposed policy. Were remarks about pornography "of a sexual nature"? Was the sentiment uttered one that could create an "offensive environment"? Did the forceful rejection of a well-known maxim of anti-pornography feminists in itself constitute a "sexist attitude"? The answer to all of those questions, lamentably, is a resounding yes. Of course, my colleagues at the union meeting assured me that the answers were no and, to placate me and assuage my concerns, inserted a phrase, probably also pilfered from UBC's policy, to assure us that the "policy is not intended to infringe upon the ability of instructors to academically discuss issues of harassment, sexism and sexuality." In short, academic freedom was allegedly safe.

In reality, what had happened was that somebody's idea of sexism and how to eradicate it was imported into a policy purportedly meant to prevent acts of sexual harassment. The levels of duplicity, misguided sincerity, and sandbox power politics involved in all of this can be passed over.

Intended or not, it seemed to me (then, and, in retrospect, now) that there was a conflation of acts and words in this policy, and the policy endangered the utterance of some words at a place that is, ironically, a privileged site for free speech. Furthermore, that speech is protected by a law that trumps local regulatory policy, namely the freedom-of-speech clause of the Canadian Charter of Rights and Freedoms.

This shaggy feminist story can be extended interminably, and was. Once we established the sexual harassment policy, we then embarked on an expansionary policy discussion that dragged on at my school for several more years and included the eradication of various other forms of harassment. But I'll cease and desist from providing the delicious details.

Whenever I gave voice to my musings about the distractions of academia, from reflections on turning colleges into factories to those on harassment policies, the reaction was uniform at the academic conferences and meetings where I spoke. The audiences tended to be a mixture of liberals and feminists. Everybody laughed with glee when I described the evils of the entrepreneurial institution, but when I got to harassment policies, the liberals furrowed their brows (some in sympathy, others with trepidation), while the self-declared feminists glowered and sometimes hooted in derision.

Before exiting from this cautionary tale, a word to the unwise. On the right, there are those who think that harassment policies and other therapeutic policies were the greatest disaster of the then *fin de siècle*. They aren't. It's important to distinguish between enemies and distractions. Harassment policies, speech codes, and the popular ideology of therapeutically treating the "whole student" and even his or her "inner student" strike me as a distraction, not a destruction of the entire educational enterprise.

But also a word to the left, to those who are offended by any criticism of "political correctness" and who are overly quick to spot a backlash of ancient sexists, racists, and homophobes once more rearing their ugly heads. My word is this: If you can't see that the excesses of the anti-sexist policies that you've created need to be reined in, I don't see how you're going to conquer the hordes of old and new fogies, both within and beyond the ivory towers, who will turn backlash into self-fulfilling prophecy.

Seen from the perspective of several years down the road, the harassment policies settled into the institution as a minor feature of the academic machinery, and harassment rates at such institutions remained as low as their murder and auto accident rates compared to the population at large. The institution as business and job training centre, however, has continued to thrive, which is why academic freedom needs attention.

●

Academic freedom — the right of the teachers to raise and discuss whatever questions they believe are relevant to life on earth — has never been understood as an absolute freedom; it has always been constrained by concepts of "teaching competence" and "professional conduct."

There are many views on offer of what academic freedom might be. One of the better-known post-modern neo-pragmatists, Stanley Fish, author of a book extravagantly titled *There's No Such Thing as Free Speech . . . And It's a Good Thing, Too*, has lately discovered that liberalism is an ideology rather than the neutral cipher it sometimes purports to be.

Liberalism, as an inclusive doctrine of toleration, it turns out, is itself intolerant of those who are themselves terminally intolerant. The inclusive university, Professor Fish finds, is a chimera; liberalism is a lie; and it is time, in his view, for plain talk. "The assertion of interest is always what's going on," he says, "even when, and especially when, interest wraps itself in high-sounding abstractions . . . Politics is all there is, and it's a good thing, too. Principles and abstractions don't exist except as the rhetorical accompaniment of practices in search of good public relations." Almost needless to add, in Fish's view, there's no such thing as academic freedom; there's only a power struggle, and by his lights, that's a good thing, too. I've no idea why Fish thinks power struggles are good things, unless he's under the delusion that his side is winning.

In a more mainstream mode, Frederick Schauer, a constitutional law professor at Harvard who specializes in what's known as "conceptual clarification," offers the metaphor of an "exemption" or an "immunity" to capture the character of academic freedom. Schauer says that, conceptually, academic freedom is "an exemption from something that everyone else has to do" or, alternatively, an immunity from, say, the proscription of certain utterances, a proscription applicable to everybody else.

He then goes on to diminish this clarification further by noting that in the United States, academic freedom "is not much of an issue" because First Amendment law protects everyone and allows everyone to say just about anything, so no special protection is required for academics. He allows that there's a slight difference in Canada; for instance, while utterances of Holocaust denial are fully protected in the United States, statutory and case law in Canada indicate that utterances of Holocaust denial are not protected, and, therefore, academics might need an exemption from such law to explore or engage in Holocaust denial. All of this strikes me as disappointing. The metaphor of "exemption" seems ill-chosen to describe what is essentially a positive teaching power protected from improper intrusion by government and others.

The idea of the teaching power is most extensively discussed by Joseph Tussman in his book *Government and the Mind* (1977), and what he says there lays the groundwork for a meaningful conception of academic freedom. Tussman writes, "The teaching power is the inherent constitutional authority of the state to establish and direct the teaching activity and institutions needed to ensure its continuity and further its legitimate general and special purposes. It is rather strange that a governmental power so visible in its operation and so pervasive in effect should lack a familiar name." He adds, "The teaching power is a peer to the legislative, the executive, and the judicial powers, if it is not, indeed, first among them."

In the broadest outline, here is how it is derived. In a democracy, power ought to reside with the citizens, who, in a constitution-making conclave, delegate certain day-to-day operations of that power to government. Furthermore, there is a "separation of powers" and a series of "checks and balances" on that delegated power, based on the intuition that unseparated, unchecked delegated power will tend toward abuse and corruption. Thus, the legislative power is not to be abrogated by the executive power or the judicial power, and its independence is not to be intruded on by other powers. As for the teaching power, we find it implicitly present in almost all constitutional documents — Tussman cites that of the state of California, which says, "A general diffusion of knowledge and intelligence being essential to the preservation of the rights and liberties of the people, the legislature shall encourage by all suitable means the promotion of intellectual, scientific, moral and agricultural improvement." The language is unremarkable, but the thought isn't the least unremarkable. It represents a long historical journey through much darkness. This declaration results in the web of offices and institutions in which the teaching power is invested.

I frequently joke with my students that, in addition to being a member of a global, trans-historical discipline, I'm also an officer of the Canadian state charged with the task of inculcating and interrogating the values, laws, and practices of Canadian democracy. The joke is no joke. I further argue that both of those functions — discipline and office — once they are appropriately vested through mechanisms of certification, appointment, and monitored performance, are protected from interference under the doctrine of the teaching power. That seems to me a tacit but logical feature of the division of powers in a democracy.

The teaching power deserves its degree of relative autonomy by virtue of its dual task, which is to inculcate citizenly virtues and to develop the critical thought at the heart of the deliberative practices of a democracy. Anything short of such a view of academic freedom trivializes the notion and probably renders it incomprehensible to the public. While everyone in a democracy has freedom of thought, imagination, and speech, academic freedom is the recognition that within the general doctrine of free speech, academic inquiry occurs within a privileged site of free speech and enjoys an articulated degree of protection and vigilance. There's a great deal more that can be said about academic freedom and how it's to be administered, but my immediate point is that such an idea only makes sense within a larger conception of forum democracy.

Of course, if a society doesn't have anything on its mind except to turn its educational institutions into little more than engines of economic growth, then the right to discuss whatever is on our minds probably doesn't amount to much.

The Music of the Spheres

Coming from a classroom on the south, or lower, side of the Capilano College campus, where I've just taught an 8:30 morning class, I'm heading up the hill toward the northside Fir Building. I have a cubbyhole office there on the fourth floor. On my way, I pass the music rooms at the base of the building. Pouring out of the practice cubicles, whose windows are partially open on this late-summer September morning, is an astonishing cacophony of sound — rippling piano scales, horn blurts, the tooting of woodwinds, and human voices running through arpeggios. I'm half-distractedly thinking about whatever happened in the classroom a few minutes ago, when I'm suddenly startled by the overlapping melodies wafting out of the bunker-like building, as if I'd never heard them before. Transfixed for an instant by the pleasure of hearing the wave of sounds, I feel as if I am listening to a local version of the "music of the spheres."

My relationship with Capilano College, over the more than twenty years that I've taught there — first politics, then philosophy — is a lot like what I feel when I hear that music. I find the sounds and the musicians reassuring: as they earnestly toot and ripple and warble, I feel reasonably certain that they're not planning to punch anyone in the nose — which is my definition of civility. The music students wander around campus, moving up and down the alpine hill like humpbacked pack animals with guitar bags and tuba cases slung on their backs, along with the other rucksack-carrying students, giving the whole place a bucolic air. (Sudden memory of singing "The Happy Wanderer" hiking song as a child in elementary school music class: "I love to go a-wandering / Along the mountain track / And as I go, I love to sing / My knapsack on my back / / Val-deri, Val-dera . . . ")

The geography of the college also contributes to that pacific sense. Capilano is located on the first ridge of hills on the north shore of Burrard Inlet across from the city of Vancouver, just beyond North Vancouver's industrial foreshore, where piles of sulphur and containers full of widgets are heaped on the docks. The college, which you arrive at by a canyon road that runs up to the top of a hill, is set within a stand of mostly cedars and firs. Beyond the college are more ridges and canyons and, farther north, range after range of mountains. A hundred and fifty kilometres north of Capilano, once you're past the mill-town at Squamish and the ski-resort at Whistler, it's pretty much pure wilderness.

Apart from my somewhat sentimental idea of the charm of the place — which, admittedly, is just plain gloomy during the rainy season, when the whole institution huddles miserably under a steady, chill drizzle for weeks on end — what I'm interested in is the main activity of the college, namely, teaching. From most of the public and media discussion of education, you'd never imagine that teaching is what Capilano and similar schools are all about, or that the teaching is aimed at developing the sort of person who can assume a place as a citizen in a democracy. Even we teachers occasionally forget that. Instead, there's an enormous preoccupation with whether students are being properly trained for various jobs and with such other diversions as whether or not the college is suitably "online." The latter refers to a concern about the use of technology in teaching, a subject I crankily regard as a euphemism for replacing teaching. But as one of my favourite newspaper columnists (John Doyle, the TV writer for the Toronto *Globe and Mail*) says when he recognizes he's just about to launch a rant, Don't get me started.

My friend Ryan Knighton and I once collaborated on a mock book called *Teaching Is Easy*. Ryan is a colleague at Capilano College, a writer who teaches in the English department. He's thirty-something, one of the new generation of instructors, with a shaved head, a gym-fit body, and a white cane to get around because he's blind. We drive to work together in the mornings since we both teach morning classes. My one-liner is "We're a car-pool, but I don't let him drive very much." We're both pretty good at irony, the alternative to which, I point out, is suicide. I also have a one-liner about teaching, which I contributed to our mock book: Teaching is easy because anything you say in class these days is "news" to the students. We both agree that the hardest part of teaching is leaving the coffee kiosk on the way to a rainy morning class because you need three hands to carry the book bag, the cup of coffee, and the umbrella. Four hands if you're also tapping around with a white cane, Ryan adds. After that, as we say, it's all downhill.

Jokes aside, the first issue of education is the conditions of teaching. Again, this is seldom publicly discussed, but there's a major difference between teaching in a university and teaching in a college, the two parts of the Canadian postsecondary educational system. Typically, in North American universities these days, introductory classes (in biology, psychology, physics, and other disciplines) are conducted in amphitheatres that can hold up to eight hundred students. From some vantage points, the professor in the pit doing the lecturing appears to be about the size of an insect, so there is often a large screen behind him (or her) on which a magnified image is projected. A good deal of the lecture occurs in half darkness because the professor is using an overhead projector to provide notes on the screen for the students to copy down. The professor will have teaching assistants to deal with the students. The teaching assistants are senior graduate students; they mark the student papers and exams, and, at what are considered "good schools," they may conduct seminars with smaller groups of students. The professors have little contact with the first-year students beyond answering a handful of questions at the end of the lecture.

The students in these huge introductory classes are fiscal cannon fodder to pay for the university's often excellent graduate schools. At best, then, you get great lecturing. And while great lecturing is nothing to sniff at, it's also a very small part of teaching. At worst (and worst may be closer to the norm), what you get is the equivalent of those schools in benighted countries where students spend the day performing, en masse, rote recitations of religious texts. I regard most of what goes on in Canadian undergraduate education of this sort as a scandal, something just short of criminal activity, but the habit is so entrenched it's seldom even remarked upon. Inevitably, sooner or later, some educational mad scientist appears on stage and proposes that there's no need for the mass lectures — the whole performance can be digitally repackaged, and the students can stay at home and watch it on their TVs or computers (thus also saving institutional janitorial costs). Worse, such dotty proposals become rational in the light of actual teaching conditions. Most of the current talk about the use of computers in teaching (or replacing teaching) is an outgrowth of this situation.

At Capilano College, I teach classes with about thirty-five students. The numbers creep up a little when there's a budget squeeze and the administration pleads with us to take in two or three extra students per course. Unlike the hermetic amphitheatres of the university, I teach in rooms — not necessarily great rooms for teaching, but often good enough that they have windows, and I can point outside to our little glade of trees and intone sentences like, "So, we all agree that the trees out there are real, right?" (It's a sentence that occurs in introductory metaphysics courses more often than one might expect.) In short, I'm able to engage in something that resembles conversations with the students. I know their names, I read their work, I mark their papers, I talk to them in my office or on the phone or by e-mail. After a few weeks, I know them well enough that I'm able to shape the lessons toward who they are and what they can understand, rather than what I, as a professor, understand. By the end of the term, I have a pretty good idea of the minds, personalities, and stories of the people I teach. I don't want to make any exaggerated claims about results, but I think these conditions of teaching produce slightly better "outcomes," as they say in the education business, than the alternatives.

Compared to the universities, the colleges, according to the unspoken wisdom that governs the matter, are second-rate schools for second-rate students who can't get into university or who can't afford to pay the more expensive tuition fees of the university. In reality, the colleges are about the only place in undergraduate education where teaching is still permitted. But I view the colleges as I do spotted owls, gloomily, as an endangered species.

I'm a pluralist on the question of how to teach. I take the position that there are lots of good ways to teach well. For example, John Dixon and I teach in what's known as the "Socratic style" (although the term perhaps flatters us). Dixon is a colleague in the philosophy department and is my best and oldest friend at Cap College. He's a tall, white-haired, bearded, outdoorsy type. In former years, when we were both more mobile, we were a familiar sight on campus, walking around together like classic peripatetic philosophers, the statuesque Dixon and his pudgy bald companion, a real Mutt-and-Jeff team. The only thing missing was the togas.

Dixon and I were both students in Bob Rowan's political philosophy classes at the University of British Columbia in the 1960s, and we both learned to teach from Rowan. I was notorious for having burst into Rowan's class one day when we were reading Plato's *Republic* and announcing, "Plato is wrong, Thrasymachus was right!", praising the world's first renowned pragmatist, who had argued that might is right, there are no eternal verities, against Socrates' wily defence of the moral life. Well, that was then. The Socratic method was reinforced for Dixon and me when we both studied briefly with the magisterial Joseph Tussman at the University of California in Berkeley. Tussman was Rowan's teacher, and Tussman's teacher was a philosopher named Alexander Meiklejohn, so there's a continuous line of transmission of both mode and thought (though, again, this probably flatters the feeble heirs).

In the Socratic manner, the fulcrum of the class rests not on the lecture but on the conversation in which we engage the students. Sometimes I "lecture" for a while, if I have something particular I want to say, although the lecturing has more the character of an improvised operatic aria than the "PowerPoint presentation" taught in business schools. There are also texts that provide the foundation for the conversation, and the texts matter. But in our reading of the books, I'm not trying to "get through" the text with a view to having "covered the material" in preparation for the final exam. The texts are usually not "textbooks" but real books by real writers, and I use them as entrances into the world and into the minds of their authors.

One of the features of Socratic-style teaching is that you don't know in advance precisely what's going to happen in the classroom or where the conversation is going to go. That doesn't mean it's loosey-goosey, ad libbing, stand-up philosophy, but it does require a certain degree of "adamant confidence," as Dixon calls it, that you can provide a measure of disciplined guidance to the conversational journey. (Our detractors occasionally describe our confidence as "arrogance.") Once we're all settled into the room and the students are nibbling on their morning muffins, I may kick it off by saying, "On the way into school this morning, I was thinking about something we said last time about whether it's possible to really be a solipsist about reality. Now, my idea is ... " And after I've rattled on for a bit, somebody in class asks a question, makes an observation, is provoked to challenge something outrageous I've said, and we're off. Sometimes

I'll say, "Well, you've read chapter two of Nagel's *What Does It All Mean?*, right? What is it about?" At other times I'll just ask, "Where did we leave off last time?" and then, like stoned people trying to remember what they were talking about five minutes previously, we'll fumble around a bit until we find the thread back into the labyrinth. Sometimes, when the class has coalesced into a group (about a third of the way into the semester) and things are going really well, I walk into the room and only have to say, "Well . . . ?" and we're on the way.

It is not the only way to teach, as I've said, and it's more exhausting or nerve-wracking than coming in with a well-planned, neatly packaged talk, complete with overhead transparencies on which the main points of the lecture can be projected onto the screen. To make matters a bit more challenging, at the start of each teaching season I try to forget everything I think about teaching and start all over again. I tend to think of my method as "non-algorithmic" teaching. That is, it's designed to be difficult for a computer to simulate (since I'm paranoid about teaching machines replacing teachers). Gradually, over the years, I've abandoned most of the technology used in teaching. I don't show movies or television documentaries, though the room is equipped with an overhead TV and various other gadgets. I don't give final exams (the students write essays), and therefore I don't need to provide transparencies for overhead projection and note taking. Lately I've stopped writing in chalk on the blackboard except once or twice a year (at the beginning to write my name, and in the middle to draw a Venn diagram if I'm talking about logic). Chalk, I've decided, is the final barrier between us and the abyss; I prefer the abyss. I don't even wander around the room. Instead, I just sit there, at a table, and we talk.

Jean Clifford, a colleague in the English department who has an office a couple of doors down the corridor from mine, teaches in a style she describes as rather different from how I teach (but she enthusiastically approves of my successes in engaging students, as I do her successes). Despite our differences, one thing we agree on is how to deal with students who miss classes and then turn up later to ask what happened. On her door she's taped up a poem by Tom Wayman (from his book *Did I Miss Anything? Selected Poems 1973–1993*) to which she refers students who have just asked,

Did I Miss Anything?

Question frequently asked by
students after missing class

Nothing. When we realized you weren't here
we sat with our hands folded on our desks
in silence, for the full two hours

    Everything. I gave an exam worth
    40 per cent of the grade for this term
    and assigned some reading due today
    on which I'm about to hand out a quiz
    worth 50 per cent

Nothing. None of the content of this course
has value or meaning
take as many days off as you like:
any activities we undertake as a class
I assure you will not matter either to you or me
and are without purpose

    Everything. A few minutes after we began last
    time
      a shaft of light suddenly descended and an
    angel
      or other heavenly being appeared
      and revealed to us what each woman or man
    must do
      to attain divine wisdom in this life and
      the hereafter
      This is the last time the class will meet
      before we disperse to bring the good news to all
    people on earth

Nothing. When you are not present
how could something significant occur?

    Everything. Contained in this classroom
    is a microcosm of human experience
    assembled for you to query and examine and
    ponder

This is not the only place such an opportunity
has been gathered

but it was one place

And you weren't here

The one thing today's students are pretty good at is psychological astuteness, which probably comes from their having watched lots of psychological talk-show television, like the *Oprah Winfrey* program. They can tell the difference between friendly fooling around and faculty hostility. I do a lot of fooling around, and I wouldn't want it mistaken for hostility. Most of the students are able to tell that I like them. When I say that teaching is easy because anything we say is news to the students, I'm simply referring to the fact that the students are inevitably ignorant (but not stupid). On the whole, it's not their fault. Most of their education, up to age eighteen, was conducted in competition with television and video games. TV and the games won.

But now they're not watching much television anymore. Oh, a few of them are, and I can refer to their experiences to make a point in class. The programs change every couple of years. For a while it was *90210*, a sex-and-soap opera for post-adolescents; then there was *X-Files*, a pernicious program encouraging belief in paranormal phenomena and conspiracy plots; then came *Touched by an Angel*, a soppy religious show that arrived at about the same time as a horrible hit song called "What If God Was One of Us?" Now there's "reality TV," a combination of game show and soft-core pornography. This is the junk that shaped their minds. But now that they're in college, TV viewing time is down; they're too busy with part-time jobs, parents, interpersonal relations, and, if we're lucky, us.

Some teachers don't like the students' ignorance and resent having to do "remedial work." I don't. If I mention Samuel Beckett's name (I may be trying to say something about existential absurdity in the metaphysics class), and I notice that they don't recognize the reference, I'm perfectly happy to stop and enthusiastically explain who Samuel Beckett is and why he's so great. I remember we're being paid lots of money, have great working conditions, good pensions, etc., so why should I resent dispelling ignorance? It's useful work.

The students, for all their ignorance, have passed through lots of filters to get here and tend to be friendly, well-behaved, and perfectly amenable to teaching. They're the 20 percent cream of the crop of their age aggregate. I regard them as the right people in the right place at the right time. Admittedly, I'm preternaturally cheerful when I'm at school and with the students — sometimes, according to my colleagues, spookily cheerful.

A few years ago, the faculty discovered the problem of "disruptive students," and several meetings and committees were devoted to figuring out what to do about it. I occasionally run into students who are nuts or inexplicably hostile, but I seldom locate any disruptive ones. Sometimes there are students chattering away in a corner of the class, distracting me from whatever I'm going on about, and I've apparently invented various clever techniques to deal with them. Mostly, the techniques have to do with cajoling them out of their own distractions. If I read someone's moving lips asking someone else, What time is it? because they're thinking about their day instead of metaphysics, I'll jump in and announce, "It's nine thirty, about a half hour left." If it's more elaborate gossip, I'll ask, "Pardon? Did you want to say something?" I have big ears and am very sensitive to sound, so I tend to hear a lot of the whispers and murmurs, which pop up on my bat-like echo-location radar system, thus making intervention fairly easy and automatic. When they arrive at class with their headphones on, listening to digital music, I always ask them what they're pumping into their heads because I'm culturally interested.

Sometimes there's a student who wants to answer every question. I deal with that through my only ground rule about public talking: you have to raise your hand to talk, and I keep a speaker's list in my head. If I see a hand for the first time that day, even if there are other hands up belonging to people who have already spoken, I move the first-time hand up to the top of the list to maximize the number of students who get to speak. The students seem satisfied with the justice of the procedure. When things are going well, they don't even have to raise their hands; I can read who wants to speak just from their eyes and eyebrows. On the whole, I'm inclined, if anything, to encourage disruption. I worry more about the "glazed-donut" problem, students who politely sit there for weeks on end and give no indication of what's happening for them.

For me, the main thing that goes on at school is what happens after we teachers close the door behind us and begin the class. I have, on the whole, shied away from the internal politics of academia, which is often a source of agony that permeates academic life. As a result, I tend to see my colleagues more favourably and charitably than some others do. Though I don't want to administer or sit on committees, and I find the meetings a chore, I admire those who are good at administration, and I'm happy to raise my hand whenever a vote is taken to support them and give them "release sections" (time off from teaching). I wander along the corridor and stop at faculty offices to chat with colleagues, who come in a diverse assortment of temperaments and states of mind, and end up at my pal Dixon's cubbyhole, where he's usually boiling a kettle of lunchtime water to make a bowl of instant noodle soup. There are about fifty or so teachers about whom I have a fair idea of what's on their minds. When I run through their names in my mind — Reid Gilbert, Yolande Westwell-Roper, Mark Battersby, Wayne Henry, Dan Munteanu, Pierre Coupey, Bob Sherrin, Bill Schermbrucker, Melanie Fahlman-Reid, and others — I have a rich album of images, personalities, and ideas they're interested in. But I'll save the encomiums for the retirement parties. The heart of the school is inside the classroom.

I only lecture twice a year — on the first day, the introduction to the course, and the last day, the Goodbye Class. Since very little has been written about actual classroom teaching (aside from professional literature on the subject, which tends to be technique- and technology-driven), I'll say a couple of things. I have an unwritten imaginary book about teaching called *The Horses of Instruction* (from William Blake's "The tygers of wrath are wiser than the horses of instruction"), but this is not the place for it.

Inside the room, after I write my name, telephone number, and the name and number of the course on the blackboard (which is actually green) and sit down behind my table, I ask, "Is there anybody here who hasn't taken a philosophy course?" I know perfectly well that almost none of them have taken a philosophy course, but when most of their hands shoot up, I affect slight surprise and say, "Oh?! Well, then I better say a few things about philosophy, and then something about how this course fits into philosophy, and then what this course is specifically about." The theme of my sermon is that philosophy is the most important subject we teach at Cap College. I say, "Well, the first thing to say about philosophy is that it's the most important subject we teach at Cap College." I allow a micro-pause for them to get the joke about my possible self-interest in this assertion, and once I've heard the chuckle, I add, "I actually mean it." Then I quickly amend that, pointing out that there are a lot of other great things taught at school, and I give some examples, but insist that philosophy seems to me the most important subject. I have two arguments for that.

The first is that philosophy is the only subject taught at school which is primarily devoted to discussing the questions that human beings have historically come to regard as the deepest, most central, and important: questions about how to live our lives, what the universe is all about, gods, selves, and all the rest. There's an internal debate in philosophy about whether these questions are intrinsic, eternal, and natural to our condition as human beings, or whether they're an historic artifact. I tend to think the latter, but for my purposes here, an agnostic view is sufficient. It doesn't matter whether the questions really exist independently of us or whether we make them up. They're the questions that people have come to care about, and philosophy is the only place in school completely devoted to them.

My second argument is that philosophy is very old, and I tell them all about my teacher, Socrates, although I quickly concede that arguments from authority and age are not as strong as arguments from good reasons. Even though I supply some dates and contrast Socrates with Jesus — pointing out in passing that it's easier to understand Socrates than Jesus (i.e., he sounds more like us) and that we have better historical evidence for Socrates' existence than Jesus's — some of them are probably left with the impression that I know Socrates personally and talk to him pretty regularly on a cellphone. All of this occasions some self-told jokes about my advanced age.

The point is simply to establish the tone and the pace of the class, to indicate that we're not merely pushing Sisyphus's stone up the hill, that we're looking for a state of mind in which it's possible to think. The semi-serious point about Socratic longevity is that most of the other disciplines taught at Cap College and elsewhere are in some way spinoffs from philosophy, and fairly recent spinoffs at that (I note that "recent" in philosophy is a word that can mean "within the last four to five hundred years"). My closer to this pitch for the importance of philosophy is that despite philosophy's importance, it doesn't provide "right answers," and, therefore, the students are not required to agree with anything I say or that other students say and, conversely, I'm not required to agree with what they say. However, I urge, we should treat our disagreements with a modicum of civility because we're all decent people. And that's about it.

The rest of the talk is practical stuff. I use the practical stuff (answers to questions like "How long should the essays be?" or "How many references do you want, and in what style?") to do a lot of "positioning," as I call it. Positioning has to do with how you want the students to think about the material, the teacher, the whole project. Most of it is jokey. I'm letting them know that I'm really available to be "the teacher," if that's what they're looking for. So I repeat my phone number several times, as if they should memorize it in case of emergencies, assure them they can phone at any time, nothing is too trivial or too large, and provide examples. The examples range from "You want to know whether to write on one side or both sides of the paper?" — and then I recite the phone number — to "You're driving along the Upper Narrows Highway at 3 AM in your Porsche, and the nice policeman stops you, tells you to open the trunk of the vehicle, and discovers the funny white powder. You don't want to discuss this with the folks just yet." Chuckles. Then I recite the phone number, as the punchline. Laughter. "I'm very good on giving advice about your legal rights, available attorneys, and bail procedures." Point taken.

If there's time the first day, I may "do" some philosophy, as Dixon and I have learned to describe it, as a sample of what's going to go on for the rest of the semester. It can be as straightforward as asking "What do we mean when we say that these chairs and tables, or those trees outside the window there, exist?" (That's when the classroom window comes in handy.) "What makes us so sure?" Or it can be that I'll point to some guy who was listening to (fill in the current fashionable blank, some rap or hip-hop group) when he came into the room and ask him, "What is it that leads to your listening to X rather than Mahler's Fourth Symphony?" which then leads to "What do you mean by 'I like it'?" which then leads to a discussion of the differences between "art" and "entertainment," which then leads to "How do we become the persons who have acquired the tastes we have?" In short, let the conversations begin.

Most of the rest of the days are devoted to doing philosophy. I spend a considerable amount of class time in metaphysics debunking unlikely beliefs — everything from astrology to Zoroastrianism — and presenting arguments for what constitute good reasons for believing in something. When students start talking about weird kinds of "energy" that they believe in, I get Mike Freeman or Stan Greenspoon from the physics department to come in for expert advice, even though the idea of reality in physics these days is stranger than any cultish beliefs in aliens, astral travel, or near- and after-death experiences. If the students are balky about fossils, radiocarbon dating, and our relationship to other hominids, a teacher in the biology department, Paul Mac-Millan, is usually kind enough to come in and explain the fine points of evolution.

I'm a moderate on epistemology. I certainly don't think we absolutely know what the world is like from a god's-eye view, independent of our consciousness and use of language, and I equally don't think that whatever you believe is "what's real for you," or that all beliefs are equally well held. I'm what might be called a "local realist": within the realm of tables, chairs, trees outside the window, and other local phenomena, what we know is good enough, and it doesn't matter whether it is absolute or ultimately relative. The knowledge of science may not be absolute either, but it's helpful, and I've no big objection to privileging it insofar as it "works." Knowledge about politics, ethics, and human relationships is shaky, and it's only possible to have better or worse arguments rather than knowledge. Claims to paranormal knowledge — from god(s) to God — ought to be resisted unless the person making the claim can provide a good reason to believe. Various knowledges and various false beliefs make a practical difference to how we live our lives. People who think God wants them to blow up buildings, other people, and themselves ought to be discouraged. Insofar as there is a politics of metaphysics, mine is fairly middle-of-the-road. The direction we're moving in is: if it's possibly the case that there are no gods to provide purposes for our lives, and if the accounts of evolution and physics are reasonably true, and if there's no good reason to believe in an afterlife, then what are the possible meanings (and selves) that we can construct for ourselves, both individually and as a society, to make our lives worthwhile?

In recent years, I notice, I've been making use of local geographic metaphors. I find myself arguing that "up here, on the hill" — since the college is on a hill — life is different from and, I imply, better than "down there, at the bottom of the hill." Down at the bottom of the hill is a big parking lot attached to something called the Real Canadian Superstore, and I portray the parking lot as a kind of hellish purgatory, where people aimlessly push their basket-carts, read no more than the statistics in the sports pages of the tabloids, or eat burgers in their overly large vehicles, and various other awful things happen. Whereas, up here, we read terrific books, talk about important stuff, meet interesting people, and get ready for great jobs, and what's more, the murder rate is lower up here on the hill than down in the lot at the bottom of the hill. A lot of other arguments flow from that — about language, the making of the self, and society — but I needn't rehearse them here. If someone notices that I'm being "elitist," I permit myself a rare political remark. I concede that the students are indeed an elite, representing only about 20 percent of their age aggregate, and that, being a democrat myself, I wish it were otherwise, but it isn't, not yet. I also note that their being an elite who will get better jobs, exercise more power, and have more leisure time than the people at the bottom of the hill is probably not a matter of intelligence, but does imply responsibility. (I then have a riff on the difference between ignorance and stupidity, but we can skip that.) I conclude, a little sadly, Well, if there is going to be an elite, I'd prefer that it be an informed rather than an ignorant elite.

There's another point to my "life up on the hill" metaphor that I usually don't talk about, but I notice it. It's that I really do believe all the stuff I say about life on the hill. Both the activity and the manner of interaction on the hill seem a model of human civilization. As Dr. Pangloss keeps insisting to Candide in Voltaire's *Candide*, life up on the hill is the best of all possible worlds . . . at least of the worlds that are possible right now. Then it occurs to me, as I wander around Cap College, listening to the music of the spheres, teaching, drinking my coffee, and holding my umbrella and book bag — and this, I realize, is what accounts for my pre-ternatural cheerfulness when I'm at school — I've come to regard life here (and at similar institutions, not all of them schools) as utopia, as the actual nearest approximation to utopia we'll experience in our lives.

I also give a talk at the Goodbye Class, in which I try to figure out what's happened in the course of the semester just concluding. It's not a very strenuous pitch, though sometimes I get worked up. Mainly, though, I'm just underscoring that goodbyes matter and that parting really is a sweet sorrow. By then, if things have gone well, the class has become a group, and the barbarians who arrived at the gates at the beginning of the semester have now become civilized. If things have gone really well, the shaft of light in Tom Wayman's poem doesn't "suddenly descend" from the heavens, but arises from the room and reveals, not a divinity, but what each man or woman among us must do.

That only happens when things are going really, really well.

Reading the Twentieth Century

Orwell's Nightmare

Each of us who reads has a list of landmark books — "landmarks" in the sense of defining moments in our own intellectual and emotional development. One such book on my list is George Orwell's memoir of the Spanish Civil War, *Homage to Catalonia* (1938). I can't remember exactly when I first read it, but I'm pretty sure it was sometime after I had actually seen the city of Barcelona, Spain, the capital of Catalonia, which I visited in 1959 as an eighteen-year-old sailor in the US Navy, and which is where Orwell's book opens in late 1936.

I still recall being both excited and charmed by Barcelona's beauty, by its broad main boulevard, the Ramblas, and its continental cafés. I noticed the ubiquitous presence of its Civil Guard police, with their guns and distinctive black matador-style headgear, but I had only the fuzziest notion of who the country's ruler, General Francisco Franco, really was. Reading Orwell's book about Spain was integral to my political education. In the centenary year of Orwell's birth, I reread *Homage to Catalonia* — as it happens, during the American punitive expedition to Iraq in April 2003.

Though I encountered Orwell's book about a quarter century after it had first been published, its concerns were still relevant then, the early years of the Cold War, and rereading it now, some sixty-five years after its publication, the book remains a powerful literary experience. More important, its dark vision, what I think of as "Orwell's nightmare," still seems to me germane to our situation today.

Why is *Homage to Catalonia* so enduringly poignant? Albert Camus's remark about what the experience of the Spanish Civil

War meant to people like Orwell puts it eloquently: "It was in Spain that men learned that one can be right and yet be beaten, that force can vanquish spirit, that there are times when courage is not its own recompense. It is this, doubtless, which explains why so many men, the world over, regard the Spanish drama as a personal tragedy."

"In the Lenin Barracks in Barcelona, the day before I joined the militia, I saw an Italian militiaman standing in front of the officers' table," Orwell begins, embarking upon his sustained narrative of a doomed revolution. The first impression, a fleeting, anonymous, but passionate encounter, no more than a firm handshake with a stranger, strikes one of the book's keynotes: "It was as though his spirit and mine momentarily succeeded in bridging the gulf of language and tradition, and meeting in utter intimacy." Immediately, Orwell provides a glimpse of the feelings of international solidarity that brought foreigners like Orwell and the Italian militiaman to the Spanish war. That militiaman, never to be seen again, "stuck vividly in my memory," Orwell continues. "With his shabby uniform and fierce pathetic face he typifies for me the special atmosphere of that time. He is bound up with all my memories of that period of the war — the red flags in Barcelona, the gaunt trains full of shabby soldiers creeping to the front, the grey war-stricken towns further up the line, the muddy, ice-cold trenches in the mountains."

Equally, from that initial anecdote, we see that Orwell matters, to use the concept in the title of Christopher Hitchens's *Why Orwell Matters* (2002), first, because he's a very good writer, of which there can never be too many. He is simply and consistently a pleasure to read, as anyone knows who has read no more than his brief essay "Shooting an Elephant," or his assessment of his own literary times and his contemporary Henry Miller in "Inside the Whale." Orwell is one of those writers who makes the rest of us feel self-conscious about writing. In his renowned 1945 essay "Politics and the English Language," and his equally famous dictum "Good prose is like a window pane," Orwell argues for transparency and a plain style. Most of what he says about the relation of language and politics is true, but, as many dissenting critics have pointed out, good prose is not necessarily, or at all times, like a window pane, and the plain style can become a guise that merely gives the impression of transparency.

What makes Orwell's prose powerful is not simply an uncluttered style, but Orwell's intelligence. Orwell's more than half-century-old essay on writing in relation to politics has continued to influence and provoke writers. For example, a notable recent "update" of Orwell's essay is provided by the most Orwell-like writer in Canada, Brian Fawcett, in his "Politics and the English Language" (1991).

Second, Orwell is one of the best political writers of the twentieth century, of which there are very few indeed. As Hitchens observes about the "very many 'creative writers' with high political profiles" who were contemporaneous with Orwell, "It is fairly safe to say that the political statements made by these men would not bear reprinting today . . . However, and by way of bold contrast, it has lately proved possible to reprint every single letter, book review and essay composed by Orwell without exposing him to any embarrassment."

The experience of the Spanish Civil War and then writing about it in "white-hot anger," as one of his biographers puts it, was the turning point of Orwell's life. As Orwell says in his 1946 essay "Why I Write,"

> The Spanish War and other events in 1936–37 turned the scale and thereafter I knew where I stood. Every line of serious work I have written since 1936 has been written, directly or indirectly, *against* totalitarianism and *for* democratic Socialism, as I understand it. It seems to me nonsense . . . to think one can avoid writing of such subjects. Everyone writes of them in one guise or another . . . The more one is conscious of one's political bias, the more chance one has of acting politically without sacrificing one's aesthetic and intellectual integrity . . . What I have most wanted to do throughout the past ten years is to make political writing into an art.

Finally, Orwell matters because of what I call "Orwell's nightmare," which I'll address momentarily.

For those who don't know, or have forgotten, the details of the Spanish Civil War and Orwell's experiences there, a brief history may be helpful. The war began in mid-1936. It was a rebellion against the elected left-of-centre Republican government, and it was led by the right-wing General Francisco Franco, who was supported by the Fascist governments of Italy and Germany. The Spanish Loyalists, as partisans of the government were also known, received support from the Soviet Union while, notably, England and France stood aside, part of their "appeasement" of the Fascist regimes. The civil war had an enormous impact on all of Europe. It was not only the prelude to World War II, but as the continent's ideological battleground, it shaped the minds of an entire generation.

Orwell went to Barcelona in late 1936, ostensibly as a journalist, but promptly signed up with one of the Marxist militias, POUM (*Partido Obrero de Unificacion Marxista*), and served on the front lines for several months. He arrived in Spain admittedly naïve about the internecine political factions that made up the Loyalist forces and, semi-inadvertently, volunteered for a group that is sometimes described as Trotskyist, and that was also politically close to the Spanish Anarchists. POUM would shortly be singled out as an enemy of the revolution and was eventually destroyed by order of the Spanish Communist Party, which was, to a large extent, controlled by the Communist Party of the Soviet Union. At the time, the Soviet Union was under the dictatorship of Josef Stalin and was in the midst of its own hideous infra-party struggle, highlighted by a series of trumped-up Purge Trials allegedly intended to rid the ruling party of the influence of Leon Trotsky, a prominent figure in the 1917 Russian Revolution. Trotsky, once an ally of Stalin, became his rival in the struggle for succession after the death of V.I. Lenin, the revolution's leader. Stalin forced Trotsky into exile and eventually had him assassinated.

Meanwhile, Orwell, while on leave from the front, witnessed and semi-participated in a sort of civil war within the Civil War that broke out among leftist factions in Barcelona in May 1937. He went back to the front a few days later, was seriously wounded at the end of May — shot in the throat by a sniper — and returned to Barcelona to recuperate, but was forced to flee Spain less than a month later, a step ahead of the police, wanted because of his political association with POUM, which had been outlawed by the Republican government. Hundreds or even thousands of POUM's adherents were arrested, jailed, and, in many cases, executed. Orwell had been in Spain, altogether, six or seven months.

I am using the word "nightmare" literally, as a very bad dream, and in two metaphoric senses: first, as a colloquial metaphor to refer to a situation that is a disaster, and then in the more encompassing sense of a dark vision. For at least ten years after the Spanish war, Orwell was visited with terrifying dreams, which often took the form of suddenly finding himself outdoors "with no cover and mortar shells dropping round me."

Much of the Spanish Civil War itself can be described metaphorically as a nightmare. Among the disasters: first, the Fascists won the war and Franco ruled Spain until his death in 1975; second, the European democracies, principally England and France, abstained from the war, partially on the grounds that the elected Spanish Republic was or would become "Red," and thus they paved the way for a more extensive world war that might have been prevented if they had opposed fascism earlier. Third, the Soviet Union indirectly participated in the war, with dubious consequences that are still argued about today, but did not succeed in forestalling Spanish, Italian or German fascism. Thus, fourth, the possibility, if there was one, of a genuinely democratic Spanish revolution was gutted. Fifth, and perhaps most painfully for the sense of betrayal it produced among combatants like Orwell, the dominance of the Communist Party among the forces of the Spanish Left precipitated a truly nightmarish liquidation of other leftist groups, complete with false accusations of collaboration with the enemy, imprisonment, torture, and execution. All of this was accompanied, as a writer of Orwell's linguistic sensitivities was aware, by a horrible mangling of language that emptied it of meaning. Finally, the conduct of the war, as Orwell's account makes plain, was itself a nightmare of battlefield suffering, inadequately armed or trained troops, failed tactics, and all the discomforts, boredom, and horrors of deadly war.

In June 1937, Orwell returned to England, a place where it was hard "to believe that anything is really happening anywhere." As he says in the bucolic but ominous concluding passage of *Homage to Catalonia*:

Down here it was still the England I had known in my childhood: the railway-cuttings smothered in wild flowers, the deep meadows where the great shining horses browse and meditate

... and then the huge peaceful wilderness of outer London, the barges on the miry river, the familiar streets, the posters telling of cricket matches and Royal weddings, the men in bowler hats, the pigeons in Trafalgar Square, the red buses, the blue police-men — all sleeping the deep, deep sleep of England, from which I sometimes fear we shall never wake till we are jerked out of it by the roar of bombs.

The bombs prophesied by Orwell would come soon enough.

Immediately upon his return, Orwell set to work, writing a tor-rent of articles, letters, reviews of new books about the Spanish Civil War, and the manuscript that would be *Homage to Catalo-nia*. His first piece, "Spilling the Spanish Beans," published at the end of July 1937, which begins with Orwell assessing blame for the state of British ignorance about the war, dubiously declares, "I honestly doubt ... whether it is the pro-Fascist newspapers that have done the most harm. It is the left-wing papers [espe-cially the Communist Party paper, the *Daily Worker*] ... with their far subtler methods of distortion that have prevented the British public from grasping the real nature of the struggle." The claim is dubious insofar as the left-wing papers had a limited cir-culation. Orwell means not the "British public" but the British Left.

That aside, Orwell's main point is this:

The fact which these papers have so carefully obscured is that the Spanish Government (including the semi-autonomous Cata-lan Government) is far more afraid of the revolution than of the Fascists ... There is no doubt whatever about the thoroughness with which it is crushing its own revolutionaries. For some time past a reign of terror — forcible suppression of political parties, a stifling censorship of the press, ceaseless espionage and mass imprisonment without trial — has been in progress. When I left Barcelona in late June the jails were bulging ... The point to notice is that the people who are in prison now are not Fascists but revolutionaries; they are there not because their opinions are too much to the Right, but because they are too much to the Left. And the people responsible for putting them there are ... the Communists.

In *Homage to Catalonia*, Orwell provides an extended if reluctant account of this political struggle. He says that "it is a horrible thing to have to enter into the details of inter-party polemics; it is like diving into a cesspool," and he twice advises readers who are not "interested in the horrors of party politics" to "please skip." I too will skip most of the details of this part of the nightmare as not germane here, but with the reminder that, for anyone who has ever engaged in political activity on the left, it is precisely the details of such arguments about tactics and strategy that are crucial.

Orwell, it should be noted, was uneasy, on literary grounds, about the chapters describing that struggle, and near the end of his life expressed a wish to revise the book. Some recent editions of *Homage to Catalonia* move the book's two extended political chapters to an appendix at the end of the book. The "political" chapters, it is thought, spoil the literary quality of the work. Rather than attempting to revise it in this way, Orwell would have done better to reread the passage about it he had written in his essay "Why I Write":

> I did try very hard in it [*Homage to Catalonia*] to tell the whole truth without violating my literary instincts. But among other things, it contains a long chapter, full of newspaper quotations and the like, defending Trotskyists who were accused of plotting with Franco. Clearly, such a chapter, which after a year or two would lose its interest for any ordinary reader, must ruin the book. A critic whom I respect read me a lecture about it. "Why did you put in all that stuff?" he said. "You've turned what might have been a good book into journalism." What he said to me was true, but I could not have done otherwise. I happened to know, what very few people in England had been allowed to know, that innocent men were being falsely accused. If I had not been angry about that I should never have written the book.

The gist of the debate about inter-party politics was that the group Orwell was associated with, POUM, was for immediate revolution, even in the midst of the war against Franco, and the Communists were not. The Communist "line," as characterized by Orwell, was roughly: "'At present nothing matters except winning the war; without victory in the war all else is meaningless. Therefore this is not the moment to talk of pressing forward with the revolution ... At this stage we are not fighting for the dictatorship of the proletariat, we are fighting for parliamentary democracy. Whoever tries to turn the civil war into a social revolution is playing into the hands of the Fascists and is in effect, if not in intention, a traitor.'" By contrast, the POUM view was approximately: "'It is nonsense to talk of opposing Fascism by bourgeois "democracy" ... The only real alternative to Fascism is workers' control. If you set up any less goal than this, you will either hand victory to Franco, or, at best, let in Fascism by the back door ... The war and the revolution are inseparable.'"

The whole of Orwell's analysis is considerably more nuanced than I've indicated. "There was much to be said on both sides," he concedes, and for much of the time he "preferred the Communist viewpoint to that of the POUM." As an indicator of Orwell's ambivalence, at one point he contemplated transferring from the POUM militia to the Communist-controlled International Brigades, which he would have done but for the situation that required him to flee Spain altogether. It was only with the crushing of leftist forces by the Communists that Orwell changed his mind and was impelled "to try and establish the truth, so far as it is possible."

Was Orwell right about the internal politics of the Spanish Civil War? Certainly he was accurate in his portrait of the brutal extermination of revolutionary factions by the Communists, and he was among the first to oppose the Communists as totalitarians, of the same order as the Fascists. Even Arthur Koestler, Orwell's anti-totalitarian friend, didn't recognize the totalitarian aspects of Communism immediately. His anti-Communist novel *Darkness at Noon* didn't appear until 1940. As Orwell says in his 1944 essay about Koestler, "The sin of nearly all leftwingers from 1933 onwards is that they have wanted to be anti-Fascist without being anti-totalitarian."

Orwell wasn't right, I think, in his tendency to conflate Fascism and capitalism, a view that echoed the Communist line through much of the 1930s. This is among the very few murky areas in Orwell's thinking, but some of the confusion can be attributed to Orwell's two-pronged program to write against totalitarianism and for democratic socialism. Was Orwell right in adhering to POUM's view that the war and revolution were inseparable? I don't think we'll ever know. The opportunity, if it was one, was irreparably lost. It's worth noting that the prominent Spanish Civil War historian Hugh Thomas, who thought Orwell's book the best firsthand account of the war, also thought Orwell was wrong about tactics. According to Thomas, "if the Republicans were to have a hope of winning the civil war, the only policy was to centralize war production, delay the revolutionary process (to avoid antagonizing the peasants), [and] establish a regular army in place of the militias . . . The anarchists and the POUM, through greater idealism, were unable to swallow such realistic stuff." But even if the Communists were right about tactics, there's not much evidence that it was necessary to suppress POUM and other groups.

In *Why Orwell Matters*, Christopher Hitchens makes much of the claim that Orwell was right about the three great issues of the twentieth century, namely imperialism, fascism, and Stalinism. Hitchens's critics have argued about whether Orwell was in fact right, and even whether those issues were the great ones of the twentieth century. His most acerbic critic, Louis Menand, challenges what he calls "the 'Orwell Was Right' button." Orwell, says Menand, "was against imperialism, fascism and Stalinism. Excellent. Many people were against them in Orwell's time and a great many more people have been against them since . . . The important question, after condemning those things, was what to do about them, and how to understand the implications for the future. On this level, Orwell was almost always wrong." Here I'm on the side of Leon Wieseltier, who chides Menand for his condescension about Orwell's anti-totalitarianism, and adds, "As it happens, a great many people were not at all against Stalinism in the years in which Orwell wrote, and if many more people have been against Stalinism since, it is in part owing to the genuinely valiant refusal of Orwell and others to desist from their denunciations of it."

Hitchens's book about Orwell has sparked the usual critical kafuffle, about both Orwell and Hitchens himself. Overall, I think *Why Orwell Matters* is helpful and interesting. Stefan Collini, a critic of the book, notes that "it is not easy to write a good book about Orwell now." Collini explains that "he has been written about so extensively, and sometimes well, that to justify devoting a whole book to him one would really need to have discovered some new material or be able to set him in some new context. The main problem with [*Why Orwell Matters*] is that Hitchens doesn't have enough to say about Orwell to fill a book, so he writes, in effect, as Orwell's minder, briskly seeing off various characters who have in some way or other got him wrong." I disagree that you would have to discover some new material to merit writing a book about Orwell. As for new contexts, setting Orwell in *our* context seems sufficient motive. And as for ragging on those who got Orwell wrong, I think Hitchens is pretty useful. Collini's criticism of Hitchens' tone is more to the point. "As always with Hitchens's work, one gets the strongest possible sense of how much it matters to prove that one is and always has been right," Collini says, "right about which side to be on, right that there are sides and one has to be on one of them, right about which way the world is going . . . right about the accuracy of one's facts and one's stories . . . There is a palpably macho tone to all of this, as of alpha males competing for dominance and display." Collini calls this style "'no bullshit' bullshit," an insistence on "no bullshit" that becomes a kind of bullshit itself.

Returning to the question of political acuity, I think that, on the whole, Orwell was right, or right enough, on the great political issues of his time, even though he may not have known what to do about all of them, any more than we do now, as we debate the politics of terrorism, "humanitarian intervention," the path of empire, and what to do about greater and lesser evils. More important than being right, Orwell's great essays, and books — principally *Homage to Catalonia*, *Animal Farm*, and *1984* — are still relevant for us as readers and citizens.

That wasn't immediately apparent upon the publication of *Homage to Catalonia*. It was printed in an edition of 1500 copies in early 1938 by the British firm Secker and Warburg. By the time of Orwell's death in 1950, it had sold a mere 600 copies, which, if nothing else, ought to hearten other under-appreciated authors. Though Orwell had achieved fame and sufficient means by the end of his life — both *Animal Farm* and *1984* were bestsellers — *Homage to Catalonia* found a readership only after Orwell's death.

What I mean by "Orwell's nightmare" isn't fully to be found within *Homage to Catalonia*, but appears most starkly in a sort of epilogue, an essay written five years or so later, called "Look-

274 • TOPIC SENTENCE

ing Back on the Spanish War." Writing from the midst of a larger
war, Orwell's retrospective view on the Spanish conflict revealed
a cooling of some passions — the internecine struggle on the
left now seemed less important, a secondary issue. But Orwell
remained deeply troubled by the lies, distortions, and propaganda on all sides when it came to assessments of the history of
the Spanish Civil War. In a passage that is key to understanding
Orwell's subsequent work and his apprehension of the future, he
writes, "This kind of thing is frightening to me, because it often
gives me the feeling that the very concept of objective truth is
fading."

Orwell's nightmare, I think, is not so much the imagination of
the future portrayed in 1984, but rather the eradication of the
past, the erasure of memory. "How will the history of the Spanish War be written?" Orwell asks. "After all, *some* kind of history will be written, and after those who actually remember the
war are dead, it will be universally accepted. So for all practical
purposes the lie will have become truth." That is, we are not here
engaged in a post-modernist debate about truth, or the parody of
such a debate frequently conjured up by self-proclaimed opponents of contemporary pragmatist philosophy. Whether or not
there is objective truth about the past to be had — Orwell thought
there was — the nightmare is that it won't matter whether or not
there is; rather, "what is peculiar to our own age is the abandonment of the idea that history *could* be truthfully written."

Although the past might be filled with deliberate lies and
inadvertent mistakes, "in practice there was always a considerable body of fact which would have been agreed to by almost
everyone." What Orwell most fears is the loss of "just this common basis of agreement"; this is precisely what totalitarianism
destroys. "The implied objective of this line of thought," Orwell
says, "is a nightmare world in which the Leader, or some ruling
clique, controls not only the future but the *past*. If the Leader
says of such and such an event, 'It never happened' — well, it
never happened. If he says that two and two are five — well, two
and two are five. This prospect frightens me much more than
bombs — and after our experiences of the last few years that is
not a frivolous statement."

Of course, now we know that the nightmare Orwell contem-
plates in "Looking Back on the Spanish War" is precisely the

subject matter he would address in his last novel, *1984*. The daily occupation of his protagonist in that book, Winston Smith, is the perpetual false rewriting of the past, and one of Orwell's greatest literary creations, the character O'Brien, tortures Smith into believing, at least briefly, that two plus two are five.

One of the most astute accounts of why Orwell matters is to be found in the 1989 essay about Orwell by Richard Rorty, the philosopher who is often taken to be the chief contemporary "denier of truth." I won't reprise the entirety of Rorty's essay, "The Last Intellectual in Europe: Orwell on Cruelty," but merely point to a few passages that have some relevance to my thesis. Rorty remarks that "Orwell's best novels will be widely read only as long as we describe the politics of the twentieth century as Orwell did . . . Orwell thought of our century as the period in which 'human equality became technically possible' and in which simultaneously, 'practices which had long been abandoned, in some cases for hundreds of years — imprisonment without trial, the use of war prisoners as slaves, public executions, torture to extract confessions . . . — not only became common again, but were tolerated and even defended by people who considered themselves enlightened and progressive.'" Rorty believes Orwell will continue to be widely read for some time. "Someday this description of our century may come to seem blinkered or short-sighted," he allows.

> If it does, Orwell will be seen as having inveighed against an evil he did not entirely understand . . . Some present-day leftist critics think that we already have a way of seeing Orwell as blinkered and shortsighted. They think that the facts to which he called attention can already be put in a context within which they look quite different. Unlike [them], I do not think that we have a better alternative context. In the 40 years since Orwell wrote, as far as I can see, nobody has come up with a better way of setting out the political alternatives which confront us.

Rorty reiterates the above point when he says,

> On my view, Orwell's mind was neither transparent nor simple. It was not *obvious* how to describe the post-World War II political situation, and it still is not. For useful political description is

in a vocabulary which suggests answers to the question "What is to be done?" just as useful scientific description is in a vocabulary which increases our ability to predict and control events. Orwell gave us no hints about how to answer Chernyshevsky's question. He merely told us how *not* to answer it, what vocabulary to *stop* using. He convinced us that our previous political vocabulary had little relevance to our current political situation, but he did not give us a new one. He sent us back to the drawing board, and we are still there. Nobody has come up with a larger framework for relating our large and vague hopes for human equality to the actual distribution of power in the world.

In one of the many "Why Orwell Matters" essays that have been written of late, Timothy Garton Ash poses the question, Does Orwell *still* matter? "Why should we still read George Orwell on politics?" he asks. "Until 1989, the answer was plain. He was the writer who captured the essence of totalitarianism ... Yet the world of *1984* ended in 1989 ... The three dragons against which Orwell fought his good fight — European and especially British imperialism; fascism, whether Italian, German, or Spanish; and communism, not to be confused with the democratic socialism in which Orwell himself believed — were all either dead or mortally weakened. Forty years after his own painful and early death, Orwell had won. What need, then, of Orwell?" Ash goes on to offer a few answers, among them: "We should read him because of his historical impact. For Orwell was the most influential political writer of the 20th century." Ash admits that saying "read him because he mattered a lot in the past" is not very exciting. He then goes on to offer "a more compelling reason we should read Orwell in the 21st century: he remains an exemplar of political writing." Ash underscores Orwell's "insight into the use and abuse of language ... the central Orwellian argument that the corruption of language is an essential part of oppressive or exploitative politics."

While Ash's reasons for reading Orwell today are true enough, my own view is that Orwell still matters because his nightmare about the erasure of the past continues to be relevant. It is true that the terms of the present political engagement may have changed. A popular expression of those changing terms is found in the title of Benjamin Barber's *Jihad vs. McWorld*. While Soviet totalitarianism is gone, we now find ourselves describing a world of insatiable consumers in the capitalist mall and a realm of bloodthirsty tribalists and religious fundamentalists possessed of a feudal metaphysics, both of which, Barber argues, are no less threats to democracy than the version of totalitarianism that Orwell depicted. Even in Orwell's time, there were alternative versions of the nightmare.

In October 1949, three months before Orwell's death in January 1950, Aldous Huxley, the author of an equally renowned dystopia, *Brave New World* (1932), wrote poignantly to Orwell:

> I had to wait a long time before being able to embark on *1984*. Agreeing with all that the critics have written of it, I need not tell you, yet once more, how fine and how profoundly important the book is ... The philosophy of the ruling minority in *1984* is a sadism which has been carried to its logical conclusion by going beyond sex and denying it. Whether in actual fact the policy of the boot-on-the-face can go on indefinitely seems doubtful. My own belief is that the ruling oligarchy will find less arduous and wasteful ways of governing and of satisfying its lust for power, and that these ways will resemble those which I described in *Brave New World*.

This is not the place to argue the dimensions of the present dangers, on Huxley's terms or on any others. It is enough to note that whether we're talking about our young people hanging out in the mall, engrossed in the virtual destruction provided by video games, or their young people indoctrinated in fundamentalist schools and sometimes persuaded to engage in the self-and-other destruction of suicide bombing, the possibility of a truthfully described past has been devoured by ideologies of utter indifference and misguided passion. Rereading Orwell's *Homage to Catalonia*, as I did, in the midst of the bombing of the region of the world known as "the cradle of civilization," and the subsequent looting of the earliest-known written records of the past, added more than a touch of bitter irony to the experience.

At the end of his essay "Looking Back on the Spanish War," Orwell remembered the Italian militiaman who appears at the beginning of *Homage to Catalonia*, and he appends a few verses written in memory of that young man. The poem is conventionally sentimental and not especially memorable except for its concluding phrase, in which the generally pessimistic Orwell allows himself to briefly imagine that "No bomb that ever burst / Shatters the crystal spirit." But in Orwell's truer imaginings, in his nightmare, the point is that even "the crystal spirit" is shattered.

Life Was A Cabaret, My Dear

I

Living in Berlin part of each year, I tend to think of Christopher Isherwood as a neighbour. Of the various addresses at which he lived in the late 1920s and early 1930s, the most famous one is Nollendorfstrasse 17, which is just a couple of blocks from the bar on Fuggerstrasse where I hang out. I imagine Isherwood as a nodding acquaintance, someone I know to say hello to when I run into him on the streets or in a local gay bar. A familiar cowlick of streaked-blond hair flops across his forehead; he flashes an ingratiating, enigmatic smile, and sometimes, at a raucous moment in the bar, we exchange the amused glance of two writers noting a potential bit of material or simply the always surprising variety of existence. As the poet Jack Spicer once said of his relationship with his predecessor Garcia Lorca, it's "a casual friendship with an undramatic ghost who occasionally looked through my eyes and whispered to me . . ."

Nollendorf 17, which I frequently pass on walks through the neighbourhood, is a five-storey apartment building. A burnished plaque on the wall near the front door records that the English author Christopher Isherwood (1904–86) lived in the city for about four years and wrote about it in *Mr. Norris Changes Trains* (1935) and *Goodbye to Berlin* (1939), which provided the basis for the successful play *I Am A Camera* and later the prize-winning stage musical and 1970s movie *Cabaret*.

More importantly, the window on the top floor, where Isherwood was a lodger, is the spot from which he looked out and saw, in the memorable opening lines of *Goodbye to Berlin*, "the deep solemn massive street. Cellar-shops where the lamps burn all day, under the shadow of top-heavy balconied façades, dirty plaster frontages embossed with scroll-work and heraldic devices. The whole district is like this: street leading into street of houses like shabby monumental safes crammed with the tarnished valuables and second-hand furniture of a bankrupt middle class."

Some three-quarters of a century later, Nollendorfstrasse isn't much different from the scene Isherwood gazed upon. The foliage of the linden trees is perhaps denser, making the street strangely dark even in summer. The cellar-shops still exist, though one or two of them have been spruced up with a rainbow flag and now sell condoms, leatherwear, and DVD porn. The scroll-work and heraldic devices on the plaster frontages remain; however, the building at number 17 received a bright coat of peach-coloured paint a few years ago. But the resemblance between then and now is sufficient that the cool, understated voice with which Isherwood announced himself to the literary world would not be out of place today. It's the voice that declared:

I am a camera with its shutter open, quite passive, recording, not thinking. Recording the man shaving at the window opposite, and the woman in the kimono washing her hair. Some day, all this will have to be developed, carefully printed, fixed.

Inside the top floor apartment, where the furniture of "a bankrupt middle class" is "unnecessarily solid, abnormally heavy and dangerously sharp," Isherwood introduces us to his first two great inventions, the landlady Fraulein Schroeder (her real name was Thurau) and the narrator "Christopher Isherwood," or "Herr Issyvoo" as she pronounces it when she rattles on about her lodgers from long-ago better days. "You see, Herr Issyvoo, in those days I could afford to be very particular about the sort of people who came to live here. I could pick and choose. I only took them really well connected and well educated — proper gentlefolk (like yourself, Herr Issyvoo)." But now, in the impending economic and political doom of the German 1930s, "Frl. Schroeder has not even got a room of her own. She has to sleep in the living-room behind a screen on a small sofa with broken springs . . . She has to do all the housework herself and it takes up most of her day." But, as she says, "'You get used to it. You can get used to anything. Why, I remember the time when I'd sooner cut off my right hand than empty this chamber . . . And now,' says Frl. Schroeder, suiting the action to the word, 'my goodness! It's no more than pouring out a cup of tea!'"

Goodbye to Berlin consists of four novella-like character sketches sandwiched between two segments of "Berlin Diaries" — the first from the slightly ominous autumn of 1930; the second from the decidedly darker winter of 1932–33, when Hitler came to power and Isherwood bid his farewell to the city.

Isherwood was a lifelong diarist, and he constantly mined, reworked, and "reconstructed" the diaries as a motherlode of source material for his books. (Two volumes of the diaries have now been published, and a third is promised, but they mainly prove that Isherwood's diaries aren't his works of literature.) *Goodbye to Berlin* is presented as the salvage of a failed, large novel Isherwood was trying to write, and the sense of it as wreckage is part of its power. Its fragmentary structure seems to anticipate the devastation about to be wreaked upon the city. It is filled with the careful observations and conversations recorded by the slightly coy narrator as he shrewdly dodges the falling bits of cornice and crashing lives around him. The book is not overtly political, but its shaded portrait of the rise of Nazism is more powerful than anything written on that subject by Isherwood's contemporaries. The book is a masterpiece; that is, it shows us something heretofore unknown about life at a particular historical moment, and it is told in an unprecedented way that gives us a different idea of what a story can be.

Isherwood wrote two masterpieces. The second is a gay, California-based novel, *A Single Man* (1964), written a quarter century after *Goodbye to Berlin*. As well, there are three or four other quite good books, including the novella *Prater Violet* (1945), about the movie industry (for which Isherwood did endless, numbing work); a follow-up to the Berlin stories, *Down There on a Visit* (1962); and a retrospective memoir about Berlin, *Christopher and his Kind* (1976).

In the opening pages of *Goodbye to Berlin*, there's a poignant vignette crucial to the identity of the narrator. "At eight o'clock in the evening the house doors will be locked," he writes.

The children are having supper. The shops are shut. The electric sign is switched on over the night-bell of the little hotel on the corner, where you can hire a room by the hour. And soon the

whistling will begin. Young men are calling their girls. Standing
down there in the cold, they whistle up at the lighted windows
of warm rooms where the beds are already turned down for the
night. They want to be let in. Their signals echo down the deep
hollow street, lascivious and private and sad. I do not care to stay
here in the evenings. It reminds me that I am in a foreign city,
alone, far from home. Sometimes I determine not to listen to it,
pick up a book, try to read. But soon a call is sure to sound, so
piercing, so insistent, so despairingly human, that at last I have
to get up and peep through the slats of the Venetian blind to
make quite sure that it is not — as I know very well it could not
possibly be — for me.

It's a superbly written paragraph, perfect for conveying both the
longing of its narrator and the loneliness of the big city. But it's
also not quite true. Because the calls from the street could very
well have been for the Christopher Isherwood who is not the narrator, "Herr Issyvoo." That other Christopher Isherwood — the
twenty-six-year-old aspiring novelist, homosexual, friend of fellow writers W.H. Auden and Stephen Spender (who were also in
Berlin in that period) — came to Berlin, at least in part, because,
as he wrote more candidly a half century later, "Berlin meant
Boys." (Today the boys no longer whistle. They use their ubiquitous cellphones, but the by-the-hour hotel is still available.)
Discovering the difference between Isherwood, the author and
person, and "Christopher Isherwood," the character, is one of
the reasons for reading Peter Parker's massive biography, *Isherwood*, published on the centenary of the author's birth.

II

Isherwood was born August 26, 1904, in Cheshire, England, to
a pedigreed family of landed gentry who owned a castle-sized
house called Marple Hall. It was, says biographer Parker, "a
symbol of everything about England" that Isherwood eventually
wanted to escape. His father, Frank, was in the military and married to Kathleen, the daughter of successful merchants. When
Christopher was seven, a younger brother, Richard, was born.
Frank was killed in World War I at Ypres, while Christopher was
at prep school. He eventually made his way to Cambridge in the

early 1920s, where he became friends with future writers Edward Upward and w.h. Auden, but dropped out of school without a degree. As Isherwood later remarked, "Upward educated me."

Isherwood turned to writing, published a first novel, *All the Conspirators*, in 1928, and was on to a second one, *The Memorial* (1932), when w.h. Auden returned from a brief trip to Berlin at the beginning of 1929. That was the first decisive moment. Auden had discovered a world that included interesting intellects and attractive boys. Isherwood was on his way. For the next four years, Isherwood lived mostly in Berlin, where he met people like Magnus Hirschfeld, the gay sexologist, and the louche sometime-archeologist Francis Turville-Petre. Auden and Isherwood were joined by another young British writer, Stephen Spender, and, as one critic later put it, the three "ganged up and conquered a decade."

Berlin is where Isherwood encountered the people who would become the characters in his books — Fraulein Thurau (the landlady who became Frl. Schroeder), Jean Ross (fictionalized as Sally Bowles), and con artist Gerald Hamilton (later turned into Arthur Norris). Berlin is also where Isherwood developed his notion of the personal "Myth," a sort of Jungian idea of how to conceive of life, and where he warily recognized the enemy "Others" (beginning with his mother, Kathleen, and extending to the Nazis; the word is capitalized, like "Boys," to mark its mythic status). Finally, "Berlin meant Boys," mostly post-adolescent boys a half-dozen years or more younger than Isherwood, whom he met in rent-bars and with whom he embarked on romantic affairs.

Once Hitler came to power, Isherwood got out of Germany and spent the next several years wandering around Europe with his Berlin boyfriend, Heinz, whom he was trying to rescue from potential military service at home. It was a twisting itinerary with stops in Prague, Vienna, and a tiny Greek island for a farcical but grim stay with "Fronny," as Turville-Petre was known. There were periodic visits to London, where Isherwood got his first movie-writing job with an exiled Viennese director, Berthold Viertel, and attempts to settle in places as diverse as the Grand Canary Islands, Copenhagen, and Sintra, Portugal, where he and Heinz tried communal living with Spender and his boyfriend for a while. Isherwood co-authored a couple of plays with Auden that got a fair amount of attention, but the most important writing he did, during a two-month stay on Tenerife, was to bang out a very good novel, *Mr. Norris Changes Trains*, a *noir*-ish book that had some affinity to the writing of his distant cousin Graham Greene, and which Leonard Woolf at Hogarth Press immediately accepted and published in 1935.

Heinz was eventually ensnared by the German bureaucracy in 1937, and Isherwood went on to other adventures and other affairs. He and Auden travelled to China and collaborated on a volume of reportage about the Sino-Japanese war. In rapid order, Isherwood published a school memoir, *Lions and Shadows* (1938), co-authored *Journey to a War* (1939) with Auden, and, most importantly, produced *Goodbye to Berlin* (1939). Both he and Auden were at the height of their reputations as their generation's literary lions when they travelled together to America in January 1939, a journey that permanently changed the lives of both men.

That was the second decisive moment in Isherwood's life. Instead of returning to England as World War II began, both he and Auden settled in the US, a decision widely viewed in British literary circles as a kind of desertion of both country and colleagues. Evelyn Waugh brutally satirizes both of them in *Put Out More Flags* (1943), and even friends like Spender and Cyril Connolly, author of *Enemies of Promise*, voiced their doubts. For all the doubts of friends and enemies, it was Auden who wrote from America in "September 1, 1939":

> I sit in one of the dives
> On Fifty-second Street
> Uncertain and afraid
> As the clever hopes expire
> Of a low dishonest decade ...

and further:

> All I have is a voice
> To undo the folded lie,
> The romantic lies in the brain
> Of the sensual man-in-the-street
> And the lie of Authority
> Whose buildings grope the sky:

There is no such thing as the State
And no one exists alone;
Hunger allows no choice
To the citizen or the police;
We must love one another or die.

While Auden preferred New York, Isherwood located in southern California. He found screen-writing work in Hollywood, but equally important, he fell in with a variety of people interested in forms of mysticism and Eastern religion, including Aldous Huxley, Gerald Heard, and, most lastingly, the Vedanta guru Swami Prabhavananda. As a pacifist (which was presumably one of his reasons for leaving England), Isherwood did wartime work under the aegis of the Quakers, which involved helping European refugees.

Isherwood would later regard much of his first two decades in the United States as "lost years." While there was a serious, but ultimately foundering, flirtation with Hindu monkhood under the guidance of the Swami, there was also a great deal of boozing, demoralizing but well-paid hack work in the movies, considerable sex (which Isherwood was very skilful at obtaining), and no substantial writing whatsoever.

In 1952, the forty-eight-year-old Isherwood met eighteen-year-old Don Bachardy, with whom he began what turned into a life-long domestic relationship, ending only with Isherwood's death in 1986. Although the relationship with Bachardy, who went on to become a portrait artist, was hardly monogamous (for either of them), the encounter was part of a slowly unfolding third decisive moment in Isherwood's life, namely, figuring out how to write again. It was only in the early 1960s that Isherwood returned to form and to his essential subject matter with *Down There on a Visit* (1962), soon followed by the first major modern gay novel in America, *A Single Man* (1964), and, a decade or so later, the memoir *Christopher and His Kind* (1976). In addition, during that period, Isherwood penned a biography of one of the Vedanta saints; wrote a bad novel about the struggle between the spirit and the flesh, *A Meeting by the River* (1967); and produced an account of his relationship with his religious teacher, *My Guru and His Disciple* (1980). To the end of his life, at age eighty-two,

Isherwood enjoyed a reputation as the author of the classic Berlin stories and as an elder of the gay liberation movement.

This is the colourful life-saga that Peter Parker, the author of a previous literary biography, *Ackerley* (1989), recounts in *Isherwood*. Parker's biography gets better than passing grades, and I don't mean that in a backhanded way. It's the fashion to write lengthy literary biographies these days (this one comes in at over nine hundred pages), and I don't think Parker can be faulted on that score, although at times the recounting of the tale seems overly long. I found some of *Isherwood* sluggish, especially the obligatory initial genealogical chapters. But for both readers who don't know much about Isherwood and those who are fans of his work, *Isherwood* provides all the necessary facts, set in context, that anyone is likely to need.

Parker notes from the beginning that Isherwood's entire writing life finds him wrestling with issues of autobiography — there are at least three volumes of purported autobiographical memoirs and three novels of closely fictionalized autobiography — yet Parker seems rather peevish about "Isherwood embroidering for effect what is being offered to the reader as candid autobiography." In his novels, Isherwood uses a genre-blurring device by which real-life persons are slightly altered into fictional characters who are given fictional names, while the narrator is identified as "Christopher Isherwood," but is also subtly fictionalized, usually for reasons of discretion, since it was impossible to frankly present his own homosexuality prior to the mid-1960s. Isherwood himself remarked on all this in a prefatory note to *Goodbye to Berlin* when he says, "Because I have given my own name to the 'I' of this narrative, readers are certainly not entitled to assume that its pages are purely autobiographical, or that its characters are libellously exact portraits of living persons. 'Christopher Isherwood' is a convenient ventriloquist's dummy, nothing more." Parker's complaints about autobiographical "embroidering" are thus a bit ironic, or perhaps simply the biographer's occupational hazard.

It should also be observed that although Isherwood is certainly writing autobiographically, he isn't really writing about himself. Rather, his "Christopher Isherwood" is a narrator telling us about other people and the world. His edge-of-stage presence is much more like the narrators in F. Scott Fitzgerald's *The Great*

Gatsby or Andrew Holleran's gay novel of the late 1970s, *Dancer from the Dance*. The material may be autobiographical, but the focus is definitely not that of self-absorption.

Isherwood's reputation as an autobiographer may have something to do with a tendency to downgrade the quality of his work. So, for example, Norman Page, the author of a monograph *Auden and Isherwood: The Berlin Years*, feels obliged to note that "their gifts and achievements were after all of a very different order ... There is a case for regarding Auden as the greatest British poet of the mid-20th century while Isherwood remains a minor novelist and autobiographer." Page later characterizes Isherwood's talents as "narrow and low-pulsed." Of course, this estimate is wrong for their time in Berlin. Auden stayed only briefly and wrote a few passable poems, while Isherwood dwelled there through the historic period of the rise of Nazism and wrote a masterpiece. Even beyond that, I suspect that eventually Isherwood's best books will rank quite favourably with those of Auden.

Parker devotes considerable space to sorting out the embroideries from the "real story." For example, he proves that Isherwood's devoted and long-suffering mother, Kathleen, was not the monster that Christopher intimated she was. Well, yes, no doubt true, but the longish demonstration of this fact — making extensive use of her diaries (a habit that apparently ran in the family) — seems a somewhat hollow biographer's triumph. Similarly, the biographer's repeated discovery that Isherwood is rather obsessed with the well-being of Christopher (and of "Christopher," the fictional character) doesn't exactly come as a surprise.

Parker is more successful with other aspects of the life. Although it's well-known that Auden and Isherwood were lifelong friends and that they had occasional sex together over a stretch of years (what's known among teens these days as "friendship with benefits"), what Parker touchingly shows is that Auden was genuinely in love with the slightly older Isherwood for a least a decade. Alas, for Auden, he was "the more loving one," as he puts it in a poem about another love. In any case, Auden eventually finds his own teenager, Chester Kallman, with whom he went on to live a stormy and booze-besotted life.

The most poignant figure in Parker's biography is Richard Isherwood, Christopher's very eccentric, and probably schizophrenic, younger brother. Richard, who lived most of his adult life with his mother, Kathleen, was an untidy mass of tics and unconscious jerks, a barely functioning alcoholic, homosexual like Christopher but unable to successfully act on his desires, and given to a rambling diary-keeping graphomania that in Christopher is turned into literature. He's a sort of mirror version of a Christopher-gone-mad, and his sad story is one of the most memorable in the book. On the whole, Christopher is protective of Richard, making over to him his entire share of the family inheritance, and remaining in sympathetic contact with him throughout his life.

Another aspect of Isherwood's life that comes through powerfully is his need for some kind of theology. Although his European friends saw Isherwood's involvement with Vedanta as "sinking into the Yoga bog," and though Christopher's adventures with the Swami really look like California hocus-pocus, Isherwood's spiritual yearnings aren't hocus-pocus. Of course, as Parker points out, spiritual discipline didn't come easily to "a sceptical, sybaritic, chain-smoking, egotistical and morally confused homosexual atheist." This particular form of wandering in the desert doesn't appear to have helped Isherwood write, but it may have tempered some of the anxiety of his exiled existence.

Finally, there is Parker's treatment of the boys. For not only did Berlin mean boys, but for Isherwood so did Los Angeles, New York, and almost everywhere else. Not only for Isherwood, though. Also for Auden, Spender, "Fronny," and dozens of others in Isherwood's circles. What's more, the desires of Isherwood and his friends are not for homosexual or heterosexual adults, but for late-adolescent males, a distinct but minority preference among gay men, albeit one with a pedigree that goes back to the ancient Greeks. As Cyril Connolly shows in *Enemies of Promise* (as does Waugh in *Brideshead Revisited*), it is a form of desire that has its social roots in the English boy's school system, and a great many boys who later lived heterosexual lives (like Connolly, Waugh, and Spender) went through extended pederastic periods that often lasted into their late twenties and early thirties.

Parker gives us satisfactory accounts of all the boys in Isherwood's life, from the first youth in Berlin to the final California companion. He flatly notes the taste for adolescents (Heinz, for example, was sixteen when the twenty-eight-year-old Isherwood met him), but doesn't indulge in either a lot of moralizing or psychologizing, which, I think, is probably the most sensible way to treat the subject.

III

Isherwood's powers as a writer included a lapidary prose style, an ability to see his friends as unforgettable characters, and a tremendous skill at portraying social situations, especially uncomfortable, psychologically complex ones. As the great American critic Edmund Wilson shrewdly said about *Goodbye to Berlin*, "Christopher Isherwood's prose is a perfect medium for his purpose. It has the 'transparency' which the Russians praise in Pushkin. The sentences all get you somewhere almost without your noticing that you are reading them; the similes always have a point without ever obtruding themselves before the object. You seem to look right through Isherwood and see what he sees." Wilson added that Isherwood's "real field is social observation, and in this field it would not be too much to say that he is already, on a small scale, a master."

The problem for Isherwood was one of perspective, and he solved it by inventing the indirect narrator named "Christopher Isherwood." He's the foil for the remarkably realized characters in the Berlin stories, like Sally Bowles and the trapped, young Jewish businessman, Bernhard Landauer. Things happen to them, while "Christopher" remains a cipher. The device was successfully employed by Isherwood in his Berlin fiction, his reportage, and his school memoir, *Lions and Shadows*.

His friends tried to talk him out of "Christopher Isherwood." Stephen Spender, in a long letter to Isherwood, complained, "I can't help protesting against the little comic-cuts Charlie Chaplin figure into which you are getting so adept at turning yourself, especially as you are now called Isherwood in these stories. The self-portrait could scarcely — even in *Lions and Shadows* — be more evasive. By sneering at the more self-pitying & even tragic aspects of yourself, you are really showing a typically English brand of dishonesty, which consists in admitting the real and then making it seem unimportant by the exercise of a sense of humour ... You are far more interesting, and rather more sinister in some ways, than you make out."

Isherwood bought the argument. "Of course you're right about

'Isherwood'," he wrote, "he is an evasion and altogether too harmless and too knowing — 'the sexless nitwit,' as somebody called him," and then promised, "I will drop 'Isherwood' altogether in the future. I always meant to."

The rest of Isherwood's writing life was centred around the struggle to get rid of "Herr Issyvoo." From the Berlin stories of 1939 to 1962 or thereabouts, Isherwood's oeuvre is an almost-complete blank. In that bleak quarter century, he managed one novel. It was called *The World in the Evening* (1954). It was written in third person, it wasn't seen through the eyes of "Isherwood," it was sort of heterosexual, and it was a disaster. It isn't entirely accurate to say the whole period was a blank. Sometime toward the end of World War II, Isherwood blearily looked up from his hangover, remembered his movie work with Viertel, and wrote a pitch-perfect novella that begins, tellingly, with the lines:

"Mr. Isherwood?"

"Speaking."

"Mr. Christopher Isherwood?"

"That's me."

"You know, we've been trying to contact you ever since yesterday afternoon." The voice at the other end of the wire was a bit reproachful.

The voice belongs to a minion at Imperial Bulldog Pictures who is trying to hook Isherwood up with the Viennese director Friedrich Bergmann. "Friedrich Bergman, you know," says the voice. "Never heard of him," replies Isherwood. "That's funny," says the flunky. "He's worked in Berlin a lot, too. Weren't you in pictures, over there?" "I've never been in pictures anywhere," Isherwood primly declares. And then, of course, he is in pictures, and in a neat novella about movie-making and pre-war Europe that's as good as anything by Nathaniel West or Budd Schulberg about the dream factory.

But apart from *Prater Violet* (1945), his novella about movies, Isherwood tried really hard to do in "Isherwood." It was something like Conan Doyle's famous efforts to get rid of Sherlock Holmes in order to write serious novels. As with Doyle, the effort to escape from what you can do was a dismal failure.

This is the most interesting story in Parker's book, and the most important one. Parker provides all the materials, but he doesn't really nail it.

Finally, in 1962, Isherwood wrote *Down There on a Visit*. It consists of four novella-length sketches and is a sort of continuation of *Goodbye to Berlin*. Again, from its opening lines, we're on solid ground: "Now, at last, I'm ready to write about Mr. Lancaster. For years I have been meaning to, but only rather half-heartedly; I never felt I could quite do him justice. Now I see what my mistake was; I always used to think of him as an isolated character ... To present him entirely, I realize I must show how our meeting was the start of a new chapter in my life, indeed a whole series of chapters." The story is a fictionalized account of Isherwood's first visit to Bremen, Germany, when he was twenty-three, invited there by a stuffy, distant relative, who is presented in the story as an important businessman.

It is also in this story that Isherwood works another turn on his narrator:

> And now before I slip back into the convention of calling this young man "I," let me consider him as a separate being, a stranger almost, setting out on this adventure in a taxi to the docks. For, of course, he is almost a stranger to me. I have revised his opinions, changed his accent and his mannerisms, unlearned or exaggerated his prejudices and his habits. We still have the same skeleton, but its outer covering has altered so much that I doubt if he would recognize me on the street ... The Christopher who sat in that taxi is, practically speaking, dead; he only remains reflected in the fading memories of us who knew him.

So now we have an author named Christopher Isherwood creating a first-person narrator named "Christopher Isherwood" who writes about a third-person "Christopher" who tells his story in the first person. Complicated, yes, but effective.

In *Down There*, Isherwood presents unforgettable vignettes about his boyfriend Heinz, who appears as "Waldemar," and a portrait of "Fronny," who appears as "Ambrose," the mad king of a private island in Greece. There is also Isherwood's first attempt to present his American life in "Paul," a story set in 1940 about a celebrated male hustler (who was also memorialized by Isherwood's fellow writers and younger friends, Truman Capote and Gore Vidal), who is interested in Isherwood's efforts at spiritual enlightenment and his relation to Gerald Heard (who appears as "Augustus Parr").

It should also be mentioned that Isherwood got a couple of lucky breaks that helped to solve the identity / narrator issue, as well as bringing him much extraneous celebrity. In 1951, when Isherwood was in the doldrums, the playwright John van Druten produced a stage version of the Berlin stories, *I Am A Camera*. (Parker doesn't make clear how this helped, but I'm certain it did.) Similarly, the 1960s stage version, *Cabaret*, and Bob Fosse's Academy Award-winning film version (starring Michael York, Liza Minelli, and Joel Grey) not only brought in a lot of money for Isherwood, but certainly helped him to write his mid-1970s memoir about Berlin.

With the Isherwood / "Isherwood" problem solved, Isherwood could, in his next novel, *A Single Man* (1964), simply create a third-person character named George, who is a closely fictionalized version of the aspect of Isherwood that was a gay, Brit-expat, English professor at a California college. Although both Vidal and James Baldwin had already published openly gay, serious novels, *A Single Man* is the first thoroughly successful one to appear in the United States, and it stands up four decades after its publication in ways that the earlier novels of Vidal and Baldwin don't. Though *A Single Man* is hardly shocking today, the *Los Angeles Times* review when it appeared was headed "Disjointed Limp Wrist Saga," a tone all too characteristic of the hatred and spite of the times. In subsequent books, like *Kathleen and Frank* (1972) and *Christopher and His Kind* (1976), Isherwood was again able to use the double-"Isherwood" narrator.

On the whole, Parker is not entirely satisfactory on the literary works, though all the material is scrupulously there — dates of publication, sources, surveys of reviewers' reception of the books, etc. But, for example, the appearance of *Goodbye to Berlin* is dispatched in a couple of pages, and Parker doesn't really explain why it's great. The "Isherwood"/narrator question is spottily handled. The problem of the relation between the life, the work, and the times is, of course, the central issue of all literary biographies. Most of them tend to be, to my mind, upside down, with the biographer committed to proving that, after all, those great imaginings are only those of a human being. Well, sure. Parker is certainly no worse than many other serious biographers, but he's hardly outstanding on this score. Nor is he particularly helpful about the literary times. Isherwood's place among other prose writers of the 1930s and '40s — Orwell, Henry Green, Waugh, Connolly, not to mention non-English writing contemporaries — is barely sketched. Not fatal flaws, I suppose, but reason to read *Isherwood* with measured judgment. Given the difficulty of doing this sort of thing credibly at all, I don't want to make too much of such complaints.

In the end, *Isherwood* does what decent biography is supposed to do. This bulky tome sends you straight to those spare, elegant books about "Christopher" and his kind.

On Czesław Miłosz (1911-2004)

I

The book by Czesław Miłosz — the Nobel Prize-winning Polish poet who died at age ninety-three in Krakow, Poland, on August 14, 2004 — that has been on my mind since its publication in English translation is called *Miłosz's ABC's* (1997–98; translation, 2001). It is one of the works from the last years of Miłosz's life, the period that he called "late ripeness." In a poem of that title, he says, "Not soon, as late as the approach of my ninetieth year, / I felt a door opening in me and I entered the clarity of early morning. // One after another my former lives were departing, / Like ships, together with their sorrow. // And the countries, cities, gardens, the bays of seas / assigned to my pen came closer / ready now to be described better than they were before." I wouldn't mind being able to say something similar to that astonishing utterance at sixty-five, much less ninety!

As Miłosz was a prime witness of the twentieth century, his "former lives" were many. He was born in 1911 to a quasi-aristocratic Polish-speaking family on a rural estate near Wilno (now Vilnius), Lithuania, a landscape and a city that appears recurrently in his poetry and prose. When I was in Vilnius about ten years ago — my father was born there at the beginning of the last century — I used Miłosz's *Beginning with My Streets* (1992) as a civic guidebook when I strolled along the black-brick-cobbled main street, Gedemino Prospect, or made my way through the narrow lanes of the former Jewish quarter, streets on which my grandfather had once walked, and whose bustle Miłosz reconstructed through his memories.

Miłosz was educated at the ancient University of Vilnius and in Paris, as much by his uncle Oscar Miłosz, a poet and diplomat, as by academic institutions, ending up with a law degree that would be briefly useful to his own later diplomatic career. By the 1930s, on his return to Vilnius, Miłosz was a young poet, the author of *Three Winters*, which had attracted some attention, and part of a literary circle known as the "Catastrophist School" for its anticipation of the coming disasters. Miłosz was working in Warsaw when the Germans and Russians invaded Poland in September 1939, inaugurating a "next life" for everyone. Miłosz heard the screams and gunfire as the Nazis liquidated the Jews in the walled Warsaw ghetto in 1943, and he witnessed the destruction of nearly all of Warsaw after the failed 1944 uprising, writing extensively about these events for the anti-Nazi underground as he made his escape to Krakow, the medieval Polish capital. After the war, his book *Rescue*, which showed the modernist influence of T.S. Eliot (whom he translated into Polish), established Miłosz among Poland's pre-eminent writers.

His reputation made him attractive to the new Communist government of Poland as he entered a third phase of his life. Sympathetic to socialism, but not a member of the Communist Party, Miłosz joined the Polish diplomatic corps, serving as a cultural attaché in Washington and Paris. It was in Paris in 1951 that Miłosz defected from the Polish regime, seeking political asylum and one more new life. In his French exile, he wrote *The Captive Mind* (1953), one of the important and early anti-totalitarian credos, joining the ranks of such books as Milovan Djilas's *The New Class*, Hannah Arendt's *Origins of Totalitarianism*, Orwell's *1984*, and Arthur Koestler's *Darkness at Noon*.

A decade later, Miłosz embarked upon a fifth and lengthy phase of his life when he accepted an appointment to the University of California at Berkeley. The transition to an even more distant exile wasn't easy. As he wrote, "Ill at ease in the tyranny, ill / at ease in the republic, / in the one I longed for freedom, / in the other for the / end of corruption. // I learned at last to say: this is / my home, / here, before the glowing coal of ocean sunsets . . . / in a great republic, moderately corrupt." It's a "corruption" about which many of us remain apprehensive at this very moment, as the troops of the empire camp in ancient Babylon.

At Berkeley, Miłosz, always a productive writer, created a cornucopia of poetry, essays, histories, and anthologies, particularly of his Polish compatriots. It was for this body of work that Miłosz received the Nobel Prize for Literature in 1980. "The world that Miłosz depicts in his poetry, prose and essays," said the Nobel committee, "is the world in which man lives after having been driven out of Paradise."

The last phase of Miłosz's life began in the same year as his Nobel Prize with the emergence of the Solidarity Movement, the workers' and intellectuals' revolt against the "workers' state" that began with strikes in the Lenin Shipyard in Gdansk, Poland. I was in Gdansk the following spring, when the shipyard workers erected a soaring, three-column, crucifix-like memorial to workers who had been shot by the regime in earlier uprisings. The Solidarity representative responsible for the erection of the memorial pointed out to me that it bore a line of Miłosz's poetry: "You who harmed a simple man, do not feel secure: for a poet remembers." Nearly a decade later, after the fall of communism in 1989, Miłosz was greeted as a hero when he returned to the region of his birth. During the 1990s he divided his time between Berkeley and Krakow, eventually settling in the city of the Jagiellonian kings. Throughout this last of his "many lives," from 1980 on, Miłosz produced a further remarkable body of work, including elegant books of poetry, such as *Road-side Dog* and *This*, a new edition of his *Collected Poems*, and volumes of essays and memoirs, including the book on my mind, *Miłosz's ABC's*.

II

Miłosz's ABC's, published when its author was in his mid-eighties, is an alphabetically organized miscellany that consists of character sketches and literary profiles, mostly of figures little known to us and long dead; descriptions of places that had meaning in Miłosz's personal geography; and reflections on broader themes, often of a quasi-theological character.

It is a difficult, obscure book for the casual North American reader, even though it's written in straightforward prose. Evidence of the difficulty is available in the hilarious democracy of Amazon.com readers' reviews, where anyone who cracks a book is permitted an opinion. One sincere soul wrote about *Miłosz's ABC's*, "I feel that this book is more written for the people he met themselves, or for their friends and descendents, rather than for outsiders like me, who don't know 80 to 90 percent of the subjects or items treated." The reviewer concedes that some comments on Henry Miller, Schopenhauer and Walt Whitman "are worth-while reading," but in the end sticks to his guns: "Only for insiders." Well, yes, but if we didn't live in a world that erases memory, history and imagination, we might all be "insiders." And, in fact, we are all insiders, once we recognize where we are, in the middle of nowhere.

Miłosz's motive in writing his *ABC's* is simply to recoup something of a world he'd once known that had almost completely vanished by the end of the twentieth century. His memory is haunted by "disappearance, of people and objects ... My time, the 20th century, weighs on me as a host of voices and the faces of people whom I once knew, or heard about, and now they no longer exist. Many were famous for something, they are in the encyclopædias, but more of them have been forgotten, and all they can do is make use of me, the rhythm of my blood, my hand holding the pen, in order to return among the living for a brief moment."

Nor does the poet have many unshattered illusions about his subject matter. As he said in a 2001 interview, "How do you write about suffering and still be able to approve of the world at the same time? If you really think about the horror of the world, the only suitable attitude seems to be to reject it." He added, "I've always regretted that I'm made of contradictions. But if contradiction is impossible to overcome, we have to accept both its ends."

Miłosz had a lovely sense of his own contradictions. In a 1985 "Confession," he reported:

> My Lord, I loved strawberry jam
> And the dark sweetness of a woman's body.
> Also, well-chilled vodka, herring in olive oil,
> Scents, of cinnamon, of cloves.
> So what kind of prophet am I? Why should the
>   spirit

Have visited such a man? Many others
Were justly called, and trustworthy.
Who would have trusted me? For they saw
How I empty glasses, throw myself on food,
And glance greedily at the waitress's neck.
Flawed and aware of it . . .
I know what was left for smaller men like me:
A feast of brief hopes, a rally of the proud.
A tournament of hunchbacks, literature.

Miłosz's ABC's, as he says, are offered "instead of: instead of a novel, instead of an essay on the 20th century, instead of a memoir. Each of the individuals remembered here sets into motion a network of mutual allusions and interdependencies linked to the facts of my century." Miłosz adds, "In the final analysis I do not regret that I have dropped names so cavalierly (or so it must seem), or that I have made a virtue of my casual way." Less modestly, one could argue that his "casual way," as well as the genre of fragments, of miscellany, of the treasure chest, that he's chosen to work in here, is the most precise method for allowing the dead to "return among the living for a brief moment."

It is not only the dead who are on Miłosz's mind, but also our condition as human beings. In "Adam and Eve," a passage on our enduring fascination with the story of the expulsion from the Garden of Eden, Miłosz says, "In our deepest convictions, reaching into the very depths of our being, we deserve to live forever. We experience our transitoriness and mortality as an act of violence perpetrated against us. Only Paradise is authentic; the world is inauthentic, and only temporary. That is why the story of the Fall speaks to us so emotionally, as if summoning an old truth from our slumbering memory." Conversely, we could say, Only the world, albeit temporary, is authentic and, like the illusion of paradise, should be eternal. The poet George Stanley, who introduced me to Miłosz's work, put it another way. Playing on the old saying "The hardest step of every journey is the first," he responded, "The hardest step on every journey / is the last, and every step is the last." The aphorism can bear one more addendum: And every step, first or last, is the expulsion from paradise.

III

The *ABC's* then, continues the project Miłosz announced in a prose poem called "Pity" in *Road-side Dog*:

> In the ninth decade of my life, the feeling which rises in me is pity, useless. A multitude, an immense number of faces, shapes, fates of particular beings, and a sort of merging with them from inside, but at the same time my awareness that I will not find anymore the means to offer a home in my poems to these guests of mine, for it is too late. I think also that, could I start anew, every poem of mine would have been a biography or a portrait of a particular person, or, in fact a lament over his or her destiny.

Faced with the tension between the poet's responsibility to bear witness to his time and his essential task of contemplating being, Miłosz returned again and again to his beginnings. In the title poem of *Road-side Dog*, he writes,

> I went on a journey in order to acquaint myself with my province, in a two-horse wagon with a lot of fodder and a tin bucket rattling in the back. The bucket was required for the horses to drink from. I traveled through a country of hills and pine groves that gave way to woodlands where swirls of smoke hovered over the roofs of houses, as if they were on fire, for they were chimneyless cabins; I crossed districts of fields and lakes. It was so interesting to be moving, to give the horses their rein, and wait until, in the next valley, a village slowly appeared, or a park with the white spot of a manor house in it. And always we were barked at by a dog, assiduous in its duty. That was the beginning of the century; this is its end. I have been thinking not only of the people who lived there once but also of a generation of dogs accompanying them in their everyday bustle, and one night — I don't know where it came from — in a pre-dawn sleep, that funny and tender phrase composed itself: a road-side dog.

Conversely, the road-side dog is the poet, his poetry barking at the passing wagons and caravans of history.

In his mid-century book-length poem *A Treatise on Poetry*,

Miłosz recalls the Krakow of "Beautiful Times," to which he would return at the end of his life.

> Cabbies were dozing by St. Mary's tower.
> Krakow was tiny as a painted egg
> Just taken from a pot of dye on Easter.
> In their black capes poets strolled the streets.
> Nobody remembers their names today,
> And yet their hands were real once,
> And their cufflinks gleamed above a table . . .
> . . . Muses, Rachels in trailing shawls,
> Put tongues to lips while pinning up their braids.
> The pin lies with their daughters' ashes now,
> Or in a glass case next to mute seashells
> And a glass lily . . .
> This is our beginning. Useless to deny it.
> Useless to recall a distant golden age.
> We have to accept and take as our own
> The mustache with pomade, the bowler hat acock.

In that same Krakow, Miłosz recalls the appearance of Joseph Conrad, fated to captain a steamer on the Congo. Conrad's tale of a jungle river was a warning, Miłosz says,

> One of the civilizers, a madman named Kurtz,
> A gatherer of ivory stained with blood
> Scribbled in the margin of his report
> On the Light of Culture: "The horror." And
>   climbed
> Into the 20th century.

IV

At the end, there's almost always a bit of slapstick to relieve what Miłosz simply called "this." Miłosz died on Saturday, August 14, 2004, at home in Krakow.

The early editions of the English-language press printed the dispatches from the Associated Press and Reuters, which, in the standard formulas of journalism, reported, "The cause of death was not immediately known." Behind the journalese was a funny moment. The AP stringer was on the phone with Miłosz's assistant, Agnieszka Kosinska, who was handling the communications traffic. What was the cause of death? they asked her. Perhaps not familiar with the protocols of the media, she was clearly puzzled. I can hear her voice, accented, in English, slightly impatient even, in the quote attributed to her after the phrase "the cause of death was not immediately known." Cause of death? she wondered.

"It's death, simply death," said Kosinska. "It was his time — he was 93."

One of the slight advantages of dying at an advanced age is that not much of a fuss is likely to be made about the cause of death. Everybody knows that, at a certain age, the cause of death is Death.

About Robert Creeley (1926–2005)

I

Robert Creeley's last book, *If I Were Writing This* (2003), begins with a "credo" poem, "The Way." Given that Creeley's particular "way" ended on March 30, 2005, with his death from pneumonia in a hospital in the obscure outpost of Odessa, Texas, at age seventy-eight, that credo poem is as good a place as any to start. "The Way," and much of what follows, brings us up to date on Creeley's position with respect to both being-in-the-world (as well as leaving it) and the subject of writing, which was inseparable from his life. "The Way" is a twenty-line, five-stanza, semi-rhymed, sonnet-like poem that moves with the elegance and swift concision characteristic of Creeley's wonderfully substantial body of work. It opens like this:

> Somewhere in all the time that's passed
> was a thing in mind that became the evidence,
> the pleasure even in fact of being lost
> so quickly, simply that what it was could never
>   last.

The most that could be expected of that evanescent "thing in mind," Creeley continues, is "Only knowing was measure of what one could / make hold together for that moment's recognition, / or else the world washed over like a flood / of meager useless truths, of hostile incoherence." He sees that it is "Too late to know that knowing was its own reward / and that wisdom had at best a transient credit. / Whatever one did or didn't do was what one could. / Better at last to believe than think to question?" he asks. Not at all, Creeley replies:

There wasn't choice if one had seen the light,
not of belief but of that soft, blue-glowing fusion
seemed to appear or disappear with thought,
a minute magnesium flash, a firefly's illusion.

Best wonder at mind and let that flickering
  ambience
of wondering be the determining way you follow,
which leads itself from day to day into tomorrow,
finds all it ever finds is there by chance.

The older Creeley diligently, and to my mind appropriately, registered "all the time that's passed" in a series of books over the last quarter century or so: *Later* (1979), *Mirrors* (1983), *Memory Gardens* (1986), *Windows* (1990), *Echoes* (1994), and *Life & Death* (2000), as well as this last one. As the various titles suggest, the poems are, among other things, preoccupied with time, memory, mortality, and the objects — windows, mirrors, echoes — literally and emblematically involved in framing those concerns. Rightly so, I'd say. In a sense, what else is there to do as a writer?

Though his poems, like those of most good poets, are resistant to simple paraphrase (or else why would poets bother to write poems?), one useful way to see Creeley is as a phenomenological poet. More useful, say, than pegging him, as is often done by critics, as a "lyric poet" or "minimalist" writer. That is, a focus of Creeley's continuing attention — as is evident from the opening lines of "The Way" — is the precise registration of how the mind, through language and other means, including the "real-time" digressions of consciousness, engages the world and the experience of being in it. Such registering is inseparable from one's being-in-the-world, as much of post-modern philosophical thought also argues.

I've long understood Creeley, since his early poems of the 1950s, as a poet with a strong philosophical intelligence. He presents an American, New England-bred, version of the Continental European existentialism in whose wake he came of age in the 1940s and '50s. The presentation of his philosophical position, as worked out over a number of years in company with, but distinct from, his friend and fellow poet Charles Olson, is indirect, oblique, and paratactical — that is, one perception follows immediately upon the last — rather than argumentative. But it's clear that Creeley's views accord with philosopher Hilary Putnam's dictum that "elements of what we call 'language' or 'mind' penetrate so deeply into what we call 'reality' that the very project of representing ourselves as being 'mappers' of something 'language-independent' is fatally compromised from the start."

If Creeley is a modernist of the "New American Poetry," whose immediate inheritance is from the generation of Ezra Pound, William Carlos Williams, and T.S. Eliot, his deepest affinity within the tradition of American poetry is clearly the moral sensibility of his New England compatriot Emily Dickinson. From Creeley's earliest poems, such as "The Immoral Proposition," which begins, "If you never do anything for anyone else / You are spared the tragedy of human relation- // ships ... " one catches the true echo of Dickinson's angular perspective and concern. In that early poem, Creeley also remarks that if you note "an unexpected thing," "to look at it is more / than it was. God knows // nothing is competent nothing is / all there is ... " That's a credo, too.

Shortly after Creeley's death, when my friend George Stanley was to give a reading of his own work and prefaced it by reading a poem in Creeley's honour and memory, it was with precision and appropriateness that he chose those haunting lines by Dickinson that begin

Because I could not stop for Death
He kindly stopped for me;
The carriage held but just ourselves
And Immortality.

302 ● TOPIC SENTENCE

So, in Creeley's "The Way," "in all the time that's passed," there "was a thing in mind." "Thing" here might mean some conception, even a necessarily hazy conception, of how everything works. Most of us have such an idea. The experience of being-in-the-world causes us to see that whatever conception we have of how everything works or manifests itself is quickly and repeatedly lost. We ourselves are lost, or at least the question of "where we are" in place and time is not finally determinable once and for all. There is "the pleasure even . . . of being lost." However we see the whole thing, we recognize that "what it was could never last." Our perspective on, and conception of, reality, that "thing in mind," cannot be permanent or final. Creeley goes on to say,

> Only knowing was measure of what one could
> make hold together for that moment's recognition,
> or else the world washed over like a flood
> of meager useless truths, of hostile incoherence.

So, again, in dumbshow paraphrase, we only can know that what we know is what we can "make hold together for that moment's recognition." There may be an accumulation of what one knows, a wisdom, but in the existential sense it is continually suborned to what one sees in the latest instant. It was the photographer Henri Cartier-Bresson who used the phrase "the instant and its eternity" as an explanation of one of the things that a work of art might investigate. The "moment's recognition" can reconfigure everything you've known. Perhaps it very rarely does, but what we're talking about is openness to the possibility. Otherwise, what you end up with is the dull perception of "meager useless truths" and "hostile incoherence." Creeley long had a sharp sense that just outside our frail efforts to make sense of things there's incoherence, chaos, and it isn't friendly.

In "The Way," Creeley uses "knowing" to mean those insights, and he contrasts "knowing" favourably to accumulated "wisdom." That flash of knowing, it turns out, "was its own reward," not a step on the way to wisdom, whatever we may have thought at the time. As in an early poem, "The Awakening," where Creeley recognizes the urgency of "moving at all . . . / because you must," he reaffirms here that whatever attention one did or didn't bring to those moments was simply what one was able to do at the time. So, he asks, is it "better at last" to have firm beliefs about how it all works rather than to constantly "think to question"?

Well, in fact, there wasn't any choice, especially "if one had seen the light" — not the light of belief, which is here treated as the rigid result of wisdom, but a light that's a "soft, blue-glowing fusion" which seems to "appear or disappear with thought." It's the light of "a minute magnesium flash," like the ones that made photographs long ago, or, better, "a firefly's illusion."

The coda of "The Way" is a gently rhymed and half-rhymed quatrain:

> Best wonder at mind and let that flickering
>   ambience
> of wondering be the determining way you follow,
> which leads itself from day to day into tomorrow,
> finds all it ever finds is there by chance.

That firefly-like "flickering ambience" is the "determining way" that Creeley follows through time. What we discover by means of "The Way" is that whatever it is we find is contingent, conditional, "there by chance." Creeley doesn't propose a world outside of time and chance.

I've stuck with this first poem for so long because it is emblematic, as it stands at the opening of *If I Were Writing This*, and because Creeley's vocabulary, syntax, and mode of seeing are dense, of high velocity, and not necessarily intended for lumpy exegesis. But I wanted to slow it down, just for a bit, so that there's no mistaking that speed for mere flash of style, and no taking the density to conceal a private or coded understanding. After exegesis, there's reading. Well, okay, maybe it's the other way around.

What follows "The Way" are three dozen or so mostly brief poems, a few longer part-poems consisting of many quick flashes, some elegies, and two or three more prosy "memory" poems — one about being in Vancouver in the 1960s, another about Allen Ginsberg and aging, one about the death of his sister.

A crucial feature of Creeley's writing is his particular sense of humour, "standing at a slight angle to the universe" (as E.M. Forster said of Cavafy). In part, it's a very hip, jazz-inflected, pot-

smoking kind of humour, in which the stoned observer discovers
that everything can be funny. But Creeley's wit goes deeper than
that — it takes the form of ontological irony, the sense at every
instant of recognizing the possible absurdity of our existence, a
recognition of how odd it is that *this* — the world, ourselves, the
ways language works — *is*. There's a snort of muffled amusement, appearing usually in a flash, that informs much of Creeley's writing.

"Drawn & Quartered," a poem that offers fifty or so quatrain-
length quick takes, is characteristic of Creeley's wry wit and cos-
mic irony. Try this:

> Hold still, lion!
> I am trying
> to paint you
> while there's time to.

I.e., before you eat me. Or this possible version of relationships:

> Am I only material
> for you to feel?
> Is that all you see
> when you look at me?

The "take" intentionally echoes children's verses, suggesting that
even as the occasions and the circumstances increasingly become
as complex as adult life can make them, there's still a sense in
which it's "as simple as that," but the underlying available irony
also allows you to mock your own hard-won simplicity. Sometimes it sounds like Old Mother Goose, a little high:

> Here I sit
> meal on lap
> come to eat
> just like that!

Repeatedly, for Creeley, there is both a celebratory astonishment at our simply being here, and a consciousness of the absurdity of being here, of existing. "Finally to have come / to where
one had so long wanted to visit / and then to stand / there and

look at it." Equally, there is the prospective absurdity, now realized, of not being here, of death. At least, in the absurdity of existence, we can make something of it, however banal or barely. So much of life is

> Like sitting in back seat
> can't see what street
> we're on or what the
> one driving sees

> or where we're going.
> Waiting for what's to happen,
> can't quite hear the conversation,
> the big people, sitting up front

That the title of this book takes the odd grammatical form of a conditional, *If I Were Writing This*, requires comment, though I'll try to refrain from a baroque perambulation about subjunctive moods, what-ifs, and the rest. My first response, upon seeing the title, is: "But you *are* writing this!" so what's going on? The title poem itself puts the phrase in quotes: "If I were writing this . . . ", a device, often used by instructors, to introduce some mild corrective. As in: "Well, if I were writing this, I think I'd put the description of *x* here, and save the comment by the mother . . . " As it turns out, the poem is about the possibility of writing and the apprehensions one feels of getting it all wrong, even as one does it:

> If I were writing this
> with prospect of encouragement
> or had I begun some work
> intended to be what it was

Eventually, amid the trepidation of beginning, he "had begun, had found"

> myself in the time and place
> writing words which I knew,
> could say *ring, dog, hat, car,*
> was rushing, it felt, to keep up

with the trembling impulse,
the connivance the words contrived
even themselves to be though
I wrote them, thought they were me.

Ah, to be in the moment where it feels like you're rushing simply
to keep up with the trembling impulse that generates the words
of the poem. In one of the pieces of the poem called "Clemente's
Images" — the images of the painter Francesco Clemente, one of
many visual artists with whom Creeley collaborated over a lifetime — it's all a play on conditionals:

If small were big,
if then were now,

if here were there,
if find were found,

if mind were all there was,
would the animals still save us?

That is, if conditions were utterly otherwise, would we be in any
less of a precarious situation in terms of our lives? Creeley frequently used the word "condition," and the notion of the "conditional," in his conversation and writing. He saw our situation as
conditional both in the sense of "temporary" (whether an eternal instant or a mere lifetime) and in the sense of being shaped
by specific conditions, by our circumstances, and he emphasized
the circumstances of relationships as much as those of time and
place.

I particularly like the longer "memory" poems in this book,
where Creeley allows himself to ramble, to let the telling be a bit
baggy, where the echoed form is the "shaggy dog story." Creeley's poem titled "Memory" begins with a recollection of Allen
Ginsberg's recalling (in *Kaddish*, I think, or in one of Ginsberg's
"shroud" poems)

. . . his mother's dream
about God, *an old man*, she says,
living across the river in
Palisades

In his mother's dream, she asks God, "How could you let the world get into such a mess?" and then, turning her waking attention to her son, Allen, she says, "he looks neglected / and there are yellow pee-stains / on his underpants." It's that recollection that produces the turn in the poem for Creeley:

> . . . Hard to hear
> God could not do any better
> than any of us, just another old
> man sitting on some bench or some
> chair. I remember it was a urologist
> told me to strip the remaining pee
> from my penis by using my finger's
> pressure just back of the balls,
> the prostate, then bringing it forward
> so that the last drops of it would go
> into the toilet, not onto my clothes.
> Still it's of necessity an imperfect
> solution. How stand at a public urinal
> seeming to play with oneself? Yet
> how not — if that's what it takes not
> to walk out, awkward, wide-legged, damp
> from the crotch down? I cannot
> believe age can be easy for anyone . . .

The poem goes on from there, although on the occasion I heard Creeley read it, some of it was lost in the audience's laughter accompanying the account of carrying out the urologist's instructions. The great things in it are, first, simply following the unlikely connections that get you from one place to the next in the poem: a memory of Ginsberg who died in 1997; A.G.'s recalling of his mother's dream of chastizing an ineffectual God; his mother's imagining the pee-stains on Allen's underpants; and then the image of pee-stains staying sharply enough in mind so that even while reflecting on God as "just another old man," there's the abrupt leap that gets us to the urologist and the account that follows from there. Second, there's the unflinching situation of, being an old man oneself, how not to pee on yourself, presented as both a self-deprecating comic antic and, more important, as a literal instance of this is how it is, this is the situation in which we'll do what we must "if that's what it takes" not to walk out "damp from the crotch down."

If I Were Writing This concludes with one last shot at it all:

> *Sit down,* says generous life, *and stay awhile*!
> although it's irony that sets the table
> and puts the meager food on broken dishes,
> pours out the rancid wine and walks away.

II

I saw quite a bit of Creeley in Bolinas, California, in the mid-1960s, I think it was, or the beginning of the '70s, when he and his wife, Bobbie Louise Hawkins, who I also liked very much, were living there. Creeley and I went for walks, on the Bolinas beach, and eventually to Smiley's bar and bait shop, one of the few indoor public gathering places in that town just north of San Francisco. A group of artists had moved in a few years previously and established a sort of community among the local residents, and somehow Bob and Bobbie and their children — I never got the exact story — had temporarily lodged here. Our conversations were easy, there were drinks at Smiley's, great meals in Bobbie's farmhouse-sized kitchen, the kids in and out.

I don't remember the particulars, but somewhere during one of our walks from the beach back to Smiley's I asked something on the order of "Why Bolinas?" and Creeley had offered an account of his relation to the place, which led me to wryly remark, "Bolinas and me, huh?" Bob laughed, repeated the phrase, "Bolinas and me." Indirectly, that conversation had some small part in a poem of that title in Creeley's *A Day Book*, quite a good poem, which he kindly dedicated to me.

We stayed friends, distantly, after that, and on each subsequent occasion, even years apart, the conversation was resumed as if there had been no interruption. Several other people, in various memorial reminiscences about Creeley, have remarked on the immediacy and presence he brought to conversations. For me, the sense of him was constantly accessible in my mind since I have an almost exact imprint of Creeley's voice and of his handling of the poetic line in my brain. I not only continued to read those slim New Directions-published volumes of his poems as they appeared, every few years, but I also retained a high regard for his prose, especially his novel of the early 1960s, *The Island*, a book of domestic disruption, hard drinking, and the particulars of Mallorca seen through the eyes of the American foreigners who are the protagonists of the story. I'd learned, by heart, a brief poem of Creeley's from his book *For Love*, which I carried about in my mind as something of a talisman and frequently recited:

The Warning

For love I would
split open your head and put
a candle in
behind the eyes
Love is dead in us
if we forget
the virtues of an amulet
and quick surprise

The last time I saw Creeley was in September 2003 at an historic literary occasion in Vancouver. Creeley, who had briefly lived in Vancouver in the early 1960s while teaching at the University of British Columbia and finishing *The Island* (he has a very good poem about the experience in *If I Were Writing This*), and Vancouver poet Robin Blaser, respectively seventy-seven and seventy-eight years old, read together at the Vancouver East Cultural Centre, and the several hundred people who filled the theatre, many of them old friends of one or both of the poets, were conscious that this was likely a one-time-only, last-time-ever, event. Creeley had written the introduction for Blaser's collected poems, *The Holy Forest* (1993), and though he had written dozens of such introductions for friends over the years, this one was notably astute and affectionate in his understanding of Blaser's place in the "company" of poets and of Blaser's poetics.

The reading was perfectly fine; both very old friends were in good form, and Creeley got to read his new Vancouver poem in Vancouver itself. It's a poem that recalls a particular "yesterday" marked by both the "freshness" of the young Vancouverites and the "faded Edwardian sitcom" of early 1960s middle-class life in western Canada. "Sometime just about then," he says, "I must have / Seen myself as others see or saw me, / Even like in a mirror, but could not quite / Accept either their reassuring friendship / Or their equally locating anger. Selfish / Empty, I kept at it." Nearly four decades later, Creeley reports, "I seem to myself still much the same, / Even if I am happier, I think, and older."

In the old days, the after-reading party would have taken place right after the reading and run well into the night, but taking account of the age of both poets and the advancing decrepitude of a good chunk of the rest of us, the post-reading get-together was held early the next evening at the house of old friends. Creeley was sitting on a living room sofa, receiving friends and various students. I positioned myself on his one-eyed good side. I explained, semi-apologetically, that I'd been thinking about certain old poems of his and wanted to ask him some leaden-footed questions about the literal meaning of some lines of a well-known poem. The poem was "The Immoral Proposition," written *circa* 1952. Without hesitation or fumbling about, Creeley recited it:

If you never do anything for anyone else
you are spared the tragedy of human relation-

ships. If quietly and like another time
there is the passage of an unexpected thing:

to look at it is more
than it was. God knows

nothing is competent nothing is
all there is. The unsure

egotist is not
good for himself.

Then we went over it, line by line, but it promptly, comically, bogged down.

I asked, "Now, what does 'another time' mean here?" and Bob replied, "Well, 'like another time'."

Ploddingly, doggedly, I asked, "Then what does it mean to say that 'to look at it is more / than it was'? 'It' is the passage of the unexpected thing, right?"

"Uh-mmm," Bob said.

"So to look at the unexpected thing — "

" — 'is more than it was,'" Bob said. In other words, what it means is what it says. Well, then, let's leave it at that. And we did. "God knows / nothing is competent," certainly not myself at that moment. But then again, "nothing is / all there is."

The Sound of . . .

I

I've been listening to music, lately. Weird music.

The other evening, for example, I was sitting in the upper ranges of architect Hans Scharoun's mid-twentieth-century chamber music hall, part of his Philharmonie auditorium complex, one of my favourite places in Berlin. I was listening to a piece by Giacinto Scelsi, a twentieth-century Italian composer (1905–1988) whom I'd never heard of, the lushly titled *Khoom: Seven episodes of a story of love and death unwritten in a distant land. Khoom* is performed by a soprano and seven instrumental players (on this occasion, singer Natalia Pschenitschnikova and musicians from the London Sinfonietta), and was one of the more than two dozen performances in the 2005 edition of the ten-day März-Musik festival of contemporary music, an annual Berlin event that takes place during the first two weeks of March.

There are two problems with talking about almost any kind of music, especially this kind of "weird music," that I'd better address immediately. First of all, this music doesn't have a convenient moniker or label. It's serious, post-classical, post-modernist, twentieth- and twenty-first-century music, often dissonant, not very melodic, marked by odd rhythms and lots of screechy, scratchy sounds. Because it arises from the tradition of "classical" music, it's sometimes simply called classical music, or the oxymoronic term "contemporary classical music" is used. But it sure doesn't sound much like Bach or Beethoven. More often it's called "new music" or "contemporary" or "modernist" music (plus all the "post-" thises and thats one can add to any label of anything these days). But that's not very helpful. After all, Nelly the Rapper's "It's Hot in Here (Take Off All Your Clothes)" is also new, contemporary, and, I suppose, post-modernist.

Second, and worse, music is generally indescribable. At least with Britney Spears and her ilk, you can describe her bare midriff and wonder what the words mean when she warbles "Hit Me One More Time" — a phrase from blackjack card games? a request for another "rail" of cocaine? allusions to an s&m relationship with Eminem? But if you've casually read any descriptions or criticism of music of any kind, you know what I mean.

In no time flat (or is that B-flat?) it sounds like this: "The somewhat dark and sombre 'D minor Suite' (No. 2) makes full use of the cello's resonant low register … The following Allemande occasionally features double-stopping (the sounding of two strings simultaneously), while the Courante is a virtuoso tour-de-force of quicksilver semiquavers. A mournful Sarabande finds no reconciliation in the anguished, angular musings of a pair of minuets and an impassioned Gigue." This is excerpted at random from the liner notes to Yo-Yo Ma's performance of Bach's *Six Suites for Unaccompanied Cello*, and even with the kindly parenthetical explanation of what "double-stopping" means, you're no closer to what it sounds like than you were when you started.

Nor do matters improve when there's a singer, as there is in the Scelsi (by the way, that's pronounced "Shell-see") piece, *Khoom*, because as often as not the singer isn't singing words but just making sounds with the human voice. In terms of writing, then, there's a real question of whether you can write anything about music at all. Unlike "pop" music, classical and new music is not especially narrative, or if there's a sense in which it is narrative (maybe anything that unfolds in time has a quality of narrative), the narrative is abstract. And the abstraction is even less describable than an abstract painting or the movements of "modern dance."

●

So there I am in the upper ranges of the chamber music hall at the Philharmonie, listening to Scelsi for the first time in my life. It's a wonderful hall, one of those buildings built, as they say in architectural lingo, "from the inside out." Outside, the Philharmonie, which consists of a full symphony auditorium and the chamber music hall, looks like a jumble of dark gold lamé boxes and tent-like swoops, haphazardly piled on top of each other. The complex was started in the late-fiftiess in a patch of Berlin bombed out in World War II, then subsequently isolated by the Berlin Wall, not far from Potsdamer Platz, one of several dispersed centres of Berlin. While the symphony auditorium was opened in 1962, the chamber music hall wasn't finished until 1987, five years after Scharoun's death. Inside, it provides unobstructed seating in the round, steeply rising in chunks and tiers, with a set of small sail-like panels dropped from the soaring ceiling (which has something to do with reflecting the sound). There's not a spot in the thousand-or-so-seat house that offers less than perfect sound and visibility. It's one of the few concert halls I've been in that calms my mild case of claustrophobia. I feel safe there, reassured by its hardwood floors and staircases. The only recent addition to the scene is a light-projected sign telling people to turn off their cell-phones, and the only thing you need is a packet of Fisherman's Friend lozenges to stave off hysterical coughing fits.

The Scelsi is on a program that includes music by British composer Jonathan Harvey, who uses a lot of live electronic sound, and Sam Hayden, another Brit, as well as an elegant piece by the famous French composer and conductor Pierre Boulez, whose eightieth birthday will be marked in Berlin later in the month with a series of concerts that he will conduct or attend. I've gotten used to hearing these kinds of sounds and have, in the last year or so, come to prefer them. I'll try to figure out how I got my taste for all this in a bit.

The Scelsi comes on at the beginning of the second half. The singer has a powerful soprano voice and is backed by several instruments, mostly strings. She's tall and lean (the other day I read the phrase, describing certain women, "toothpicks marinated in Chanel"). Beyond that, there's little to say except that it's electrifying, a sustained passion that lasts through seven pieces. If Scelsi says it's about love and death, "in a distant country" yet, I'm inclined to believe him. No, nothing describable, other than the soprano's shriek, meshing, clashing, interweaving with the nearly unbearable tautness of the strings. If I write another sentence attempting to describe it, it'll turn into the liner notes cited above, except it'll be even less helpful since I know less about music than the erudite liner-note writer.

There are two things I can say. First, I can distinguish between the various pieces and my level of interest in them. I'm not especially taken with the Jonathan Harvey, though I recognize the intelligence behind the music. Pretty much ditto for Sam Hayden. I like the Boulez; its gracefulness interests me. But the Scelsi is riveting. It makes me pay attention. Something is happening, and even if I don't know exactly what, I know I'm involved. And that's the second thing I can say: Having heard the Scelsi, I know and feel something I didn't know previously, didn't know before I entered the chamber music hall and climbed up to my spot in section D left. Whatever it is I claim to know now, it's abstract, almost unarticulatable, but has something to do with everything I think about the meaning of life, and I'm slightly changed as a result of having heard it.

II

I'm trying to remember when I first consciously heard music. I was seven years old and on holiday with my mother at a resort in Wisconsin called The Dells, not far from our home in Chicago. The holiday had been paid for by her brother, Irving, a successful accountant. In the evenings, the guests assembled in the resort restaurant and a floor show was provided, featuring a handsome young lounge singer named Jimmy Spitalny, whose signature closing piece each evening was a song called "Bewitched, Bothered, and Bewildered." It had a slow lilting melody and went,

> I'm bewitched,
> bothered,
> and bewildered . . .
> by
> you.

The "by you" came with a dying fall that I thought very sophisticated, the "you" tossed off slightly ironically and yet perfectly capturing the pain of being in love. I developed an instant crush on Spitalny, and of course had no idea that he was a very obscure entertainer who'd managed to secure a summer gig at a very obscure lower-middle-class resort.

But I didn't remain completely naïve. In my early teens, although I faithfully watched and listened to the weekly television show *Hit Parade* (with chart-topping songs like "The Tennessee Waltz" — "I remember the night . . . and the Tenn-es-see Waltz" — sung, or "covered," as they say, by Snooky Lanson), I also recall the pale yellow cover of the booklet that sombrely announced the scores of Chopin's *Preludes*, whose simple rhythms I utterly failed to navigate at the spinet piano my mother had insisted we purchase. I wasn't much better with the Stephen Foster nineteenth-century songbook.

It was some years later — I was in my twenties, had just gotten beyond Elvis Presley and was about to be plunged, along with the rest of us, into the Beatles, the Rolling Stones, Paul Simon, and the 1960s — when the poet Robin Blaser introduced me to modernist music in San Francisco. That meant Igor Stravinsky, Erik Satie, and the group of early-twentieth-century French composers known as Les Six. There were also recordings of Virgil Thompson's music for Gertrude Stein's opera *Four Saints in Three Acts* and, a related piece, William Walton's settings for Edith Sitwell's *Façade*. We went to a concert in Berkeley, California, one evening, and Blaser pointed out to me an elderly man tottering down the aisle toward his seat, the composer Darius Milhaud, one of the legendary Les Six (Georges Auric, Arthur Honegger, Francis Poulenc, Louis Durey, and Germaine Tailleferre were the others).

There's a long period after that, several decades, in which I listened to music only sporadically. Apart from the ubiquitous sound of pop songs, I knew the names of the famous classic composers, Bach, Beethoven, Mozart, and had at different times heard some of their music, but it wasn't until the early 1990s that I discovered Gustav Mahler (1860–1911). I can't remember the details of encountering Mahler, but as soon as I heard his symphonies, with their mixture of late romantic longing, snatches of pop music that included everything from hurdy-gurdies to military marches (there was a barracks near his central European boyhood home), and the first dissonances of the new century, I immediately recognized that he was the bridge between Romanticism and Modernism, something that was also noted by the young Viennese modernist composers of his late years (Berg, Webern, Schoenberg). As it happened, just at that time, in post-Wall Berlin, the Berlin Symphony Orchestra, conducted by Claudio Abbado, was giving a series of performances of all of Mahler's major works at the Philharmonie, and I attended several of them.

One of the things that is obvious about Mahler's music is that, somehow, it tells you something about the twentieth century; it conveys, indirectly, the feelings of romantic yearning of the late nineteenth century that would be blown to smithereens on the battlefields of World War I, whose sounds Mahler anticipates. The mantra I'm operating from while hearing all of this is a remark of Robin Blaser's, made long after we'd seen Darius Milhaud in Berkeley, a remark about living in your century. Blaser said, "A lot of people lived in the twentieth century without having lived in the twentieth century."

What he means is that it is possible to have lived in a particular period without really living "in your time" — that is, without experiencing the culture, science, or politics of the era. Like living in the twentieth century without reading Joyce or Beckett, or hearing about Einstein, or thinking about apartheid or feminism. Blaser, of course, wasn't referring to people who had been prevented from "holding one's time in thought" through economic and political oppression or other circumstances of isolation, but to those of us extravagantly privileged people for whom access to literature, visual art, music, and the rest is no further than your local bookstore, art museum, or concert hall. To not hold one's time in thought (I think the phrase is from philosopher Richard Rorty, out of Hegel), to not live in one's century, is to live in the world without engaging the world, and if you don't encounter the complexity, velocity, density of the world, then what's the point of going through the whole painful business of living at all? Better, as one of the gloomier Greeks said, not to have been born.

About a year ago, my current cultural mentor in Berlin, Thomas Marquard, handed me a pile of CDs of Luciano Berio's *Sequenzas* to listen to. Marquard, who is a friend of Blaser's as well as of mine, is, at least to my untrained ear, an almost concert-class violinist. I've heard him play Bach and Telemann in at-home concerts in his apartment (we live in the same building in Berlin). He'd recently heard a performance of the Berio works for solo instruments, and his enthusiasm was contagious. I duly listened to these wonderfully strange pieces and was easily hooked. The question I repeatedly asked myself, with considerable puzzlement, is, How come I've never heard this stuff before or, just as bad, never even heard *about* it?

Something similar had happened to me with modern dance several years earlier: Once the classic picture breaks up, you see odd movements by dancers and suddenly learn something about human bodies and how we move in relation to each other that you didn't know before. The world and your own time are revealed in ways you hadn't suspected. And so it is with these sounds. There is a surprise in hearing them that makes you say, "Ah, so that's *another* way the world is," an astonishment at the variousness of reality.

For the next several months I attended a lot of concerts, mostly with Thomas and other friends, sometimes by myself. One of the attractions of this music for me is that I find it to be a relief from words. I spend most of my days reading words, or thinking in words, or writing them. In the evening, when I'm too tired to read, music, abstract "weird" music, wakes me up again. It allows me to think without words.

The most powerful of the concerts took place in late 2004, when I heard, for three nights running, the piano pieces of German composer Karlheinz Stockhausen, performed during the "Festival Weeks" series, which is held at the Berlin Festspiele House and other venues. The seventy-six-year-old composer was present at the performances, in mid-audience, operating the electronic soundboard, while various of his disciple-pianists hammered away at, tinkled, elbowed, muttered, and threw themselves into the instruments before them. Again, no attempt at description of the music, just the recognition that Stockhausen (enough of a living legend that people often ask you if he's still alive) had crafted a very large aural world within the world. I'm using the word "aural" in both its senses simultaneously: pertaining to the ear, and aura as felt ambience. The slogan for me here is: The transcendent occurs *within* the world. That is, these are experiences that transcend normal, everyday experience, but since we now pretty much know that there isn't a transcendental world beyond time and space, such experiences must occur here, in this world. Stockhausen's "world" enlarges the world.

I soon heard other important "new music" composers —

Gubaidulina, Saariaho, Kurtág, Nono, Rihm, Carter — as well as younger local composers like Enno Poppe, in the profusion of musical events and series with which Berlin abounds. The most extraordinary of the events was a mixed-media performance of dance, live music, and singing by a troupe led by Moroccan-Belgian choreographer-dancer Sidi Larbi Cherkaoui, from the company Les Ballets C de la B (Contemporary Ballet of Belgium), held at the Hebbel Theatre, another of the places in the city marked by intelligent, innovative programming.

The Cherkaoui piece, *Tempus Fugit*, combines North African Arabic music and Corsican folksongs (so the sound is Mediterranean), and its narrative elements, structured around fragmented episodes, seem to reflect a world of immigrants and refugees crossing Europe's increasingly permeable borders. The whole piece is powerfully melodic, at times funny, and emotionally moving even though the narrative is non-linear. About as much of a description as I can offer is that it's my idea of what an avant-garde non-Broadway musical might be like, if there is such a genre. I went back a second night just to make sure that it was as great as it seemed to be, since a lot of this stuff balances on an aesthetic knife-edge between plain silliness and magnificence. The second time was better than the first. My local sophisticated CD store, Fidelio, of course, had a copy of Jean-Paul Poletti and Le Choeur D'Hommes de Sartene's *Fiori di Memoria*, and soon I was listening at home to the Corsican folksongs that had inspired Cherkaoui.

Interestingly, all the "new music" didn't take me away from "old music," but, on the contrary, often led me back to it. I went with Thomas to a concert at the Philharmonie that included a piece for clarinet and orchestra written by the ninety-something American composer Elliott Carter, as well as an oratorio performance of Bartok's one-act opera *Bluebeard* (1911). When I expressed my pleasure at the Bartok, Thomas said, knowing that I like string groups, "Well, you ought to hear Bartok's string quartets," and promptly loaned me a CD of them. That somehow led to Bach's sonatas and partitas for solo violin (c. 1720), and from there to Yo-Yo Ma's version of Bach's cello suites. The curriculum continues to unfold.

And then, as I've related, some months later I heard Scelsi's *Khoom*.

III

When I got home from the Philharmonie that night, I googled
Scelsi (what else does one do these days but "google"?), accompanied by my now familiar sense of, How come I've never heard of
this guy? plus an equally familiar bemusement about how it's possible to be so ignorant despite having lived a relatively long life. If
Scelsi's music is "weird," so is the composer. Scelsi, according to
the thorough biographical essay by T.M. McComb on www.clas-
sical.net, was born in 1905 to a wealthy, aristocratic family on
an estate outside Naples, and from the beginning was relieved of
such onerous duties as wondering where the next meal was coming from or earning a living.

Scelsi's first music, for the piano, an instrument on which he
was apparently a virtuoso performer, reflected his early-twentieth-century training in Vienna with a teacher associated with
Alban Berg. I'm not going to go through his entire musical career
here, but I just want to register a couple of moments. For the most
part, until his death in 1988 at age eighty-three, Scelsi was relatively obscure, rarely performed, considered a musical outsider
even by the avant-garde, and personally increasingly reclusive.
He was rather phobic about photos, uninterested in interviews or
contacts with many people (though he was friends with the poet
Henri Micheaux), and preferred to speak French.

During World War II, Scelsi's marriage broke up, and he went
through some sort of psychological breakdown. His therapy,
according to McComb, "eventually consisted of playing a single
note on a piano over and over again," and this therapy, along
with his deepening, even mystical, interest in the musical ideas
of the East, especially India, led to his developing a new style of
music. As Scelsi's biographer puts it, during Scelsi's long recovery,
the key was playing and listening to "his single note . . . to the resonance and decay, and most importantly the lack of uniformity
even within a single sound. This is really Scelsi's most profound
realization: that a single sound is not a musical point in any real
sense, it is a dynamic entity shaped by a variety of influences."
He set this realization "to music in a way no one else has ever
done," McComb claims.

In the mid-1950s, when Scelsi was fifty years old, he settled in

Rome after extensive travels in India and Nepal, where he had learned a considerable amount about yoga and mysticism. In the Italian capital he produced many of his masterpieces, even as he increasingly withdrew from social contact. During the 1960s and 70s, Scelsi wrote vocal music, including *Khoom* (1962), whose text consists of phonemes and words made up by the composer, a technique he had already used in an earlier piece, *The Birth of the Verb* (1948). *Khoom* marked the beginning of Scelsi's collaboration with a Japanese singer, Michiko Hirayama, whose voice was an inspiration for much of Scelsi's subsequent vocal writing. In the same year, Scelsi began composing a series of songs, *Canti del Capricorno*, written specifically for Hirayama's voice as an instrument.

A couple of nights later, as part of the MärzMusik series, the Capricorn songs were being performed at a concert in the Philharmonie's chamber music hall. They were to be sung, I noticed in passing, by a Japanese singer, backed by a string bass, saxophone, and drums. Earlier in the evening there was a performance of the music of a local composer, Walter Zimmerman, whose work focuses on the notion of the instrumentalists themselves singing. If not exactly to my taste, it's an interesting idea and was part of the festival's thematic focus on voices.

After the break, I was back in my familiar spot in the chamber music hall when an elderly Japanese woman in a red gown and black cape appeared, accompanied by four German musicians in standard-issue intellectual black. They took seats in an unlit background, while the singer was spotlighted. Her name, I saw in the program, was Michiko Hirayama. It was Scelsi's singer from Rome, now eighty-two years old, and from the moment she began, unaccompanied, it was clear that she was both the muse and voice of this song-cycle that Scelsi regarded as having been dictated to him, just as Orphic poets understand themselves to be simply messengers or transmitters of their poems.

Again, there is no description of the music, at least none I'm capable of providing. An elderly woman in a red gown, occasionally accompanied by a single musician — the bassist, the saxophonist, or the two drummers together playing bongo-like instruments — but mostly on her own, her powerful voice shifting between two or three music-stand locations on the small chamber hall platform, the sound filling the auditorium.

My attention didn't waver, nor did that of most of the rest of the audience. What happened? What was it about? Again, there's the knife-edge between silliness and splendour. An old woman screeching meaningless phonemes, or a supernal voice charting all the intimations of what it is to be human and mortal?

At the end, the majority of the audience thought it was the latter, and there was not only applause but a very rare standing ovation. Thomas told me that the pianist Evgeny Kissin, a favourite in Berlin, once received one, but generally Berlin audiences are parsimonious about rising in tribute to a performer. Later on I ran into David Moss, a musician and one of the people responsible for organizing the festival's voice events, someone whose judgment I'm inclined to trust, and he confirmed that I'd heard something special. Hirayama appeared once more, for a fourth or fifth call, fell to her knees and kissed the floor of the chamber music hall.

IV

Part of what was on my mind during the MärzMusik series was a recent article about contemporary music by the (London) *Guardian* columnist Martin Kettle. "When did the music die?" Kettle pugnaciously asks in his lead. "And why?" Kettle notes that, of the moderns, Dmitri Shostakovich and Benjamin Britten both died thirty years ago. Aaron Copland and Olivier Messiaen managed to stagger on until the early 1990s. "But apart from these?" Kettle asks dubiously. Is there really anything in modern music worth listening to? Anything that anybody really wants to hear? Isn't it mostly elitist junk?

"I can see them already," Kettle sneers. "The protestations on behalf of the half-forgotten and semi-famous, the advocates of Henze and Berio, the followers of Tavener and Adès. Perhaps there will be a good word for Golijov or Gubaidulina, for Piazzola or Saariaho." Kettle parenthetically allows that these are enthusiasms that he sometimes shares. But driving the main point home, Kettle adds, "And maybe, even now, there remains someone who believes that Stockhausen should be mentioned in the same breath as Bach, the last of the true believers clinging to the shipwreck of modernism."

Kettle waxes nostalgic for a minute about some Puccini he heard on the radio recently, and then challenges readers to "answer this question: what is the most recently composed piece of classical music to have achieved a genuinely established place in the repertoire? I mean a piece that you can count on hearing in most major cities most years and a performance of which is likely to bring in a large general audience."

The thrust of Kettle's argument is that "modernism" killed the popularity of classical music. Instead of popularity, modernist theory led to the awful dissonance of Arnold Schoenberg, and it's been downhill ever since. Until then, crowds were happily going to hear Beethoven, Mozart, Brahms. Along came big, bad musical theory and the "deliberate renunciation of popularity." The "public," says Kettle, "looked elsewhere, to what we are right to call, and right to admire for being, popular music." Then Kettle looks around for a few signs of melodic spring and declares that "the need to create something beautiful that excites the public and goes beyond its experience is too strong to be frustrated indefinitely."

I guess the place to start in this blustery farrago is with the specious notion of names that might be mentioned "in the same breath as Bach." As my violin-playing friend Thomas quickly pointed out to me, even Bach's name wasn't mentioned in the same breath as Bach (or whoever the equivalent was back then) during his lifetime. When Bach died in 1750, he was relatively unknown. Other composers, like Mozart, paid serious attention to Bach in order to learn from his genius, but there wasn't a clamouring public for Bach's music until the early 1800s in Berlin, some two or three generations after his demise, when Bach was rediscovered thanks to some intelligent local cultural impresarios. The same thing is true for other "classics." As one of several letter writers replying to Kettle noted, both Beethoven and Mahler were "composers who suffered huge problems in getting their music recognized."

Actually, the little mini-bio of the obscure Scelsi that I read on the Internet makes exactly the sort of same-breath mention Kettle is looking for: "The fact that Scelsi could write such fine violin music (arguably the finest in this idiom since Bach) … " I suppose that counts as a mention "in the same breath as Bach," for whatever such mentions are worth.

What they're worth is very little. This sort of name-game is mostly nonsense. In terms of who is capable of listening to what, it's fairly easy to chart. There is a literate public, which constitutes a small fraction of the large not-so-literate general populace, that knows, a century later, what to make of the early modernism of Mahler, Bartok, Dvorak, Stravinsky, and Satie. There is an even smaller musically trained elite audience that can knowledgably listen to Stockhausen, Berio, Carter, and the rest of the contemporary roster of "new music" composers. The audience is limited: a couple of thousand people in each of the major cities of Western Civ. How these composers will stack up in two or three generations is something to leave to musical history.

The insidious idea in Kettle's piece is the conflation of popularity with an idea of good or interesting music. Surely it wasn't Schoenberg who sent people to the music hall or the jazz speakeasy. They were already there. Wasn't it the Broadway musical that knocked out opera, rather than Stravinsky? And when was the concert hall filled with the masses rather than a select segment of the relatively well-to-do? As the writer of another letter to the *Guardian* remarked, "At no stage in my lifetime (longer than Martin Kettle's) has classical music been anything other than a minority interest." The whole notion of serious music seeking general popularity hasn't made much sense since church music in the seventeenth century, and even then, after church, the peasants were probably humming other tunes down at the local inn.

I think Kettle's remark about "the need to create something beautiful" is a sly reference to some contemporary neoclassical composers who write recognizably melodic music in toe-tapping rhythms. Kettle shouldn't be allowed to get away with this, or be ceded ownership of the "beautiful," since works like Scelsi's *Songs of Capricorn* are, among other qualities, beautiful. In any case, the attempt to reproduce eighteenth- and nineteenth-century classical music in the twenty-first century as often as not comes off as mere pastiche, something like those contemporary sequels to Jane Austen novels written in an imitation of Austen's style.

In the end, plaintive cries like Kettle's are simply wrong-headed. Composers aren't trying to be popular; they're trying to hold their time in sound. And sometimes in silence.

V

The MärzMusik series wrapped up on a Sunday evening in mid-March at the Philharmonie main hall with a performance of Berlin composer Dieter Schnebel's *Symphonie X*, on the occasion of the composer's seventy-fifth birthday. It's a three-hour extravaganza for a full orchestra, electronic devices, and pockets of musicians stashed in corners of the furthest upper reaches of Scharoun's hall. The symphony was composed in the early 1990s, but Schnebel had recently returned to it and written a new movement, which had its premiere at this performance.

From the festival's first multi-media evening, where the London Sinfonietta played Cage, Ligeti, and a sampling of young composers while Britain's Warp Pictures provided punkish video accompaniment, to the Schnebel finale, MärzMusik was striking as an expression of what I think of as "the mind of the city." That is, the state of culture is measured by the intelligence of its artists and organizers. In this instance, the figure behind MärzMusik Joachim Sartorius, a writer and cultural organizer of saturnine appearance. I first met him some years ago at an Academy of Art poetry reading, where Sartorius appeared, in one of his many roles, as the translator of American modernist poet John Ashbery, who was reading that night.

Ever since, I've been aware of him as a rather unobtrusive presence who shapes much of the city's mind. Of course, there are a dozen or more similar people who run museums, dance companies, and theatres. When all of it is working well, there's a kind of cultural critical mass, and some fifteen years after the fall of the Berlin Wall, the city is as vibrant a cultural centre as is to be found in Europe. Of course, none of this comes without complaint. Since Berlin is a voluble, disputatious, endlessly critical city, Sartorius has the physical appearance of someone with slightly bowed shoulders who bears the weight of the various criticisms and carpings that inevitably attend those who are responsible for anything. If we're feeling generous, we can regard the criticism and maybe even the carping as part of the civic intelligence that makes for events like MärzMusik, where someone listening to "weird" sounds of music can discover a Giacinto Scelsi.

New York Poems

Tattoo

When Thomas goes to the bathroom at the crowded New York Japanese restaurant on 9th Street, where we're about to have dinner on my first evening in town, the guy at the next table (the tables are tightly packed, cheek to jowl), in his late twenties, less than a foot to the left and opposite me, who is holding hands with a Japanese-American woman (do I detect something punkish about her? a streak of colour in her hair, unusual eye makeup?), immediately says to me, in French-accented English, "Eet's per-fect." He's referring, I realize, to the plain blue tattoo of an anchor on my left forearm, visible because I'm wearing a short-sleeved shirt on this clammy, foggy, about-to-rain late April evening.

What he sees as the perfection of my tattoo is not only its simplicity, almost handmade amateurishness, but also, he enthusiastically points out, its ironic, hip, even if unintended, derisive commentary on the current, or recent, fashion of baroquely over-elaborate tattooing (and body-piercing) that briefly swept Western society. As he's cataloguing the virtues of my tattoo, I envision, in a flash, the tattoo/piercing shops one can now find in almost every neighbourhood in any metropolis, in some apocalyptic future, all shut down, boarded up, the wave of fashion passed. Then, just as suddenly, I imagine the metaphor "wave of fashion" literally, a receding tsunami rolling back down one of the avenues (Broadway, 4th, 3rd, streets I've just crossed on the walk to the restaurant), the tattooing fad over, and the minor art of it, not unlike poetry, reduced again to slightly disreputable tattoo *parlours*, like the one in which I acquired my blue anchor on Market Street in San Francisco in 1962. But my Frenchman (if that's what he is) is enchanted, seeing my perfect tattoo as something like the prototype of *all* tattoos, or a *Critique of Pure Tattooing*, and me as the primitive, ancient, but still living bearer of the tattoo archetype.

"I got it very long ago," I say to them (she is pouring *sake* into shallow, translucent, miniature bowls), "so the irony was before its time," whereas the time of the tattoo's inscription is in a past retrospectively defined by sincerity, "true love," and tattoos as marking rites of passage, rather than being seen, in a post-apocalyptic New York Japanese restaurant in 2005 (three and a half years after the "9/11" destruction of the World Trade towers), as decoration or, worse, a post-modernist signifier *avant la lettre*!

I try to explain, using sailor talk, that it is an "unfouled" anchor as contrasted to a "fouled" one, i.e., one with a "line" (a rope) entangled in its prongs, but I see that the point of the distinction I'm making is incomprehensible to them, though they're according me the polite attention one gives to any antiquarian rattling on about his specialty. I manage, just barely, to refrain from boasting that I've written a book about this particular tattoo and what it means to me.

Then there's a blink in timespace, Thomas returns from the toilet, food comes, the four of us share some mutual sympathetic clucking from our respective tables as well-intentioned fellow diners; and later, as we're leaving, saying our farewells, I ask him where he's from, thinking it might be Quebec (the immediate thought of any mainly Anglo-Canadian who hears English spoken in a faintly French register), and he says, "Switzerland." "Switzerland," I repeat, which Thomas, as he remarks afterwards, outside the restaurant, had already picked up on (since Switzerland is the first thought of any European who hears English spoken in French-German tones), and the Swiss guy adds, somewhat mournfully, "I've been in New York five years, but I'll never looze ze ac-cent." Yes, some things are almost indelible.

On a Grecian Hot Cup

There is for me, invariably, upon arrival in another place — in this case, New York — an always slight surprise to be in the company of all these people: in the streets, on buses, in restaurants, working, or homeless on the Bowery dragging plastic bags of their possessions past store after shabby store selling restaurant-bakery-pizza equipment. There's the irrational recognition, as though I'd totally forgotten, that *everybody* has been living more or less complete lives (even if fragmented beyond repair), filled with concerns, interests, internets, right up to the very moment of my seeing them, *now, here.*

At 7 AM, I awaken in clammy hotel sheets, dress, go downstairs for coffee, passing at bottom of stairs a large, at least one-and-a-half metres high, white plaster reproduction of the Statue of Liberty, guarded by a red velveteen rope strung between gold stanchions, as if verifying the patriotism of this small off-Soho hotel — and though I'm determined not to make *too much* of it, I would be curious to know who decided on its acquisition and under what circumstances.

One could say, It's just a tourist-thing, that plaster Statue of Liberty, to reassure tourist-guests in the hotel that this, the *sign* of New York, of America, confirms that we *are* in New York, America, just as one could say about everybody and their lives up to this point, Well, of course they've been living their lives, complete with interests, affairs, heartbreaks, right up to the instant you encounter them, how could it be otherwise? That is, it's temptingly easy to dismiss odd perceptions, even one's own, and to simply gloss over the moments when you recognize the strangeness of life itself, or that in some ways it's really weird to have a replica of the Statue of Liberty in a hotel corridor. One *could* say, I suppose, well, this and that, *whatever,* but I don't, I don't say whatever, and I'm even leaving aside the wall-mirror at the bottom of the staircase in which is etched the old skyline of New York. I'm leaving it aside since it raises the constant question of the missing and/or present towers, etc. Which is to say that, whether anything is noticeable or not, interesting or boring, so much depends on what you bring to seeing it. Especially

328 ● TOPIC SENTENCE

so in these first hours of seeing, where potentially useful leads, i.e., digressions leading to unexpected discovery, are inversely proportional to the degree of knowledge (in this instance, almost total ignorance), so that anything might be interesting, and is the very reason for travel as against the over-familiar inattentions of home.

So, I'm looking for a cup of coffee (while all this is in / on my mind). I pass the guy behind the glassed-in desk clerk space (the place is run by stolid men in their thirties and forties from, where? Iran? India?), exchange morning greetings, go out, walk around the block, air clammy chill, might rain or not, just to map out coffee shops, bakeries, newsstands, tobacconists in the immediate vicinity (a grocery across Bowery, on Spring Street, seems the likeliest possibility), though in the end return to hotel coffee shop to get a couple of cups of coffee to take up to my room. The desk man comes out of his enclosure, goes down the two steps into empty coffee shop (a coffee shop in which I'll never see a customer during the several days I'm living in the hotel), pours coffee into paper hot cups, and, when I ask him where he's from, tells me, Egypt. "Are *all* of you from Egypt?" I ask, referring to the three or four men I've seen running the place. "Yes, all," he says, but he's taciturn, not very forthcoming, though when I ask, "When did you come to New York?" he says, "About ten years ago, 1995." And when I ask, "Are you from Cairo?" he says, "No, not from Cairo, a smaller place," which he doesn't name, assuming, probably correctly, that its name would mean nothing to me. "But was life difficult there, in Egypt?" I persist. "No, not difficult," he replies, dashing my anticipation of a refugee's gruelling tale, and finally, when I say, "So, Mubarak was president then," referring to the past and present holder of the presidency of Egypt, he sighs, "Always Mubarak," and that subtle political sigh is as far as he's prepared to go before the conversation peters out.

Then I'm at the elevator doors, paper hot cups of coffee awkwardly in hand, pressing elevator button, the staircase, skyline-etched mirror, and Statue of Liberty installation behind me (I decide, arbitrarily, that the replica has been inherited from previous hotel owners . . .), and at last I'm in my hotel suite drinking morning coffee, reading, as it happens, the mid-twentieth-century British philosopher A.J. Ayer on the subject of perception and the existence of an external world, his little book resting on the surface of the not-very-solidly balanced octagonal glass table in the kitchen area, next to a window looking out into the six-storey airshaft of the hotel, which is adjoined to the shell of an old building next door that has been gutted and is under reconstruction. The paper hot cups on the table have a crude fàcsimile of an antique Greek design on them, but I'm busy tracking a pigeon that has settled on a nearby fifth-floor, vertiginously narrow ledge just outside my window (not vertiginous to the pigeon, of course), and it's only on second or third glance, as I'm about to look at the age-browned page of Ayer I'm fitfully reading, that I actually notice the cup, and only then that I stop scanning, roving, sampling, and lock into focus, once and for all, the paper hot cup.

Within the mock-antiquity design of the cup there's a picture of a Greek maiden in a loose, light shift pouring bath water from an amphora onto the back of a naked crouching person, sex somewhat indeterminate, but it's got to be another young woman, right? (because women servants didn't bathe male youths, did they? only men servants — oh, something more to look up.) The point or *punctum* of the drawing, copied from ancient Greek vase painting, is a single short curved line that delineates the buttocks of the crouching bather — so, it conveys a sense, a meaning, even a desire, but what's it doing here? in the hotel coffee shop (and now on my table)? How does ancient Greece fit into the décor or personnel of the hotel with its Statue of Liberty motif, etched-glass New York skyline (pre-"9/11"), Egyptian men? Who gave the stolid guys running the hotel the particular deal on paper hot cups depicting ancient Greeks at their bath?

In addition to the picture, the cup has a cobalt blue marble-ized background, a drawing of Doric columns at the cup's seams framing the bathing scene, and linked labyrinthine decorative bands running around the cup at top and bottom — all signifiers of antiquity, while the message on the far side of the cup, a motto inscribed in a sort of plaque, says, unsurprisingly, if slightly disappointingly, "It's our pleasure to serve you," so the picture is an illustration, then, of *service*, of being served a cup of coffee.

And one could say, Well, that's that, the hot cups are simply what the restaurant-goods supplier offered, something a bit classier than merely plain white paper hot cups; the Egyptians running the hotel made no particular judgment, or they liked the curved buttocks, in any case purchased several dozen gross of cups on offer, and so on. And Keats, likewise, could have said, It's just a Grecian urn, and thus we would be spared all the rest, "unravish'd bride of quietness / . . . foster-child of silence and slow time," right on down to "When old age shall this generation waste / Thou shalt remain, in midst of other woe / Than ours . . ." And the debatable claim, allegedly conveyed by the images of the urn, that "Beauty is truth, truth beauty" would remain undebated. Yet now, old age having generations wasted, in midst of woe other than theirs, it is not only the reawakened scenes of the urn or hot cup, but the context in which they emerge, the *context* that imperils truth and beauty, and permits poetry in the ruins of New York.

Prose Poem

For a few minutes, maybe a half hour or so, while sitting at the table in my hotel room, writing, I experience a gathering, intensifying patch of euphoria, or as my old pal Larry Fagin, whom I'll soon be visiting, says, That moment when it all snaps into place. It's a familiar but rare state of compositional joy I've sporadically experienced over the years, in other cities, at other writing tables.

It happens very early in my brief trip to New York, less than twenty-four hours after arrival. I've barely had a glimpse of the city that I last saw decades ago (before the destroyed towers had been built), no more than an evening's walkabout in the tangle of streets around the intersection of Houston and Bowery, guided by my friend Thomas, whom, ostensibly, I've come from Berlin to meet. The rough idea is that we'll spend a few days together in New York; he's at the end of a longer American journey, he'll show me around since he knows the city, accompany me to the art museums, that sort of thing, and then we'll both fly back together to Europa.

So, I've seen a few streets and noted the welter of advertisements-cum-ideological-messages on hoardings along the Bowery, e.g., "Life getting too complicated? Uncomplicate," says the ad for Levi's 501 blue jeans pitched to sophisticated young urbanites, the company self-proclaiming itself the sign of redemptive simplicity in a confusing, changing world. We've had dinner in a Japanese restaurant on 9th Street where a Swiss guy at the next table admired the tattoo on my forearm. I'm getting a sense of direction, of this island slanted on a northeast-southwest axis, and I'm learning to cross the streets of New York (different from crossing the streets of Berlin), in the middle of which Thomas occasionally pauses, as a several-ton vehicle bears down on us ("Don't worry, they stop," he assures me; yeah, but what if they don't?), to take advantage of the vista to point out to me a distant famous building — the Chrysler, the Empire State Building, or the missing World Trade Center towers.

And more ads for concerts, politics, products, a TV movie, already shown a few days ago according to the date on the dozens of pasted-up announcements, "Ring of Fire," about the former boxer Emile Griffith. On the poster there's a painting of a handsome brown man, almost nude, slumped over on a stool, representing Griffith, presumably only moments after he'd killed Benny (Kid) Peret in the ring in 1962, in a bout I'd seen "live" on TV. And what made it more than just another boxing death was that Peret, before the fight, at the weigh-in, had called Griffith a *maricon*, a faggot, all this decades ago, a brief version of which story I tell Thomas, who, as a Berliner, is bereft of this particular American cultural reference, as we're walking along Bowery, turn right into Spring Street, the story updated in the *New York Times* just the other day, in an interview with the now nearly seventy-year-old Griffith, who continues to coyly bob and weave around the question of his sexual tastes, as if it really mattered that we know what they are. And forty years later, is America (not New York) any less hysterical about homo?

I've slept, woken, gotten coffee, and am making notes about a paper hot cup with a facsimile drawing from an antique Greek vase when my mind recognizes itself to be levitating, lifted in delirium. I pause only to note in the same notebook in which I'm writing about the Greek cup, about the Swiss guy and our conversation about tattoos, this quick phrase: "New York poems (prose poems, I think)."

And with that, all uncertainties are momentarily stilled. The question always is, Why are you anywhere? What am I doing in New York? And the tentative, unsatisfactory answers, I'm meeting Thomas, or, Well, I'm getting on and I've never seen the great art museums in New York, and since Thomas is going to be there, all that, while true enough, is subsidiary to the sentence, "I'm in New York to write poems. New York poems," which I utter aloud, even as I'm euphorically writing pre-poem notes. Simultaneously, from other multiple directions, I'm receiving instructions on the order and number of the pieces (about five), and the rules about the usage of New York materials, e.g., no ripping off, appropriating what I don't know about New York, no pretense to know, as Larry Fagin will put it later, "New York's secrets." And finally, the form: "prose poems, I think."

I'm in the foyer of a little apartment building on 12th Street the next day, between 1st Avenue and Avenue A, across the street from a public school, looking through a small square of smoky glass in a reinforced metal door until I see the face of Fagin seeing me. He comes through the door and we hug to make up for the years we haven't seen each other, as many years almost as since Emile Griffith killed Kid Paret, and out on the sidewalk, Larry asks, "Plain or fancy?" I say, "Plain," and we begin to walk up a few blocks to his neighbourhood coffee shop, where we'll get coffee and settle in.

As we're walking, I glance over at Larry, unconsciously adjusting the image of him I had from when I last saw him, as one invariably does upon seeing someone after a decades-long hiatus. I always thought of him as a kind of quick bird, a sparrow or maybe a bright-eyed young crow or grackle, with a crow's rasp of laughter, and now, striding alongside him, even as I'm registering his familiar beak, I begin to notice that he's bundled up a bit, as have I, against the spring chill, but no, wait, it's not so much that we've bundled up — after all, it isn't *that* chill — but that we're both simply more *bulky* than long ago, and if we're still in any way birdlike, we probably look more like pigeons painted by, say, Rubens. Plus, since we're semi-aware of parodying old guys walking along, reminiscing (we're not really old guys, are we? but young at heart, ha-ha), you could say we appear to be Damon Runyonesque, Rubens-like, tattered, plump old birds (have I ever actually read Damon Runyon?).

Larry is instantly at home in his neighbourhood coffee shop (which, I begin to gather, is what stands in for the cafés of Berlin, since New York isn't, I've noticed, a café city), greeted by and immediately bantering with the old crone Asian woman who runs the place, the two of them familiarly squawking at each other as we settle into a booth, as coffee and Danish are duly set before us. It takes no more than the mere mention of Berlin (where I now live part-time) or Paris (Larry was there too, about the same time I first went) to set us off, and Larry is telling me the story — I had passingly mentioned the poet Gregory Corso, whom I had met in Paris in 1959, which reminds Larry — of the time he and Greg Corso, along with Larry's girlfriend of the time and the actress Jean Seberg, had *double-dated* one evening in Paris. "Jean Seberg!" I say, astonished to hear her name (while at the same time registering that I haven't heard the term "double-dated" in eons), and Larry cackles, too, as we both consider a night on the town with the gamine-like star of Jean-Luc Godard's *Breathless*, her name or image (elfin, cropped blond hair, high cheekbones) now known probably only to film buffs. "And she was in *Jeanne d'Arc*, wasn't she?" one or the other of us (probably me) recalls, Otto Preminger's failed film, "Yes, yes." Her troubled life reprised in a flash within the course of a quick anecdote, right on through to her suicide death years later (when? late-seventies? age forty).

Then we gab away non-stop for the next two hours, until Larry has to go off to meet some students to whom he teaches writing, private lessons for individual aspiring writers, as well as some writing courses at the legendary New School, and the flow of talk, opinions, reminiscences veers wildly yet smoothly, instant shifts in sub-topics without loss of comprehension, from Paris in the late 1950s to Language Poetry (no, he reassures me, I don't have to worry about having missed something in having more or less missed LangPo, as it's retrospectively known), to the San Francisco poetry scene in which we were mutually engaged in the mid-1960s, to what it's like being an intellectual in New York in 2005 (like, almost, Don't ask). "And the Muse?" I ask, "is she still alive?" Yes, he reports, knowing immediately to whom I'm referring, and gives me a blow-by-blow account of visiting her, with another poet friend, a couple of years ago in, good god, East Oakland, California, still drug-addled, not quite rescuable, yet looking surprisingly great at, what, sixty?

When we were young, and yes, these two elderly gents in a New York coffee shop on a Monday morning approaching noon

334 ● TOPIC SENTENCE

were once young and could even "run the table," as they say, in select San Francisco pool halls, she was the young woman all the straight younger poets in our circle were slightly in love and lust with, one of the last protegés of our dour mentor, Jack Spicer, and the author of a few poems of crystalline purity and beauty. A kind of goddess or muse. Alas, other crystalline substances attracted her attention, and for the long, long interim, right up to the latest sighting, she was on and off, in and out of the needle-strewn purgatory (how she would snort in derision at that sen-sationalizing phrase!) of her own and her dealers' making, but making no more poems.

So that's the itinerary of the talk, and it's like stirring up some pond, with smoky clouds of pond bottom rising up through the pond waters and then resettling to the bottom once more. But the main pleasures, above and beyond the particular topics, are —

The pleasure of concentration: the locked-in attentiveness and intensity of conversation with Larry in the midst of the general fragmentation, of travel disorientation, of people constantly chattering on cellphones in public places, of everybody — wait-resses, bus drivers, clerks — multitasking, affording you, how-ever competently, a fraction of their focus. At its most extreme, for example, at the neighbourhood grocery on Spring Street that very morning, where the clerk, mid-twenties, "Middle Eastern looking," as the police profilers would say, talks on a cellphone (in a Middle Eastern language) through the entire transaction so that I don't get one instant of his direct perception, and as I'm leaving, an elderly Asian woman holding a can of beans says to him, "Bean," or an approximation of it, and he says, "Beans. What kind of beans?" (an utterance way beyond her capabilities in what's known these days as "global English"), disappearing among the shelves with her, all the while uninterruptedly yak-king away into his cellphone. Whereas, talking to Larry is like a two-man luge team swerving down the icy chute.

The pleasure of coherence: to find that, after all these years, the old friend, now in his late sixties, is completely and utterly in pos-session of his faculties (notwithstanding the title of Paul Simon's song, "Still Crazy After All These Years"), totally sane, engaged, witty, the works. I mean, there's no way of knowing in advance, it could be dope, off-the-wall obsessions, fetishes, that old "I've seen the best minds of my generation destroyed by . . . "

The pleasure, and this is the punchline, the pleasure of a coincidence. "So, what are you teaching at New School?" I ask. "Right now, only one course," Larry says, "The Prose Poem."

"The prose poem?" I say. "What a coincidence! That's just what's on my mind right now." At which invitation, Larry provides me a little précis on the subject, and, as always, much of it is news to me. Sure, I know something about it — Baudelaire, Rimbaud, an American twentieth-century tradition from Gertrude Stein's *Tender Buttons* to John Ashbery's *Three Poems* and Jack Spicer's *Heads of the Town Up to the Aether*, as well as other prose poem writers in other languages, the most important of whom for me is the recently deceased Polish poet Czesław Miłosz and his late book, written in his eighties, *Road-side Dog*.

Yet even though there are great prose poems (usually by writers who generally write verse poems), it's an unstable, self-deprecating form, seemingly for people who can't really write in poetry lines and have to forego the real poem's armada of multiple story-telling through enjambment, metre, rhyme, and the rest, retaining maybe only some semblance of the breath and the poetic principle. It's a hybrid, a decayed, neither-this-nor-that form, such that, even now, every discussion of it begins, So what exactly is a "prose poem"? a question to which there's no satisfactory answer. How to distinguish it from the scrap, note to oneself, aphorism, vignette, sketch, essayette, journal writing, or shaggy dog story? Not possible.

"But you write prose poems," Larry recalls. "You wrote 'Topic Sentence,'" he says, citing a piece I wrote around 1970, a piece about learning to write composition at school and how the writing itself subverts not only all the rules of composition but one's entire being, and which, again quite coincidentally, is a piece of writing I'd just been revising in the last month, although I'm not sure I'd ever thought of it as a prose poem. "That's a prose poem," he declares, like the guy at passport control putting the stamp of arrival in your passport. Bang!

Trompe l'oeil

When Thomas asked me, "What would you like to do in New York?" the only practical thing I could think of was "See some paintings," although the more accurate answer would be, simply, "See New York," plus "meet some people." In any case, the infrastructure of my five-, six-day tourist visit to New York is provided by the notion of seeing art, visiting the museums, just like other tourists, the Cloisters, Frick Collection, Guggenheim, the Met, MOMA, and, as it happens, our friend Douglas Crimp is giving a lecture on Daniel Buren's installation at the Guggenheim, which will lead to dinner with Douglas, meeting some other people, I'll check in with my old friend Larry Fagin, and in the course of doing all this, getting from place to place, riding on buses, subways, walking, eating in restaurants, I'll get to see something of New York and find out what's on what's left of my mind.

So that's what we do. The seeing of New York takes various forms. For example, it can be as oblique but ordinary as the Middle Eastern clerk at the grocery on Spring Street (Spring Street is also where we catch the subway to go uptown), whom I see each morning around 7:30, 8 o'clock, when I buy cigarettes or pastry to go with my morning coffee, and just as the first time I saw him, this time, too, through the entire transaction, he's talking away on his cellphone, even while punching up my purchases on the cash register, telling me the total, bagging them, except this time the connection is unexpectedly broken, and he looks in puzzled consternation at the little handheld phone. "Got cut off," he says, and I ask, "Who're you talking to?" or "Where are you calling?" and he says, "To my wife. In Yemen," "Yemen?!" I say with astonishment, and in that one step forward, from being peripheral to his attention to being within it, that's what I mean by "seeing New York." "Well, have a good one," I say on my way out, which is what the American customs guy at the airport said to me on my way in.

Or, just one more example, Thomas and I are taking a long, beautiful bus ride all the way through the city up to the northern tip of Manhattan to see the Cloisters Museum, and we have to change buses in Spanish Harlem, where the ads are in Spanish and everybody, from the guys in a doorway behind the bus stop to a trio of Sunday-dressed six- or seven-year-old boys in spotless white suits, is speaking Spanish. The bus stop ad, for Bud Lite beer, says, in Spanish, "You can have it all," and features a woman dancing in wild abandon, and the soft-core porn focus of the erotic photo of her is a gleaming bit of hipbone pointing to her crotch, and as I'm noting the incessant devilry of the ad makers, the vast sociological analysis-intelligence poured into or wasted on these commercial appeals, the bus rolls up. The driver of the bus, like the previous driver, is a large black woman, and I might as well get this in now: all the bus drivers I'll see in New York are very large African-American men and women who display such imperturbable calm and competence as they deal with countless tourist requests for information, lurchings of aged and disabled people, crazies, all the while piloting these huge vehicles through swaths of traffic, that I begin to think of them as not only pillars of the community but giant Bodhisatvas getting the populace from place to place, if not toward enlightenment, at least to the next stop.

And in fact, just a few streets into this leg of the journey, a skinny black guy with a straggly, youthful beard and wearing a white hoodie under a sort of parka appears outside the doors of the bus and is, I realize, begging the Amazonian bus driver for a ride though he doesn't have the fare, and in the end she opens the doors, lets him aboard, he effusively blesses her in the name of the Lord, heads down the aisle, but he almost can't leave well enough alone and has to come back to the driver and pronounce a further benediction, "God *bless* you! Yes, he does!" to which she replies, matter-of-factly and with precise wit, "God oughta bless you with some money to pay for this ride." This infinitesimal encounter, while the Hudson River and its soft, wooded bluffs on the far shore roll by as the bus heads north, is exactly what I think of as "seeing New York."

At the Frick Collection, housed in a mansion on East 70th Street, just off Central Park — we've come down from the Cloisters by subway and taken a short walk across the narrow rectangle of the park, which runs from 59th Street to 110th — Thomas is particularly taken with a strange eighteenth-century work of art by Jean-Étienne Liotard, a Swiss painter. He calls my attention to it. It's called *Trompe l'Oeil*, but I'm too busy thinking about three

Rembrandt paintings in another room to do more than glance at it, and it's only somewhat later that I actually look at Liotard's odd creation. Here's what you see: there's a piece of raw brown board, with its wavy grain-lines going across it, and attached to the board are four objects: two small, slightly chipped, grey ceramic bas-relief plaques, both of a nude woman and a winged child, Cupid and Venus, hung on bits of string tied around screws driven into the board, and below the ceramics are two bits of drawing, both of women's heads, on ragged-edged scraps of paper awkwardly pasted to the board. And it's only on second, third, or even further glance that you see it's not a board, screws, string, ceramic plaques, and pasted-down drawing scraps, but a hyper-realistic *painting* of a board, screws, string, plaques, even the shadows of the plaques, and drawings, intended to deceive the eye and make you think the objects are real.

I've seen examples of this curious little sub-genre of painting before, but without paying more than cursory attention (that's the story of my life: not paying attention!), mildly amused by the optical illusion, the tricking of the eye caused by the *trompe l'oeil* painting. But it's not until the next morning, just before I'm off to visit Larry Fagin, as I'm having morning coffee, sitting at the writing table in my hotel room, reading philosopher A.J. Ayer on the subject of perception, notebook at hand, that I'm unexpectedly led to one of those double takes that can cause you to re-evaluate anything from the smallest notion or trivial preference to the entirety of your life.

I'd thought of A.J. Ayer as a rather typically dry linguistic philosopher, associated with a long-since-faded 1930s analytic movement known as "logical positivism," which argued that the only reliable reality was that provided by science, and everything else was more or less meaningless metaphysics, poetic piffle, but now, reading a general introduction to the subject, *The Central Questions of Philosophy*, that Ayer wrote in the 1970s, toward the end of his life, I find him to be a perfectly reasonable, urbane, interesting guide to the question of what's real. The part I'm reading, about perception and reality, just happens to be the very thing on my mind in my own work as a philosophy teacher at a small college near Vancouver, which is where I'm generally to be found when I'm not living in Berlin or, as I'm doing at present, "seeing New York." I frequently pester my students with questions like,

How do we know that the tables and chairs and people in this room, the trees outside the window, and so on, are real? And if they say, We just know, or, Our senses tell us, a position known as commonsense or naïve realism, I can ask, What does "we just know" mean? or remark, But aren't our senses often fooled, for example, by optical illusions or *trompe l'oeil*?

Ayer asks, How do various philosophers, a long, reputable line of them, "come to assert that the access to physical objects which we believe that we obtain from the exercise of sight and touch is not direct?" How can they maintain that physical objects are not perceived directly but through a medium or conception of some sort, variously called "ideas," "impressions," "representations" in the eighteenth and nineteenth centuries, right down to present-day notions of "sense data," "qualia," or "percepts," as Bertrand Russell and Ayer himself call them? That is, how do we know that it isn't all in our heads, or that external reality, whatever it is, can't really be known, and all that we can know is what's mediated through our senses and minds? The argument Ayer slowly constructs is readable, but dense, and I frequently pause to look up, rest my eyes, have a sip of coffee, glance out the window into the building-well.

When I look up I see, on the slanted angle of wall directly facing me, one of several artworks decorating my hotel room, the usual unremarkable sort of nondescript drawings and watercolours of gardens, landscapes, vases. And this one is unremarkable, too. It's a watercolour of a large, plump vase filled with some leafy plant, in front of which is a china coffee pot, cup, a spoon, some other objects (perhaps a sugar bowl?), on a wooden tray. I've glanced at it innumerable times already, I guess, in the day and a half or two I've lived in this hotel room, but it's only now, maybe it's because I'm reading Ayer on perception, that I notice there's something odd about it. Although its pastel colours and the domestic still life it portrays are subdued, it seems a bit too realistic, too three-dimensional. Now that I've gotten up, moved around the octagonal glass table to get a closer look, now that I'm looking at it from a centimetre away, I see that it doesn't *seem* three-dimensional; it is three-dimensional. The leaves of the plant in the vase or round-bellied pot are not just painted, but cut out and stacked in several layers, and so are all the other objects in the piece, the coffee pot, the cup, sugar bowl, spoon, tray, the whole thing is a painted paper cut-out sculpture of sorts, at various levels within the narrow glassed-in frame or picture box. It's signed by Trisha Hardwick, and this reverse-*trompe l'oeil* has somehow landed as a decoration in a modest hotel room in Lower East Side New York. And couldn't some post-modern cultural studies critic write an entire work on the sub-genre of Hotel Room Art?

That's when it strikes me that *the whole thing, life itself, is a trompe l'oeil!* A trick of the eye. Or rather, there is at least one perspective from which to see the possibility that most of one's understanding of what it all means, what it's about, might be a kind of optical illusion, that whatever I now think about my life, politics, art, the nature of the starry universe, time, death, is potentially revisable, as all writing is permanently revisable, in the light of subsequent experience. After all, didn't I, at previous times in my life, see the world primarily through some ideological framework or prism, from early childhood wonder / terror to midlife versions of Marxism, literature, and eros, prisms that I currently see as having been partial and/or distorting? Or I think of others who took it that their firm beliefs (about Victorian mores, say, or Greek glory) were indubitably true and not refractions of the ideological constructions of their era, went to their graves secure in their apprehension of reality. Not possible now. Not possible not to always be aware of the possibility that we have almost no idea of what it's about. It's not skepticism, and I'm a local realist myself, but the recognition that uncertainty is the medium in which the human condition floats.

Now, I'm going to skip the running conversation/argument that Thomas and I are having about art as we pad through the lush rooms of the Frick, gaze at the Grecian vases in the Met, searching in vain for an image of a maiden pouring bath water from an amphora, or trudge up the six-storey circular ramp of Frank Lloyd Wright's rather unsuitable Guggenheim Museum building, which currently features a Daniel Buren installation that consists mainly of a six-storey mirrored square column and little kelly-green stripes running along the outer rim of the six-storey ramp, an installation I'm not much interested in, but then, as someone with a more than minor case of vertigo, my judgment is probably not to be trusted when I'm in a space that's largely a six-storey atrium / abyss. I mean, thanks, but I get enough abyss in everyday life.

Nor am I going to go into the history of modern art, which began with the Armory Show in New York in 1913 or Marcel Duchamp, who sort of single-handedly invented it when he attempted to put an inverted porcelain men's urinal, the most notorious of his "readymades," in an art show, which thus raised the question "What is art?" for all subsequent art, performance, installation, since it suggests that anything might be art if it's called "art" and placed in an appropriate *context*, like an art gallery.

No, I'll just skip that, though I thoroughly enjoyed Doug Crimp's lecture at the Gugg in defence of the so-called decorative, or rather, the accusation of the decorative in art, which, he suggested, might be a coded accusation of homosexuality, and into which he wove the story of himself working as a young, gay, curatorial assistant in the Guggenheim in the early 1970s, when an earlier large Daniel Buren piece, a cloth hanging I think, occupying all six stories of the abyss, was at the very last minute, the night before the opening, pulled from a group show of somewhat similar artworks for some obscure reason. What lingers in mind is Crimp's passing reference to the New York poet and sometime art critic Frank O'Hara (who died in 1966, less than a year after the death of my poetry teacher Jack Spicer, both of them dead at age forty), who said, "You just go on your nerve," ... no, I'm going to leave all that aside and stick to my little insight about *trompe l'oeil*.

Thomas and I walk around New York, and now I more frequently see *trompe l'oeil*. It is often art or even the institutions in which art is displayed, like, say, the Cloisters Museum, which is a simulacrum or theme-park version of a medieval monastery, or, for that matter, *trompe l'oeil* is also the glass globe paperweight, a sort of art toy, with a unicorn in it, that I buy, with childlike enthusiasm, in the museum shop, something produced and marketed on the basis that the Cloisters has among its possessions the set of fifteenth-century tapestries portraying the hunting and capture of the mythical unicorn. Inside the transparent globe there is a handful of translucent bits, so that when you turn the object upside down and then set it down rightside up again, there's a snowstorm of these bits in glowing green as they catch the available light, like a shower of magical fairy dust falling onto the plastic unicorn, and my eye sees it with the same innocent wonder I had at age six.

But, as well, *trompe l'oeil* in "life." When we come back from uptown, approaching Cooper Square, we see that a bearded man, almost nude except for a loincloth, standing atop the stoplight mountings at Cooper Square, is tied to a cross and apparently being crucified. As we walk closer, into the gathering crowd that's assembled under and around him and on the far side of the street, along with a half-dozen police vehicles and more arriving in a wail of sirens, it gradually becomes clear (how does it gradually become clear?) that the man, his arms tied to the makeshift cross, naked except for an American flag wrapped diaper-like around his midsection, is performing a street-theatre protest against the American war/occupation in Iraq. Surely, I think, as Thomas takes a few digital photos of this surprising imagery, as are other people in the crowd, this is tomorrow morning's cover photo on the tabloids. But (I'll just parenthetically remark) as it turns out, it isn't the next day's cover photo, and I can't even find a mention of the event in the *New York Daily News* or the *Times*, but this is another issue altogether I'm thinking about, about the messages in New York and which ones do or don't attract notice. For now, though, just the momentary *trompe l'oeil* illusion of a crucifixion in the streets of New York.

And what to make of two black guys appearing in the subway car, singing in two-part harmony, "I have seen the light / Hallelujah"? just like black kids sang two- and four-part harmony in the hallways of the high school I attended a million years ago, time itself the ultimate *trompe l'oeil*, but what light, I wonder, have they seen, as they pass the hat? Is it the light that the poet Robert Creeley, whose death I'm mourning, unbearable absence, the light he talks about when he says, "There wasn't choice if one had seen the light / not of belief but of that soft, blue-glowing fusion / seemed to appear or disappear with thought"? Have I seen the light, or seen the *trompe l'oeil*? In any case, Hallelujah.

Or, speaking of those who have seen the *trompe l'oeil* of revelation, there are the Jews in their *yarmulkes*. At first I barely noticed, seeing a man on the street, uptown, around Park Avenue and 70th, wearing a small black skullcap, the ones Jewish men put on when they're about to pray in synagogue or at some ritual observance at home, and subsequently I sporadically glimpsed other such men, on the streets, in museums, restaurants, wearing *yarmulkes*, as they're called in Yiddish (in Hebrew it's *kippah*), though they're usually not worn in public, as far as I know.

But I really didn't pay attention until one morning, a day or two before our departure, Thomas and I were having breakfast in a restaurant with an acquaintance of his, a pianist, currently somewhat down on his luck, who, in order to earn a living, had to give piano lessons to the bratty children of the well-to-do, often recently enriched, Jewish families of the professional classes on the Upper East and West Sides. The pianist launched into a minor tirade, bitter but persuasive in its details, about the barbaric nouveau-riche behaviour of these Jews and their children — thousand-dollar-an-hour lawyer-mothers complaining about the cost of his seventy-five-dollars-an-hour lessons — all of this delivered by him with a sophisticated awareness that the very mention of such things could be construed as in itself a form of anti-Semitism. "Yeah," I said, not discouraging him, "I've been noticing Jews wearing *yarmulkes* in public. What's that all about?"

Later that day, or maybe the day before, I've got the sequence mixed up now, when Thomas and I were roving through the Met, there appeared one, then two, and, shortly afterwards, a third man, not together but individually, in some masterpiece-crammed gallery, in their forties, well-dressed, wearing, discreetly but insistently, *yarmulkes*. Not radical ultra-orthodox messianic Jews who always wear their *yarmulkes* in case, I guess, the Messiah appears on the spot, but regular ordinary middle- and upper-middle-class Jews. Hey, what's going on? I wondered. How come they're wearing *yarmulkes*? I'm a Jew, but I'm not wearing a *yarmulke*, and I've been a Jew, a "bad Jew" admittedly, but a Jew, way longer than them, so, what's the deal? By which point I was saying some of this to Thomas, as we were passing a Rubens or a Titian. "It's some kind of statement, I guess, maybe something about Israel," I mused. "Some kind of 'Jewish Pride' thing." But why now? Why at a moment, considering the situation in the Middle East, that might be described as one not of Jewish pride, but of "Jewish shame"? But, no, I'll put aside my own tirade about the "moral failure" of Israel, the desecration of the Holocaust that Israeli politics has become, and just stay with the odd sense of the apparition of New York Jews in *yarmulkes* in the Metropolitan Museum, as though they were strolling in a nineteenth-century Jewish neighbourhood in Wilno or Buda-pest or Berlin, on Sabbath eve, about to don the paraphernalia of worship. Though they're subtler than other displays of religious identity, I don't like these *yarmulkes* any more than I like see-ing Muslim women in North America wearing hair-hiding head-scarves, buttoned up from head to toe, all of them mock-humbly proclaiming themselves more holy than thou, holier than me.

Finally, the swiftest bit of *trompe l'oeil* of all, quick as a thought. Thomas and I are wandering about in midtown Man-hattan, north of Times Square, he's pointing out the various tow-ers and their architectural features to me, something I might not notice at all but for his interest in them, I would just see them as "tall buildings." We're on our way to have lunch on a park bench in the south end of Central Park, when, on a crowded sidewalk, in the mid-day pedestrian flow, various uniformed young people are handing out a small object the size of a business card, which, it turns out, is advertising new non-stop direct flights from New York to Berlin, and there's the funny coincidence that we happen to be people who are shortly flying, if not by direct route, pre-cisely from New York to Berlin. On one side of the packet there's a Delta Airlines plastic card announcing the new service ("Good goes around," Delta informs us), and on the other a plastic Coca-Cola business card ("Make it real"), and in between, glued to the two cards — somebody, some agency, as always, thought this up, that's what astounds me — when I fold it out is a miniature map. It's a little map of the streets of New York, and when I turn it over, on the other side, it's a map of Berlin. I say to Thomas, almost at the instant that the *trompe l'oeil* is appearing in my mind, "Wouldn't it be nice if you could just turn the New York map side over" — and I turn it over — "and you'd be in Berlin? or turn over the Berlin map" — and I do — "and you'd be back in New York?" A little *trompe* idea that lasts no longer than a chuckle as we amble on toward lunch in Central Park.

Death in Central Park

A few weeks before I went to New York, while I was in Berlin, I had a dream in which my father (who died in 1975) appeared before me and announced that this would be his last visit or the last time he'd see me, but when I anxiously and/or tearily protested, he lightly said, "Well, maybe I'll see you in Central Park," and, still in the dream, I'm pretty sure, I thought to myself that the dead are surprisingly frivolous. "I love you," I said to my father before he gave way to other dream scenes, big empty warehouses, maybe the hangar-like art display spaces at the Hamburger Bahnhof museum in Berlin, big enough for small airplanes, and an artist friend of mine is pushing a heavy, black leather, stuffed ball in rehearsal for a performance piece, while in the background there are uniformed men from World War I in puttees and gas masks, fog or gas rising at their ankles, and so on.

Just to forestall any false sense of suspense, when a few weeks later I was in Central Park in New York, I did not, as far as I can tell, meet my father there, nor was there any corresponding image or incident that connected in some oblique way to the dream. But then, I don't put much stock in dreams, though the rare powerful and coherent ones, like the one with my father, encourage a sort of superstition, in this case about the possibility of the dead making contact with us, and since I'd told Thomas about this dream before I got to New York, once we were in Central Park it was in some corner of our minds, an amusing possibility, a possible poetic manifestation.

So I don't think dreams have meaning, or much meaning, and there's little to be had from them as foretellings or premonitions, the historical and traditional functions of dreams, or by a Freudian interpretation or, for that matter, any other psychological reading. Dreams, if not just junk-image subconscious recycling, images processed through a narrative mechanism innate to the brain, ought to be regarded, at best, as proto-artworks of the unconscious, and like artworks, though they make use of the dreamer's own biographical materials, they don't necessarily tell us anything about the meaning of the dreamer's life, only something about the meaning of the artwork, in this case, the odd

346 • TOPIC SENTENCE

suggestion that the dead, of whom we have innumerable images, haphazardly visit our world but are capricious, frivolous, careless, especially about us, the still living. I'm tempted by the view of my teacher, Jack Spicer, who said that even dreams are not patient enough for poetry; according to him, only the dead are patient enough, and poets are like the dead.

The Renaissance phrase in Latin has it *Et in Arcadia ego*, which can be read as "And (even) in Arcadia I am," spoken by Death. That is, even in the most bucolic space imaginable, Greek Arcadia or New York's Central Park or the Tiergarten in Berlin, for that matter, death is omnipresent, and as it happens, as we're crossing the park, amid joggers, strollers, trees, ponds, children, birds, burgeoning life, the elderly lolling on benches, it occurs to me that if my father is unlikely to turn up, there's always the possibility that it is Death itself who will meet me in Central Park.

In Central Park, at the south end, just above 59th Street, we find a park bench in front of a trickling waterfall coming over blocks of black stone, spilling into a pond. We walked up from the Museum of Modern Art, stopped at a sandwich shop (soup for Thomas, a panini for me), and took our lunch into the park to eat, found a free bench, sat in the sun, as did others who had come out of nearby towers, some still yattering into their cellphones (a woman speaking Spanish two benches down). In the park, fewer signs, fewer messages than in the ideological streets.

What one sees, then, are all these lives, somehow unexpected, minds filled with memories, ideas, intentions, at the moment of our mutual encounter, except for the children, who don't necessarily know it's a "park" or "lunchtime," who don't yet have most of the categories and names for objects that weigh us down, but move through the largely undifferentiated phenomena in a kind of lightness of being. I accept with a mild despair that I'll never know what's going on in the minds of all these people in the park, much less the rest of the earth's inhabitants, though I'm also occasionally grateful to be spared the utopia of total transparence we sometimes imagine. I'll know only the minutest fragment of all these lives — I have some idea, say, of what's on Thomas's mind, of who he is, or I have a sense, however partial, of the clerk at the Spring Street grocery who's forever talking on a cellphone to his wife in Yemen.

All these lives, but from the anticipatory perspective of death, all these deaths. My father does not appear in Central Park, the dead do not contact us, notwithstanding a few psychics on TV who assure us otherwise, nor do we contact them. But in old age, I think about the dead, I mourn the death of Robert Creeley, whom I'll never see again, or I get involved in the argument about the slighting obituaries on the occasion of the recent death of Jacques Derrida, author of *The Work of Mourning*, but think to myself, However it comes out, this particular grumpy argument, it won't matter a bit to Derrida, who is no more, and I anticipate, worry about, the deaths of my agemates, my friends, myself, or sometimes I think, again with a mild despair, of *all* the deaths, of the senselessness, arbitrariness of so many of them. I can cut into the imagery, find an example at any moment I choose, arbitrarily, the first thing that comes to mind is not the televised camcorder images of bodies flying out of the burning World Trade Center towers that September morning but, on this viewing, the cemetery on a hillside near the Polish-German border at Seelow (Thomas. took me there) containing the corpses of twenty-year-old Russian soldiers slaughtered in one of the last battles of World War II, sent across the Oder River in insane human waves. I'm looking at the gravestones, names written in Cyrillic, there is no end to it all, but there is an end to each. The dead, in a sense, are only *in us*, but ontologically there's a further sense in which we see the sheer idiocy of death. No wonder that even atheists demand resurrection.

If there is just one of the now-dead New Yorkers who might appear in Central Park, sauntering past the park bench where I'm eating my panini, it's a slight, lean man in his late thirties, who casually turns and says to me, "Hi. How's it going?" And while struggling to match my faint recollection of his image — high forehead with a widow's peak of hair, tomahawk-shaped nose, bright eyes — with the person now before me, I stutter, "Frank? Frank O'Hara? You know me?" "Sure," he says, "you wrote the letter to the *New York Review of Books* in 1966 about my poems, didn't you?" "Yes, yes I did," I say, always having hoped that O'Hara had seen that letter, which was published a mere three months before his accidental death, and then, remembering that O'Hara was an acquaintance of my friend, the poet Robin Blaser, add, "Robin gave me your poems to read," as I'm vainly trying to recall whether it was O'Hara's *Meditations in an*

Emergency or his *Love Poems (Tentative Title)* on whose behalf I was protesting (the latter, in fact), but in any case, the protest worked, since the critic, whom I had petulantly chastised for virtually ignoring O'Hara's work, gracefully replied by printing the O'Hara poem I'd requested. "How is Robin?" O'Hara asks, genuinely interested, as if he'd been meaning to phone him any day now. "Oh, he's fine. It's his eightieth birthday in a couple of weeks." "Well, I'm just on my way to see Larry," O'Hara says, referring to his painter friend Larry Rivers, "maybe you'd like to come along," adding, "I just have to stop at the museum for a minute," meaning, of course, MOMA, where he worked, and I rise from the park bench.

Then Thomas and I stroll out of the park, back into the immediacy of life, into the messages of the streets, leaving behind death in Central Park. "Life is random," "Enjoy uncertainty," "Give chance a chance" the ads for a music machine say in the rotting subway station, water dripping from the rusted steel beams overhead into the ear-splitting squeal of the cars on the tracks, or on the train the "poem of the week" is Emily Dickinson (Dickinson!!), and though I would have preferred "Because I could not stop for Death / He kindly stopped for me," nonetheless, they've chosen her account of how she "stepped from plank to plank" (walked the plank?) until she acquired "that precarious Gait / Some call Experience," and Levi's 501s again remind of us of such complications as "Movies became films / Medium became *grande*" (a cultural in-joke about fancy coffees), so, is "Life getting too complicated? Uncomplicate."

But the most insistent of all the messages, the ultimate message, plastered everywhere on hoardings, posted on public transit (along with the poem of the week), broadcast over the subway public address system, is "If you see something, say something," meaning, as everyone is meant to know, each person must be alert to the threat of terrorism, to the unending "war on terrorism," to "unattended," as they're euphemistically called, bags or rucksacks, to suspicious acts, characters, anything. "If you see something, say something." And there are two things to note: 1) how seamlessly the terror warning has been translated into the language of all the other advertisements and messages, and 2) the irony, since we, or at least I, am *always* seeing something and saying something.

In the Spring Street grocery, on the morning of my departure from New York, the clerk is talking on his cellphone, in Arabic, to his wife in Yemen while he's toting up my purchases, putting them into a paper bag (which advertises a forthcoming summer movie), making change, it's become a little routine we have, and I cut in, asking, "How's Yemen?" He brightens, and without breaking pace, or so much as a blink, translates my message, and a second later replies, "Yemen says hello."

Sonnet About Orpheus
(Miroir)

In the Mirror of the Real   each scene
found in negation   not the lake
of the heart   not the body torn to pieces
by the Furies   not the tongue of Orpheus

In the Mirror of the Real   reversals
doubles, endless folds, oppositions   the actual
trees, stones, stars, lakes   reflect
the dead, the "irreparable," the under-

world. Eurydice not a person   but the cry
of Orpheus: "Eurydice   O harsh
  justice!   Eury-
dice"   when he looked back and saw
poetry   can't bring the dead

back to life   In the Mirror of the Real, both
the underground of the world   the under-
side of his body   back and forth through the
  black
liquid of the mirror   look, Eurydice,

no hands! No looking
back!

Acknowledgements and Credits

Topic Sentence is a book of recombinations (and revisions) of earlier writing as well as a prospectus of future texts. I'm grateful to the many editors who have worked on these writings, especially Brian Fawcett, Rolf Maurer, and Audrey McClellan.

Credits are presented in the following format: title of piece and approximate date of writing, followed by bibliographic citation of publication or posting.

Before

"Topic Sentence," 1970–2006, in Stan Persky, *Wrestling the Angel* (Vancouver: Talonbooks, 1977).

"Lake," 1961, in *Wrestling the Angel*.

"The Day," 1969, in Stan Persky, *The Day* (Vancouver: Georgia Straight Writing Supplement, 1971); reprinted in *Wrestling the Angel*.

"Reasonable Beings," 1970, in *Wrestling the Angel*.

"Chicago Blues," 2004, in Stan Persky, *The Short Version: An ABC Book* (Vancouver: New Star Books, 2005).

"The Hedge," *circa* 1985, at www.dooneyscafe.com, May 1, 2006.

During

"Autobiography of a Tattoo," 1996, in Stan Persky, *Autobiography of a Tattoo* (Vancouver: New Star Books, 1997).

"Eros and Cupid," 1985–90, in Stan Persky, *Buddy's: Meditations on Desire* (Vancouver: New Star Books, 1989, 1991); reprinted in Alberto Manguel, ed., *The Gates of Paradise* (London: Flamingo, 1993); "Death" and "Epilogue," in *Buddy's*.

"A History of Homosexual Desire in Montreal, 1642–1992," 1992, in *Sodomite Invasion Review* (Don Larventz, ed., Vancouver, 1993).

"On Certainty," 1993, in Stan Persky, *Then We Take Berlin: Stories from the Other Side of Europe* (Toronto: Knopf Canada, 1995; Toronto: Vintage Canada, 1996); reprinted in Alberto Manguel and Craig Stephenson, eds., *Meanwhile, in Another Part of the Forest* (Toronto: Vintage Canada, 1994).

"Rereading Paul Monette's *Borrowed Time*," 2003, in *The Short Version*.

"Feasting with Oscar: From *De Profundis* to Post-Queer," 2005, at dooneyscafe.com, October 2005.

After

"Sonnet About Orpheus (Scar)," 1999, in *Tads*, No. 6 (Vancouver, 2001).

"The Translators," 1991, in *Then We Take Berlin: Stories from the Other Side of Europe*; reprinted in Karen Mulhallen, ed., *Paper Guitar* (Toronto: HarperCollins, 1995), and in Barbara Moon and Don Obe, eds., *Taking Risks* (Banff, AB: Banff Centre Press, 1998).

"The Horses of Instruction," 1996, 1997, 2004: "The Secret of Happiness," in *Autobiography of a Tattoo*; "Academic Freedom and Its Distractions," in Sharon Kahn and Dennis Pavlich, eds., *Academic Freedom and the Inclusive University* (Vancouver: UBC Press, 2000); "The Music of the Spheres," in *The Short Version*.

"Reading the Twentieth Century," 2003–05: "Orwell's Nightmare," at dooneyscafe.com, April 28, 2003; "Life Was a Cabaret, My Dear," at dooneyscafe.com, June 26, 2004; "On Czesław Miłosz," at dooneyscafe.com, August 2004; "About Robert Creeley," at dooneyscafe.com, March 2005; reprinted in *Jacket* at www.jacketmagazine, October 2006; "The Sound of . . . ," at dooneyscafe.com, March 2005.

"New York Poems," 2005, at dooneyscafe.com, June 2005, and published in *Descant* (Karen Mulhallen, ed.,Toronto, 2007).

"Sonnet About Orpheus (*Miroir*)," 2002, at dooneyscafe.com, February 2002.

S | MARQUIS

MEMBER OF SCABRINI GROUP

Québec, Canada
2007